MIMESIS AND THEORY

*Cultural Memory*
*in*
*the*
*Present*

*Mieke Bal and Hent de Vries, Editors*

# MIMESIS AND THEORY

*Essays on Literature and Criticism, 1953–2005*

René Girard

*Edited and with an Introduction by*
*Robert Doran*

STANFORD UNIVERSITY PRESS

STANFORD, CALIFORNIA

2008

Stanford University Press
Stanford, California

Printed in the United States of America on acid-free, archival-quality paper

Library of Congress Cataloging-in-Publication Data

Girard, René, 1923–
   Mimesis and theory : essays on literature and criticism, 1953–2005 / René
Girard ; edited by Robert Doran.
      p.   cm.—(Cultural memory in the present)
   Includes bibliographical references and index.
   ISBN 978-0-8047-5580-1 (cloth : alk. paper)
   1. Literature, Modern—History and criticism.   I. Doran, Robert, 1968–
II. Title.
PN511.G48 2008
801'.95—dc22

                                         2007038390

# Contents

## *Editor's Note*

This book brings together virtually all of René Girard's uncollected articles on literature and literary theory. A few of the earlier essays could not be included because of space constraints. Seven essays were originally written in French. I have translated six of these, which appear for the first time in English in this volume. One translation has been reprinted. The remaining thirteen essays were originally written and published in English. In order to assist the reader in contextualizing the material, the essays have been arranged in chronological order, with the original date of publication appearing in brackets after each essay's title.

I would like to express my gratitude to Professor Girard, who warmly encouraged and supported this project from its inception to its completion. I would also like to thank Eric Gans for his insightful comments and suggestions on several of the translations, which no doubt improved their accuracy and readability. Any errors are of course my own. Thanks also to Thomas Beebee, who generously offered his comments on my editor's introduction.

I am very grateful for funding I received from the Dean of Faculty Research at Middlebury College, which allowed me to hire two Middlebury students as research assistants. These two students, Caroline Vial and Melissa Cassis, did a fantastic job in support of this volume, and I thank them wholeheartedly for their painstaking work.

# Editor's Introduction: Literature as Theory

For over thirty years, René Girard has been one of the most influential thinkers in the humanities. His works have been translated into numerous languages and have been the subject of a constant stream of commentary. The bibliography of secondary sources dealing wholly or in part with his oeuvre now numbers in the hundreds of articles and over fifty full-length books. In 1990, a research colloquium (COV&R—Colloquium on Violence and Religion) was formed in order to further the study of Girard's thought. Its annual meeting brings together theologians, literary scholars, philosophers, psychologists, and anthropologists from Europe and North America.[1]

Best known for his ideas about archaic religion, myth, and the Bible, which he developed in a stunning series of publications starting in the 1970s, Girard's writings on literature have to some extent been overshadowed by his work in religious anthropology. This is unfortunate, for literary studies has always been at the center of Girard's professional career, and the mainspring of his thought—his theory of mimetic desire—evolved out of his reading of literary texts.

This volume of René Girard's uncollected writings on modern literature and literary theory is thus long overdue, for in addition to presenting some of Girard's best and most powerful work, which deserves to be better known, this anthology offers a panoramic view of Girard's unique ideas on the place of literature in modern intellectual life—that is, of his views on how literature relates to the domains of social science, cultural theory, psychology, philosophy, and religious studies. Particularly for those for whom Girard's contribution to literary studies is restricted to his first book, *Deceit, Desire, and the Novel* (*Mensonge romantique et vérité romanesque*, 1961), these essays will reveal, more consciously and more explicitly, the interdisciplinary matrix that informs Girard's approach to the literary text.

In this introduction, I will draw out the implications of Girard's critical approach by situating it in its historical and intellectual context.

## Literature and Theory

René Girard was born in Avignon, France, in 1923. During his formative years, he studied at the Ecole des Chartes in Paris, where he was trained as a medieval archivist. After receiving his diploma in 1947, he was recruited to teach French in the United States, and he decided to stay, taking a Ph.D. in History from Indiana University in 1950. Soon after, Girard sought employment in departments of French literature. A year in the Romance Languages Department at Duke University was followed by an appointment at Bryn Mawr. In 1957, he joined the faculty of Johns Hopkins University, where he was granted tenure and published many of his most important works. He left Johns Hopkins in 1971 to become a Distinguished Professor in the English Department at the State University of New York at Buffalo. He returned to Johns Hopkins in 1976 as the John M. Beall Professor of the Humanities. In 1981, Girard moved west, becoming Andrew B. Hammond Professor at Stanford University, where he was affiliated with the departments of French and Italian, and Comparative Literature. He officially retired in 1995, but returned to teach courses at Stanford in 2000, 2003, and 2004. Girard was elected to the Académie Française in 2005.

Girard's career coincides with a crucial period in the development of literary studies in the United States. He witnessed firsthand the revolutionary changes of the 1960s and 1970s, which reshaped the field and led to a seismic shift in what had hitherto been a rather conservative discipline. Girard was a co-organizer, along with Richard Macksey and Eugenio Donato, of the famous 1966 conference held at Johns Hopkins University (where he was a professor of French at the time) entitled "The Languages of Criticism and the Sciences of Man."[2] This conference, which brought to prominence such thinkers as Jacques Lacan, Roland Barthes, and Jacques Derrida, was a watershed event in the reception of French thought in the United States, for within the space of a few years these names would come to dominate the critical landscape. Though Girard would soon cast a wary eye on what he saw as a new orthodoxy, this initial burst of interdisciplinary enthusiasm no doubt encouraged Girard to explore the more far-reaching implications of his own thought.[3]

Subsequently, Girard's name became associated with the avatars of "French Theory." His 1972 monograph, *Violence and the Sacred* (translated in 1977, one year after the translation of Derrida's *Of Grammatology* appeared), became a touchstone of the critical theory genre and made a name for him in the United States.[4] This book, which featured lengthy critiques of Freud and Lévi-Strauss and made reference to Derrida and Lacan, was interpreted by many as being part of the "post-structuralist" movement in French thought.[5] However, the convergence was more coincidental than essential. Girard had arrived at a similar crossroads as these other thinkers, but he had come on a different path and was traveling toward a very different destination.

At first, Girard welcomed this new expansion of literary studies. Inspired by the linguistic theories of Ferdinand de Saussure, structuralist criticism had created a bridge between literary studies and the human sciences. In a 1966 article, "Critical Reflections on Literary Studies," published in *Modern Language Notes* (and included in this volume), Girard spoke about "renewal" and the need to reconfigure literary studies so that it could more effectively dialogue with other disciplines and approaches. At that time, Girard was a defender of the critical avant-garde, which was under fierce attack from the literary establishment: "In the [human sciences] we see a new enemy, and not the opportunity they offer to renew literary studies, to emerge finally from the crisis which engulfs us." Feeling that the type of criticism practiced in the American academy (and, in France, at institutions such as the Sorbonne) was stale, reactionary, and in desperate need of revitalization, Girard thought that the *nouvelle critique* would be able to lead literary studies out of its "crisis."

In the 1950s and 1960s, literature departments in the United States were dominated by New Criticism, a type of formalism or aestheticism which isolated the literary text from non-literary disciplines and methodologies. In France, on the other hand, literary history was the dominant force. Strongly influenced by nineteenth-century positivism and diametrically opposed to New Criticism, literary history concerned itself primarily with the study of context and authorial biography, paying relatively scant attention to the literary works themselves. While Girard found useful elements in these two rival methodologies, he rejected both the anti-scientific aestheticism of the former and the scientific anti-aestheticism of the latter.

Girard's own approach to the literary text is quite unique in the annals of literary criticism, for it does not so much draw on a particular critical school as it derives its ideas from the texts it comments upon. This does not mean that a particular theoretical content is abstracted from the imaginative work, in the way that Camus' *The Myth of Sisyphus* can be seen as making explicit the "philosophy" behind *The Stranger*, or that Sartre's *Nausea* can be considered a literary supplement to *Being and Nothingness*. In these examples, literature is seen as merely illustrative of a thought that is non-literary in nature. What Girard is aiming at, however, is the notion that the imaginative text can be as "critical" as the critical text, and can even usurp it. Girard thus reads literature to illuminate psychoanalysis or structuralism, rather than the other way around. The imaginative or narrative text is critical, in the sense that the best of these contain profound insights into the human condition. What is required, then, is a manner of reading that involves a complete redefinition of the role and purview of literature.

Thus, what Girard offers us is not a theory of literature or a theory that makes use of literature for some other end, but literature *as* theory. This does not, however, involve reducing literature to abstract statements; nor is it a matter of imposing a theoretical model on a text that is dutifully expected to conform to it. Girard sees the literary text as an embodiment of an intuitive understanding of the human condition, providing the tools necessary for both its own analysis and the analysis of literary criticism itself.

One can, I believe, discern three basic principles that underlie Girard's critical practice: (1) the literary work reveals significant structures or forms of human comportment, which can be considered on a par with any of the human sciences (psychology, anthropology, sociology); (2) there is a dynamic and essential relation between author and work; and (3) literary theory and cultural theory are one, in the sense that the great literary text is concerned with what is essential in the human experience from the perspective of a specific historical moment. The first principle could be described as "structural"; the second as "existential"; and the third, "historical." Though generally underemphasized in relation to the universal structures of human interaction that he develops in his mimetic readings, the historical aspect of Girard's thought is a crucial part of his critical approach. Girard was trained as a historian, and all of his work is infused with an acute awareness of the historical dimension of the texts he treats. One can perceive this most directly in two of his early essays, included in this volume: "History in Saint-John Perse" and "Classicism and Voltaire's Historiography."

I will now present a general outline of the structural level, often called the "theory of mimetic desire" or simply "mimetic theory," which, as mentioned above, developed out of an engagement with literary texts.

### Mimetic Theory

I will only briefly discuss Girard's theory here, given the rich secondary literature on the topic.[6] However, I think the best general introduction to mimetic theory is contained in Girard's postface to his book on Dostoevsky, entitled "Mimetic Desire in the Underground" (included in this volume).

It is generally accepted that all cultural transmission (language, customs, values) is a product of imitation. However, there is one type of imitation that is systematically excluded from the concept of imitation: *the imitation of desire.*[7] On Girard's account, we do not desire spontaneously, but according to another person; we imitate the Other's desire. Desire does not have its origin in the self or in the object, but in a third party. Put another way: there is always a level of social mediation between my desire and its object.[8] Imitative or mimetic desire can therefore also be termed *mediated* desire—a desire that is never fully my own. Girard thus replaces an object-oriented conception of desire (which he alternately terms "romantic," individualistic, or rationalistic) with an intersubjective or "inter-individual" conception predicated on the power of the social.

The consequences of this seemingly simple idea are enormous, and they stem from the relationship between the imitator and the mediator, or model, of desire. In traditional and pre-modern societies, which are based on rigid hierarchies and strict lines of authority, the distance between models and imitators tends to be very large or even absolute (the models may also be mythical, or may derive from an earlier civilization). In such societies, mediation is itself a function of hierarchy, and thus there is little possibility for mediators and imitators to become rivals or otherwise come into conflict with one another. Girard calls the type of mediation that predominates in these societies "external," since the mediator generally lies outside the realm of the imitator's sphere of action. External mediation most often takes the form of explicit veneration or admiration.

Within a specific caste or peer group, the possibility for imitation to lead to rivalry is ever present, due to the social and spatial proximity of the actors. Girard terms this type of mediation "internal," for it involves relations within a given sphere that can give rise to conflict. In internal imitation, the mediator is both a model of and an obstacle to desire. He embodies the double-bind "Imitate me; do not imitate me"; that is to say, with a single gesture he designates the object to be desired even as he reserves it for himself. In our modern world, where class distinctions are much weaker and no longer place limitations on desire, imitation, particularly of the internal variety, is far more widespread and pervasive. The more the individual frees himself from the formal expressions of authority (tradition, religion—the imitation of transcendental models), the more his imitation is turned toward his neighbor, thereby multiplying the interfaces and increasing the intensity. In other words, the more "individual" we become—the more we exalt ourselves as autonomous, self-sufficient, original, and spontaneous—the more we are in fact determined by others. Though modern societies do institutionalize types of imitation that are openly expressed (such as economic competition or the notion of the role model), the imitation of our peers is most often hidden or disavowed. Individualism does not release us from the chains of mimesis; it makes the chains invisible even as it binds us more tightly. In his essay "Innovation and Repetition" (included in this volume), Girard shows how the shift from imitation being perceived as positive and originality as negative, to originality being perceived as positive and imitation as negative, occurred virtually overnight, and came about as a result of the Enlightenment concept of the individual.

As egalitarianism began to take hold in the wake of the French Revolution, writers and thinkers became horrified at the idea of being lost in the crowd. The notion of the individual was no longer tied to the rise of the bourgeoisie, as it was in the eighteenth century; the true individual was now the *exceptional* being. This anti-bourgeois hyper-individualism reaches its zenith in the Romantic subject, which counterposes a heroic individuality to the indistinct mass of uncomprehending others. The failure of the Romantic hero to halt the march toward social leveling finds its dialectical double in the post-Romantic antihero (Flaubert, Dostoevsky). But this inverted subjectivity retains the same sordid dialectic between self and other, the individual and the social, which persists all the way into the existentialist thought of Heidegger and Sartre.[9] Ultimately, Girard argues, individualism is a religious form of anti-religion. The "secularization" of the modern world does not herald the transcendence or abandonment of religious structures, but their perversion. The search for individuality reveals itself to be a latter-day theology of the self: the replacement of God by the human subject, which is affirmed as the locus of all meaning and authority (Nietzschean pride). But it is at this moment that the specter of the Other reveals itself most powerfully and unwelcomingly. In Girard's view, the greatest modern authors are those who are both attracted to but who are ultimately able to see through the individualistic illusion that endeavors to place a god-like self beyond the influence of others.

Like many twentieth-century thinkers, Girard is attempting to overcome the inveterate solipsism of the philosophical tradition, both ancient and modern, in which the "Other" is invariably reduced to an aspect of self. Emmanuel Levinas's ethics of alterity and Jürgen Habermas's intersubjective discourse ethics also represent attempts to overcome solipsism. Though there are points of contact, Girard differs from these thinkers in that he does not aim to found an ethics or a politics, but to discover the true nature of human interaction. That is to say, he is concerned neither with the ethical meaning of existence that the presence of others entails, nor with the normative character of communication; it is actual human comportment as a function of the concrete relations between Self and Other that Girard seeks to explicate. Girard's anthropological perspective puts the ethical meaning of this interrelation in brackets, as it were, in order to better understand its various implications. For Girard, mimetic desire is always an opening toward the Other, and thus any "Girardian ethics" would have to start there.

In Girard's major works of religious anthropology—*Violence and the Sacred, Things Hidden since the Foundation of the World,* and *The*

*Scapegoat*—he expands his mimetic insights into a full-blown genetic theory of culture. An explanation of these works lies outside the scope of this introduction; but suffice it to say that the mimetic theory always lies at the heart of Girard's thinking.

## Mimesis and Psychoanalysis

Sigmund Freud is perhaps Girard's most important interlocutor, for it was Freud who put the concept of desire on the intellectual map, as it were, obliging all subsequent reflections on the human psyche to take his theory into account. Prior to Freud, the concept of desire had been considered the province of novelists and poets, and Freud himself tells us that he was greatly influenced by his reading of literature and myth. Curiously, Girard does not mention Freud in his first book (*Deceit, Desire, and the Novel*), precisely where one might have expected it. In fact, this was a conscious strategy on Girard's part to avoid his study being lumped with the mass of commentaries on psychoanalysis.[10] He wished to completely separate the mimetic theory of desire from Freud's vision. However, he soon realized that a dialogue with psychoanalysis would not only be fruitful, but necessary.

It is Freud's use of myth, particularly of the Oedipus myth and the myth of Narcissus, that Girard has found most intriguing from the perspective of desire. Let us first take the theory of the Oedipus complex. Girard accepts the Oedipal logic that there is a triangular relation between self, object, and obstacle, but reproaches Freud for not seeing the essential role of imitation in this paradigm. Freud weds himself to the notion of an incest-patricide drive that expresses the innate desire of the male child for the mother. What Freud does not realize, though he often comes close, according to Girard, is that the child's desire is modeled on that of the father; hence the child's imitation is prior to and generative of his conflict and rivalry with the father. Girard interprets Freud's doctrine of the Superego (or Ego ideal) as compensating for this inability to see the father as a model in the Oedipus complex. Ultimately, Girard sees the fatal flaw of psychoanalysis as its inability to overcome solipsism. Contenting itself with the positing of intra-psychical relationships (those between Ego, Id, and Superego), psychoanalysis refuses to follow the path to the Other that Freudian notions like "identification" should have necessitated.[11]

Girard's substantial article on Sartre ("Bastards and the Antihero in Sartre," included in this volume), written just a few years after *Deceit, Desire, and the Novel*, offers a glimpse into Girard's thinking on psychoanalysis well before his formal engagement with Freud in *Violence and the Sacred*. Prompted by the appearance of Sartre's autobiographical essay *The Words* (*Les mots*) in 1964, Girard is moved to reconsider Sartre's entire oeuvre, both philosophical and literary, in terms of its own concepts. Girard locates the birth of the Sartrean antihero in the young Sartre's Oedipal veneration of his grandfather, as described in *The Words*. Sartre identifies with and admires his grandfather; he desires all that his grandfather desires; he desires *to be* his grandfather, who is his model. At some point, Sartre feels the need to assert his own self, which he does by rejecting all that his grandfather represents. But this rejection is only a more extreme form of imitation. In his earlier works, such as *Nausea*, Sartre employs the figure of the antihero to manifest his rejection of the bourgeois values embodied by his grandfather. But the antihero is always a hero in disguise, for in denouncing all the others, the antihero is claiming that he is the only authentic being. Sartre thought that he was dispossessing himself of his Superego—that is, of his relation to the transcendental model, the father-figure—by rejecting the grandfather and embracing the role of the antihero. But, as Girard writes, Sartre is in fact the "proud owner of an inverted Superego. . . . The anti-Superego is a super-Superego that increases the demands of a Superego whose tyranny it claims to reject."[12] In a nutshell, what Girard seeks to show is that behind the gesture to rid oneself of the model one always finds the will *to be* the model, a will that is unaware of itself. Girard uses dialectical turns of phrase to express the paradoxical nature of human desire, and in particular its "bad faith" (*la mauvaise foi*), a Sartrean concept that Girard here turns against the master.

In essence, Girard accuses existentialist "bad faith" of being in bad faith. Existentialism is a rejection of bourgeois individualism in the name of an individualism more extreme and more "bourgeois" than the one it critiques. Girard argues this point with panache in his "Memoirs of a Dutiful Existentialist: Simone de Beauvoir" (included in this volume). Commenting on de Beauvoir's assertion that for her "the idea of salvation had survived the disappearance of God," Girard writes: "How can we save ourselves, concretely, in the absence of God, if not by surpassing our fellow human beings in all sorts of worldly endeavors?"

Though he rarely theorizes it explicitly, the concept of "bad faith," or "self-deception," is fundamental to Girard's conception of the psyche and to his theory of mimetic desire. In "Marivaudage, Hypocrisy, and Bad Faith" (included in this volume), Girard defines bad faith as the "obvious fact that we are not always clearly aware of our deepest motivations." The dynamic of mimetic desire presupposes a minimal awareness of its operation; otherwise, its truth would not be so violently repressed or denied, as in internal mediation. If everyone were always aware of the true nature of their desires and their relations with others, they would not behave paradoxically or contradictorily. Furthermore, as Girard argues in his essay "Narcissism: The Freudian Myth Demythified by Proust" (included in this volume), "You must be a dupe of your own comedy to play it with conviction." That is to say, any strategic advantage in the realm of desire is necessarily the product of a self-deception—and this is no more effectively shown than in the phenomenon of *narcissism*.

Girard credits Marcel Proust as being his guide for his deconstruction of Freud's notion of narcissism. In his essay on Proust and Freud, mentioned above, Girard provides perhaps the most explicit demonstration of his idea that literary intuitions are coequal—and often superior—to corresponding reflections in philosophy and the human sciences.[13] As in the Oedipus complex, Freud sees narcissism in terms of a pathology of the self: the narcissistic person (quintessentially artists and women, according to Freud) retains something of the "natural" narcissism of the child, and thus can be said to be "immature." Contrary to Freud, Proust shows that, paradoxically and contrary to all appearances, one can be simultaneously self-oriented and other-oriented. Girard notes how Proust's narrator experiences an intense attraction to a group of girls (*une bande à part*) who ignore him, realizing that it is because they ignore him that they fascinate him. The flaunting of the narcissist's lack of desire—the aura of self-sufficiency projected by the narcissist—captivates the observer who dreams of the autonomy of which the narcissist appears to be a shining example. Desiring the Other's autonomy is a contradictory enterprise doomed to fail, thereby confirming the narcissist's superiority and increasing his or her prestige. Narcissism is thus revealed as a *strategy* to attract desire, rather than as a psychological condition. The narcissist's self-desire is really a mimetic device that allows the narcissist to be both the mediator and the object of desire.

In reality, the narcissist is no more autonomous than anyone else. The narcissist too is influenced by the others he spurns, for his self-love increases when it is reflected in the Other's admiring gaze. More properly speaking, then, this phenomenon should be termed "pseudo-narcissism," for narcissism is ultimately a form of reciprocity masquerading as non-reciprocity.

## Author and Text

Unlike the criticism that followed in the wake of the 1966 conference, which associates author-centered approaches with a discredited historicism, Girard places great emphasis on the figure of the author, rejecting both the formalist reduction that separates the author from his or her work and the overestimation of the author in literary history. For Girard, it is not a matter of reconstructing the author's intention as the key to the work, but of reading the work as a key to the intentional structures. Girard almost never comments on this or that aspect of a particular work, or on a work in isolation. More interested in the arc of an author's thinking as it evolves over time than in the particularities of a given text, Girard will often read the later works of an author as the interpretative key to the earlier works.[14] For example, in his essay on Victor Hugo, "Monsters and Demigods in Hugo" (included in this volume), Girard will treat a late work of the author, *The Man Who Laughs*, as emblematic of a contradiction that is present in Hugo's work from the beginning, thereby revealing its true orientation. Girard notes that Hugo's lifelong obsession with monsters and disfigured beings reveals a relation of identification which, when interpreted systematically, is really an identification with Satan. Hugo casts himself in the role of Satan when he realizes he cannot be God. Girard writes: "Hugo does not admit it to himself, but he always tends toward divinizing Satan." In divinizing Satan, Hugo divinizes himself, thereby revealing the dialectical sleight of hand. Hugo remains blind to this operation, which is inscribed in his constant inversion of elementary images: darkness is exalted in terms of light; physical monstrosity is redeemed by moral beauty.

The proximity that Girard sees between the author and his fictional hero is of a different order than that conceived by literary history. For Girard, the relationship is symbiotic and existential. The fictional hero is an extension of the psychic reality of the author, a kind of alter ego which can have a causal impact on the author him- or herself, usually as an image of the author's bad faith. As Girard observes in "Marcel Proust" (included in this volume): "The book made the author no less than the author made the book." Hence Girard's contention that in the greatest authors the act of writing itself leads to a self-revelation or *conversion*.

In the conclusion to *Deceit, Desire, and the Novel*, Girard describes what he calls "novelistic conversion": moments of disillusion in which the protagonist, in league with the author, realizes the futility of his mimetic pursuits and renounces the world in some way. Girard sees this motif recurring at the end of novels such as Cervantes' *Don Quixote*, Stendhal's *The Red and the Black*, and, most paradigmatically, Proust's *Remembrance of Things Past*. It is possible to read Proust's great novel as a sort of allegory of novelistic conversion. The last installment in the series, *Time Recaptured*, reveals the truth of the work from the perspective of its denouement, which is both the denouement of the author's existence as well as the denouement of the novel. This double denouement is a classic example of the feedback loop between author and work that Girard considers essential to the creative process. In his essay "Conversion in Literature and Christianity" (included in this volume), Girard writes:

Thus, we have two perspectives in Proust and other great novels of novelistic conversion. The first perspective is the deceptive perspective of desire, which is full of illusions regarding the possibility of the hero to fulfill himself through desire. It is the perspective that imprisoned him in a sterile process of jumping from one frustrated desire to the next over a period of many years. [ . . . ] The second perspective is one that comes from the end of the novel, from the omega point of conversion, which is a liberation from desire. This perspective enables the novelist to rectify the illusions of the hero and provides him with the creative energy he needs to write his novel.

In other words, the creative process allows the author to discover his own bad faith or self-deception from the perspective of desire. Without the experience of self-deception no conversion is possible, and without a conversion there is no liberation from self-deception. Of course, to be self-deceived concerning the nature of one's desire is already a higher form of consciousness—quite distinct from mere naïveté or simple deception—since in self-deception there is always the implicit recognition of a truth.[15]

Not all literary conversions are novelistic. In his formidable essay on Racine ("Racine, Poet of Glory," included in this volume), Girard interprets *Phèdre*, Racine's last worldly drama before turning toward religious subjects, as a work of conversion. In his heroine, Racine uncovers the full truth of the dialectic of glory—that desire enslaves power—of which his earlier dramas offered only a vague and incomplete idea. Racine's intuitions with regard to non-reciprocal desire, a hallmark of his oeuvre, receive their full measure of understanding only in *Phèdre*, whose revelations place Racine before a spiritual choice.

The religious connotations of the term "conversion" are important to Girard's thinking. Though Girard is not suggesting that literary conversion is a form of religious experience, he does want to imply that this type of conversion represents an opening to religion, for the path that leads from literature to Christianity is one that has great historical resonance—Saint Augustine being the first and most spectacular example. Ultimately, literary conversion is the recognition of the failure of desire—the failure of self-fulfillment through desire, which is at the root of modern individualism and the consumer society—and as such it constitutes a renunciation of the world.

## Text and Interpretation

In the late 1970s and 1980s, with the ascendancy of Derrida and Foucault, Girard sought to distance himself from the development of "theory" in literary studies, thus reversing his initial enthusiasm for the critical avant-garde in the late 1960s. This shift in perspective is chronicled in detail in his essay "Theory and Its Terrors" (included in this volume).

Though generally considered at odds with one another, mimetic theory and deconstruction nevertheless have points in common, and the relationship between Girard and Derrida has been explored in depth.[16] In some ways, Girard's hermeneutic stance is not unlike that of deconstruction. They both refuse the transcendental authority of the author, and they both reject abstract theorizing, preferring to develop their insights through the careful reading of texts. Both overturn the priority granted to "critical" or "theoretical" writing. And both seek to subvert conventional readings, exposing presuppositions of which we were previously unaware. Where they part company is in their attitude toward the signified or the referent. Deconstruction asserts the autonomy of the text—the free play of the signifier—thereby cutting it off from the referent-signified, which is seen as being produced (rather than reflected) by the text. This is a restatement, with different metaphors, of Heidegger's dictum "Language is the house of being," which is to say, there is no such thing as meaning corresponding to something like reality, and therefore everything can be seen—and read—as a "text." In Derrida's words, "There is no outside to the text" (*Il n'y a pas de hors-texte*).[17] The written text is liberated from reference and thus from truth, since any putative "referent" is always already a text.

Girard sees deconstruction, like structuralism, as a variant of New Criticism—that is, as a formalism, an evacuation of content in favor of linguistic play. In "Theory and Its Terrors," Girard observes: "Saussurian linguistics became a means to confirm and reinforce the expulsion of 'content.' The 'signifier' corresponds to 'form,' the hierarchically inferior 'signified' becomes the new word for 'content,' and the despised 'referent' the new word for reality." Girard reproves formalist exclusivity for its implicit nihilism, arguing for a return to content, a return to historical, social, and psychical meaning. This is not to say, however, that Girard has not found certain thinkers in this tradition compelling. Girard professed great admiration for Derrida's early essays, and in particular for "Plato's Pharmacy." However, as much as he found Derrida's thought stimulating and necessary, he considered subsequent developments unhealthy and counterproductive. The liberation of literary studies, of which Girard himself had been an ardent advocate in the late 1960s, had come at the price of a new servitude.[18]

While deconstruction explodes the subject-object dichotomy by subsuming it into language—a language without "subjects," properly speaking—Girard deconstructs subjectivity through the dialectic of desire, the dialectic between Self and Other. From a certain point of view, a Girardian reading of a text can be considered more radical than a deconstructive reading, for the deconstructive approach ultimately takes the text at face value. It cannot accuse the author of bad faith, because it considers meaning to be immanent. Though Girard puts into question the regulative value of authorial intention, he nevertheless does not separate the author from his or her text. Texts can be read against their authors, just as they can be read against themselves.

Like Derrida's deconstructive readings, Girard's approach has appeared to some as inimical to the aesthetic aspirations of literature. However, Girard is not at all opposed to rhetorical or stylistic analysis, as evidenced by his examination of metaphor in his article on Racine (mentioned above) and of oxymora in "Love and Hate in Chrétien de Troyes' *Yvain*" and "The Passionate Oxymoron in Shakespeare's *Romeo and Juliet*" (both included in this volume). But in Girard, such analyses are always calibrated to discover the real-world significance behind what appear to be merely "poetic" or "literary" devices.

If one takes a longer view, one can see Girard as harking back to the earliest examples of literary criticism—ancient poetics and rhetoric—in which the anthropological and cultural resonances of the verbal arts were always part and parcel of "literary" analysis.[19] Plato's denunciation of mimesis in the *Republic* connects poetic creation with an analysis of human nature. Aristotle's notion of *katharsis* does not denote a merely "aesthetic" condition, but relates to psychology, religion, and medicine.[20] Longinus's fragment on sublimity (*hypsos*) is as much a treatise on human finality as it is a manual on "rhetoric," strictly speaking. In the broadest sense, then, classical aesthetics was inextricable from anthropological concerns, and no one exemplifies this classical approach better in a modern context than does René Girard.

The attempt to poeticize philosophy in Nietzsche, Heidegger, and Derrida represents a desire to return to the primordial (pre-Socratic) unity between the will to know and the will to create. Girard finds this unity in literature itself. Girard sees the uniqueness of literature in its ability to reconcile universality and particularity in ways that philosophy cannot easily match. As modes of discourse concerned primarily with the human passions, literature and myth are able to offer man perhaps the only truth man can offer himself: a truth that is specifically human. Thus, for Girard it is not a matter of bowing before an a-temporal, non-human reality, but, on the contrary, it is one of grasping human reality through its most pertinent representations, which are in most cases literary, mythical, or religious.

Hence, Girard does not see literary intuition or religious anthropology as cumulative in the sense of the positive sciences. Nor does Girard see the dialectical movement of history as evidence of a vain attachment to outmoded forms of thought. To a historical relativism gone awry, Girard counterposes a perennial wisdom that slowly makes itself known. It is a matter of following the dramatic unfolding of the human adventure in terms of mimetic structures—always changing, always remaining in some sense the same. It is possible that we may be regressing in terms of our understanding of our world, as increasing specialization erects barriers to thought and as cultural leveling extends even to the elites. But Girard holds out hope that the university will continue to provide access to the great texts of all cultures—a true *universalism*—without losing the specificity of the Western tradition grounded in its Greco-Judeo-Christian heritage.

MIMESIS AND THEORY

# History in Saint-John Perse [1953]

All the critics have observed that in commingling history with his works Saint-John Perse has entered into an area long scorned by poetry. Indeed, in the eyes of contemporary poets—who evince only disdain for what is not pure consciousness, that "closed palace of mirrors, made fecund by a solitary lamp,"[1] or who, on the contrary, seek their marvels in that which escapes this consciousness and which does not rise to the level of concepts—what is more lacking in its apparent abundance, or even more suspicious, than the historical event? Should we not be surprised, then, to see Paul Valéry and André Breton—these two stars whose rival forces of attraction appear impotent here—come to agreement in praising the qualities of an author as indifferent to the *art poétique* of the former as to the *mots d'ordre* of the latter?[2] Of course, not everyone has welcomed Perse so warmly. Some doubted, as Denis de Rougemont reminds us, that a "pure delight" would be able to "stand the test of time."[3] What some saw as an enigma or a curiosity, and what led others to suspect Perse's intentions, has only been the subject of passing remarks. It is nonetheless clear that one cannot determine Perse's place in contemporary poetry, even provisionally, so long as we are unable to understand precisely what it means to speak of a "historical presence" in his work.

Perse does not write "historical poems." In his work, history does not furnish a "subject," that is, a specific historical event that provides the setting for his poems. *Anabase* seems to constitute an exception, since the entire work appears to be situated in the remote past. But history is in need of precise points of reference, and critics have endeavored—in vain—to determine the spatial and temporal identity of the world described by the poet. The works of the second period, which begins with *Exil* in 1942, could be the subject of inquiries as fruitless as those concerning *Anabase*, if their autobiographical details did not appear to provide verifiable reference points. Thus we know that the "subject" of these poems is present in the same manner as in *Anabase*. It is therefore the form—that is to say, the essence—of this poetry that is affected by history.

When one selects a page at random from the poetry of the second period, it is apparent that the past presents itself in multiple ways: in the use of archaic terms and turns of phrase, and above all in the constant usage of historical or legendary images and metaphors:

And a bird of pink ash, which was a burning ember all summer, suddenly lights up the crypts of winter, like the Phasian bird in the Books of Hours, Year One Thousand.[4]

(Et un oiseau de cendre rose, qui fut de braise tout l'été, illumine soudain les cryptes de l'hiver, comme l'oiseau du Phase aux livres de l'An Mille.)[5]

The second part of the image, its explicative part, is precisely the one that contains the larger share of the unknown; the first bird, which one more word would have allowed us to identify, is suddenly compared to a second bird, about which we know next to nothing. We were almost confident about the bird, and then it inherits a bit of the mystery and anguish associated with the year one thousand. Perse's historical image thus plays exactly the opposite role as that of the historian. For neither can the historian do without images. If his work is not bejeweled with images, it is because most of them are implied. The second part of these images is always taken from the present, a present that a convention—which is most often tacit—allows us to consider as perfectly transparent, and even the source of a light that can always accompany us in the exploration of the shadowy regions of the past. Thus, the historian always assimilates the medieval bird to a modern bird—an assimilation without which no historical knowledge would be possible. It is the opposite that occurs in Perse's poems. One could almost speak of an "anti-image" and of its "obfuscating function." The past casts its shadow over the poem.

Could one not even be more precise and say that the past casts its shadow over the present? Indeed, we know that the subject of the poems of the second period is contemporary. The "bird of pink ash" is an American bird. Such a formula could obviously not be applied to *Anabase*, but our desire to reach conclusions that are valid for Perse's entire oeuvre must not blind us to the differences made possible—if not probable—by the long time span separating the two periods of Perse's poetic production. Thus, without invoking *Anabase*, we will endeavor to show that the role of history is not limited to giving the present an aura of the past in order to transfigure it. Let us take, for example, the third stanza from *Pluies*, which is particularly rich in historical images:

Sisters of the warriors of Assur were the tall Rains striding over the earth:
Feather-helmeted, high-girded, spurred with silver and crystal,
Like Dido treading on ivory at the gates of Carthage,
Like Cortez's wife, heady with clay and painted, among her tall apocryphal
    plants . . .
They revived with night-dark the blue on the butts of our weapons,
They will people April in the mirrors' depths of our rooms!
Nor would I forget their stamping on the thresholds of the chambers of
    ablution:
Warrior-women, O warrior-women towards us sharpened by lance and dart-
    point!
Dancing-women, O dancing-woman on the ground multiplied by the dance and
    the earth's attraction!
It is the weapons by armfuls, helmeted girls by cartloads, a presentation of eagles
    to the legions,
A rising with pikes in the slums for the youngest peoples of the earth—broken
    sheaves of dissolute virgins,
O great unbound sheaves! The ample and living harvest laid over into the arms
    of men!

(Sœurs des guerriers d'Assur furent les hautes Pluies en marche sur la terre:
Casquées de plume et haut-troussées, éperonnées d'argent et de cristal,
Comme Didon foulant l'ivoire aux portes de Carthage,
Comme l'épouse de Cortez, ivre d'argile et peinte, entre ses hautes plantes
    apocryphes . . .
Elles avivaient de nuit l'azur aux crosses de nos armes,
Elles peupleront l'Avril au fond des glaces de nos chambres !

Et je n'ai garde d'oublier leur piétinement au seuil des chambres d'ablution :
Guerrières, ô guerrières par la lance et le trait jusqu'à nous aiguisées !
Danseuses, ô danseuses par la danse et l'attrait au sol multipliées !
Ces sont des armes à brassées, ce sont des filles par charretées, une distribution
    d'aigles aux légions,
Un soulèvement de piques aux faubourgs pour les plus jeunes peuples de la
    terre—faisceaux rompus de vierges dissolues,
Ô grandes gerbes non liées ! l'ample et vive moisson aux bras des hommes
    renversée !)[6]

Even if, for the sake of rigor, we maintain that this rain is not any old rain and that it refers to a present authenticated by certain autobiographical details found in the poem, we must admit that the present plays quite a meager role in this long citation. In this instance, what we have termed the "obfuscating function" of the image does not act on the rain and its hypothetical present, but on the other images that conjure up a half-dozen different "pasts": Assyria, Carthage, the Mexico of the Spanish conquest, Rome, the French Revolution perhaps . . . Some of them are not identifiable with any certitude. What is important here is the clashing of these worlds that we are unused to seeing referred to *together*.

The predominance of certain "geographical"—tropical or oriental—images should not mislead us. From the perspective that we are discussing, it is not necessary to distinguish what Perse annexes in space from what he annexes in time. It is certainly not useless to note the relations that combine the poet's images with the traveler's experience; but it is not what A. Rolland de Renéville calls the "balancing act between East and West" that determines his art.[7] It is the universalist and planetary character of these images that is fundamental. They envelop the whole of human history: from "the rising of great fossils flush with dripping marls" (l'affleurement des grands fossiles aux marnes ruisselantes)[8] to the American West and its "unstoried plains straddled by pylons" (vastes plaines sans histoire enjambées de pylons).[9]

We understand why the label "exotic poet" is not appropriate in this context. Exoticism is always a dialogue between two worlds, the Western world and the world that negates it. As mistreated as it is, Western civilization still holds a central place in exotic literature, for the world one opposes to it exists only in and for this opposition. In Perse, the West is truly torn, because it enters into the whirlwind of cultures and civilizations evoked by these images.

It is obviously not in the literary domain, but in the sciences of man that this shift in perspective—from exoticism to Perse, from a more or less self-conscious dualism to an intentional pluralism—first triumphed. We know what its consequences were. As historians and anthropologists started to refuse to study other civilizations from our own perspective, they discovered that the only thing that gave an appearance of unity to the human adventure considered in its entirety was precisely this perspective. To renounce it meant discovering a world made up of disparate fragments. Civilizations appear as worlds that cannot communicate with one another. They come into being, live, and die, only to be replaced by others just as ephemeral and isolated as they were. We also know what kind of pessimistic reflections have been associated with this historical metamorphosis. For every civilization that believes itself the keeper of the secret of human destiny, proclaiming that it is its duty to fulfill it, we can oppose the rival claims of countless civilizations, all of which are defunct. There is no more absolute; man is condemned to the relative. Historical relativism as a theme of despair has perhaps attained its most perfect literary expression in André Malraux's *The Walnut Trees of Altenburg* (*Les noyers de l'Altenburg*):

If the destiny of humanity is History, then death is part of life; but if not, then life is part of death. . . . If mental structures disappear forever like the plesiosaurus, if civilizations succeed each other only to cast man into a bottomless pit of nothingness, if the human adventure only perpetuates itself at the price of an implacable metamorphosis, it matters little that men hand down their concepts and techniques for a few centuries: for man is an accident, and the world is essentially a product of forgetting.[10]

It is perhaps in light of these transformations of history that we should consider Perse's oeuvre. It is doubtless not a simple coincidence that the doors to the past are reopened for the poet at the precise moment when everything that was about to become clear is once again enveloped in darkness—the moment when Hegelian history collapses, a history that in a certain sense put the past at the service of the present and provided reassuring certitudes of eternity to a modern world defined by Jules Monnerot as: " . . . uniformly reassuring and flat, laid out and spreadable, which science *accounts for* and technology *manipulates*."[11] The new vision of history is only pessimistic with respect to the modern myth of a world without mystery which poetry has never accepted.

We thus see how historical relativism can become an ally for the poet and the artist. In the late works of Malraux, historical relativism plays the same combative role that psychoanalysis played in the hands of the surrealists in the previous generation. This theme, which is constantly presented as overflowing with despair, moves through the work like a breeze announcing a storm in a heavy atmosphere. A comparison between Perse and Malraux would no doubt be instructive. One might observe a surprising agreement in themes and images between the poet and the prose writer.

We now see how Perse's oeuvre is able to display the scientific and historical knowledge of its author without having the presence of the poet's suspicious erudition imply a collusion with the worldview ascribed to him by the positivists. Although most modern poets flee from a world they do not believe they can reclaim from the specialist, Perse will look for ammunition in the very heart of this world. If, in facing his work, "the West shrinks back in horror in the consciousness of its hideous vulgarity,"[12] as André Gide writes, it is because once we have negated the Hegelian vision of history that promised us eternity, we see that this world is but one world among countless others, reduced to nothingness by a merciless confrontation. Like other modern poets, Perse finds in these worlds the beauty of memories.

In Perse, the image is only arbitrary with respect to a worldview it negates. Chaos is still its only truth. Whereas Surrealist arbitrariness goes off in all directions—for it is concerned with discrediting all modes of Western thought—Perse's arbitrariness prefers historical and anthropological sequences. Surrealism denounces the world's dearth of reality, Perse its dearth of time.

Nevertheless, it is not a question of limiting Perse's oeuvre to this first negation. The poet assumes the historical relativity, but he does not limit himself to it. It constitutes but the first moment in the dialectic of the image.

If we reread the beginning of the third part of *Pluies*, we can observe that the heterogeneous character of these images and their "obfuscating function" are so obvious that it becomes possible to negate them. Images always offer themselves as "explications," and so we end up by wondering if our refusal to grant them this role is not merely due to our ignorance of the rule that presides over their organization. In fact, only analysis will allow us to distinguish the moments of this dialectic of the image. Many factors that are foreign to Perse's world contribute to lending immediacy to the impression of its homogeneity.

Considered from an exclusively "plastic" perspective, the images of the above-quoted passage do not surprise by their strangeness, but by their exactitude. The great majority of them adhere rigorously to their object. The poet is describing the falling rain. At first, we see the rain whipped by the wind: "Rains . . . feather-helmeted, high-girded, spurred with silver and crystal" (Pluies . . . casquées de plume et haut-troussées, éperonnées d'argent et de cristal); we hear its "stamping" (piétinement); we see it fall straight and heavy like a thousand sharpened points, "warrior-women, o warrior-women towards us sharpened by lance and dart-point" (guerrières, ô guerrières par la lance et le trait jusqu'à nous aiguisés), and then bounce in droplets on the ground, "dancing-women, o dancing-woman on the ground multiplied by the dance and the earth's attraction" (danseuses, ô danseuses, par la danse et l'attrait au sol multipliés). Then the parallelism of these pointy objects evokes the images of the "sheaves" (faisceaux, gerbes) and the "harvest" (moisson). Only the historical aspect of these images is disconcerting; nevertheless, what is exacting and striking about them in the descriptive mode appears to authorize these perpetual jumps in duration, which nothing can legitimate.

On the other hand, one can observe that when one of the parts of the image is an object or a natural phenomenon, the other is often taken from the realm of human activity. In the previous example, the rain seemed to evoke only human gestures or man-made objects. Elsewhere, Perse will associate man with natural objects and even chemical elements, which are apt to show what is most "inhuman" in nature: "Nitre and Nitron are themes of exile" (Le nitre et le natron sont themes d'exil).[13] This perpetual assimilation of nature to man and man to nature clearly suggests an order by which the chaos of historical images will be arranged.

Another element of homogeneity is the discreet but sufficient logical apparatus that seems to organize the poem. With respect to this type of rhetoric, Roger Caillois has observed that it is intended "to consolidate the enumerations or, if you like, to insidiously guarantee their well-foundedness."[14] Such is obviously the role of the phrase "nor would I forget . . . " (et je n'ai garde d'oublier . . . ) in the third part of *Pluies*. We must also take note of the use of disjunctive and conjunctive terms, "and . . . ," "well . . . ," "but . . . ," "here is . . . " (et . . . , or . . . , mais . . . , voici que . . . ), which suggest that far from being used arbitrarily, the diverse elements of the poem logically correspond to one another. Still more important is the manipulation of the verb tenses, which always seems to reflect the exigencies of the poem's own duration. In our example, the shift from the past to the future is always rational with respect to a present situated in the middle of the rainy season. This present follows the rain's fall, from its initial moment, "The banyan of the rain takes hold of the city" (Le banyan de la pluie prend ses assises sur la ville),[15] to the return of pleasant weather, "The banyan of the rain loses its hold on the city" (Le banyan de la pluie perd ses assises sur la ville).[16] All throughout the poem we find this alternation between past, present, and future, which gives the impression that the poet is uniting elements that he does not want to leave dispersed in time. But this time is that of a lived duration—or its equivalent—which has nothing to do with the prodigious mental leaps that the historical images impose on the reader. Nevertheless, the reader is gradually led to perceive only the lived duration, in which even the historical images will be quite naturally inscribed.

Another very important element of homogeneity is the repetition of sounds in words with different meanings, so much in favor in poets, like Péguy and Claudel, whose works are defending a position:

Warrior-women, O warrior-women towards us sharpened by lance and dartpoint!
Dancing-women, O dancing-woman on the ground multiplied by the dance and the earth's attraction!

(Guerrières, ô guerrières par la lance et le trait jusqu'à nous aiguisées!
Danseuses, ô danseuses par la danse et l'attrait au sol multipliées!)

Here again, Roger Caillois saw that "the extreme diversity of meanings strangely matches the extreme similarity of sounds."[17]

We would not be surprised if the poem—when it no longer shows itself as fragments separated by analysis, but as something one apprehends in its aesthetic totality—does not leave an impression of chaos, but rather of order; the sovereign ease with which we shift from one world to another obliges us to contest the reality of this shift; we believe that we see immobility behind the perpetual movement, an absolute behind all the relativity.

It is the appearance of this absolute that allows us to explain why the word "rite" is so often used with regard to Perse's oeuvre. Whether they are images or representations, most of the human gestures described in the poem derive from a civilization other than ours; they have meaning only when linked to the absolute they embody; once they are cut off from this absolute, they become absurd. It is necessarily in this state that these gestures attain modern historical consciousness—or Perse's poem—since the absolute values of the civilization that begat them did not survive its confrontation with other absolute values stemming from various sources. The more these gestures become absurd, the more difficult it is for us to accept them as such. These signs have a meaning, and the art of the poet consists in suggesting a meaning that will embrace all of them. The impression left by their original meaning is, however, too profound for their relation with the second meaning to be anything but indirect, magical, incantatory, ritualistic.

many things on the earth to hear and to see, living things among us!
celebrations of open-air festivals for the name-day of great trees and public
    rites in honor of a pool; consecration of black stones perfectly round, water-
    dowsing in dead places, dedication of cloths held up on poles, at the gates of
    the passes, and loud acclimations under the walls for the mutilation of adults
    in the sun, for the publication of the bride-sheets!

(beaucoup de choses sur la terre à entendre et à voir, choses vivantes parmi nous!
des célébrations de fêtes en plein air pour des anniversaires de grands arbres et
    des cérémonies publiques en l'honneur d'une mare ; des dédicaces de pierres
    noires, parfaitement rondes, des inventions de sources en lieux morts, des
    consécrations d'étoffes à bouts de perches, aux approches des cols et des
    acclamations violentes, sous les murs, pour les mutilations d'adultes au soleil,
    pour des publications de linges d'épousailles.)[18]

In the same way, Perse's poetry gives the impression of a world ordered by a system of *castes*. When considered outside of the society in which they are practiced, many human activities lose their meaning. Once again, the absurd appears when the historical perspective is broadened. This is what perturbs us when we read these long lists of "trades" of which

Perse is so fond. These trades are taken from multiple civilizations, or are simply invented by the poet. However, the more our consciousness of the absurd is sharpened, the more intense is our need for an intelligible world. Clearly, these rather unbelievable trades cannot be organized into a coherent social system, that is to say, into a system based on imaginable economic or political realities. It is thus necessary for the social to organize itself in terms of something exterior to itself. This is precisely what happens in a caste system in which the social is a reflection of the religious. Thus we are brought back to this absolute that is always lurking behind the absurd.

The foregoing remarks on caste and rite will allow us to extend our conclusions to *Anabase*, which does not feature this perpetual clash between incompatible worlds on which our analyses have been based thus far, but which seems, on the contrary, to present the picture of a homogeneous civilization. The homogeneity is of the same type that one finds in Perse's other poems. It is "beyond" heterogeneity. That which is image in *Exile* or in *Pluies* is often representation in *Anabase*. The absurd gestures are passionately described, as if they were the only ones possible. The sacred emerges behind these gestures, a sacred which, the closer one flirts with nothingness, the more strongly it imposes itself.

ha! all conditions of men in their ways and manners; eaters of insects, of water fruits; those who bear poultices, those who bear riches; the husbandman, and the young noble horsed; the healer with needles, and the salter . . . he who makes it his business to contemplate a green stone; he who burns for his pleasure a thorn-fire on his roof . . .

(ha! toutes sortes d'hommes dans leurs voies et façons : mangeurs d'insectes, de fruits d'eau ; porteurs d'emplâtres, de richesses ; l'agriculteur et l'adalingue, l'acuponcteur et le saunier ; le péager, le forgeron . . . celui qui trouve son emploi dans la contemplation d'une pierre verte ; qui fait brûler pour son plaisir un feu d'écorces sur son toit . . . )[19]

Perse's poetry thus moves toward the "positive" only through an excess of "negativity." This explains how Perse could inspire judgments as diverse as those of Pierre Jean Jouve, who writes, "The content remains in a powerful state of nothingness in which one tries to decipher the world; and we cannot discern any presence greater than man's affliction,"[20] and that of Caillois, who holds that "Out of the innumerable images that the centuries have brought together in long solitary chronicles, that distances have distributed over the continents in large independent frescos, he creates a world which is for the first time one."[21] The contradiction between these two judgments is only apparent; but Caillois is wrong, it seems to me, to speak of an "encyclopedic poetry"; the being of this poetry is grasped only through nothingness; it is not composed of a simple accumulation of details; indeed, only objects of the same nature can be added up into a sum. It is thus clear that Perse's poetry does not venture outside the framework of contemporary poetry, but it accomplishes in its superabundance what so many others seek to achieve in asceticism. Beyond the appearances and their illusory richness, one discovers "a great poem born of nothing, a great poem made from nothing . . . " (un grand poème né de rien, un grand poème fait de rien . . . ).[22]

Indeed, this immobile center in the midst of movement, this timelessness in duration, is simply the result of a second negation. The negation of a world whose meaning was given by the rationalist philosophers is succeeded by the refusal of the broken world left behind. The poet cannot renounce the search for the meaning of the world. He is among the "great adventurers of the soul" (grands aventuriers de l'âme)[23] . . . "interrogating the whole of the earth over its area, to know the meaning of this very great disorder" (interrogeant la terre entière sur son aire, pour connaître le sens de ce très grand désordre).[24] And we must not see this refusal as a contradiction with what preceded it—a caprice, a need to escape from "the real," because history cannot force us to make its vision of chaos our own. History is the first victim of its own "scientific rigor." The more history wants to scrutinize "the facts," the more man appears imprisoned within his civilization. It is clear that history cannot find at the end of inquiry the human freedom that it had scrupulously ruled out at the beginning. But with the elimination of this freedom, the notion of freedom itself is threatened:

Fragments of beautiful stories adrift in spirals, in the sky full of errors and erring premises, went turning around to the scholiast's delight.

(De beaux fragments d'histoires en dérive, sur des pales d'hélices, dans le ciel plein d'erreurs et d'errantes prémisses se mirent à virer pour le délice du scholiaste.)[25]

The poet puts the freedom of life back into the historian's inhuman world. The serenity with which he flies over obstacles that should be insurmountable suggests a divine power, a direct contact with some absolute situated behind the poem. Indeed, only the reliance on a reference point lying outside the world would seem capable of ordering this chaos. But this single cause to which we believe we can ascribe the always similar effects that we have observed in the elements of the poem—this ability to reconnect what is disconnected—is obviously neither above nor exterior to the poem; it can only define itself in aesthetic terms. The poem has no "truth" other than itself. Its world is thus "one" only in the sense in which we see a solid disk when the propeller blades rotate fast enough. It is a matter of knowing how to invest them with a movement that will turn them into objects of plenitude and immobility. This is Perse's secret, a secret that the preceding remarks lay no claim to having exposed. It is certainly not a question of reducing this art to a mechanical or dialectical process. However, it is still possible to isolate some of the elements that go into his poems and to observe that, however arbitrary they may appear at first, the ambiguous relations that develop between these elements correspond fairly exactly to the equivocations of modern consciousness, in which a cumbersome history denies access to those absolute values of which modern consciousness feels so strongly the need.

*—Translated by Robert Doran*

## 2

# Valéry and Stendhal [1954]

Paul Valéry's preface to *Lucien Leuwen* in the *Complete Works* of Stendhal is too rich to be exhausted by a single reading.[1] It requires at least three readings. The first reveals a Stendhal that the disclosures of Henri Brulard hardly allow us to suspect. On a second reading, we find the old Valéry and his inventory of favorite themes. But behind the appearance of serenity and detachment we can detect another tone, bitter and intense, which awakens a curiosity one might have thought satisfied. A third reading is thus required if we are to investigate the relation between Stendhal and Valéry. It is the reflections prompted by this reading that the present essay explores.[2]

Stendhalian egotism is based on the belief in two Egos: the first, the social Ego, is simply a mask that we don as our public face; this fiction is all too easily confused with the natural Ego: the only true expression of a nature that one can expend great effort resisting but which cannot be eradicated. This natural Ego, Valéry observes, "can only be known to us by those of our reactions which we consider or imagine to be primal and truly spontaneous."[3] Valéry is convinced that "in order to distinguish the natural from the conventional, a convention is indispensable." If Valéry is right, then Stendhal's assertions that he reveals the most intimate part of his being to his reader are vain, and what the realist novelist calls *true* must always be based on an arbitrary decision:

Literary Egotism consists . . . in being a little more *natural* than nature; a little more oneself than one was a moment or two before the idea came into one's head.

When we furnish our impulses or our impressions with a conscious *agent* who, by deferring, waiting expectantly upon ourself, and above all by *taking notes*, draws his own portrait more and more clearly, *perfects* himself from work to work *as his talent for writing develops*, we substitute an imaginary character for ourself and finish imperceptibly by using him as a model.[4]

If Stendhal is a liar through an excess of sincerity, Valéry believes himself to be sincere, at least to the extent that he recognizes the inevitable lie. "In literature the true is inconceivable,"[5] Valéry affirms. If art is artifice, fabrication, and illusion, then there must be a truth somewhere that it cannot reach. This is indeed Valéry's credo. Valéry shows the same contempt for the two Egos that he says are arbitrarily distinguished by Stendhal. Beyond the "personality" of the "spontaneous" or "natural" Ego, the individual must look within the depths of his being for the true self that grounds appearances. The hero of Valéry's youthful writings, Monsieur Teste, broke the bounds of the natural Ego to arrive at the "pure" or "absolute" Ego. Teste drinks directly from the wellspring of his freedom and thoughts. At this point, all that interests him is his proper "functioning." Whatever derives from the inferior Ego—passions, ambitions, loves, hatreds, even art, all that the existence of others is made of—leaves him perfectly indifferent.

The preface to *Lucien Leuwen* never mentions this extraordinary man, but there is not a single reflection in Valéry's presentation of Stendhal which does not have its contrary in some aspect of his portrait of Monsieur Teste. Nevertheless, nothing appears to suggest a similarity between the two, not even the label "individualist," which, according to Valéry, can only refer to the will to make oneself *unique*. If one detects this project in Stendhal, it would seem to be at an embryonic stage; *vanity*, that is, the desire to be greater than others, would, according to the theorist of egotism, win out over *pride*, which flatters itself as *incommensurable*. On the contrary, Monsieur Teste is shaped only by pride, since he has "refused to be a great man." If he is not to betray his essence, then, he must have nothing in common with anyone. Now, let us first make sure that he has nothing in common with Stendhal; they are easy to compare, since the two are perfectly symmetrical.

Stendhal considers himself original; by his conduct, his manners, and his words, he strives to attract the attention of his contemporaries and posterity; as for Monsieur Teste, he never tries to make himself noticed, and presents the image of some very ordinary man. Stendhal is interested in business and politics, whereas Monsieur Teste never opens a newspaper (a remarkable fact for a stock-market speculator). Stendhal often feels pity for the oppressed; nothing in Monsieur Teste, according to the confessor of Teste's wife, "is oriented toward charity." Eroticism plays a major role in Stendhal; his life and his art are profoundly affected by amorous relationships; for Monsieur Teste, on the contrary, love is, even in the most favorable of circumstances, merely a diversion. Stendhal thinks of himself as "sensitive" and "passionate," vulnerable to outside influences; Monsieur Teste's solitude is inviolable, since his inner world is coextensive with his vision and understanding. Stendhal speaks and writes continuously; he is looking for salvation in art; Monsieur Teste willingly keeps silent; he writes sparingly and is contemptuous of art. From the *Soirée avec Monsieur Teste* to the preface to *Lucien Leuwen*, writings separated by more than a quarter century, the use of almost identical expressions reveals that Teste and Stendhal are not only dissimilar, but exact opposites. Valéry discovers a Stendhal who "vaguely reminds him of Punch"; as for Teste, "When he spoke he never lifted an arm or a finger; he had *killed his puppet.*"[6]

If it were a matter of proving that these two intellectual worlds do not intersect, the goal has been accomplished and even largely exceeded. We are now convinced to the point of seeing in Stendhal and Monsieur Teste two symmetrical and opposed halves of the object, *individualism.* But how can Monsieur Teste claim *incommensurability,* since he has a contrary, Stendhal, with whom it cannot be denied that he has the most direct relationship? Monsieur Teste is the *antithesis* of Stendhal.

The two moments of this dialectic are contained in two major currents of modern thought. The enthusiasm of the positivist psychologists and Taine (who did a great deal to "resurrect" Stendhal) was perhaps misplaced, but their point of view obviously served the interests of a Valéry always anxious to underline the differences that contrast him with Stendhal. He insists on Stendhal's "positivism," his rationalism, his respect for science, and his admiration for the geometer Lagrange. Here one need only emphasize that the egotist's natural Ego, like that of the associationist psychologists, is thrown into a world of which it is only a miniscule part. For Valéry, on the contrary, it is not the world that is primary, but the pure Ego. This Ego, the source of all light, which nothing can tarnish, is not accessible to science, because there would be no science without it; our knowledge of it is of a mystical nature; only through a true asceticism can this Ego conquer itself. On the surface, these two worlds appear very different, but one is simply the reverse of the other. Indeed, it suffices to change the first term in order to shift from a world imagined by science to a de facto solipsism. Either a wholly determinate nature will be the only reality, or it will be the scientist's thought that will penetrate this nature through and through. In either case, it is a matter of a perfectly intelligible world. Valéry recognizes only one common trait between Stendhal and Monsieur Teste, but its importance is paramount: this "habit of the mind which consists in seeing the 'vague things' as identically worthless" is the hinge on which both individualist systems turn. Whether one's starting point is consciousness or the world, one need only follow this initial prejudice to its extreme logical conclusion in order to eliminate the ambiguous relations between subject, world, and other which constitute true subjectivity. Between a social Ego that belongs to everyone and a natural Ego that is difficult to conceive as free, it is hard to see how the egotist's vanity and pride can be satisfied. Thus, between Valéry's spontaneous but foolishly gregarious Ego and his pure Ego, whose indomitable force would not tolerate the limitation that the presence of another pure Ego would impose on it, we cannot know *who* can delight in the pride of being unique. Under cover of the exaltation of subjectivity, Valéry and Stendhal enclose themselves within rational alternatives that destroy it.

The presence of all of these anonymous Egos can only be explained in terms of the objective of the system's creator. The individualist is interested in only *one* subjectivity, his own, and by debasing all the others he will lift his own subjectivity higher than it already is. The abstract pattern of the two Egos is simply a trap to ensnare the subjectivity of the other.

In both cases, the others have only the inferior Ego. No one, save the creator of the system, is in full possession of his superior Ego. It is the weapon that he uses to humiliate the inferior Ego. It is all about proving to the others that they are unaware of true existence: in Stendhal it is the passions; in Valéry, it is a contemplation that approaches mystical ecstasy. The gulf that divides the two Egos is merely the distance—indeed the very real distance—that separates the individualist's subjectivity from all the others. In deciding that he *alone* is in possession of his superior Ego, and thus the only one capable of bridging this divide, the individualist gives himself the illusion of having interrupted the reciprocity of the relations between himself and the other. Explaining the rules of his game in the "Letter from a Friend," Valéry articulates in a single formula the secret of the failure and renewal that all "individualist" systems have in common. Speaking of those "intellectual" professions in which "the principal instrument . . . is the opinion of you held by others,"[7] he affirmed that for those who exercise these professions, "each of them founds his own existence on the nonexistence of the others, who must however be forced to agree that they do not exist . . ."[8]

The other is thus reduced to an inferior Ego which, in its weakness, can never know the superior Ego that negates it. The two Egos must therefore never be present simultaneously. Pride, however, cannot come from the one pure Ego, which does not even suspect the existence of others; this Ego is not solipsistic because it is alone; it can only discover itself as unique *in comparing* itself with the inferior Ego reproduced in an infinite number of copies. Thus Valéry's prose works do not derive only from the inferior Ego, since directly or indirectly, they always communicate a revelation that lies beyond this Ego's weak powers. Nor do they spring from the one pure Ego, because this Ego would then be obliged to recognize the existence of the others to whom his works are addressed. The prideful subjectivity, the one that writes solipsistic literature, defies the system it posits because it requires the simultaneous presence of the two Egos, or perhaps the *perpetual shifting from one Ego to the other*. The figure of the narrator in *Monsieur Teste* fulfills this role; the narrator is more extraordinary than the hero, since he is close enough to the true light to reflect a few rays in our direction, but the very existence of the text is proof that he is not above the vain concerns of the work of art and of communicating with others. We find the same ambiguity in the works of Stendhal. The social Ego, for example, reveals the mundane concerns of the author or his financial problems. This does not keep the natural Ego from expressing its surprise when it discovers that such pathetic problems are the fabric of the other's existence. The individualist sees no contradiction in the fact that he attributes to himself what he denies to all others. Certainly, no one can deny him the right to shift from one Ego to another or to contest the reality of this movement, because in order to posit the existence of two distinct Egos, *it is necessary to have measured the distance that separates them.* But the individualist is at once judge and the one who is judged, and he never creates obstacles to individual salvation that he has not himself *a priori* overcome. However authentic the experience of its creator may be, the entire system appears necessarily arbitrary to the eyes of an outside observer. This is precisely what Valéry, in the above-quoted passages from the preface to *Lucien Leuwen,* demonstrates so brilliantly with respect to Stendhal. Only a convention that the egotist himself has established can distinguish what belongs to one Ego or the other.

Perhaps Valéry does not believe that he is vulnerable to this kind of critique. The two Egos are easily distinguishable in his work, for he leaves everything, or almost everything, to the pure Ego, and reduces the other to nothingness. Monsieur Teste—whose pure Ego infinitely conceals itself and will not allow itself to be either seen or conceived, since it is the source of all objectivity—writes in his "Log-book": "away with everything, so that I may see."[9] It is on this apparently impregnable position that Valéry builds his dogmatic system. But if this Ego is simply an "absence," this absence remains "divine." If, following Sartre, we create a true *nothingness* and identify man's being with his deed, Valéry's distinction between being and seeming will prove just as arbitrary as Stendhal's distinction between nature and culture. Sartre's perspective, whatever its intrinsic merit, places Valéry's critic in a position that is comparable to the one occupied by Valéry himself with respect to Stendhal. It is simply a matter of showing that the two doctrines are equally *vulnerable,* and for the same reasons; for the second is the inversion of the first. If the truth Stendhal is seeking rests on the belief in an absolute accessible to introspection and transferable to the work of art, Valéry's artificiality is based on the belief in an absolute that the work of art must finally renounce. Now if we eliminate any reference to the absolute, then the insistence on being false reveals itself to be just as vain as the insistence on being true. If we discern in Stendhal "a certain calculation," Valéry is now no longer above suspicion. If Stendhal is "three or four times too true," Valéry is three or four times too false. Stendhal lies through an excess of sincerity, but Valéry endeavors to hide the fact that he cannot always lie. Stendhal wants to make us believe that his work reproduces a preexisting truth; Valéry refuses to admit that the only truth he possesses resides in the created work. Some identical consequences follow from these two attitudes. The Ego that Stendhal so easily attains is not a free Ego, because a passion whose effects one could control is no longer a passion; on the contrary, the Ego that Valéry exhausts himself trying to reach is the only one that is free; in both cases, no one is ever *responsible*. The individualist well knows that he cannot interrupt the absolute reciprocity of his relations with others; he prepares for a counter-offensive: whether he is always or never himself, he is insulated from possible attack.

Perhaps the negative theology of the Ego that Valéry has substituted for Stendhalian egotism wins out over the rival faith in terms of its subtlety, but it does not solve the problem; it secures no path from the finite to the infinite. The comparison between Stendhal and Monsieur Teste shows that the "refusal to be anything" is first of all the refusal of highly determinate beings, such as Stendhal, and this refusal remains just as determinate as they are.

Valéry may have an answer to all this, for the rapprochement that we have effected between Valéry and Stendhal is not without presuppositions. It recognizes an objective value in literary criticism that is rejected by the author of the preface to *Lucien Leuwen*. Even if we do not agree with this view, we must account for a critical mistrust that no doubt goes beyond the level of simple observation. Valéry's study of Stendhal constantly recalls Monsieur Teste, but in Valéry's eyes, literary criticism is simply a way of rehashing the same old ideas. If criticism is constituted by violent oppositions, it is not because the critic is incapable of certain nuances or that the subject treated has none; it is due to the fact that the writer commented on is only there to serve as a foil. Thus, the Stendhal that Valéry paints for us is likely not the *true* one. The creator of this enemy of the theater Monsieur Teste has made his essays into such contrived dramas that even the least attentive reader will never confuse the good with the bad characters. The good characters, Descartes and da Vinci, resemble Monsieur Teste so closely that no one would ever think of treating them as true representations. Like Pascal, Stendhal is counted among the bad characters, and it is possible he has been refashioned to fit this unfortunate role. On the other hand, let us not forget that if the real Stendhal precedes Monsieur Teste by a half-century, the Stendhal of Valéry's preface to *Lucien Leuwen* comes thirty years after him. Perhaps the movements of the dialectic that we have traced only occur in Valéry's mind and follow a path contrary to the one we have outlined. The Stendhal of 1926 would then simply be an anti-Teste created for the needs of the moment, a counter-model for the education of the true individualists. It would thus be ridiculous to compare Valéry with a Stendhal of his own creation.

It is obvious that Valéry takes great liberties with Stendhal; he considers him outside of any historical context. The décor is there but the substance has fled. We see Stendhal bustling about in the "days of the last stagecoaches and the first railways";[10] however, it would seem that in this world in which technical progress starts to accelerate, only the ideas are not transmitted. Stendhal's ideas will all be considered perfectly *original*. Valéry refuses nothing to Stendhal that he does not grant to da Vinci or Teste; Stendhal too "will depend only on himself." Monsieur Teste, as we know, has quite simply rejected "the opinions and customs that arise in communal life and in our relations with others." He never wonders if the distinction between the individual and the collective is not based on a convention analogous to that which grounds the relation between nature and culture; but what difference does it make, since the scales are in balance; in both cases history is eliminated, and the two adversaries, Stendhal and Monsieur Teste, face off in a space closed off from the rest of the world.

On the contrary, it matters a great deal, because what remains a privilege in the case of Monsieur Teste, our contemporary or close contemporary, becomes a serious constraint for a century-old Stendhal. The public which, by definition, shares the "customs that arise in communal life," will not notice what Monsieur Teste owes to the collective. The subjectivity of Valéry's hero is infused only with the historical present, with values so contemporary that the reader would most likely not be able to perceive them on his own. But when the need arises they will be defended, and defended all the more vehemently because these values support the conviction that *one depends only on oneself*, a conviction that makes every reader like Monsieur Teste. Stendhal, on the other hand, is weighted down with dead values and outmoded prejudices. This is easy to see when Valéry treats Stendhal's feelings toward Napoleon or the clergy. He establishes a complicity with the public that seems to exclude *only* Stendhal, even though no French person who lived during the Restoration would have understood the meaning of these winks of complicity that he lavishes on the reader.

Napoleonic mythology is foreign to Valéry and his intellectual world. We would not criticize him for emphasizing it if he were merely presenting the reaction of a twentieth-century reader to a Stendhal he finds dated. But Valéry judges, and judging is most comfortable when it is ahistorical. This does not by any means prevent Valéry from appealing to history and its vicissitudes when they can serve his argument. "Fortunately, Beyle inherited from the century into which he was born the inestimable gift of liveliness."[11] This is probably just rhetoric, but Valéry is also attempting to link the author of *The Charterhouse of Parma* to the author of *Candide* and *Zadig*, evidently in order to envelop Stendhal with the aura of insignificance which, according to Valéry, permeates all that Voltaire thought and wrote. It is as if he were saying to the initiates: here are two writers happy to be brought together. To show that he is making a great effort to adopt a perspective so different from his own, Valéry enumerates the advantages of the association that he has in mind: "Stendhal, with his taste for opera-buffa, must have delighted in Voltaire's little novels, which will always remain marvels of racy vigor and terrifying fantasy."[12] Henri Brulard refuses to be abused in this manner; after all, his opinion of Voltaire is not so different from Valéry's: "From as far back as I can remember, I have always had the greatest dislike for the writings of Voltaire; they seemed childish to me. I can say that I have never liked anything Voltaire ever wrote."[13]

Valéry finally reduces his victim to silence with an effort to lure Stendhal's posterity into the quicksand of vaudeville and operetta. At this point, Valéry senses that the reader is shocked.[14] He mistakes only the object of this emotion, however. It is not the boldness of the defiler of literary idols that provokes this emotion, but this confidence suddenly placed in causal reasoning which—we understand the scruple—requires the *appearance* of capriciousness: "Only the relations and kinships that are surprising are real."[15]

The Stendhal who must confront Monsieur Teste under such unfavorable conditions is nonetheless very much alive. Through his ferocious commentary, Valéry makes an individual appear that is not perhaps the *real* Stendhal—insofar as the real Stendhal is available to us—but who is nevertheless not made out of whole cloth, since we *recognize* him:

Beyle played a dozen parts in his private theater—the dandy, the coolly rational man, the connoisseur of the fine arts, the soldier of 1812, the man in love with love, the politician and historian. [ . . . ] Like an actor on tour with his wigs, beards and costumes, his Bombets, his Brulards, his Dominiques, his ironmongers . . . In *Memories of a Tourist*, made up as a prosperous traveling salesman, he talks as people do in a public conveyance; plays the economist, gives his views on administration, criticizes and suggests improvements in the plans for the layout of the railways of the future. He enjoys frightening himself about the espionage system of the police, is suspicious of the postal service, uses codes and signs so transparent that they would be comic if the fears were not fictitious and if he didn't want to be frightened.[16]

The Stendhal described in this passage can only be the contrary of the individual without substance that is Monsieur Teste. Valéry did not imagine this Stendhal, but rather crashed into him; it is against Stendhal and thus partly through him that Valéry has created his hero. We have to catch this clever writer in the trap of his own talent's making; one escape route is thereby blocked, but there is another by which he believes escape is possible.

    Up until now we have identified Valéry with Monsieur Teste without asking for Monsieur Teste's credentials. For Valéry recognizes that he has changed since the time when he read *Lucien Leuwen* "with passion." It was 1894, the year that preceded the publication of *Monsieur Teste*: "I cared little about plot or action. I was only interested in the living system to which every event is related. I mean the disposition and reactions of a particular man."[17] The author of *Monsieur Teste* had to uncover the secret workings of this system in order to be in a position to construct its contrary. This is tantamount to admitting that Stendhal served as a negative guide. We do not doubt that Valéry was one of those "non-conformist" readers who, better than Beylism, kept the spirit of Stendhal alive by sending him "to the devil." And perhaps he now looks upon Monsieur Teste with a gaze as "amused" as the one that skimmed through *La vie de Henri Brulard*. In this contempt for the "vague things" that Stendhal shares with Monsieur Teste, Valéry recognizes a "precious but dreaded quality." A closer study of his essay would perhaps reveal that Valéry would never think of renouncing a kinship to which he draws the reader's attention so visibly in the text. The meaning of the text will thus escape us to the degree that the author tends in our direction. There are certain youthful positions of Valéry, which, far from being confirmed by the critique he wages in this essay, fall perhaps under the very condemnation that he has pronounced against Stendhal. Since Monsieur Teste is never mentioned in the preface, we cannot know if Valéry places himself on the side of the antithesis or the synthesis. Valéry always claims to be "charmed" by the very qualities that Monsieur Teste would find the most repugnant. He is no doubt having fun with his readers, but we must still decide on what grounds he is joking in this instance. Is this equanimity required by the genre of the preface, prescribed by the absurd but salutary rules of literary practice or, on the contrary, should we see it as proof of a real critical detachment? The more we reflect on particular critical formulas, the more we hesitate to define their field of application. Stupidity, as we know, is not Valéry's strong point,[18] and he cannot be unaware of the stimulative effect he has on his reader when he writes: "It is a law of nature that one can only protect himself against an affectation by means of another affectation."

Monsieur Teste thus remains present, but it is no longer clear what role he plays when he is juxtaposed with Stendhal: adversary or accomplice, supreme judge or the accused. A third character has emerged in this intellectual comedy, Valéry himself, and his relations with the other two characters appear extraordinarily complex.

Let us first remark that the passage from the "Letter from a Friend" mentioned above testifies to the fact that Valéry did not wait until the preface to *Lucien Leuwen* to consider Monsieur Teste from a certain distance and even with a certain irony. Monsieur Teste undertook the paradoxical task of expressing the inexpressible, but its failure was a foregone conclusion. This character remains a literary creation. Is not the work of art always artificial, untruthful, and concerned only with the seduction of the reader? One can thus effect a rapprochement between Monsieur Teste and Stendhal without affecting Valéry the individual, or perhaps even the essence of Valéryism. In this respect, the preface to *Lucien Leuwen* is neither more nor less ambiguous than is the preface to *Monsieur Teste*. Though he never disassociates himself from his writings, Valéry knows how to subtly frustrate those who would use his writings against him. In his preface, he reminds us that any rapprochement between Stendhal and himself can only happen in the realm of art, that is, in the realm of the inferior Ego. It matters little to Valéry that this "law of nature" makes Monsieur Teste take the opposing tack to everything Henri Beyle does. Indeed, the only thing that interests him is the moment when laws no longer apply. And let us not believe that we are catching Valéry off his guard by giving to Stendhal the very privilege of immunity Valéry claims for himself. He has anticipated our move; the true Stendhal remains intact, as he asserts at the end of his preface: "He is too radically himself to be reducible to a writer."[19]

But we were far from suspecting the existence of this sacred wall that Valéry now erects around his victim when, a few moments earlier, reading between the lines of the text, we thought we had discovered a "desperate ambition" behind a "comedy of sincerity." At that moment, we were opposing vanity to pride, the project of being a great man to that of being incommensurable. We naïvely thought that we had learned something essential concerning Stendhal. We see that after having made use of his critical instrument, Valéry now questions its value. We would like to believe at this point that the "psychological" discoveries accessible to objective reflection are *second-order* truths, but Valéry is on the wrong track when he criticizes Stendhal for delighting in these discoveries, in effect blaming Stendhal for indulging in what Valéry's own criticism is designed to stimulate. Indeed, this "ambition" and "comedy" to which Valéry deigns to dedicate this essay are standard Stendhalian truths. We are thus forced to conclude the following: the Valéry who criticizes Stendhal for his penchant for psychology is not the Valéry who indulges in it; nor is the Valéry who disdains history the Valéry who manipulates it for his own benefit. We now understand why Valéry entertains these ambiguous relations with his works. He can dress up like Monsieur Teste whenever he chooses, then disguise himself as a man of letters or a literary critic. Like Stendhal, Valéry plays many roles at once; it is the critic who wastes his time in showing us a Stendhal truer than the Stendhal Henri Beyle describes in his writings; as for Monsieur Teste, he is contemptuous of these impure *divertissements*. There is nothing here that should surprise us. We are simply using a concrete case to verify this perpetual shifting from one Ego to another by which we have defined "individualism."

We will no longer allow ourselves to be led astray. Whatever the cleverness of his maneuvers and the rapidity of his changing disguises, we know that Valéry cannot score points against Stendhal without leaving himself open to attack, and that he will not be out of danger so long as the enemy remains vulnerable. As has been shown with respect to Stendhal and Valéry himself, Valéry cannot hide this *second-order* truth from us: the reversal of the egotist credo—the shift from one belief system to another—does not affect the essence of literary individualism. It is not a matter here of reducing Stendhal and Valéry to a fascination before the Other that would result in an overly simplistic account of their writings, but to show that the defensive systems created by this common anxiety are very close to one another, in that they retain from contrary modes thought only that which can serve an identical end. Valéry is not unaware of a secret fraternity with an author who is in many ways very different from him; Valéry's deftness at discovering the weak points betrays him as the one whom Claude-Edmonde Magny has so aptly called Stendhal's "accomplice."[20] Valéry even goes so far as to point out the effort and simulation in love that Henri Beyle brings to his art, which Valéry himself considers only a *second-order art!* It is this exasperating intimacy that transforms Stendhal into this *Other* on whose non-being Valéry must found his own existence. Dogmatic in its appearance of spontaneity, profoundly unjust behind the laudations required by the genre, the preface to *Lucien Leuwen* constitutes a symbolic destruction of Stendhal and his oeuvre. We must not look here for the fruits of a self-assured criticism; it is something else that makes this text invaluable: Valéry is playing a tight game with an opponent who has anticipated his every move.

—*Translated by Robert Doran*

# 3

# Classicism and Voltaire's Historiography [1958]

Voltaire was convinced that his surest claim to eternity lay in his historical writings, and he kept revising them until the end of his life. This judgment, like some other judgments of Voltaire, has not been ratified by posterity. We admire *The Century of Louis XIV*, but we read Saint-Simon and Betz. We salute the *Essay on Mores* (*L'essai sur les moeurs*), but the Benedictine historians are the founding fathers of modern scholarship.

Voltaire heartily disliked both the passionate memorialists and the patient Benedictines. But whereas we feel that these two groups of historical writers deserve our admiration on separate, perhaps opposite grounds, Voltaire directed the same fundamental criticism against all of them. He ridiculed them for writing too lengthily on unimportant subjects.

To the modern student, this criticism seems futile to the point of absurdity. We have too much respect for Voltaire—or not enough—to take it seriously. Is not thoroughness the first virtue of an historian? Can anything be insignificant in his eyes? Should not history aim at the "integral resurrection of the past?"

—No, answers Voltaire. The noblest task of the historian is to eliminate the superfluous, so that whatever facts are really worthy of being handed down to posterity will stand out majestically. The heroic deeds of reigning princes are not the only such facts, as they were for Voltaire's predecessors; the criteria of historical choice are different, but the principle remains intact.

We should not be surprised. The principle of historical choice, after all, is identical with the law of classical proportion. History must observe that law or it will not be classical. And Voltaire is determined to achieve immortal fame by making history classical. His remarks on the genre are of special interest to the critic of classicism. Not so much because of what Voltaire thinks, as because of what we think. In the case of history, our professed admiration for the classics conflicts with a sentiment which, in most of us, is more intense: devotion to *scientific principles*. It becomes difficult to ignore the gulf between the modern and the classical spirit.

Voltaire makes a distinction between the *histoire générale* from which all "details" must be ruthlessly extirpated and the *histoire particulière*, history of a war, or of a reign, where they can be introduced, although sparingly.

Such details require great artistry. It is very difficult to retain one particular event in the multitude of these revolutions which throw our planet into confusion. So many enterprises, alliances, wars and battles succeed each other that, after a century has elapsed, what appeared in its day sublime, important, unique is replaced by new happenings of greater interest to contemporaries, and the past is forced into oblivion. Everything is lost in this immensity; everything becomes a dot on the map. Military operations cause as much tedium as they did anxiety when the fate of the nation depended upon them.[1]

If the historian is not brief, if he does not prune his facts as sternly as a Versailles gardener his hedges, his readers will, sooner or later, abandon him. Our quotation is from a reply to the Maréchal duc de Richelieu, who had just sent to Voltaire a thirty-two-page letter on his own contribution to the wars of Louis XV. Voltaire explains politely to the Maréchal that all this material cannot be used. Of course, this grand-nephew of the great cardinal wants the lion's share of immortality. We should be reasonable, Voltaire warns, or we shall defeat our own purpose. If we try for too much immortality, we might end up with none at all.

Voltaire speaks from personal experience. He felt strongly tempted, at times, to give up history, deluged as he was under egotistical memoirs, pedantic disquisitions upon trifles, endless dissertations on forgotten incidents, long-winded panegyrics and naïve chronicles which no stretch of the imagination could bring under the heading of *générales* or *particulières*. Voltaire did pursue his task, but the price, in his eyes, was exorbitant. Certain pages of the *Essay on Mores* cost him "weeks of reading and research."

Voltaire was a conscientious historian, even by our own standards, but why did he find slightly unworthy of himself chores which are the daily bread of the modern historian? We might accuse him of being lazy if, everywhere, traces of his activity did not belie the accusation. There is not, it seems, one field of human endeavor which has been completely neglected by Voltaire. And it is, of course, this universality of interests which explains the impatience of our modern historian. All intellectual pursuits have the same importance in the eyes of Voltaire. He will not let any single one detract him from the others. He refused with indignation an enthusiastic disciple of a scientist friend, Madame du Chatelet, when she suggested that he should abandon poetry and dedicate himself solely to physics.

The classicist resents verbose historians because they are going to make it impossible for the *honnête homme* to venture into the past. A few will dedicate their entire lives to history; the others will have no history at all. No matter which group one decides to join, one will not be an *honnête homme*. The *honnête homme* will disappear, for he cannot do without history; but he can do even less with nothing but history. The survival of the *honnête homme* depends upon sound historical choice, upon the law of classical proportion.

It is the classical rules which make it possible to be interested in everything, indifferent to nothing. All classical arts and disciplines are sections on a sphere with the *honnête homme* at its center. Strict genre distinctions prevent any overlapping detrimental to the harmonious formation of the individual. All classical restrictions, including classical brevity, correspond to some need of the *honnête homme*. Even the classical concern for posterity, often viewed nowadays as a proof of inordinate vanity, is a form of self-denial. The writer's point of view shall be that of the reader farthest removed in time; therefore, it is the most alien to his own preoccupations. Thus, it will be certain that all points of view are taken into account. What will appear, a century from now, like a dot on the map, should be represented as a dot on the map. Just as the classical architect renounces small ornaments on a great palace because its façade is designed for the beholder at the end of the park, the classical historian eliminates details because he writes for the *honnête homme* of tomorrow and for the *honnête homme* of all times.

Classical society is totally present in each of its component parts; it is geared to the individual. To use one of the modern jargons, we might say that, thanks to classical self-restraint, the *honnête homme* can receive all cultural stimuli and react appropriately. Classical society provides the *maximum amount of intellectual communication* or, in classical French, *le commerce des esprits*. It greets geniuses as different as Newton, Leibnitz, Montesquieu, and Rousseau with the same alacrity. In no other society do ideas meet a deeper echo, do new forms evoke a greater response. Ultimately, it is the writers and artists themselves who benefit from their own self-restraint.

When the conversation is general, wit and talent will be immediately appreciated by all the guests. A brilliant salon depends not only on wit and talent, but on everyone's good manners. Let any person talk endlessly about his favorite subject, let him resort to pedantic, esoteric terms, or to intimate confessions in an effort to retain the undivided attention of the other guests and the salon is destroyed. One such egotistical guest immediately breeds others who will also try their own devices upon the audience. Soon the salon is fragmented into small groups which ignore each other.

Thus, under the pressure of insatiable egos, the classical world "explodes" and its fragments—our fields of specialization—move farther and farther away from each other. This is what Voltaire fears. We might speak of an expanding universe as the physicists do. The image is bad, however, because it is an image and, as such, it will always comprehend its object, even the fastest-expanding one. The expanding cultural universe, on the other hand, is the one which no mental image, no individual mind can ever hope to comprehend. As Western man conquers the material world, he is losing his grip upon his cultural world. *Who* can be proud of what we still call *our* culture? In every field, a few specialists write esoterically for their own kind, for the only ones who, from the point of view of a harmonious individual development, do not need their writings. The various disciplines speak such different languages that they not only ignore each other, but sometimes cancel each other out without even being aware of it. For those who are repelled by the narrow pragmatism of the various specialists, there is nothing but small talk or the silence of infinite space, the interplanetary void.

In the twentieth century, classical rules have become so alien to us that Paul Valéry, an ultra-romantic in disguise, has proclaimed their excellence anew on the grounds of arbitrariness. In Valéry's eyes, the scrupulous observance of meaningless rules is the *summum* of aesthetic refinement. Valéry's boundless egotism prevented him from understanding the *raison d'être* of classical discipline. Intellectual life is a form of social life, and there is no social life without a process of give and take. If the writer does not efface himself in front of his public, he may gain a temporary advantage, but ultimately he himself will suffer. If Richelieu demands too much immortality, immortality will be denied to him. If writers, through unclassical means, claim the undivided attention of the public, they will face, one day, the interplanetary void of a specialist's culture. Specialists of literature will be writing enormous studies about writers, but the intense feeling of presence which was taken for granted in classical society will be gradually replaced by the familiar *angoisse* of our contemporary world. This unnatural *angoisse* may help us to understand what the classical writers meant when they claimed that they were being faithful to human nature.

In the name of nature, the classical writers set up rules which the romantics, again in the name of nature, discarded. Nature, it seems, cannot be the same in both cases. The romantics must have "discovered" a new, more modern, more complex, and more complete nature. But our quotation from Voltaire's letter could be signed by any romantic or post-romantic writer. If it dealt with the individual rather than the collective past, it could be signed by Proust. *Everything is lost in the immensity of the past*: Voltaire's historical method and *Remembrance of Things Past* originate in the same observation. Who said that the classical writers lived in eternity, that their time was not as destructive as ours, that they knew nothing of relativity?

It is the same nature to which Voltaire and Proust are faithful, but the literary consequences are diametrically opposed. Where does the difference lie? It is almost too immediate to be readily perceived: the classical writer respects the reader's nature; the romantic is thinking only about *himself*. The classical writer wants to adapt literature to the limitations which finite existence imposes upon the *commerce des esprits*; the romantic is trying to rescue *his own* existence from the immensity of the past.

The classical writers are aware that civilization is an *unnatural* development. Being unnatural, it will not survive unless it patterns itself closely after nature. As natural growth is a harmonious and balanced one, both in the individual and the species, so must be cultural growth. The *honnête homme's* relationship to his cultural milieu must be like that of any healthy living creature to its natural environment. And classical society is like a living tissue, each cell of which is capable of performing all the exchanges necessary with the life of the whole. But this orderly growth, in nature, is promoted through destruction, violence, and death. In the cultural world, there is no law of natural selection. In order to achieve the same ends as nature, man must resort to the opposite means of self-restraint and *politesse*. In a classical society, nature and the most extreme social refinement are inseparable and complementary. They will become contradictory only after the romantics "discover" nature.

The classical relationship to nature is an organic one; the romantic relationship is that of an image to reality: art becomes an absorbing spectacle which is set up without much regard for the absorbed spectator. The classical disciplines carefully apportioned the whole of human personality; the *honnête homme* was a harmonious synthesis because his literature was analytical. When each discipline, each author wants the whole sphere for himself, when literature itself becomes a synthesis, the reader's personality becomes "analytical," fragmentary, mutilated, "specialized."

Voltaire's conception of the historian's *politesse* may be a little narrow, but it is not the frivolous ideal it is sometimes made out to be. Our various cultural cancers and the curious symptom of *angoisse* now spreading to more and more sectors of our intellectual life may be the price which we have to pay for the total abandonment of classical self-restraint.

The criticism of lengthiness against fellow historians is, therefore, perfectly legitimate within the classical framework. Both our extreme subjectivism and our extreme objectivism deem it superficial. From Voltaire's viewpoint, it is the opposition between these two modern attitudes which is superficial. Voltaire, let us remember, makes no distinction between the memorialists and the Benedictine historians, between those who are so engrossed in themselves or so engrossed in their science that they are blind to everything else. Philosophers and poets often fancy themselves to be the last line of defense against the inhuman world of science. But behind the philosopher's or the poet's search for a new, unsullied language which shall belong to no one else, as well as behind science's search for unlimited power—and unlimited destruction—Voltaire would denounce the same driving force, the unbridled ego. His interpretation of our cultural malaise would not separate the aesthetic and methodological factors from the moral ones. *Le moi est haïssable*; Voltaire is not as far from his enemy Pascal as he is from the twentieth century. If he were, we could not call him a classical writer.

But Voltaire's battle was already lost. The *honnête homme*, so much more modest than the Renaissance man, was becoming a preposterously ambitious ideal in the already fast expanding culture of the eighteenth century. The last *honnête homme*, Voltaire, is also an international phenomenon of feverish creativity. This is the paradox of Voltaire. All his life he clamored for fewer books; but his complete works number close to a hundred volumes and he wrote letters to posterity by the tens of thousands. Voltaire himself was the victim of romantic egotism. All he could do was to keep out the lyricism that usually accompanies it. But Voltaire could be as petty as a Saint-Simon, a Benedictine monk, or a romantic poet. And, ironically, it is often when he indulged in his pettiest moods that Voltaire achieved immortality. Non-classical posterity rewarded him when it should have punished him. Voltaire would not understand. He did not suspect that, when all literary *terrains d'entente* are abandoned, the exhalations of the embittered ego provide, at least for a time, a new and paradoxical one. This ignorance is Voltaire's innocence, and it is his classicism.

# 4

# Pride and Passion in the Contemporary Novel[1] [1959]

Romanticism is a literature of the self and for the self. With Rousseau and the first romantics, love and passion were no longer treated for their own sake; these literary themes were called upon to glorify and justify a self perpetually threatened with anonymity and disintegration in the new democratic society. The first romantics tried to reach their goal by asserting the eternity and intensity of the passionate sentiments aroused in their beautiful souls by a chosen woman.

This chosen woman played a very minor role. When that point was not clear enough, the romantic did not hesitate to suggest, with a deep sigh or a sly wink, according to the mood of the moment, that the beloved was not quite worthy of the tribute rendered to her. It was the romantic soul, overflowing with beauty, which transfigured the object of its passion. The romantic was God, and his love was a communion with himself.

In the first years of the nineteenth century, the spiritual effects of the French Revolution were still largely limited to men. Women could still accept the purely passive role which was bestowed upon them. The romantic women writers, however, were not far behind men in their egotistical appetites. With a Mme de Staël and, more strikingly still, with a George Sand, a new woman emerged, infinitely more threatening to male supremacy than her libertine grandmother in the rococo boudoir.

The romantic love myth, like all myths, did not attempt to survive by coming to terms with reality, but by exaggerating its most chimerical features. As real women began to lose some of their femininity, as they started, in other words, that upward climb which led them to the position of prestige and power we see them "enjoying" today, the fictitious woman of literature became more and more frail and gracile, more consumptive and retiring. As the century wore on, however, the celebration of this sublimely passive and self-sacrificing creature sounded a note of increasing melancholy. The term of this dual evolution was reached with the plaintive, elusive, transparent, and slightly insignificant Mélisande of the symbolist Maeterlinck.

Most writers, by that time, had rejected the romantic love myth and ushered in the twentieth century, with its many new attitudes toward sexual passion. These range from the sex cult of D. H. Lawrence, the *amour fou* of André Breton, and the delicately diabolical *immoralisme* of Gide to the various shades of "neo–Don Juanism" propounded by Messrs André Malraux the Conqueror, Henry de Montherlant the Conquistador, and, more recently, by Albert Camus, the crusader of the *absurde*. Sex, as a rule, came to replace love. But sex, too, could be a tool of self-justification. The means were different, but the end was the same. Earlier romantics had gloried in the eternity of their attachment to an irreplaceable woman; the later ones exulted in the eternally renewed vigor of their desire for an undetermined number of sex objects. No doubt could be left, this time, as to the relative importance of the sex partners. The interchangeable character of the objects enhanced the unity and superiority of the desiring subject.

The new type of glorification did not seem to conflict with autobiographical truth. Twentieth-century writers openly acknowledged the temporary nature of their amorous attachments; they were heralded, together with Freud and his disciples, as prophets of a new sexual truth, as the liberators of mankind. The romantic love myth was constantly ridiculed. The mythical character of the new literary constructions remained almost unsuspected during the first half of the century. Since the war, however, it has become more and more visible, as new generations of writers, through a new process of literary overbidding, moved farther and farther away from the truth of their society.

Let us take, for instance, the case of Don Juan. This personage cut a strange enough figure in the world of Colette and Marcel Prévost, but he looks downright eerie among the heroines of Simone de Beauvoir, Françoise Sagan, and Vladimir Nabokov. The persistence and general acceptance of the Don Juan theme in such dreary surroundings calls for serious reflection. Something must hide behind the shopworn mask of Don Juan, something more arresting than the face of Roger Vailland's hero, *Monsieur Jean.*

Women may not all have been virtuous in the Spain of the Golden Age, but they were, at least, severely restricted in their freedom by stern duennas and gentlemen armed to the teeth. The game of numbers which Don Juan played in such circumstances was not devoid of sportsmanship. If this hero could exchange his hell for the Parisian literary circles of the twentieth century, he would probably throw away his cape and rapier in disgust. Speculating, perhaps, that the fish, unlike his former game, tend to disappear as their pursuers multiply, he might well join the anglers on the banks of the Seine rather than his misguided disciples in the city nightspots.

Don Juan concealed his true nature from his prospective victims; he presented himself as a virtuous and sincere young man; he had only one witness, the inconsequential Sganarelle. Monsieur Jean behaves quite differently; he wants the whole world for a witness; he publicizes his fickleness far and wide. He is especially eager to impress beautiful women with his promiscuous disposition.

Monsieur Jean says that he is Don Juan, and Don Juan said that he was not. Shall we conclude that the only difference between the model and the disciple is the greater truthfulness of the latter? We should realize, on the contrary, that the only thing common to Don Juan and Monsieur Jean is the intent to deceive. The two heroes are trying to hide their identity. Monsieur Jean has no right to present himself as a reincarnation of Don Juan. Don Juan was always free, and Monsieur Jean never is. He is not free, even as he goes from mistress to mistress, for he is in constant danger of losing his freedom.

When Don Juan failed, his wound was quickly forgotten. He was the victim of virtue or of insuperable physical obstacles. When Monsieur Jean fails, he is the victim of *indifference.* Modern vanity dreads nothing more than sheer indifference. Indifference cannot turn Monsieur Jean into a new Tristan, but it exerts upon him a horrible and weird fascination.

The modern egotist is *almost* convinced that he is God. As such he should be invulnerable to all, and all should be vulnerable to him. Any exception to this rule shatters the confidence of Monsieur Jean. Confronted by an indifferent woman, the modern seducer immediately suspects, with *angoisse* in his heart, that she, and not he, is the Divinity. His instinct warns Monsieur Jean that the now completely emancipated woman has exactly the same metaphysical appetites as he does. She, too, wants to be God, and she will be fascinated by the appearance of invulnerability. This appearance will be provided by the mask of Don Juan. Monsieur Jean wears this mask in order to fascinate his partner before she fascinates him. Success makes him almost believe in the reality of the role. Don Juan had only others to deceive; Monsieur Jean is also trying to deceive himself.

The real ancestor of Monsieur Jean is not Don Juan or Valmont, but the twentieth-century *dandy* who was the first professional indifferent. Baudelaire viewed the dandy as a relic of the aristocratic past; Stendhal defined him, more correctly and less romantically, as a child of democracy. The dandy displays his indifference in order to attract idle desires, just as a magnet attracts iron shavings. This Mephistopheles in a top hat wants to be the capitalist of desires; there is nothing aristocratic in such an undertaking.

The dandy does, indeed, look like a gentleman when compared to our recent heroes, but it is a question of perspective. Monsieur Jean, too, advertises his indifference. The product is the same, but the technique is different. It has become, like all advertising techniques, more brazen and impudent with the passage of time. Attracting other people's attention to the fact that one could not care less is a problem for which it is increasingly difficult to find new solutions. Dandyism was still compatible with a certain refinement and good taste, which are notably absent from the works of Montherlant. And Montherlant was still compatible with a certain restraint, which is notably absent from the works of Roger Vailland.

The erotic relationship has turned into a battle of equal and identical selves trying to outdo each other in their display of callousness and insensitivity. Since the two partners are haunted by the same mirage of divine autonomy, the first who reveals his desire will never be desired, and he will see his dependence turn into utter enslavement. This *marivaudage* for the atomic age is also a caricature of Hegel's "dialectics of the master and the slave." Each one is staking his freedom against his partner's freedom. The deciding factor is not physical courage, but the power of dissimulation, the old *hypocrisy* of the Stendhalian novels.

*La loi*—the law—of Roger Vailland is but another name for the implacable dialectics of egotistical desire. The game played in the villages of Southern Italy is a symbol of the relationship which prevails among the young, and the not so young, all over our idle and spiritually empty middle-class world. Unlike a Stendhal or a Proust, however, a Roger Vailland does not rise above his mediocre little hell. He enjoys it thoroughly, and he wants us to share his admiration for the winner of the game. This winner, however, is even more of a dupe than the loser, for the simple reason that much can be learned from defeat and nothing from victory. Stendhal and Proust have proved the first point long ago; Roger Vailland is busy proving the second.

Wherever "the law" reigns supreme, reciprocity is impossible. Desire breeds contempt, and contempt breeds more desire. The heroes of many current best-sellers aspire to a sentimental communion which cannot and will not be achieved. And yet these heroes have no higher value than this erotico-egotistical *ekstasis*. They are bound to be disappointed. We know, now, what would happen to Emma Bovary if she left Charles in Yonville and bought herself a sports car.

Many of these new novelists seem to share their heroes' belief in the supreme value of individual "differences." Each adolescent is convinced that his "uniqueness" alone prevents him from merging harmoniously with an equally unique partner. It is clear, though, that everybody is a carbon copy of everybody else. The lovers cannot agree because they all pursue the same chimera of a ready-made divinity. Modern erotic fascination is a fascination for the Identical conceived as absolute Otherness. Far from being the fruit of concrete differences, the opposition is both absolute and nil: it is the opposition of an object and its image, identical and reversed, as we see it in the mirror. The sociologists confirm that the sexes are becoming more alike. And homosexual obsessions are perhaps a paroxysmal form of this very general malady. It is not, therefore, in spite of, but because of his homosexuality that Marcel Proust managed to give such powerful and universal expression to the modern erotic predicament.

The uniformity of youth, in certain milieus, is never acknowledged, but it transpires in the very inability of the contemporary novelist to individualize his characters, in the impression of grayish uniformity which they leave in our minds. The laws of fascination produce rigidly geometrical patterns, which explain why a Françoise Sagan is attracted by the art of the ballet. All the characters appear to be the victims of some latter-day Racinian fatality; the counterpoint of their passion recalls, indeed, those plays of Racine which are most impregnated with the spirit of the Court. Orestes loves Hermione, who does not love him . . . Hermione loves Pyrrhus, who does not love her . . . Pyrrhus loves Andromache, who does not love him . . . It would seem that a spiritual disease formerly limited to a small social elite is now invading a materially secure middle class.

This middle class has not yet found its Racine or its Proust. But it may soon have its Dostoevsky in the author of *The Fall.* A neglected aspect of this relatively neglected work by Albert Camus concerns the hero's sexuality. This hero, Clamence, is a progressive lawyer, an indefatigable signer of manifestoes, and a successful lover. He defends the innocent and seduces the beautiful with the same serene conviction of his spiritual and physical excellence. One day, however, he is summarily dismissed by a new mistress after giving a rather unfavorable account of himself. His boredom immediately turns into that horrid fascination which absent-mindedness or sheer perversity insists on calling love. Unsoothed by this linguistic anomaly, Clamence turns toward the forgotten art of ethical self-examination. He might accuse an unjust society, he might curse the "human condition," but he bypasses these traditional scapegoats and puts the blame, instead, on his own monstrous egotism. No wonder the work has baffled the critics.

Gone is the naïve Don Juanism of *The Myth of Sisyphus. The Fall* is a vigorous attack on the hidden smugness of post-war sermonizing literature, including, probably, Camus' own. The need for justification which possesses Clamence is infinitely more complex than the self-centeredness of the French classical moralists. It is inhabited by an inner contradiction. Self-concern is always looking for reassurance, and it binds us to others as powerfully as, but less harmoniously than would love. It is both the *amour-propre* of La Rochefoucauld and the *alienation* of the Marxists.

Individualism is not the unifying factor which the Promethean thinkers have described. Whatever it embraces in its search for justification immediately begins to disintegrate. The present exaltation of sex, like the exaltation of love in a former era, is not a cure but a symptom of a spiritual disease which has been steadily worsening since the beginning of Romanticism.

Desire, in our world, is exalted in the abstract, but concrete desire is shameful. It brands one as inferior to the desired object. We have already seen that Monsieur Jean conceals his desire in order to stimulate the desire of his partner. Desire, however, does not belong to "inner life"; it is essentially dynamic, and concealment is tantamount to suppression. Willpower is brought in, and it may well interfere with the normal fulfillment of desire. The distance is small, indeed, between the strategic refusal to abandon oneself in the presence of the desired woman and the inability to do so when the time has really come for such abandonment. The impulse of desire has become inseparable from its own suppression. Julien Sorel, the great technician of seduction, is a secret brother of Octave, the impotent hero of Armance. The Jake of *The Sun Also Rises* is a secret brother of all the super-virile figures created by Hemingway. The conquerors of Malraux are haunted by the fear of sexual impotence. They, too, want to eliminate all *passivity* from *passion,* and they are left empty-handed. The successful Clamence is still another victim of the Stendhalian *fiasco.*

The complete invulnerability that is the dream of Monsieur Jean is equivalent to complete impotence. This equivalence explains, perhaps, why our present literary stage is almost evenly divided between the swaggering seducers and the pitiful wretches. These antithetic heroes are the two halves of our truth. But a half-truth is not the truth; it is not even the most effective weapon against the truth. The novelists of the half-truth—it does not matter which half—are all romantics in disguise.

Our swaggering seducer suppresses his desire when the woman he intends to seduce is looking at him. He may soon discover that he is really paralyzed by the gaze of this woman. He could preserve his freedom if the woman, for some reason or other, were not conscious of his presence. Julien Sorel wishes that Mathilde could not feel his kisses. In Proust, the only experience of sexual pleasure takes place when Albertine is *asleep*. In Dostoevsky, the hero may kill his beloved in order to possess her.

With more ordinary heroes and in more ordinary circumstances, the woman will not lose her consciousness, and the only recourse is to hide from her view. The closest thing to physical possession, in such a predicament, *is to see without being seen*. Monsieur Jean is now metamorphosed into a Peeping Tom. The theme of the *voyeur*, already important with Dostoevsky and Proust, becomes essential in contemporary fiction, and even in contemporary thought. Jean-Paul Sartre's *pour-soi* feels "deprived of his world" when someone is looking at him. Unseen, he wants to see, and we find him, at one point, peeking through a keyhole. *Being and Nothingness* contains a phenomenology of the Peeping Tom caught in the act. The heroes of Jean Genet are all *voyeurs*. And, from the barrels and garbage cans of Samuel Beckett only wide-open eyes emerge.

Until recently, the *voyeur* was a theme or a character in the novel; he was not the novel itself. With *le nouveau roman*, however, we have a direct expression of the *voyeur*'s worldview. Action is nonexistent, and almost all impressions are visual. Objects are never described as they appear to the man who handles them, but as pure spectacle. The novelists of *le nouveau roman* devise the techniques and situations of what Sartre would call the *transcendance* of the object.

In Michel Butor's *La modification*, the hero is sitting in a train from the beginning to the end of the novel; he stares with the same indiscriminate avidity at the objects and human beings gathered in his compartment or stored in his memory. Sex is rarely present as a theme, but it pervades the description of the apparently least sexual objects. There is a vague obscenity in these prolonged and insistent descriptions. Everything is seen through the eyes of the *voyeur*, and the readers themselves are turned into *voyeurs*. The contemporary man should not find it difficult to play a role in which modern life is already casting him. Glued to his movie or television screen, fed his daily dose of scandals, always watching and never acting, he too has become a Peeping Tom.

The two most recent novels of Alain Robbe-Grillet, *The Voyeur* and *Jealousy*, are masterpieces of the *nouveau roman*. The hero of *Jealousy* is so much alone at the center of his visual world and so much intent on the spectacle he is watching that he never reflects upon himself, and we might almost believe that he is absent from his novel. The narrative in the personal mode connects with the most impersonal description. The hero keeps registering the smallest details present in his field of vision. Among the various objects there are two human beings, and they are treated exactly as if they were objects.

There is no common human denominator in *Jealousy,* and there does not seem, at first, to be any human feeling. Gradually, however, a pattern of relationship emerges; it is the classical triangle of the bourgeois drama. The two human beings are the wife and a friend of the hero; the wife may be having an affair with the friend. The hero is jealous, and the flavor of *angoisse* which permeates the descriptions reflects his suffering. The minute depictions of trivial objects, the obsessive returns of apparently insignificant notations, crystallize into a personal symbolism of hatred.

The philosophical critics have not exhausted the meaning of *Jealousy.* They emphasize the technique at the expense of a content which they do not judge worthy of their attention. They fail to perceive that the chief interest of the book lies in the tension and contradiction between the solipsistic technique and the psychological content. This tension is already present in the title, *Jealousy,* which refers both to the hero's jealousy and to the Venetian blind from behind which he is peeking at the alleged lovers. Robbe-Grillet's man is as far from true solitude as he is from communion. He lives in what a page of Kafka's *Journal* calls the *Grenzland zwischen Einsamkeit und Gemeinschaft* (the frontier between solitude and community). The omnipotent consciousness of the philosopher is really a prison. Individualism is divided against itself. We are always coming back to that truth.

Sexuality is not, as Freud believed, the mainspring of our life; it is a mirror in which the whole of existence is reflected. Contemporary fiction holds this mirror up to us. What we see in it, more plainly with each passing year, is the failure of the Promethean project.

# 5

# Stendhal and Tocqueville [1960]

Persuaded as he was that all European nations were traveling toward democracy at various rates of speed, Stendhal gave to a faster-moving America the passionate attention of a man who is trying to catch a glimpse of his own future. The novelist read many travel accounts and political essays on the American democracy. In a review of Basil Hall's *Travels through North America*, we learn that he leafed through "hundreds of volumes" in order to get a clear idea "of the only republic which functions correctly in the nineteenth century." The quality of the works was often poor, however, and this conscientious survey of travel literature resulted in a good deal of "yawning."[1]

Stendhal did not yawn, assuredly, when he chanced upon the first two volumes of *Democracy in America*, which were published in 1835. We find a reference to the work in a marginal note on the manuscript of *Lucien Leuwen*, which Stendhal abandoned in October 1836. The passage opposite the note is typically Stendhalian in its rather negative appreciation of the American experiment. The hero, Lucien, is the son of a rich French banker and a very refined young man. Several times in the novel he rejects, like other Stendhalian heroes, the idea of settling in the United States. Lucien is a liberal, but the disadvantages of democracy are great when one is not capable of earning "even the price of a cigar." Lucien is not ready to exchange a brilliant social life for an honest government. America is fine for the downtrodden people, but there is no good opera house. Democratic life breeds an "excessive morality" and destroys the aesthetic refinements.

There are reasons to believe, moreover, that the pressures for conformity limit personal freedom. Where public opinion reigns, the majority is the tyrant. Paying court to one's grocer and butcher may be worse, in the end, than paying court to M. de Talleyrand. Democracy, Lucien feels, is "too harsh for his sensibility." Commenting upon this last statement, the novelist wrote: "M. de Tocqueville has been paid by the government to spread this opinion among the French. Fortunately for the government the truth was sufficient to the task."[2]

Tocqueville, of course, was not subsidized by the government to write a tendentious report on America. Tocqueville, however, had left for the United States on an official mission to investigate the penitential system. This fact, of which Stendhal was perhaps cognizant, could not fail to arouse his suspicion. And Stendhal was not a man to voice his suspicion with restraint, especially when writing for no one but himself.

Tocqueville belonged to an important aristocratic family; he enjoyed all the social advantages that the novelist lacked; he was received in the fashionable salons, both *légitimistes* and *orléanistes*. He was a relative, by marriage, of M. de Chateaubriand, the founder of a romantic school which Stendhal found pompous and hypocritical. A rather solemn and melancholy young man himself, Tocqueville could easily pass for a latter-day René with a touch of the 1830 dandy. By all appearances, the young sociologist was a perfect product of what Stendhal often called, using the English phrase, "our age of cant." To make matters worse, Tocqueville seemed promised to a brilliant political career under the July monarchy. His liberal ideas were tempered by a nostalgic respect for the traditions of the French past. Such a mixture was the ideal recipe for success under the July monarchy, but it could not fail to strike Stendhal as the height of priggishness and opportunism.

Tocqueville is a profound observer but a rather humorless man. Stendhal, on the other hand, is always looking for the lighter aspects of people and events. Stendhal loves to shock his readers; he is addicted to the most extreme statements, and his critics are still wondering if they must place him on the far left or the far right of the nineteenth-century political spectrum. All they know is that he is nowhere in the middle. And the middle is precisely where Tocqueville appears to be. How could there be any points of contact between the two writers?

A closer examination will reveal, I believe, that the spectacular differences between Tocqueville and Stendhal are a question of temperament and style rather than substance. Tocqueville's appreciation of America appears much more favorable than Stendhal's. But the marginal note in *Lucien Leuwen* reveals that there is a large measure of agreement between Tocqueville and Stendhal *in the eyes of Stendhal himself.* The novelist is obviously shocked to find himself on the side of an Alexis de Tocqueville, and this shock explains, if it does not justify, the content of the marginal note.

Both Stendhal and Tocqueville view America as the paradise of the common man; both Stendhal and Tocqueville believe that the European intellectual and man of leisure who would settle in the America of 1835 would find the place a bit dull. Both Stendhal and Tocqueville are intellectuals and men of leisure. Tocqueville feels, however, that his own situation must not interfere with his opinions. He identifies with the common good. Stendhal would feel like a hypocrite if he were to identify with any good but his own. In case of doubt, Stendhal will inveigh *against* the common good, just to make sure that he is really *sincere.*

An identical outlook is reflected by two strikingly dissimilar temperaments. Stendhal, in his mature years, is no more of an extremist than Tocqueville is a moderate, at least in the vulgar sense of the word. Stendhal always adopts the position most likely to disturb what he calls *la sottise.* He is a *Jacobin* with the royalists and a royalist with the *Jacobins.* He swings gracefully from the extreme right to the extreme left with the demands of contradiction. *La sottise,* as everyone knows, belongs to both extremes, but it always appears greater to Stendhal on the extreme he has just visited. Stendhal, in his novels, is always visiting one extreme wearing the spectacles of the other. The critics do not always consider that these Stendhalian volte-faces are incompatible with a genuine political commitment. Stendhal expresses with a passionate irony and Tocqueville with moderation a thought which really transcends the political quarrels of the time.

Stendhal opposes the world of *vanité,* which is essentially the modern world, to the *passion* of former ages. Passionate man is full of energy; his desires are genuinely his and he never compares himself to his neighbors. The distinction between *vanité* and *passion* is often misunderstood; it must not be confused with the romantic distinction between gregariousness and individualism. *Vanité* includes many features of what we would call individualism. The man of *vanité* is always claiming a self-sufficiency which he is unable to achieve. He constantly compares himself with other people and, afraid that they might be superior, he secretly copies their manners and borrows their desires. In the social order, the spirit of *vanité* produces arrogance and fear among the privileged few, envy among everybody else. The political battles fought in the name of freedom and tradition are usually spurred by *vanité*.

Tocqueville does not speak about *vanité* and *passion*, but he distinguishes between two ideas of freedom: the modern idea, which is the source of revolutions, is universal and abstract; the aristocratic idea is purely individual and selfish:

> The aristocratic idea of freedom gives to its worshippers an exalted conception of their individual value and a passionate love of independence. Egotistical energy and power are enormously increased. The individuals possessed by this freedom frequently become capable of the most extraordinary actions.

This description cannot but remind us of the passionate heroes of the *Italian Chronicles*. These short stories take place in the Italian city-states of the fifteenth and sixteenth centuries. Tocqueville has the French rather than the Italian aristocracy in mind when he writes about aristocratic freedom, but this difference is secondary. Aristocratic freedom and passion flourish at the same time and in the same type of society. The individual is stronger when society is weaker, when men are not automatically protected by law and order. In France, aristocratic freedom was already well on its way to destruction with the pre-totalitarian monarchy of Louis XIV. Like Stendhal, Tocqueville has read Saint-Simon, who presents the *roi-soleil* as the grave-digger of the old society. The Court of Versailles took the noblemen away from the land and turned them into domestic servants and courtiers. Deprived of any concrete superiority, the aristocracy clung all the more tenaciously to the honorific aspects of its role, thus creating resentment among the commoners. Inequality became more and more marked in etiquette and social manners as it steadily decreased in the economic and political fields. People became obsessed with each other's standing. In *The Old Régime and the Revolution*, Tocqueville maintains that "while the citizens and the noble had grown more like each other, the distance between them had increased; their mutual resemblance had rather alienated than united them."[3] The whole argument can be summed up in an often repeated Stendhalian axiom: "The smaller the social difference the greater the affectation it creates."

Tocqueville emphasizes the psychological causes of the French Revolution and defines their effects in terms reminiscent of Stendhalian *vanité*. The modern idea of freedom is really a passion for equality. Like *vanité*, it rests on a comparison and it cannot be assuaged; it feeds, so to speak, upon itself. As people claim more and more loudly their individual rights, they really become more and more spiritually dependent on each other.

Amongst democratic nations men easily attain a certain equality of conditions: they can never attain the equality they desire. It perpetually retires from before them, yet without hiding itself from their sight, and in retiring draws them on. At every moment, they think they are about to grasp it; it escapes at every moment from their hold. They are near enough to see its charms, but too far off to enjoy them; and before they have fully tasted its delights they die. To these causes must be attributed that strange melancholy which oftentimes will haunt the inhabitants of democratic countries in the midst of their abundance, and that disgust at life which sometimes seizes upon them in the midst of calm and easy circumstances.[4]

Here again, the readers of Stendhal will recognize some recurrent Stendhalian themes: the empty restlessness of *vanité* and this sadness which overcomes all those who succumb to the mania of comparing oneself to another . . .

The hatred of equality springs, of course, from exactly the same source as the passion for equality. Far from being immune to the modern disease, the social elite are the first to contract it, and they are often the most severely stricken. The lower classes should not be denied, therefore, the equality they seek; they often have more *passion* left in them, more energy and more genuine attachment to freedom than the privileged few and the wealthy bourgeois. Tocqueville has harsh words for his own class in *Democracy in America*:

Nothing is more wretchedly corrupt than an aristocracy which retains its wealth when it has lost its power, and which still enjoys a vast amount of leisure after it is reduced to mere vulgar pastimes. The energetic passions and great conceptions which animated it heretofore leave it then; and nothing remains to it but a host of petty consuming vices, which cling about it like worms upon a carcass.[5]

This description fits perfectly the ridiculous courtiers of *The Charterhouse of Parma*. The aristocracy is no longer a class; it has become a party. Far from denoting a genuine adherence to tradition, the reactionary policies of the aristocracy reveal that the modern mentality is taking hold. Only a man of *vanité* can attempt to defend arbitrary privileges by appealing to public opinion. The aristocrats of the Restoration have adopted a bourgeois morality in order to convince the bourgeois that they "deserve" their privileges. They become middle-class in order to fight the middle class. Stendhal notes, with sarcastic glee, that the post-revolutionary aristocrats display all the morose virtues of democratic and Protestant Geneva.[6] Tocqueville, at this point, takes a less cynical approach. He is too much of an aristocrat himself to suspect the motives of the aristocratic conversion to virtue. But he notes, too, in his own humorless way, the paradox of an aristocracy which adopts bourgeois morality in order to fight bourgeois political principles. "It may be said, though at first it seems paradoxical, that, at the present day, the most anti-democratic classes of the nation principally exhibit the kind of morality which may be reasonably expected from democracy."[7] Even when their interpretation differs, Stendhal and Tocqueville remain in perfect agreement on the facts to be interpreted.

The novelist and the sociologist bring to bear upon the actions and sentiments of their contemporaries the same acutely pessimistic insight, but they do not draw from their severe judgment the classically reactionary conclusions. Democracy, for the factions, is all good or all bad; for Tocqueville and Stendhal, democracy is an almost inextricable mixture of the good and the bad. Every disadvantage of the new regime becomes an advantage when it is viewed from a different perspective. Public opinion may stifle individualism, but it will promote an efficient and honest government. Exceptional men will be fewer or may even disappear entirely, but the general level of education will go up. The pressures for conformity will be almost irresistible, but the material lot of the average man will improve tremendously. Individuals will be restless, but this restlessness can be channeled into peaceful types of competition. Agricultural production will increase; industries will develop . . .

Whereas, in Europe, most conservative elements denounced the weakness of democracy, Stendhal, like Tocqueville, was concerned about its excessive strength. Former tyrants could coerce only the body; modern tyranny might take a more subtle form; it might corrupt the minds and souls of individuals; it might sap their will and make them incapable of opposing the all-powerful majority. Unless the rights of the minorities are jealousy preserved, democracy will easily turn into what we would call to-day the totalitarian state. Tocqueville, like Stendhal, paints in somber colors the fate of the true individualist in the modern age:

They have swept away the privileges of some of their fellow-creatures which stood in their way, but they have opened the door to universal competition: the barrier has changed its shape rather than its position. When men are nearly alike, and all follow the same track, it is very difficult for any one individual to walk quickly and cleave a way through the dense throng which surrounds and presses him. This constant strife between the propensities springing from the equality of conditions and the means it supplies to satisfy them, harasses and wearies the mind.[8]

Faced by great obstacles, truly ambitious men will be strongly tempted to adopt an antisocial philosophy and to resort to antisocial behavior. In a country like France during the period of transition, a combination of obstacles proper to inequality and to equality renders the rise of the individual particularly difficult. Energetic young men coming from the newly educated lower classes must face both the entrenched privileges of the few and the envy of the crowd. This ferment of disorder is especially potent as long as the memories of the Napoleonic era remain alive in the French people. Tocqueville describes the conditions which produce a Julien Sorel, the hero of *The Red and the Black*:

The reminiscence of the extraordinary events which men have witnessed is not obliterated from their memory in a day. The passions which a revolution has roused do not disappear at its close. A sense of instability remains in the midst of re-established order: a notion of easy success survives the strange vicissitudes which gave it birth; desires still remain extremely enlarged, when the means of satisfying them are diminished day by day. On every side, we trace the ravages of inordinate and hapless ambition kindled in hearts which they consume in secret and in vain.[9]

*The Red and the Black* is not the clear-cut Jacobin novel which some critics have described. Stendhal's political vision is full of nuances and subtleties which evaporate in the dry atmosphere of nineteenth- and twentieth-century partisanship. Tocqueville helps us to perceive some of these

nuances. Tocqueville may be read as a social exegesis of the dramatic situations in Stendhal's novels. We can almost feel that the novelist himself rec-
ommends this practice when we meditate on his brief but eloquent homage to the sociologist in *Memories of a Tourist*: "The faculty of the will is
more and more lacking in Paris," Stendhal writes; "our people do not read
the good books anymore, Bayle, Montesquieu, Tocqueville; all they read
is the modern nonsense and for the sole purpose, besides, to appear well
informed."[10] The essay was published in 1838. We can see that Stendhal
quickly recovered from the shock of his first contact with Tocqueville. He
now excludes his work from "the modern nonsense"; he associates the sociologist with Montesquieu, a writer for whom he has the greatest admiration. Tocqueville is the only one of his contemporaries, to my knowledge,
on whom Stendhal ever bestowed such an honor. The readers of Stendhal
who remain puzzled by the apparent contradictions of this witty author
should turn toward Tocqueville for a key to his political vision.

# 6

## Memoirs of a Dutiful Existentialist:
## Simone de Beauvoir[1] [1961]

Mme de Beauvoir's existence has always been governed not by Heideggerian *Angst*, as orthodoxy demands and as earlier writings seemed to indicate, but by a relentless drive to *happiness*. Those Americans who still regard French existentialism as a school of idleness and Buddhist-like indifference to things mundane should read *Memoirs of a Dutiful Daughter* (*Les mémoires d'une jeune fille rangée*, 1958) and *The Prime of Life* (*La force de l'âge*, 1960). If these two volumes do not correct their misconceptions, nothing ever will. Mme de Beauvoir gives us the key to her whole life in a sentence which would have delighted the sociologist Max Weber: "In my case, the idea of salvation had survived the disappearance of God, and my strongest conviction was that each person must see to his own salvation." This is an excellent definition of that modern spirit, competitive and puritanical, which erects philosophical systems as well as industrial empires. It is no small pleasure to sit down in a comfortable chair and to watch Mme de Beauvoir save herself through hundreds of pages of lively prose and a few decades of feverish activity. As a little child, she had formed the project of visiting even the tiniest corners of the globe, down to the last ditch and the smallest clump of trees. During her many travels, she is haunted by the fear of missing *something*, and she leafs frantically through; she *compulse frénétiquement* her various guidebooks. When she is in Marseilles, she goes on solitary excursions, and she walks longer, faster, and farther than anybody else. She reads everything, from *Was ist Metaphysik* to *Fantomas* and *Chéri-Bibi*; she sees all the plays, goes to all the exhibitions; in addition to philosophy, she studies music, painting, sculpture, geography, and physiology. She gives courses and she writes a great number of books. She practices winter sports and she learns how to ride a bicycle. Her capacity for absorbing what she calls "happiness" is truly frightening. And the salvation she pursues is typical of our age, insofar as it is a strictly individual one; she must build her happiness all alone, *toute seule, sans secours*. Even anti-capitalism is approached with typical capitalistic avidity. Mme de Beauvoir is too intelligent, of course, not to perceive the dark dialectical implications of this voracious appetite.

How can we save ourselves, concretely, in the absence of God, if not by surpassing our fellow human beings in all sorts of worldly endeavors? Early in life, Mlle de Beauvoir was one of those little female prodigies who win all the prizes in school and get the *mentions très bien*, thus poisoning the lives of their more relaxed brothers and cousins. These female prodigies are one of the truly national institutions of France. Academic achievements of children are a major field of competition between families of the middle class. The girls are usually ahead of the boys because they are more eager to please their fathers. Immediately after the *baccalauréat*, however, they are expected to abandon all intellectual pursuits in order to become wives and mothers. Competition is suddenly shifted to other fields. Little geniuses with their heads full of trigonometry and Kantian philosophy are often seen never to open another book for the rest of their lives.

Being a particularly brilliant subject, Mme de Beauvoir could not stand the thought of forsaking the *mentions très bien*, and she simply refused to be reconverted to home life, thus manifesting for the first time that spirit of rebellion which made her famous and which is still alive in her. However much we admire this valorous feat, we must not exaggerate the scope of the revolution. Mme de Beauvoir rejected only the moribund aspects of French bourgeois morality, and for the sole purpose, moreover, of upholding more vigorously its one essential tenet, which demands that everything be turned into a competitive examination and that everybody try to run away with the first prize. Mme de Beauvoir, as we all know, has been running away with first prizes ever since that initial exploit. To such a woman, existentialism and Marxism were two more academic subjects, which she mastered as easily as the others and which exerted considerably more influence on her than trigonometry and Kantian philosophy would have, had she agreed to become an ordinary housewife and mother. The dutiful daughter became a dutiful existentialist. Mme de Beauvoir is probably less a revolutionist than she thinks, but she is a good writer and a brilliant Left Bank intellectual. It is only in France, perhaps, that such a person could become the spokesman for the growing class of progressive and intelligent career women. Mme de Beauvoir is the voice of all the other feminine first-prize winners. She reinterprets the traditional culture of France from the perspective of the career woman; she expresses a viewpoint entirely novel to the French social set-up in a language worthy of a long intellectual past.

Mme de Beauvoir perceives and formulates some of the conflicts inherent to the situation of a career woman, but she denies the existence of others; and these unsolved conflicts add fuel to the fire of righteous indignation, which burns high and bright in the heart of this remarkable woman each time *alienation* seems to threaten her precious freedom. Mme de Beauvoir and Jean-Paul Sartre never married, because they were afraid of *alienating* each other. *Alienation* lurks again when Mme de Beauvoir feels overwhelmed by undifferentiated sexual desire. Can a woman remain free to choose her lovers with her head rather than with her senses? Can she remain faithful to the chosen one within the precisely defined limits of a sexual lend-lease program? Strait is the gate between *alienation* to society and *alienation* to instinct. But Mme de Beauvoir, like a Cornelian heroine, wins all her battles; she can experience the ecstasy of dark passion, while remaining perfectly dignified and independent: "Amorous joy should be as fatal and as unexpected as the swelling of the seas, as the blossoming of a peach tree" (La joie amoureuse devait être aussi fatale et aussi imprévue que la houle des mers, que la floraison d'un pêcher). She goes into a frenzy of self-surrender while keeping a watchful eye over her Adversary, the little devil *Alienation*. This, undoubtedly, is the neatest trick of the past two or three thousand years. Sartre, among others, has devoted several hundred pages to proving that love cannot be like the blooming of the peach tree. But Sartre, obviously, is far behind Mme de Beauvoir in the pursuit of happiness.

Mme de Beauvoir's free, happy, and spontaneous love does not come from Sartre, but from Rousseau, Mme de Staël, and Lamartine, as well as from George Sand and the young Alfred de Musset (the Musset who had not yet encountered George Sand). The modern career woman is really a romantic in disguise. At times, it is true, she sounds more like M. Jules Romains than Lamartine. But M. Jules Romains, too, is a romantic in disguise. We keep reading the name of Jean-Paul Sartre in *The Prime of Life*, but all we hear is *Jallez*, or perhaps *Jerphanion*. There was already a faint flavor of *bonne volonté* in the less pessimistic passages of *The Roads to Freedom* (*Les chemins de la liberté*). Perhaps all existentialists from *Normale supérieure* must sound like M. Jules Romains when they turn from negative to positive thinking.

Mme de Beauvoir really succumbs, in parts of *The Prime of Life*, to the old myth of romantic spontaneity. The myth is not absent from the Sartrean notion of freedom, but it is Sartre's greatness that he tried desperately to chain this uncontrollable dragon, and he gave it as limited a place as he could in his philosophy. He could not destroy the myth, however, and this explains, perhaps, why it can wage such a powerful counter-offensive in the recent books of Mme de Beauvoir. Since *The Mandarins*, the myth has successfully reoccupied all the positions from which Sartre had painfully extirpated it; it proliferates luxuriantly; it blooms everywhere like the flower of the peach tree. With Sartre's waning influence, Mme de Beauvoir is reverting to a much more naïve, more elemental, and often quite charming form of romantic individualism.

As a curious consequence of this evolution, the heroic years of *Nausea* (*La nausée*) turn, under the pen of Mme de Beauvoir, into the exact antithesis of this famous book. Unlike Roquentin, who believes that "adventure" is "bunk" and that traveling is a bore, Mme de Beauvoir and her companion meet the unexpected at every turn and embrace it passionately. The Sartre we have all imagined brooding somberly about *la contingence* was really drinking *manzanilla* to the sound of the guitar in the sidewalk cafes of Old Madrid; he was eagerly exploring Barcelona's picturesque Barrio Chino; he was greedily snapping mental pictures of bullfights and tricorned gendarmes. It is difficult to assess how much irony entered into the creation of this *anti-nausée*.

Let us follow the two happy tourists into the Prado Museum. Before meeting Mme de Beauvoir, the unfortunate Jerphanion—pardon me, Jean-Paul Sartre—was afflicted with a decidedly middlebrow outlook on the art of painting. He paid more attention to the "story" of a picture than to its style; he commented glibly upon the sentiments expressed by the characters, and he fell into a deplorable silence when it came to shapes and colors. He even presumed to like a painter as contemptible, in the modern scale of values, as far "out," we might say, as Guido Reni. *Horresco referens.* Mme de Beauvoir, needless to say, put a quick end to that heretical nonsense. She taught her friend true spontaneity, and he became so well trained that he automatically exclaimed "C'est de l'Opéra" whenever confronted by a figurative painting. Having rid himself of his ignorance, he embraced the rigid faith of a neophyte, thus providing an even nicer background for Mme de Beauvoir's delicate nuances of taste. One of these fine points is the author's fondness for Titian, a master widely suspected of operatic tendencies. This subversive inclination reveals a great indifference to established values; it fits in nicely, too, with Mme de Beauvoir's role as the extoller of "happiness" and "life" versus Sartre's intellectualism.

Are the "monsters, demons, and cripples" of Hieronymus Bosch preferable to the "cruelty" of Goya's portraits and to the "black madness" of his later work? So many enchanting beauties make it difficult to exercise the faculty of judgment, and the Mme de Beauvoir of 1929 decided that Bosch was supreme; the Mme de Beauvoir of 1959 rectifies this gross error and puts Goya first. Both preferences are spontaneous, of course, since the only sentiments Mme de Beauvoir is willing to entertain are those which are "spontaneously provoked by their object." It must be noted, however, that Mme de Beauvoir was all for Bosch when the dominant aesthetic was surrealism, and that she shifted her allegiance to Goya when everybody looked at this painter through the eyes of André Malraux. Like so many writers addicted to spontaneity, Mme de Beauvoir gives us the impression that whatever is fashionable today will remain fashionable forever. As a matter of fact, she almost convinces us that there is no such thing as fashion. Her severe criticism of her own pre-existentialist period contributes enormously to that feeling of eternity. Humanity was still at the groping stage in 1929; even its elite had not yet reached the definitive answers on every subject. Mme de Beauvoir constantly points out how much *idealism* in that antediluvian period, how much of the bourgeois, was still present in her revolt against the bourgeoisie. We never quite manage to understand when and how the author finally rid herself of the disease, but we know that the cure must have been successful and complete because the opinions of the present are not submitted to the same searching criticism as the opinions of the past. There is nothing relative, nothing *historically* or *socially* conditioned about Mme de Beauvoir's latest word on marriage, happiness, Guido Reni, Hieronymus Bosch, the Barrio Chino, and *Was ist Metaphysik.* What will happen the day *Was ist Metaphysik* is toppled from its present eminence? What will happen the day Guido Reni is exalted again? It is to be feared that the force of one age will turn into the weakness of another and that many pages of Mme de Beauvoir's memoirs will sound more and more, with the passing of time, the way M. Jules Romains began to sound after the opening of the Second World War.

But other pages will remain. As the war approaches, historical events take precedence over the search for happiness. The 1940–44 period is the best part of the book. There is less tourism, less surface exploration, and more progress in depth. It is impossible not to admire the Mme de Beauvoir of the Occupation years, and not to sympathize with much of what she writes and does. She never loses her sense of values, and she never abandons hope. She never allows her revulsion for the mad and chauvinistic world of the early forties to turn into the paralyzed fascination evidenced by so many works of art of the period. At its best, *The Prime of Life* is a hymn to individual freedom and to the life of the intellect; at its worst, it is a *summa* of the French intelligentsia during the *entre-deux guerres* and the Second World War; it is a description of its way of life and a repertoire of its opinions and intellectual fads; it is, at any rate, a priceless document for future historians of taste. It also contains an enormous amount of information on the genesis of Sartrean ideas and of Sartrean literature—even though Roquentin is constantly, and perhaps significantly, misspelled as *Roquantin.*

Mme de Beauvoir, anyway, is not thinking of posterity; she is thinking of the present, and the present is hers, whatever criteria we may choose in order to decide the matter. *The Prime of Life* is a charming book, and its success is well deserved. Once again, the first lady of existentialism is running away with the first prize.

# 7

# Marcel Proust [1962]

Marcel Proust was born in 1871 of a Catholic father and a Jewish mother into a family of solid Parisian bourgeoisie.[1] He was a gifted but sickly and neurotic child who, from an early age, displayed marked homosexual tendencies. After brilliant but desultory studies at a Paris *lycée* and at the university, the young man began to circulate in the intellectual and artistic upper class; he published a few minor essays, a thin volume of rather "decadent" prose, and some translations of John Ruskin. He also frequented assiduously certain salons of the old and aristocratic Faubourg Saint Germain. During that period, Proust doubtless felt and behaved like some of the bourgeois snobs he later created in *Remembrance of Things Past*. On the death of his mother in 1905, however, Proust literally renounced the world and dedicated the rest of his life to the creation of what is, perhaps, the masterpiece of French literature in the twentieth century. After more than a dozen years of continuous and often heroic labor, pursued under the most deplorable conditions of health, Marcel Proust died at the task, leaving the last uncorrected volumes of his novel to be published posthumously, his literary fame already assured not only in France but in the entire world.

Like Montaigne, and more than Montaigne perhaps, Proust could have boasted that he himself was the substance of his book. This does not mean that Marcel Proust and Marcel, the hero and narrator of *Remembrance of Things Past*, are identical in the vulgar empirical sense, but that from a higher and more spiritual viewpoint, they are one. The book made the author, no less than the author the book. The earlier works, however brilliant they may appear, are nothing but preparatory exercises and rejected first drafts of the great masterpiece. Any attempt to understand Marcel Proust, the man and his work, must therefore begin, as it must end, with *Remembrance of Things Past.*

In the beginning is Combray, a sleepy little provincial town of the Ile de France, where Marcel (the narrator) spends the happiest moments of his childhood at the home of his paternal grandparents. Combray is a world of tradition and ritual rigidly caught in a complex middle-class hierarchy reminiscent of a latter-day feudal order. The village, still surrounded by the remnants of a perfectly circular medieval wall, lives apart from the rest of the world, not in time but in eternity, like a haven of poetry and joy which no evil can touch.

Combray is threatened, however, like every other paradise of childhood innocence. The dark forces of *snobisme* and erotic passion are seeking to destroy it. *Snobisme* makes its first appearance with Legrandin, a friend of Marcel's family who succumbs to a morbid fascination for the local gentry; sexual desire is introduced by Mlle Vinteuil, whose abnormal relationship with a woman friend turns the life of her father, the great musician Vinteuil, into a horrible martyrdom. From this point on, with the narrator himself or, exceptionally, with Swann, a wealthy bourgeois socialite, at the center of the stage, the great novel drifts further and further away from the blissful peace of the first Edenic descriptions. As we plunge deeper into the world of social ambition and sexual desire, a spirit of futility pervades. Marcel never begins the novel he plans to write. Eternity gives way to the hostile and corrosive time which Robert Champigny describes in his remarkable essay.[2] The spirit of Combray seems utterly destroyed.

Throughout the novel, the desires—innocent as well as perverse—of Marcel and of the other characters are described in quasi-religious terms. Behind the coveted *something*, there is always a *someone* endowed with an almost supernatural prestige. Marcel yearns after a kind of mystical communion, with an individual or with a group, dwelling, he believes, in a superior realm of existence and entirely separated from the vulgar herd. This *metaphysical* desire takes a different form in the various stages of the novel. Just as Combray huddles at the foot of its medieval church, so the first Marcel lives in the shadow of his parents, or of Swann, or of the great writer Bergotte, all of them towering figures whom the child imitates religiously in the hope of becoming one of them. Later on, through sexual desire and social ambition, Marcel again seeks *initiation* into a new and mysterious existence which he believes to be preferable to his own. Now, however, the benevolent gods of Combray have been replaced by malevolent ones—the smart hostesses who stubbornly refuse to send the passionately awaited invitation, the flighty boys and girls who inflict the torture of jealousy upon their admirers in inverse proportion to the pleasure they provide. Proust's metaphors, which he rightly saw were the most essential and original element of his art, reflect this change in the "religious" atmosphere of the novel. The images of Combray, usually borrowed from the Old Testament and medieval Christianity, express a vigorous but naïve faith. The world of *snobisme* and erotic passion, on the other hand, is associated with black magic, with the bloody cults of fetishism, and with such perversions of Christianity as witch-hunting and the Inquisition.

When the goal of initiation is reached, the awe-inspiring idol invariably turns out to be as dull as anybody else, and the divine flavor evaporates. We do not have to ask why possession kills such a desire, for the answer is obvious enough. Nothing human can satisfy it. The real question is harder to answer: Why is Proustian desire of this sort—Why, that is, is it metaphysical? The answer lies in the psychology of man, as Proust understands it.

A child's veneration for his parents is intelligible enough. What surprises us is the adult's veneration for other adults, in which something infantile evidently remains. This is precisely what is suggested by an important scene at the very beginning of the novel. When Marcel goes to bed at Combray, he cannot go to sleep unless his mother comes up to his room and kisses him good night. The parents try not to accede to this demand, because their child is nervous and sickly; he must build his "will power" or he will never become a "real" man.

One particular night, however, Marcel is so unhappy that he breaks the sacred family law and comes downstairs, begging for a last kiss. Instead of meting out the expected punishment, his father shrugs his shoulders and tells the mother to spend the whole night with her frightened little boy. Marcel is relieved, but he knows that something irreparable has happened. By transgressing the law they themselves have laid down, the parents have stooped to the level of the child and turned his weakness into their own. Marcel has lost faith in the gods of Combray. But this is no normal process of growing up, nor is it the end of the search for salvation through magical means. The child has to resort to other gods who will maintain, in their dealings with him, the unyielding domination which, up to that fateful night, was characteristic of his parents. Marcel's entire emotional life will become a *repetition* of the sleepless nights of Combray.

Included, of course, in this parental *Götterdammerung* is the Law itself: bourgeois respectability, associated, in Marcel's eyes, with the world of the family. Once this has fallen, immorality and idleness must be worshipped in secret. The illusion of the sacred will be present whenever Marcel feels systematically excluded from pleasures which the family would consider forbidden. Here is a Puritanism in reverse, which is open, no doubt, to a psychoanalytical interpretation; but we must beware of considering Marcel a truly separate psychological entity. We have isolated him here from his fictional context in order to show that he systematically distorts reality. Let us now put him back into his context and it will become clear that reality, in the form of the snobs, contributes to provoke this distortion.

The snobs act as if the salon were not simply a place where people like to congregate for the purpose of gossiping and absorbing *petits fours*, but a sacred little world, entirely separated from the big one and infinitely more desirable. In this view, the salon is a temple of esoteric mysteries of which the snobs constitute the initiates, mysteries which would be diluted and lost if they were imparted to the unworthy. The rejected outsider is thus made to feel a victim of some earthly and mundane damnation. No wonder that these exclusive little cliques look to Marcel, prone as he is to metaphysical desire, like the *hortus conclusus*, the enclosed garden of mystical literature. He may himself be ill, but the snobs around him seem diabolically intent upon making his illness worse—worse because social ascent in *Remembrance of Things Past* entails spiritual and physical degradation. Urged on by his desire and constantly turned toward a sterile future, the narrator is rendered incapable of real action or contemplation. Recollections from his happy childhood have become stilted and dryly factual.

One day, however, the original Combray comes back, through a curious phenomenon of *affective memory*. After a long and dreary·day spent in seeking his so-called pleasures, the narrator comes home and his mother serves him a cup of tea and one of those cakes which the French call *madeleine*. Marcel wearily dips the cake into the tea, and as the soaked crumbs touch his tongue, he feels miraculously delivered from his wretchedness. His bedridden aunt used to offer him tea and *madeleine* in the days of Combray. The renewed sensory impression provides a material bridge between the past and the present; the world of Combray springs back to life in all its original freshness.

The *madeleine* resurrects the serene and joyful Combray, huddled about its beautiful gothic church and protected from outer darkness by its perfectly circular wall. In retrospect, this Combray appears closer to the enchanted garden Marcel seeks than to all the experiences that follow. The salons are to Combray what a caricature is to the original. Combray, like the salons, is a world of ritual, but less self-consciously and less rigidly so; Combray is jealous of its identity, but not to the point where outsiders become systematically excluded. Between Combray and the rest of the world there may be perpetual misunderstanding, but there is no open conflict, as in the salons. Yet there is enough likeness between the two worlds to mislead an inexperienced observer like Marcel into thinking that the identity possessed by Combray must be possessed more abundantly by the salons. Their claim to being the "enchanted garden" appears a more substantial one.

This is a mistaken conclusion. Behind the tantalizing *noli me tangere* of the snobs there is actually nothing but anxiety and restlessness. Mme Verdurin and her friends mimic a passionate attachment to their own "little clan," but, in reality, they are fascinated by the haughty Guermanteses, whom they profess to despise. All that unites the snobs of one salon is envy of another salon from which they feel excluded and which, in consequence, becomes the sole object of their desire. Far from being independent, the salons can be understood only in this "dialectical" relationship, whereas Combray is intelligible in and by itself. That is why there are many salons but only one Combray.

Lured by the false promise of the salons, the narrator unknowingly turns his back on his true goal, the enchanted garden. A snob cannot find rest, even at the "top" of society, since there is always a place where he will feel unwanted and which he will therefore desire. The moment society crouches at his feet the Proustian snob loses interest and turns elsewhere, even toward the underworld, like the baron de Charlus seeking his pleasure in the gutter. Consequently, whenever the snob moves forward, the enchanted garden recedes. In a world of insiders, everyone imagines himself an outsider. But since no one admits this truth, everyone becomes necessarily both deceiver and dupe, victim and torturer, excluding every other on the grounds that he himself feels excluded. There is an element of imitative magic in this behavior and also a panic fear that one's own state of deprivation is going to be perceived, and the narrator undergoes it no less than the other characters in the novel: he learns to hide his true feelings; he learns to wear a mask of self-satisfaction and contempt.

Why should everyone feel individually guilty about a feeling of inadequacy which is, in reality, universal? To answer this question, we must go back to Combray. Marcel has rejected the bourgeois morality of his parents except for one essential tenet which he is unable to question: he still believes that he must be a "real" man, self-reliant, independent, and strong. But what does it mean to be a "real" man in a positivistic world from which all things transcending the human have been banished? It means, in the last resort, that humanity must assume the attributes of divinity. This consequence of "God's death," seen clearly only by Nietzsche and Dostoevsky before Proust's time, is perhaps obscurely at work among those characters in the novel who are constantly seeking mystical union with a pseudo-divinity and must therefore be, at least subconsciously, committed to self-divinization.

According to Nietzsche, God's death, by propelling human pride to new heights, will lead man to surpass himself and become a superman. Dostoevsky is of a different mind. Man is not a god, Dostoevsky asserts, and the individual man's inner voice will always tell him this truth. But this existentially irrefutable truth is powerless against the unanimous voice of a Promethean society always urging its members to arrogate the functions of the divine. The result, for the individual, will be inescapable frustration. "Divinity" becomes what one knows one does not have but what one must assume *les autres* (the others) do have. Each would-be superman will believe himself the only limited being in a society of demigods, and in his delusion will seek salvation from his divinized but envied fellowmen, with tragic and grotesque consequences for all concerned.

Proust is not prepared to take a direct part in this philosophical debate, possibly because, for him, God is simply too dead. But his snobs, like the Dostoevskian characters, would feel less inadequate if they were not so proud, if they did not expect the impossible from themselves. And the religious imagery of *Remembrance of Things Past* tells a story which is not fundamentally different from Dostoevsky's own, and it tells it all the more objectively and strikingly because Proust does not perceive the metaphysical or even certain of the ethical implications of his vision, because he never abandons the level of "psychological" analysis. His shortcomings in the realm of existence, so shrewdly detected by Ramon Fernandez, here contribute to the value of his work.[3]

For Proust, as for Dostoevsky, transcendence, which, in the past, separated the worshipper from the worshipped, now separates individuals from each other and forces them to live their relationships at the level of a corrupted religiosity. Everyone is led by *amour-propre*, Proust writes—by a self-centered love that leads *outward*, turning us into the slaves and imitators of others. Crushed under the weight of our Promethean pride, *amour-propre* has become like a centrifugal planisphere. As this centrifugal pride lures the narrator with the fallacious promises of *snobisme* and sexual passion, it takes him further and further away from Combray.

One may, of course, find moments of relief from this diabolical mechanism, ecstatic moments of peace provided by the contemplation of beautiful landscapes or by the great works of artists such as Bergotte the writer, Vinteuil the musician, and Elstir the painter. But they cannot shut out actuality for long.

The grandmother, who has accompanied the narrator like a luminous angel of love and innocence during the years of his youth, falls ill and dies a horrible death. Then Bergotte dies. Then Albertine is killed in a riding accident after breaking away from the apartment where the morbidly jealous Marcel has held her a virtual prisoner. This last catastrophe marks the beginning of the worst period in the narrator's life. The sting of desire is gone, but instead of peace, apathy replaces it; the narrator resigns himself to a life of spiritual emptiness and ennui. Art itself has lost its power. Marcel gives up his long-cherished plans to "reform his life" and become a great artist.

After a long period of illness, and for want of a better purpose, Marcel accepts an invitation from the Guermanteses. Upon his arrival, he again experiences a sudden and extraordinary blossoming of affective memory. The uneven cobblestones of the Guermanteses' courtyard take him back to a certain piazza in Venice; a little later, in an antechamber, the glossy surface of a starched napkin reminds him of his life in Balbec, a Channel resort where he had met Albertine; still later, he finds his whole childhood enclosed in the pages of a novel by George Sand, the same one which his grandmother had given him many years before.

Once again, the present and the past are bridged; time is replaced by a sensation of eternal youthfulness, in violent contrast to the horrible spectacle of degeneration and decay offered by the guests of the Guermanteses, some of whom have aged so that Marcel hardly recognizes them. Marcel knows that his own body is going to die, but this does not trouble him, for his spirit has just been resurrected in memory. And this new resurrection, unlike the first one, is permanent and fruitful: it will be the foundation of the great work of art which Marcel had finally despaired of writing.

All directions are henceforward reversed in the existence of Marcel, all plans inverted: the quest for the "enchanted garden" has shifted from the outer to the inner world, from the future to the past, from dispersion to unity, from desire to detachment, from possession to contemplation, from disintegration to aesthetic creation. The outward and downward movement of pride is succeeded, as Richard Macksey points out, by an inward and upward movement leading back to Combray, back to the true center of the personality.[4] Affective memory is only one aspect of a spiritual conversion which will not fail to provide the energy needed for the great work of art. The reader cannot doubt that the promise has been fulfilled this time, because the novel which is about to be written is also the one which is coming to a close.

~

Was *Remembrance of Things Past* born of a revelation identical, or similar at least, to the one just described, which forms the subject of the last volume? Critics have traditionally said that it was, but this viewpoint has been weakened in recent years by the publication of unfinished manuscripts dating back to a period which, in the novel, is depicted as one of relative inactivity. Proust published very little between the dilettantish *Pleasures and Regrets* and *Remembrance of Things Past*, but we know now that these years were not spent in idleness. The three-volume *Jean Santeuil*—a somewhat heterogeneous collection of fictional texts in various stages of completion—has convinced several critics that *The Past Recaptured* owes little to the actual creative experience of Marcel Proust. On the other hand, although it is true that Marcel Proust had had some experience with the art of the novel when he finally plunged into *Remembrance of Things Past*, this fact does not prove that *The Past Recaptured* is pure invention. A comparison between the recently published manuscripts and the finished novel suggests that a real break did occur in the aesthetic life of Marcel Proust and that the event was, on the whole, faithfully recorded in *The Past Recaptured*.

In *Jean Santeuil*, we recognize the setting, as well as some of the characters, of *Remembrance of Things Past*, but the style and spirit are different. Many brilliant pages of descriptive prose remind us of the good writers of the period, but the religious metaphors, so constant a feature in the later novel, are few. Love is present, but it is rosy and sentimental. As for *snobisme*, it is only an ugly fault that Jean Santeuil, the hero, condemns severely, even though he, a bourgeois, frequents the most aristocratic salons. Pursued by snobbish enemies, Jean Santeuil is always rescued at the last minute by protectors as well born as they are powerful; he therefore rises like a bright new star in the glittering firmament of society.

One need not be a great psychologist to suspect that the Cinderella outlook of certain of these chapters reflects the irrational hopes and fears of a *snobisme* of which Proust had not yet divested himself. The moral indignation of the Proustian hero is no proof to the contrary, for moral indignation may simply be one snob's way of expressing his resentment against other snobs who happen to stand in his way, rather than a true insight into the nature of *snobisme*. All the barriers of society come crashing down at the feet of Jean Santeuil simply because he is a young man of remarkable talent and infinite charm, appreciated at his just value by almost equally talented and charming aristocrats. *Snobisme* thus plays a lesser role in *Jean Santeuil* than in *Remembrance of Things Past*, and is more vigorously condemned. On this ground, some observers have concluded that it is a "healthier" novel, more "rational" in its outlook on people and society.

They also note that its world is "closer to ours." This last remark may well be true—but Jean Santeuil's apparent health and rationality stem from Proust's failure to *perceive* the irrational and magical elements of his own approach to reality. *Snobisme* becomes universal in *Remembrance of Things Past* not because Proust is still obsessed with society, but, on the contrary, because he has seen that it is a truly universal disease and he can now as-similate, at least metaphorically, all its manifestations into the particular phase of it with which he is personally best acquainted.

Jean Santeuil is an ideal figure happily frolicking in the "enchanted garden" of Proustian metaphysical desire. This does not mean that Proust himself had reached his mystical goal at the time he wrote the novel, but only that he was still identifying it with the salons, to which Jean Santeuil has gained unobstructed access. Santeuil is therefore not so much a faith-ful image of what Proust really felt, as of what he hoped he would feel fol-lowing frequentation of the salons and imitation of his current idols. The society Santeuil moves in—very different from that in *Remembrance of Things Past*—is divided in two halves: the first, which belongs to the hero and his aristocratic friends, is good, beautiful, and luminous; the second, which belongs to his enemies, is dark, ugly, and sinister. This Manichean division means that introspection and observation are working separately, in the two separate halves of the world, at the expense of depth, color, and life. The hero's half is characterized by an empty and insipid perfection; the "enemy's" side by shadowy figures and grimacing caricatures.

How were the two halves of the Manichean world finally reconciled? This process can be followed rather closely thanks to some essays written by Proust just before *Remembrance of Things Past* and published in 1954 under the title *Contre Sainte-Beuve*.[5] In a chapter entitled "Conclusion," Proust expresses his conviction that he will never be a great writer. Then he notes that, at long intervals, he perceives certain new and mysterious bonds between people, things, or widely separated moments of his life, all of which had previously appeared unrelated. Perception of such synthesis is intensely pleasurable and is accompanied by a vivid impression of truth, but it shatters whatever confidence the writer had ever had in his literary talent.

In *Remembrance of Things Past*, this same somber mood is attrib-uted to Marcel during the period immediately preceding the aesthetic illumination. "Conclusion" must be read from the viewpoint of the yet to be written *The Past Recaptured*; it is really a very early draft of this volume, although conceived at a much earlier stage of the experience, at a time when the Proustian "dark night of the soul" was still very dark indeed. But since it is more directly autobiographical, this "conclusion" reveals the purely literary aspects of the "dark night," which are omitted from *The Past Recaptured*; it shows us the two halves of *Jean Santeuil*'s Manichean world gradually coming together.

Professor Vigneron has shown that this literary drama is an echo of the real tragedy which Marcel Proust was living at that time.[6] His mother was dead and he thought that his conduct had been responsible for this tragic event. He felt an irrepressible urge to confess his guilt in letters to his friends and even in the pages of *Figaro*. His despair was so intense that it frightened his friends. His already failing health being further impaired, Proust gave up his social life and retired to a cork-lined bedroom in his apartment on the Boulevard Haussmann, where much of *Remembrance of Things Past* was written. In *The Past Recaptured*, Proust insists that a great vision must be born in suffering. This and similar statements have been too much overlooked by those who feel that the effects of suffering on creative writing cannot be determined empirically. Guilt feelings, especially, do not enjoy a good reputation in our contemporary world. When they are not felt to be downright contemptible, they are viewed as symptoms of mental disturbance. But Proust felt differently; he was obsessed at the time with the structure of *Crime and Punishment*, which he recognized not only in all the novels of Dostoevsky and in those of Flaubert, but in *Don Quixote* as well. And Proust may well be right, in his own case as that of these other novelists. If it is true that the aesthetically false division of the fictional world as presented in *Jean Santeuil* is a product of what I call *metaphysical desire*, and if it is true that metaphysical desire is a product of pride, we may have to conclude that whatever injures pride, whether it be guilt, suffering, or remorse, constitutes an important factor in the spiritual metamorphosis which turns a superficial writer into a great one. The two worlds of *Jean Santeuil* cannot come together unless Marcel Proust recognizes *himself* among the snobs. This is the price which must be paid for the alliance between introspection and observation. The experience is both a "sickness unto death" and a resurrection, for it is both the end of metaphysical questing and the end of metaphysical enslavement. The creator, at least temporarily free from an absorbing and sterile future, can turn back toward the past and breathe the flavor of the sacred in past desires without the torture of actual yearning, and he can cast a lucid glance upon the errors and absurdities of this past. As Jacques Rivière perceived, the lyricism of the novel is inseparable from its psychological truth. *Jean Santeuil* and *Remembrance of Things Past* illustrate Simone Weil's distinction between those works of art which remain second-rate, however brilliant they may be, because they do nothing but "enrich" their author's personality, and true masterpieces, which originate from an impoverishment, a mutilation of the inauthentic self.

The novelist's handwriting suggests that a sharp break occurred in his life just before *Remembrance of Things Past.* The change is so striking that even a casual glance can determine whether a page was written before or after the fateful period. All the available evidence confirms, therefore, the truthfulness of *The Past Recaptured.* The only departure from autobiographical truth is an apparent one—namely, the failure to mention previous contacts with the art of the novel. Proust modifies the letter of his experience in order to reveal the spirit. The metamorphosis of the writer had to be presented as a solemn entrance into literature, in order to acquire symbolic weight. It would be quite wrong to imagine a conflict between this aesthetic requirement and the autobiographical dimension of the novel. The novel uncovers a spiritual autobiography which is both more beautiful and truer than the literal one.

It is a fact that *The Past Recaptured* was entirely conceived, if not entirely written, before any other portion of the novel. This conclusion is, therefore, both an end and a beginning. If the novel is a "cathedral"—as Proust himself suggested—*The Past Recaptured* is the choir toward which all architectural lines converge and from which they all originate. Each event differs in meaning according to which "end" of the novel it is observed from. There are always two perspectives which must be brought together. Ideally, therefore, the novel should be read twice with such a double reading as Charles S. Singleton has recommended for the *Divine Comedy*, which is also both the record and the fruit of a spiritual metamorphosis. In the first reading, we become acquainted with the progress of the hero; in the second, we fully appreciate for the first time the viewpoint of the artist born from *The Past Recaptured*. But no novelist can expect so much attention from his readers. It is imperative, therefore, that the two perspectives be introduced and distinguished from the start. And yet it is impossible to reverse the chronological order. Proust solved the difficulty by extracting a small fragment of his conclusion and grafting it onto the beginning of the novel; the scene of the *madeleine*. This scene, as we first meet it, seems to fall from heaven and to return to it, for it has no immediate consequences for the narrator's existence. It provides an image of a reality that is in the past from the viewpoint of the author, a promise of a reality that is yet to come from the viewpoint of the narrator. The *madeleine* is thus the *Annunciation* of *The Past Recaptured*. The novel has indeed the structure of a cathedral, since, like a cathedral, it has the structure of a gospel.

The Proustian experience is often labeled Platonic, because memory plays a great role in it and because the word "idea" is used repeatedly in *The Past Recaptured*. Platonism, however, evokes the notion of a serene and unbroken ascent toward the Ideal, bearing little resemblance to what happens in *Remembrance of Things Past*. Almost to the end, the dynamic element of the novel is *amour-propre*, which leads outward and downward from the relatively high starting point of Combray. This direction is reversed only *in extremis*, and the change cannot be logically explained. All we can say—and this remains an impression rather than a demonstrable fact—is that the downward movement had to be pursued *in extremis* before it could mysteriously reverse itself. Similarly, Dante went down to the bottom of his Inferno and, as he kept descending upon Satan's own body without ever turning around, suddenly found himself climbing toward Purgatory and Paradise.

The only possible analogy for the Proustian experience has been noted by Georges Poulet, and it is that of Christian grace.[7] Critics like Georges Cattaui and Elliott Coleman have underlined the Christian aspects of *Remembrance of Things Past*.[8] Others have protested, pointing out that Proust never made any effort to live according to Christian morality and probably did not even believe in God. This biographical fact does not, however, alter the aesthetic one, which is simply that, although Proust was an agnostic, his masterpiece espouses the Christian structure of redemption more perfectly than the carefully planned efforts of many conscientious Christian artists. Though the Christian significance of *Remembrance of Things Past* remained metaphorical for him, he viewed this metaphor as his supreme aesthetic achievement. After the naïve biblical symbolism of Combray, after the infernal imagery of *Cities of the Plain*, comes a third dominant religious symbolism in *The Past Recaptured*, the Johannic and Apocalyptic symbolism of spiritual metamorphosis. *The Past Recaptured* is a second birth and a last judgment.

None of this should scandalize a believer, or an unbeliever for that matter, especially in an age when the search for analogies between the creative experience and the most exotic mythologies has become an accepted topic of research. Even if Christianity were a myth, it would still be less exotic than most, and we cannot reject out of hand, therefore, the possibility of its being relevant to certain forms of aesthetic experience. Mary Magdalene sitting by the empty tomb, the Emmaus pilgrims walking away from Jerusalem, are at first unable to recognize Christ, who is speaking to them. This evangelical theme of a divine presence unidentified and yet effective—unidentified perhaps because it is particularly effective—is a familiar one to Proust. He makes use of it in his novel in a non-religious context, but with the usual metaphysical overtones.

The Christian form seems to be present in Western literature whenever the hero-creator is saved from an idolatrous world by a spiritual metamorphosis which makes him able to describe his former condition. The work records its own genesis, in the form of a fall and redemption. For Proust, as for Dostoevsky and Dante, the fall and the redemption are opposed, yet dialectically joined. But the opposition is less radical for Dostoevsky than for Dante, and still less radical for Proust. The metaphysical significance is lost first, then the ethical; to Proust, finally, the revelation is primarily aesthetic, but it remains as irrational as ever. Or perhaps it should be called super-rational, because, far from bringing irrationality in its wake, this illumination provides the rationality and order which a truly great art demands. Irrational subjective elements are finally distinguished from objective reality. Literature is raised to a level where most romantic and modern antinomies lose their relevance. *Remembrance of Things Past* is both poetic and didactic, lyrical and psychological, aesthetically autonomous as well as existentially truthful. A humanist like Albert Thibaudet feels no less at ease in the Proustian novel than a Christian like Charles du Bos.[9] Henri Peyre finds Romanticism in its pages, and Jacques Rivière invokes the classical tradition.[10] Georges Poulet is right to call *Remembrance of Things Past* a *Summa*, because all types of experience are explicitly or implicitly present in it. This universality is the fruit not of a weak eclecticism, but of an authentic synthesis in which beauty and truth, so often enemies in the art of the nineteenth and twentieth centuries, are reconciled. In some of his late theoretical pronouncements, Proust, who was not an abstract thinker, may still talk the language of the symbolist and the subjectivist; he may still oppose his truth to the truth of his readers; but this false prudence evaporates in the great moments of insight. As the novelist descends deeper into himself, he also descends into the hearts of all men. He cannot doubt, then, that truth itself is one.

# 8

# Marivaudage, Hypocrisy, and Bad Faith [1963]

Most readers take it for granted that Marivaux gives us a complacent picture of the society in which he lived and that his optimism is particularly reflected in his heroines, the delightful *ingénues* of the plays and novels. Working upon the assumption that Marivaux himself shares our nostalgic longing for the rococo boudoir, the people whose business it is to stage his plays try to extract the maximum amount of "charm" from the leading actress, and they sacrifice everything else, including the text, to this one grandiose achievement. Because we never listen to Marivaux's plays, *marivaudage* has become synonymous with flirtatious chatter and the author's purpose has always been misunderstood.

The first Marivaux is the playwright, and he is not well known because only a few of his plays are ever staged. There is a second Marivaux, the novelist, who is even less well known than the first. André Gide once included *The Life of Marianne* (*La vie de Marianne*) among the ten works of fiction which he would take with him to a desert island, but he added that he had never read it. The critics are all agreed that the book is *important,* but they cannot say why, even when they *have* read it. And there is still a third Marivaux whom no one is bold enough to call important because he has not been fully reedited since the end of the eighteenth century. This last Marivaux writes essays which recall the pessimistic moralists of the seventeenth century. His motto could be countersigned by La

Rochefoucauld: "*Amour-propre,*" this Marivaux writes, "is to our minds what form is to matter; the one supposes the other." The same attitudes and reactions which keep recurring in the plays and the novels are ascribed in the essays to this *amour-propre,* which is also called *vanité.* The heartless coquettes of these essays look very different, at first, from the *ingénues* of the plays, but they are really the same characters; and they will be perceived as such if we bear in mind that the "happy ending" is demanded by the genre of the comedy. The conventions of the theater disguise somewhat, but do not suppress the ruthless character of Marivaudian *amour-propre* as it is defined in the essays. In this theater the true nature of sentiments based on egotism is obvious in the essential role played by "pique" and in the absence of genuine tenderness. What concludes the amorous battle is really an alliance between the rival *vanités,* and the mutual admiration society thus formed looks plausible enough as a substitute for requited love so long as its durability does not have to be tested; we can be sure, of course, that no such test is forthcoming, since the play is at an end.

In his *Marivaux par lui-même,* Paul Gazagne maintains that the earthiest aspects of love play a greater role in Marivaux than we have been so far willing to recognize.[1] This view is correct, but only because physical possession is a matter in which *amour-propre* is deeply involved. The coquette is not genuinely sensuous, and she never misbehaves, Marivaux writes in one essay, unless she finds it absolutely necessary in order to retain the undivided attention of her lover. So small, indeed, is the role of the senses in Marivaux's world that a woman deprived of physical charm will score more triumphs than a truly beautiful one, provided she believes herself irresistible, provided, in other words, she is endowed with the most inflated *amour-propre.* In Marivaux's battle of the sexes, the two partners succeed in impressing each other insofar as they manage to be impressed with themselves.

This means, of course, that a life of *amour-propre,* in Marivaux's sense, is a life of make-believe, but a very special kind of make-believe. The Marivaudian hypocrite tries "to deceive himself so that he can better deceive the others." The seventeenth-century moralists were already preoccupied with *hypocrisy,* but they were prevented by their rationalist outlook from interpreting it primarily as a process of self-deception. The problem was never clearly formulated, but it was generally felt that the only man who cannot be deceived by hypocrisy is the hypocrite himself. The trouble with this commonsense viewpoint is that it makes all distinctions between the hypocrite and the vulgar liar impossible. A certain confusion between these two equally but differently unpleasant characters is indeed visible at the end of Molière's *Tartuffe*, when the religious hypocrite turns out to be a common criminal sought after by the police. Marivaux judged Tartuffe quite unsatisfactory as a portrayal of the hypocrite. His own Tartuffe is a man who plays his role so well that he confuses it with his own nature and manages to convince himself that he is genuinely religious.

In *Les sincères*, the heroine is a marquise who prides herself on her sincerity and lack of *coquetterie*. This marquise has a maid who adorns her mistress with great care in the morning, and is rebuked on the grounds that vanity is a woman's worst fault. The maid then studiously neglects the coiffure of her marquise, whose beauty suffers. The noble lady ceases to complain, but she becomes sullen and mean, whereas she had been cheerful and kind until then. Understanding her mistake, the maid resumes her first practice, whereupon the marquise resumes her little sermons, but her good looks being restored, she recovers her serenity. This marquise wants her servant to be a coquette in her place and for her sake so that she can be both pretty and self-righteous.

The process of self-deceit, which involves two characters in *Les sincères,* can also take place within a single individual. The Marivaudian psyche is always divided between a servant and a master, between deceiver and deceived, such as we find in this play; every coquette, for instance, is really two women in one; there is a first woman in her who uses all the feminine tricks in order to attract a crowd of admirers, and there is another one who superciliously denies these same admirers the customary benefits of a patient courtship; she can thus enjoy her dubious popularity in the serene belief that she remains innocent and respectable. This second woman does not hesitate to stigmatize *coquetterie*—the *coquetterie* of other women, of course—and, in so doing, she acts with the utmost "sincerity."

This division of the Marivaudian psyche recalls, somewhat, the modern division between the "unconscious" and "consciousness," but the separation is less rigid, less complete. Between the two halves of this psyche there is the same collusion as between the marquise and her maid in *Les sincères*; these two halves, in a sense, are not even separate entities; the deceiver and the deceived can shift roles so swiftly that the shift is not perceived by the subject himself, just as masters and servants shift their roles in *The Game of Love and Chance* (*Le jeu de l'amour et du hazard*) in order to tease, test, and deceive each other. The servants have become the silent accomplices of their masters; they are not their equals, yet, and their rivals, as in Beaumarchais, but the distance between the two classes has diminished. This modified master-servant relationship pervades both the social structure, in a world of disintegrating aristocracy, and the inner life of the individual. Marivaudian society, like the Marivaudian psyche, is never really one, nor is it ever really two. This hesitation between unity and duality expresses itself in a back and forth motion between these two poles. Within and without, the dialectical game is the same; it permits a number of unstable combinations, which keep reappearing as plot structures in the plays and as harmonic variations on the theme of self-deceit both in the novels and in the plays. The process of self-deceit is never so complete, therefore, that the truth cannot be acknowledged, if *amour-propre,* which is always shifting its grounds, demands it. The tricks with which a character manages to deceive himself become quite transparent to him when they are employed by others, which means that this character can be successively capable and incapable of understanding the same fact.

The coquette wants to think of herself as a virtuous woman, and she wants to enjoy the pleasures of *coquetterie;* in most instances, she ends up choosing the twilight zone between vice and virtue. Her two objectives are poles apart; we assume that she will land in the middle and get nothing. She is neither truly modest nor frankly promiscuous. The outward face of her ambiguous moral attitude—its objective correlative, as some would say—is that kind of erotic teasing which was no less effective with the eighteenth-century male, if Marivaux can be trusted, than it is in our day. The coquette does, therefore, land in the middle, but she gets everything. In a world of universal self-deceit, the prerequisite of worldly success is more self-deceit. The rule is a general one, as the example of the Paris shopkeepers will reveal. These shopkeepers want to make money, but they cannot bear to think of themselves as dishonest men. What will they do? They will charge a little less than they could and a lot more than they should. They, too, choose the fertile middle-ground between good and evil, and Marivaux explicitly points out the similarity with the coquette.

The shopkeepers want to be both respectable and rich, and the richer they get the more respectable they appear. Are they sincere? Their attitude is not one of good faith *stricto sensu*; but it is a mitigated good faith which does not strictly abide by the moral law and which makes allowance for their greed without conflicting too openly with religion. The shopkeeper steers a middle course. He is a Christian and he is a businessman; the two are contraries; one is hot, the other is cold; people must make a living and yet they must save their souls. What will they do? They will look for a compromise.

This "mitigated good faith" (*bonne foi mitigée*) recurs frequently in the essays under slightly varying names. The expression recalls the famous "bad faith" (*mauvaise foi*) of Jean-Paul Sartre, and the resemblance is not solely in the language. In both cases, moral ambiguity is resorted to in order to evade a difficult choice. Nothing is more Marivaudian than the illustration of "bad faith" Sartre gives in *Being and Nothingness*: a girl, who does not want to notice that her companion is holding her hand, will talk passionately about her beautiful soul and she will completely forget her unimportant body. In *Les sincères,* the very ideal of sincerity is the object of a critique very similar to Sartre's own. Marivaux often describes "mitigated good faith" as a state of lukewarmness, halfway between the hot and the cold, like Sartre's viscous consciousness, a product of bad faith, which stands halfway between the liquid and solid states. The eighteenth-century writer limits himself to psychological observation, but his "mitigated good faith" is so universal that it tends to acquire the same "ontological" significance which Sartre claims for his "bad faith." The analogy between Marivaux and Sartre has been noted by Gabriel Marcel in a brief preface to an anthology of Marivaux's theater which is more precious than many ponderous volumes of criticism and historical research.

Both Marivaux and Sartre want to retain moral responsibility and yet still account for the obvious fact that we are not always clearly aware of our deepest motivations. They can accept neither the psyche of the rationalists, which is completely transparent to itself, nor the psyche of modern depth-psychologists, which is completely opaque. They must reject both the glaring light of the first and the total obscurity of the second for an intermediary *chiaroscuro* in which things are only dimly seen and confused with each other. In order to account for the ethical middle-of-the-road, these writers must settle for a psychological middle-of-the-road which is infinitely more subtle than the two extremes and often makes both of them look like gross simplifications of a complex reality. This psychological compromise shocks our common sense and frustrates our desire for clear-cut solutions, but it is not the easy way out like the ethical compromise for which it tries to account; it forces the two writers into verbal acrobatics, and it exposes them to the risk of being perpetually misunderstood. Sartre resorts to a technical jargon, which professional philosophers, at least, will understand, and Marivaux creates his *marivaudage,* which, to my knowledge, has never been fully understood by anyone. His contemporaries were unwilling to accept his psychology and they accused him of being "mannered"; he protested, to no avail, that the peculiarities of his style were caused not by a desire to appear original but by the nature of his observations. *Marivaudage,* both as dialogue in the plays and as monologue in the novels, is an attempt to reveal the process of half-conscious self-delusion at the very moment it is taking place and from the perspective of the half-deluded subject himself. In the novels the chief victim of "mitigated good faith" is also the narrator. This subjective technique may be partly forced upon Marivaux by the evolution of the psychological novel in the eighteenth century, but it answers perfectly the novelist's purpose, which is, I believe, to test the reader's psychological acumen. Sartre, too, in the name of his "characters' freedom," has formulated a theory of implicit revelations which is primarily destined to develop the reader's power of self-awareness.

This technique has failed in both cases, but Marivaux's failure is the more complete, because Sartre, misunderstood as he is by the public at large, can always count on those knowledgeable readers who are perfectly aware of what he is trying to achieve because they interpret his novels and his plays in the light of his theoretical writings. Marivaux could be interpreted in the light of his essays, but almost no one bothers to read them.

Let us try to read the beginning of *The Life of Marianne* in this new light. Marianne, a charming orphan girl, is entrusted by a priest to M. de Climal, an old man of pious demeanor, who immediately tries to seduce her with a gift of expensive clothes. Marianne's landlady, a hearty and vulgar laundress named Mme Dutour, advises the girl to take the clothes and whichever presents will follow; Marianne, she believes, can put off indefinitely the old man, who is quite feeble and easy to dupe. Marianne rejects this bluntly immoral counsel with a great show of indignation, but she accepts the clothes on the grounds that an innocent girl like her does not have to understand the implication of such a gift. She does not break with Climal until the young, rich, and elegant Valville surprises the old man at her feet in the act of declaring his love. Afraid that Valville might resent her composure, which is remarkably unruffled for the occasion, Marianne rushes, a little belatedly, to the priest, in order to expose the vile maneuvers of her unworthy protector. M. de Climal is confounded, and Marianne, who portrays herself as an innocent victim, triumphs. But the story is more ambiguous than our résumé suggests, because it is told by Marianne herself. This heroine's super-Tartufferie is never clearly spelled out for the benefit of careless or myopic readers. The presence at her side of the obviously sinful Climal, and her success in vindicating herself in everybody's eyes, appear to resolve the ambiguity in favor of Marianne. But appearances are misleading. The most doubtful characters in Marivaux's novels are also the most charming and the most successful; Jacob, the hero of *The Upstart Peasant* (*Le paysan parvenu*), is a male Marianne: money, beautiful women, social prestige, and, above all, self-esteem are the reward of his "mitigated good faith." The success story of these crafty scoundrels does not indicate Marivaux's approval of moral turpitude, as Marcel Arland believes, or even less his blindness to it, as Sainte-Beuve and Brunetière imagined, but rather his discouragement with men in general and his society in particular, not without a little admixture of *Schadenfreude*. Far from applauding the conduct of his heroes, Marivaux, like a Flaubert or, again, like a Sartre, silences his own feelings in order to let the evidence speak for itself.

Can we prove that this interpretation is the right one? The critic Le Breton felt tempted to read the novels as we do, but he finally espoused the traditional interpretation of Marivaux as an immoral or amoral novelist because he could find no evidence to support the other view. He was looking for a type of moral judgment which is rigorously impossible in such novels as Marivaux's. The creator of Marianne and Jacob never speaks in his own name, and Le Breton looked in the wrong place for a moral judgment, but he was certainly right to look for it. If Le Breton had read the essays, he would have learned that Marivaux was not only cognizant of the subtle form of evil typified by Marianne, but eager to portray it *as evil:*

I do not want to criticize those faults so obvious and blatant that they are defense-less against my satire; they are too easy a butt for my jests and I leave them alone. I do not hit a man when he is down. But oh! how I hate, how I detest those vain and deceitful people whose tricks are so clever, whose impostures are so well de-vised that almost everybody sides with them and one does not know how to cast upon them the opprobrium which they deserve.

The "faults so obvious and blatant" are those of the cynically greedy but good-hearted Mme Dutour, and even of the frankly lecherous Climal; the clever impostor, with whom everybody sides, is Marianne. When Mari-anne finds it difficult to convince the priest that Climal's intentions are not pure, she invites him to touch her dress, ostensibly to prove that such an expensive gift cannot have been bought out of charity, but her real intent is more sinister. The reader who knows how Marivaux felt about Molière remembers Tartuffe and his awkward attempt to disguise his compelling desire behind an alleged concern for Elmire's dress:

Elmire: What does your hand there?
Tartuffe: I am only feeling your dress: the material is very soft.
(*Le Tartuffe*, 3.3.917–18)[2]

Marivaux's scene is a clever reversal of Molière's. Far from being overcome by passion, like Tartuffe, the almost pathetic Climal, and the other second-rate hypocrites, Marivaux's feminine Tartuffe arouses the passion of others in order to further her devious ends. She instinctively knows that no man is really immune to her charm, and the priest, for all his saintliness, is also a man. The circumstances are such that they appear to justify the hypocrite. Unlike Tartuffe and Climal, the girl is perfectly invulnerable to criticism, because she never clearly formulates her immoral purpose, *even to herself,* her self-righteousness remains flawless.

The invulnerability of Marianne extends, of course, to the readers of the novel, who do not realize that the real villain is she rather than Cli-mal, who dies repentant a little afterwards. Indeed, her impostures are so well devised that everybody sides with her, including posterity. Everything turns to her benefit. When Marivaux wants to hint at the truth, he must show his heroine practicing at least some limited form of introspection, and this activity, in itself laudable, tends to vindicate rather than incrimi-nate the hypocrite. The task of "casting opprobrium" upon a clever girl like

Marianne has proved even more difficult than Marivaux anticipated, and this misunderstood writer can consider himself lucky that his heroine has not quite succeeded in casting opprobrium upon him.

If the creator is thus the victim of his own creation, he must also be, at a deeper level, the victim of his own contradictions. Why is Marivaux thus obsessed with the coquette? He is certainly not the benign admirer of feminine graces portrayed by some of his biographers, but neither is he the detached and austere moralist whom he tries to impersonate in his essays. When Molière decided to portray a man at war with the world, he created Alceste, who is under the spell of a coquette. This profound vision may provide the one key to unlock all the diverse aspects of Marivaux. We have much to learn from the almost incredibly subtle distrust of the Self practiced by Marivaux, but his overly suspicious attitude certainly does not suggest a man who is at peace with himself. This man ought perhaps to be pictured as an Alceste who never dared criticize his Célimènes too openly because he could not tear himself away from them, as one who resented their persecution in proportion to his own weakness. Hence the hidden venom in his writings. It was Marivaux's belief that Molière could easily be surpassed as a psychologist, but this judgment may prove to have been hasty; in the debate between the two writers, the last word may well belong to the author of *Le misanthrope*.

# 9

# Formalism and Structuralism in Literature and the Human Sciences [1963]

The fairy godmother of literary studies, the positivist, has bequeathed to it two gifts of unequal value. The first is truly priceless: it is the *method* that still supports and will always support the editing of texts as well as the critique of the knowledge amassed by literary history. The second gift is the idea of a literary science on a par with the natural sciences, such as the late nineteenth century had conceived. Already with symbolism there is a reaction against this pervasive idea. At first the reaction is purely defensive. Scientific dogma is dismissed in the name of *le rêve*, individual fancy, and simple literary pleasure; but since Renan we know that *the truth is perhaps sad*. And this sadness permeates even the word "impressionism": the only domain that the artist still claims as his own is that of the impression, that is to say, the surface, the superficial; the substance of things is now a matter for the serious people, for the scientists.

With Valéry, Claudel, and T. S. Eliot, literary positivism will come under fierce attack. This great science is unable to account for the creative experience, and it is the creators themselves who assert this fact. For example, positivism perpetuates the legend of "old La Fontaine" as an absent-minded fellow who wrote fables for his own amusement. Valéry destroys this legend by using it to justify his own poetic practice. The art of the fable writer is far from being simple. Perhaps La Fontaine appeared to be absent-minded to non-artists because he was in fact absent-minded, that is, he was absent-minded in everything else but art because he was not, in other words, an absent-minded artist. No matter how much laymen and literary historians delight in his anecdotes, La Fontaine's critic, for his part, must not allow himself to be distracted by the great care that La Fontaine brought to his art through anecdotes. In his critical essays, Valéry sketches a veritable "Copernican revolution," whose principle Wellek and Warren would later formulate, with as much judiciousness as rigor, in their indispensable *Theory of Literature*:

The natural and sensible starting point for work in literary scholarship is in the interpretation and analysis of works of literature themselves. . . . But, curiously enough, literary history has been so preoccupied with the setting of a work of literature that its attempt at an analysis of the works themselves has been comparatively slight in comparison with the enormous efforts expended on the study of environment.[1]

To take Taine's famous triad (*race, milieu, moment*) completely seriously would be to negate the specificity of the literary text; this procedure is always about reducing the work—posited as unknown—to that which it is not—posited as known. Absolute knowledge would translate into a radical negation of the work, a disintegration whose residue would be called sources, influences, hereditary factors, etc. The critic who reacts against the excesses of positivism strongly affirms the primacy of the work. It is in England and America that this idea of primary evidence has the strongest influence; it brings about an entire movement that results in New Criticism.

Among the contributions of this movement we should mention its victorious struggle, during the interwar period, against the abusive application of simplified versions of psychoanalysis and Marxism to literature—"application" in the sense that we say we "apply" a cataplasm to the back of a sick person. Here again it is a matter of "reducing" literature to something that it is not. The more general the ultimate term of analysis—whether it is called "Oedipus complex" or "decadence of the bourgeoisie"—the less revealing it is.

However, in order for the "Copernican revolution" to occur, it is not enough to stigmatize the errors of "reduction"; one must truly resituate the center of gravity within the work, a center which had hitherto been situated everywhere but in the literary work. The work must no longer be the doormat of passive influences, a "reflection" of the outside world, or the trace of some "complex." The work can thus only define itself in terms of an organizing force exerted on language and on the reader's perception. This amounts to saying that the work is *form* or perhaps *structure*, in or not far from the sense that Saussurean linguistics has given this term.

Saussure himself does not speak of structure, but his disciples have adopted this term. According to Louis Hjelmslev, for example, structural linguistics is based on the hypothesis that makes of language

. . . an autonomous entity of internal dependences or, in a word, a structure. . . . The analysis of this entity allows us to constantly separate parts that reciprocally condition each other, where each part depends on certain other parts and would neither be conceivable nor definable without these other parts. Structural analysis reduces its object to a network of relations, while considering linguistic facts as being "in a network."[2]

After 1930, and particularly after World War II, the use of the term "structure" is generalized in the human sciences as well as in literature. The sociologists picked it up from Max Weber, who perhaps got it from Spencer and Marx. The *Gestalttheorie* psychologists come later, followed by the ethnologists, led by Claude Lévi-Strauss. A group of French psychoanalysts aligned with Jacques Lacan worked toward the reformulation of Freud's thought in terms of structures. In all of these thinkers, Saussurian linguistics played a primary role. One should also mention the first writings of Georg Lukács, such as *Signs and Forms*—later repudiated—which gradually circulated under the influence of scholars such as Lucien Goldmann, and which contributed to the "structuralizing" of Marxism. Only by resolving the general problem of structures on a philosophical as well as a methodological level can one understand the trajectory of this great intellectual convergence.

This has not yet been done, even if the linguists and the social scientists recognize that their disciplines do not evolve in a vacuum. In 1933, Nikolai Trubetzkoy wrote: "Our time is characterized by the tendency in all disciplines to replace atomism by structuralism. . . . Contemporary phonology is not isolated. It is part of a larger scientific movement."[3] But literary critics have generally shied away from debates around the term "structure," and, with few exceptions, the meaning of the word remains somewhat vague in literary studies. The slightest contact with the human or social sciences immediately conjures up the specter of "reductive" criticism.

Are these fears justified? There can only be a "reduction," properly speaking, within a univocal causal relation; however, this is just the type of causality that the structural vision eliminates. What disappear are the metaphysico-material substances and entities susceptible of furnishing a principle of universal explanation. Certainly structuralism tolerates the appeal to such a principle, but its internal logic does not lead fatally in its direction, in the manner of the earlier historico-social or psychoanalytico-literary experiments. There can no longer be any turf battles between the different disciplines, at least not at the operational level, for the only things that remain are structures and structures of structures, often called "worlds" or "worldviews." This concept does not imply any hierarchical organization of structures; these structures maintain relations of reciprocal expression which exclude neither oppositions nor contradictions, and which, far from suggesting an *a priori* solution, no longer allow us to pose the question of origins.

These relations of expression indicate that structure, in the sense that interests us here, is essentially meaningful. The structural field is meaningful, and it is meaningful without having all of its articulations necessarily correspond to the mode of linguistic articulation. The literary work signifies perhaps more effectively, more substantially, differently, or even signifies something different than other structures—but it *signifies*. It is perhaps by *opposing* literature to these various structures that one will approach the essential in literary criticism, but it is certainly not by isolating it from them or by renouncing signification altogether.

An excessive fear of "reduction" can lead the critics who advocate the primacy of the work to a rejection of meaning. Therefore, one tries to bring the non-meaningful structures to the fore. But this quest turns out to be delusive. Either the structure will be immediate and very apparent, or it will be mediate and hidden. The first solution has the advantage of avoiding any hint, even a faint one, of the mistrusted "depth psychologies." But it is difficult to understand what distinguishes "structure" or "form" from good old composition, in the sense of the most banal *explication de texte* practiced by every French schoolchild. If the best part of the artwork, its form, offers itself without effort, then there is no longer any critical method, nor is there any real investigative process on the part of the critic. To avoid negating itself, modern criticism must become a search for the implicit, a hermeneutics.

But how to formulate the implicit in purely aesthetic terms? There is the desire to endow literary criticism with a language that would not owe anything to extra-aesthetic meanings. One describes the form—or the structure—with the help of images borrowed from the fine arts and architecture, images such as "texture," "tensions," "equilibrium," etc. These metaphors are of great interest, but using them exclusively has a weakening effect; for it should be obvious that they cannot be as meaningful as the original language, the language of the work itself. The principle of the return to the work of art should not make us forget an even more fundamental principle: the literary work is language, and is thus condemned to signify. It is perhaps true that painting and sculpture avoid some types of signification, but this is in order to conquer others through the obstacle of material substances. The verbal arts, freed from or deprived of these obstacles, are constantly threatened by prolixity; nevertheless, they realize their essence not in refusing to signify but in striving to attain the richest meanings.

Merleau-Ponty once observed that formalism has so little regard for form that it detaches form from meaning. In this sense, the watchword of the "return to the artwork" easily leads to formalism. The slogan itself is irrefutable, but an overly narrow interpretation transforms it into a veritable literary isolationism. In the same way that not long ago the respect for objective methodology culminated in scientism, here the reaffirmation of the primacy of the artwork culminates in aestheticism and formalism.

One must not define this formalism by the importance it accords to notions of form or structure, but by its ignorance of structures *outside the work of art*, a refusal that isolates the aesthetic structure from other meaningful structures and that makes the notion of structure lose its fecundity.

Contemporary formalism presents itself as purely methodological and anti-philosophical, yet it remains linked to the aesthetic and intellectual movement associated with symbolism. It sees the work of art as the only possible refuge from a hostile world, a world entirely dominated by the laws of positive science. Thus, this attitude remains determined by the positivism it strives to contest. And it falls back into the dualism of form and content, that is, into that which the notion of structure endeavors to overcome.

The structure—let us say the form—is once again opposed to a content judged derisory since it derives from something other than *pure* art. The exigency of form is almost always linked to an ethics of "non-commitment" (*dégagement*) which readily defines itself in opposition to Sartrean or pseudo-Sartrean "commitment" (*engagement*). In short, one finds here the old opposition, which is now more entrenched and systematized, between realism and *l'art pour l'art*, or between naturalism and symbolism. "Non-committed" criticism always takes committed criticism to task for its normative character, without realizing that it is condemning itself in the same stroke. Mallarmé paid homage to Zola, but contemporary formalism has made the separation between politics and aesthetics a veritable dogma—and this at a time when Bertolt Brecht's Berliner Ensemble was creating a very different kind of theater, with which we are all familiar.

There are subjects that are proscribed because they are considered rebellious to form. It is difficult to understand why. Thus, there are also privileged subjects, subjects recognized as natural vehicles of formal beauty. The thing-oriented and positivist conception of content results in a thing-oriented conception of form itself. The domination of formalism by positivism is thus absolute. One ends up with a critique of subject matter infinitely more extreme than that of Boileau. Indeed, it is not possible to tolerate a social or political "content" under such a dubious pretext as one finds in Boileau's *Art poétique*:

There is no serpent, no odious monster
Which the art of imitation cannot transform into a pleasing sight.[4]

This extreme distrust of meaningful structures is all the more surprising given that even the systematic recourse to these structures does not imply an abandonment of formalism; it allows for a development and enlargement of structural description. In the first essay of *Sur Racine*, Roland Barthes shows how the language of psychoanalysis, so disappointing when it is applied to an author, can assist a criticism strongly centered on the work in drawing out the aesthetic structures.[5] Here, psychoanalytic references do not lay the groundwork for a potential psychoanalysis of Racine—who is nowhere mentioned in Barthes' text, either as an individual or even as an author. Nor is it a matter of psychoanalyzing fictional characters. Rather it is a matter of locating certain fundamental conflicts and of using them as a starting point to define the "tragic functions" of Racinian theater.

Like psychoanalysis, philosophical systems are sometimes helpful in deciphering the aesthetic structures. However, these systems no longer have a normative character, but rather an operative one. Their presence does not represent a return to the old "philosophical" critique, which aimed at abstracting the "ideas" of the writer. Sometimes these "ideas" have only a slight relation, or no relation at all, to the hidden philosophical framework that interests interpretative criticism. Nor should one believe that this type of critique is systematic. It is all the less systematic in that it succeeds in transforming all systems into an interplay of structural grids. By contrast, criticism that is highly systematic does not uncover any philosophical structure in the works it treats; it is unaware of its own philosophical prejudices.

To make structural conception into something more than a Platonic wish, one must appeal to the languages of structuralism: to psychoanalysis, philosophy, sociology, or even to the dialectic of primary images developed by Gaston Bachelard. Is this tantamount to adopting a revolutionary attitude? Does this mean turning the venerable institution of literature upside down? Certainly not, for it has not been sufficiently observed, or observed at all, that the great writers were the first to describe *structures* in the modern and scientific sense of the term.

In order to remove the aura of mystery that still shrouds structural description, one need only think of the famous Vauquer pension in *Le père Goriot*. Balzac does not merely present us with a simple accumulation or combination of heterogeneous objects; in every detail the pension is present in its entirety, though always in a different way. The architectural details, the furniture, the utensils, the habits of the pensioners, their gestures, their speech—all of this refers to a larger meaning that defines the pension as a totality. Meaning emerges from objects and then returns to them, conferring on them additional significations. Description is thus never a simple inventory; it is not linear, but circular. Its starting point is absolute ignorance—the reader's—and it moves toward absolute meaning, an infinite series of dialectical movements that go from the parts to the whole and from the whole to the parts, in order to gradually reveal their reciprocal conditioning. There is a phrase in Balzac's description of Madame Vauquer that aptly describes this dialectical movement of structural description: *Her whole person explains the pension, as the pension implies her person.*

Like all authentic works, the *Comédie humaine* is not only structured, it also describes the structures; and this is perhaps the most novel and characteristic element of what we call "realist" art—at least in its most brilliant practitioners. This art is very different and even opposed to the current theory of realism, which is positivist and anti-structural, with its notions of "objectivity," "copy," and the famous scalpel planted in the bleeding heart of Emma Bovary—by Sainte-Beuve, not by Flaubert.

The great modern novelists, and most particularly Marcel Proust, already give us interpretive criticism of their works, since they bring out and explicitly formulate certain structures which were implicit in previous works. Do the ethnologists and the sociologists realize that Combray is a model of structuralist description? One can certainly make the relations described by Proust more explicit; one can even mathematize these relations to a certain point, but the essential is already there. Physical circularity symbolizes spiritual circularity; the structure's interiority symbolizes its autonomy. But Combray cannot define itself as a spatial entity. It is not geography that interests the novelist; he reminds us of this when he compares the imperfect and concrete circularity of Combray with the depiction of cities and towns in medieval painting, whose perfect and ideal circularity is always evocative of the celestial Jerusalem. The structure is neither an object nor a collection of objects, and yet the description is necessarily composed of objects; it will thus be indirect, allusive, symbolic.

Proust seeks to describe Combray as an enclosed space, with all that this implies: human warmth, security, the poetry of childhood, but also ignorance and a lack of awareness of others. There are no structures, the specialists tell us, without a certain "resistance to change." And these same specialists add that one cannot introduce a single new element into a structure without changing it in some fundamental way, that is, without upsetting the relation between the whole and the parts. One could say that these properties of structures determine the conservatism of the inhabitants of Combray and their profound mistrust of anything new. One cannot indicate the presence of an "unknown dog" to Aunt Léonie without her endeavoring to situate it within the structure. Her disquiet reveals that in her eyes the well-being and permanence of Combray depend on this process of integration. Here we have a quaint caricature of a profound truth. Now a bit more serious is the problem that Swann's mundane life poses for Combray. There is a Swann who is a part of Combray and whose personality is quite determinate, that is, strongly structured. The great-aunt rejects any news about Swann that tends to replace the Swann that is familiar to her with an unfamiliar, worldly Swann. It is not the object *in itself* that counts, but the meaningful structure in which it appears. An unfamiliar Swann cannot introduce himself into Combray without bringing about radical change, without upsetting a whole system of social hierarchy, without exploding, in other words, a certain worldview that we can describe from the outside as provincial, narrow, and bourgeois, without ever fully "defining" it.

The great-aunt does not know that she systematically rejects facts that are incompatible with her "worldview." We never perceive the structure that governs our existence. It is this truth that Jacques Lacan's anti-Cartesian *cogito* expresses: "I think where (or) I am not, thus I am where (or) I think not" (Je pense où je ne suis pas, donc je suis où je ne pense pas).[6] If one does not want "unconscious" structures, one must at least allow for "latent" structures.

Even if he does not ignore any of the people or objects that figure in the novel, a plainly positive observer would still not be able to grasp the structure. The relatively small amount of information that would be gleaned through this kind of observation would be perceived from the outside, and thus would be labeled as "prejudiced"; that is, it would be defined negatively. The positive reading will always lack the essential element, that is, it will always lack the principle of unity that organizes objects and integrates them into a signifying totality. The strangers who pass through Combray are considered "barbaric" by the locals; "the spirit of the place" eludes them. Having only analytical and positive reason at their disposal, they are not able to perceive the structure. They are not "initiated" into Combray's secret, which is, moreover, not definable in any direct manner. The difficulties that the novelist encounters when he speaks to us of Combray are of the same order as the misunderstandings between Combray

Formalism and Structuralism 89

and the external world. An art that is not simply structured but structuralist always studies itself as much as and more than it studies its object.

In some sense the novelist's predicament is similar to that of the literary critic facing the work. In order to "initiate" the reader, he must describe the structure *qua* structure, that is, he must understand it from the inside. The poetic element depends on interiority, which is not an object; interiority can only apprehend itself metaphorically. And only the outside world can furnish metaphors. To reveal the inside, the novelist makes an appeal to the outside, but he does so according to a very different mode than the one that characterizes positivist and explanatory reason. This essential but paradoxical fact must be emphasized. The metaphors that gradually weave together the network of significations that we call Combray derive from areas of inquiry that have since been conquered by structuralism: ethnology, sociology, psychopathology, the history of religion, etc. Aunt Léonie's nightstand becomes a church altar. In order to awaken some of Combray's inhabitants from their private reveries, it is necessary to resort to procedures that Proust compares to those of the alienist doctors. A parallel is made between the slaughter of a chicken and the sacrifices of primitive religions. The aunt's whims evoke the intrigues and passions of Versailles during the time of Saint-Simon. No domain of reality should be excluded under the pretext of "purifying" the poetry or for fear that it might evaporate in the air of the outside world. It is not by withdrawing himself that Proust will articulate the closure of Combray; it is by opening himself as much as possible and by discovering that the relative closure and autonomy of Combray have their analogues in the various domains of anthropology; in order for these qualities to be expressed, one must not isolate oneself and one's art from all that is not Combray; one must appeal to the incredible diversity of human history.

It is not by getting worked up about some abstract notion of the essence of Poetry that one will assure the richness accorded to it by the principle of the primacy of the work; it is by appealing to significations, no longer as explanatory principles but *as significations*. In short, it is a matter of truly renouncing positivism and of recognizing that the most diverse areas of human reality can only signify in the manner of works of art. One must multiply relations and comparisons between significations in order to render each of them ever more meaningful, without, however, hoping to attain the type of evidence that is the province of the natural sciences. Such evidence is based on a process of verification to the detriment of signification; it thus impresses itself on the observer the least inclined to understand, the least endowed with good will.

We have just discovered structuralism in novelistic works that are fifty and one hundred and fifty years old. We will see, conversely, that the structural disciplines will adopt a set of problems and a style of interpretation that the specialists of the novel will judge to be typically novelistic. After having found Lévi-Strauss in Proust, we will now find Proust in Lévi-Strauss. In *The Savage Mind* (*La pensée sauvage*), for example, Lévi-Strauss meditates on the problem posed by the almost infinite variations of Australian customs within a common sociological pattern. The interpretation he proposes irresistibly recalls the analyses of Parisian society in *Remembrance of Lost Time* (*La recherche du temps perdu*):

It was desired and conceptualized, for few civilizations seem to equal the Australians in their taste for erudition and speculation and what sometimes looks like intellectual dandyism, odd as this expression may appear when it is applied to people with so rudimentary a level of material life. But lest there be any mistake about it: these shaggy and corpulent savages whose physical resemblance to adipose bureaucrats or veterans of the Empire makes their nudity yet more incongruous, these meticulous adepts in practices which seem to us to display an infantile perversity . . . were, in various respects, real snobs. They have indeed been referred to as such by a specialist, born and brought up among them and speaking their language. When one considers them in this light, it seems less surprising that as soon as they were taught accomplishments of leisure, they prided themselves on painting the dull and studied water-colors one might expect of an old maid. . . . Each group was no doubt actuated by the only apparently contradictory incentives of being like others, that is, of constantly elaborating themes only the general outlines of which were fixed by tradition and custom.[7]

Evoking images of the Verdurins and the Guermanteses in this context would certainly not betray the spirit of Lévi-Strauss's analyses. After having read Lévi-Strauss, how can one believe that the dialogue with the structuralized human sciences implies a secret retreat toward nineteenth-century scientism? Indeed, social scientists hostile to structuralism were the first to note his literary style—in order to criticize him for it. And it is just this kind of challenge that pleases a Jacques Lacan. He defines neurosis as a "solecism," and, in a text originally addressed to students of literature, he writes: "The [psychoanalytic] symptom *is* a metaphor, whether or not one wants to admit it, just as desire *is* a metonymy, even if we mock it."

It would seem that generalized structuralism, in a Lévi-Strauss or a Lacan, can very well result and does in fact result in a generalized formalism. In order to escape from this formalism without abandoning phenomenological empiricism and without resorting to a philosophical *coup de force*, it is perhaps necessary to reflect on the experience of the structuralist himself. How does the one who perceives the structures differ from the one who does not? Lévi-Strauss asked himself this question in several of his studies:

It was not until anthropologists [ethnologists] appeared on the scene that we discovered that social phenomena obeyed the laws of structural organization. The reason is simple: the structures are only apparent from the perspective of an outside observer.[8]

As we have seen, the novelists have preceded even the ethnologists on the path toward contemporary structuralism. Thus, Lévi-Strauss errs, and doubly so, since exteriority, if it is a necessary condition, is certainly not a sufficient condition for the structuralist experience. As we know, not all transatlantic tourists make good ethnologists. Exteriority gives the whole but not the parts, and one can no more have a structure without the whole than one can have a structure without the parts. Interiority gives us the parts but not the whole.

Pure exteriority corresponds, precisely, to the tourist's vision, to a superficial overview. Pure interiority gets lost in the details. In order to perceive the structure, that is, the reciprocal relation between the whole and the parts, one must, paradoxically, connect exteriority with interiority. Interiority is not given to the ethnologist; he must patiently conquer it by penetrating into the intimacy of the ethnic groups he seeks to understand.

But *who* puts the required patience of the ethnologist to the test? Is it the "savage," whom the "civilized" consider a legitimate and permanent cause for scandal? Or is it the ethnologist himself, who is powerless to perceive the structures because he is himself structured? The great-aunt is closed to Swann because she completely belongs to Combray. Between structuralism and us there is nothing but structures. For example, it is our native language that makes it difficult for us to master foreign languages; children, who are less solidly structured than adults, are the better linguists.

Being a part of Western civilization imposes a vision of the "savage" that is as false and as reassuring as the image of Swann cherished by the great-aunt of Combray. Let us remember that she always reasons as a "positivist." She only wants to know the facts, and the facts arrive in abundance, but they only reveal the usual significations of Combray; they cannot modify her "worldview." It is not because positivist reason has gone beyond the structures that it misconstrues them; on the contrary: it impresses itself on those who are so strongly structured that they are unaware of being structured. At the level of perception, positivist reason always expresses itself as an unconscious imperialism. It cannot see the other's interiority because its own interiority is invisible to it.

In order to grasp a structure from the inside, one must accept the experience that the great-aunt refuses; one must be able to renounce, to a certain extent, one's own structure, one's own worldview. The structuralist vision involves something other than pure intelligence; it is based on a metamorphosis that is existential and even spiritual. In *Tristes tropiques* as well as other writings, Lévi-Strauss himself has posed the problem much more fully than in the previous quotation:

Since, in a word, it is the same type of operation which in psychoanalysis allows us to win back our most estranged self, and in ethnological inquiry gives us access to the most foreign other as to another self.[9]

The "operation" that reveals the Other in his truth, that is, insofar as he is structured, will obviously reveal our own structures and will reveal them to us as Other; for this operation consists in extricating oneself, in freeing oneself from one's own structures. Structuralism does not stop functioning when the ethnologist directs his analyses toward his own civilization, Western civilization. And it is perhaps in this return that the most profound meaning of the ethnographer's vocation will be revealed.

Proust describes structures in his works; in so doing, he has freed himself from his own structures, and this is the experience he describes in *Time Recaptured*. The analogy with psychoanalysis is in fact stronger than in the case of ethnology. Indeed, the Ego, the Ego of Combray, which Proust's novel aims to reconquer, is unfamiliar, not because it belongs to the other, but because, with the passage of time, it has ceased to belong to the novelist. The interiority conferred on the child is subsequently lost by the adult. Once again, it is a matter of reconquering an alien interiority by taking a position completely outside of one's own structures.

The narrator is assisted by objects that are really more like relics to him, since they remain integrated into the structure of Combray; they retain their meaning, which is attached to Combray. For it is not enough that they have been perceived at Combray; it is also necessary that they not have been perceived since Combray, that they have never been integrated into subsequent structures, into the successive Egos of the novelist-narrator. The sudden perception of the object will lead to quasi-perception of the old structure. But the first contact, that of the *petite madeleine*, is not as productive as what we find in *Time Recaptured*. The object-relic cannot fully play the role of concrete mediator. The narrator is not yet ready for the decisive experience; he has not yet emptied the cup of pseudo-pleasures and pseudo-knowledge that the world offers him; new desires, new projects, and new passions will always bring about a structuring of reality and a perpetuation of ignorance. There is no Time recaptured except at the end of a long period of disillusionment and suffering. Lost Time must define itself as a slow but irrevocable process of "destructuration." The security of Combray gives way to a world that is fascinating, but also empty and cruel. The original misconstrual of structures thereby hardens into a refusal of knowledge accompanied by a hatred for the misunderstood Other. The high-society salons, which are veritable caricatures of interiority, treat the unfortunate Swann with a ferocity that the great-aunt would not have been capable of. Destructuration does not automatically insure the revelation of structures, even over the long term. Only in the case of the narrator does it result in a structural vision. Thus, destructuration appears retrospectively as a negative stage on the path to truth. It is analogous to what the psychoanalysts call "transference" and to what the mystics call the "descent into hell."

The experience of Time recaptured and, more generally, the structural perspective, is joined with the fundamental experience of the Western world, that of death in a too limited world followed by resurrection in a greater world. Thus, the Proustian novel discovers the structure of death and resurrection that characterizes the great works of Western art, thought, and religion. We should also note that the great visionaries of the Judeo-Christian world—Moses, Saint Paul, Saint Augustine, Dante—men torn between several "worldviews" (Egypt and Israel, Israel and Greece, Greece and Rome, the ancient world and the medieval world . . . ), in the final analysis belong to none.

The experience of these few isolated geniuses, coming from a remote or more recent past, is not without a certain relation to the collective destiny of the world we call "modern." The rapid disintegration of national, cultural, and religious boundaries in the modern world appears only superficially to result in the eclecticism of the Roman Pantheon. The ideas of "mixing" or "blending," which are essentially thing-oriented concepts, cannot describe the phenomena that we are witnessing. The clash of "worldviews" can only result in their mutual destruction. Images of "uprootedness" evoke the most visible consequences of a global spiritual evolution as rich in promises as in perils. All that worries us in the evolution of the contemporary world recalls the process of "destructuration" articulated in the Proustian novel. The paralysis of action, the weakening of creativity, the partial enervation of desire dissimulated under a veritable frenzy of entertainment—all are today collective phenomena. And the counterpart to these negative aspects is an always more radical opening toward true subjectivity and to the Other.

This opening to the Other can appear either as the realization of promises that remain abstract at the level of religion, or as the announcement of a turn toward religion so radical that it makes even the religious man turn away. Structuralism is certainly linked to this spiritual adventure. The word is fashionable; it is thus already ridiculous, or it will be tomorrow. And the laughter is indeed legitimate in the face of certain excesses. However, behind the fashion there are deeper meanings which ridicule cannot adequately probe. Commanded by neo-positivism to prove its existence, the structure remains silent, and for good reason. But neither can poetry prove its existence to those who see only words, or music to those who hear only noise. The term "structure" aims at a type of understanding that one would want to define as *aesthetic*, but whose generalization and systematization requires a rethinking of the field of aesthetics properly speaking.

Far from bringing literature within the reassuring dimensions of a clearly defined "specialty," far from favoring a turning back toward familiar truths, or those that appear so, the notion of structure recalls humanists to their oldest and highest vocation, which is universal.

—*Translated by Robert Doran*

# 10

## Racine, Poet of Glory [1964]

From the birth of a metaphor until its death, there is a single, continuous process. The original semantic field gradually falls away, and at some point we lose sight of it altogether. Over the course of its history, the metaphor has changed its meaning, but in so doing it has fallen back to the level of a univocal and thus fully arbitrary sign; in other words, it has lost its mediating function.

Racine does not invent; he reinvigorates metaphors by bringing together the two domains of language to which they owe their existence as metaphors. In short, Racine invites them to rediscover their mediating function. This is a poetic operation that can remain purely verbal; its mechanism is thus quite obvious. In the phrase "seared by a greater flame than e'er I lit" (brûlé de plus de feux que je n'en allumai [*Andromache*, 1.4.320]),[1] it is not an image that recalls the *précieuses*—and such images are still frequent in Racine—which arrests our attention; it is the almost too clever reinsertion of this phrase back into its literal context. Pyrrhus did in fact set Troy ablaze; the mad lover is a true fire raiser.

At every stage of poetic creation, the dramatic or quasi event resounds with the rhetoric of preciosity. For example, in *Iphigenia* there is a metaphorical relationship between the sentimental and social levels in the relations between Eriphyle and Achilles. Defining one of these levels means necessarily sliding to the other, because the metaphorical relation remains inscribed in language. Eriphyle is "ravished" (*ravie*) by Achilles in every sense of the term. The tragedy reminds us of the game in which one mimes well-known expressions for the audience to guess. But in the Racinian game the phrases themselves are given, and it is perhaps a matter of uncovering a second meaning. Whatever the case may be, Racinian art reveals itself from the outset as being equally theatrical and poetic.

Indeed, the example of Eriphyle suggests a second meaning. In the prisoner who contorts with rage and desire at the feet of her master, we do not see the animation of a rhetorical figure, but a woman of flesh and blood, drawn to the very violence to which her ravisher subjected her. If rhetoric takes precedence in the creative realm, in the eyes of the spectator it is real violence that precedes and determines desire. The two domains of the metaphor disappear behind the synthetic unity that defines the "the morbid passion of Eriphyle." On the contrary, "seared by a greater flame . . . " is very nearly a play on words because the two domains appear to be simply juxtaposed. We do not perceive the synthesis that would push the original meaning into the background. In other words, the more successful the operation, the less visible it is.

Domination and servitude, sacred and profane: these are the two essential polarities that characterize the rhetoric of precocity. The lover calls himself a *slave* of his *mistress*; he genuflects at the feet of the *divinity*. These two systems correspond to the division of Racine's profane tragedies into the historical and the mythological. In *Phaedra*, myth acts as a dramatic extension of the language of love. The heroine's passion expresses itself in terms of religious worship:

My mouth implored the goddess, but my heart,
Hippolyte; I saw him everywhere,
Even in the midst of sacrificial smoke,
And gave him all, a god I dared not name. (*Phaedra*, 1.3.285–88)

(J'adorais Hippolytus : et, le voyant sans cesse,
Même au pied des autels que je faisais fumer,
J'offrais tout à ce dieu que je n'osais nommer.)

However, the duality of history and mythology is not essential. The role that the cult of the Emperor plays in *Britannicus* and *Berenice* allows us to grasp the profound unity of all the elements. In these two plays, the metamorphosis of the master into a divinity and the slave into a humble worshiper occurs before our very eyes. Berenice affirms that she would have doubtless chosen Titus even if he "lacked the grandeurs that clothe him" (loin des grandeurs dont il est revêtu [*Berenice*, 1.4]), but the political power of the emperor and the sacred character of his office always take center stage in the poetic expression of desire.

Have you not seen the splendor of last night?
Did not his greatness captivate your sight?
The night of crackling flames, the pyre, the torches,
The eagles, fasces, people, soldiers, arches,
The consuls, senators, the crowd of kings,
Whose brilliance all from my beloved springs;
The gold and purple, glittering with his glory,
The laurels witness to his triumph's story;
The myriad eyes one saw from every side
Gazing their fill at him, unsatisfied;
His royal stance, his fascinating airs;
With what respect, what reverential stares
Did all in secret pledge their loyalty! (*Phaedra*, 1.5.301–13)

(De cette nuit, Phénice, as-tu vu la splendeur ?
Tes yeux ne sont-ils pas tous pleins de sa grandeur ?
Ces flambeaux, ce bûcher, cette nuit enflammée,
Ces aigles, ces faisceaux, ce peuple, cette armée,
Cette foule de rois, ces consuls, ce sénat,
Qui tous de mon amant empruntaient leur éclat ;
Cette pourpre, cet or, que rehaussait sa gloire,
Et ces lauriers encor témoins de sa victoire ;
Tous ces yeux qu'on voyait venir de toutes parts
Confondre sur lui seul leurs avides regards ;
Ce port majestueux, cette douce présence . . .
Ciel ! Avec quel respect et quelle complaisance
Tous les cœurs en secret l'assuraient de leur foi !)

---

Yet at this very moment, Italy
Prays for Titus; with sacrifices they
Are hallowing the first fruits of his reign. (*Phaedra*, 1.5.319–21)

(Cependant Rome entière, en ce même moment,
Fait des vœux pour Titus et, par des sacrifices,
De son règne naissant célèbre les prémices.)

In the same way that he played on the double meaning of the word "fires" (*feux*) in *Andromache*, in *Berenice* Racine plays on the double meaning of the word "empire." However, a third meaning emerges out of the interaction between these two, eclipsing both of them. Here we are dealing neither with hollow rhetorical oppositions nor with the brutality of politics in the Roman Empire. Berenice is not physically a slave to Titus; she does not burn incense at the foot of his statue. It is not a matter of the real power of the Emperor, but of the prestige that this power confers on him, or in Racinian terms, his *glory*. The master/slave and god/worshiper relations evoke the concrete aspects of glory as much as the fascination it exercises. Imperial omnipotence furnishes everyone, and Berenice in particular, with a personal reason to adore the emperor. Glory is revealed through the fusion of the two domains of metaphor. Because of its naturalness the process frequently escapes us. Indeed, it constitutes the poetic equivalent of a historical process. In Roman history absolute imperial power does, in fact, result in the cult of the emperor.

Racinian glory is radiance; it is the dazzling light that is reflected in the faces turned toward a glorious being. Berenice's desire is drawn to Titus's incomparable glory; Eriphyle is captive to Achilles' glory, which is brutally inscribed in her flesh. Desire is defined as *lack of glory*. Berenice always considers herself inferior to Titus. She witnesses his apotheosis as a simple spectator. The relative baseness of Racinian desire is evident in a passage from *Britannicus*, which is curiously similar to Berenice's speech. Nero anxiously wonders if he will be able to supplant Britannicus with respect to Junia. Narcissus seeks to reassure him by invoking the imperial glory that the young girl has not yet experienced:

But now, my lord, that her wide-opened eyes,
Observing close the splendor of your throne,
Will see around you kings, who've lost their own,
Merged in the crowd, her lover too with them,
All vying for the honor of a glance
That you may deign to cast on them by chance;
When from this pinnacle of glory, she
Beholds you come to sigh her victory;
Lord of a heart, be sure, already moved,
Command she love you and you will be loved. (*Britannicus*, 2.2.449–58)

(Mais aujourd'hui, seigneur, que ses yeux dessillés,
Regardant de plus près l'éclat dont vous brillez,
Verront autour de vous les rois sans diadème,
Inconnus dans la foule, et son amant lui-même,
Attachés sur vos yeux, s'honorer d'un regard
Que vous aurez sur eux fait tomber au hasard :
Quand elle vous verra, de ce degré de gloire,
Venir en soupirant avouer sa victoire ;
Maître, n'en doutez point, d'un cœur déjà charmé,
Commandez qu'on vous aime, et vous serez aimé.)

Once again we can observe that the seducer's charm becomes one with sovereign authority—a magical double power which the term "glory" is uniquely able to express. Narcissus is wrong about Junia, but his expectation is not unreasonable, as the example of Berenice shows. However, if Junia is indifferent to Nero, and if this indifference augments the desire of an emperor obviously covered in glory, should we not renounce the idea of defining *all* desire as lack of glory?

Indifference is itself a sign of glory; it belongs to those who desire nothing outside the perfect circle of their own existence. Glory is sovereign autonomy, absolute self-sufficiency; glory is therefore as much the contrary of desire as its object: Glory *is* indifference. Between indifference and desire there is a relation that *Phaedra* puts particularly into relief. The heroine dreams of Hippolytus's young glory, which is indifferent to love. Certainly Phaedra's desire intensifies when she learns that Hippolytus loves Arcia and that she loves him, but there is no contradiction here. If the circle of glory appears to close around "indifference," all the more reason for it to close around happy lovers who are self-absorbed and indifferent to others.

As the supreme obstacle and the only real object of passion, indifferent glory erects an invisible rampart around whoever possesses it. Glory is intangible, invulnerable, inaccessible. The one who desires cannot encounter these attributes of glory—even in a grossly material form—without coveting them passionately. Acomat is not unaware of this blind weakness of desire, and he cunningly plays on it in order to inflame Roxane's passions:

I pitied Bajazet, and praised his charm,
Hinting he was, although so close at hand,

Yet jealously kept hidden from her eyes.
What can I tell you more? Roxane, roused,
Had now no other wish than seeing him. (*Bajazet*, 1.1.138–42)

(Je plaignis Bajazet, je lui vantai ses charmes,
Oui, par un soin jaloux, dans l'ombre retenus,
Si voisins de ses yeux, leur étaient inconnus.
Que te dirai-je enfin ? La sultane éperdue
N'eut plus d'autre désir que celui de sa vue.)

As one can see, the sadistic desire to break through obstacles does not essentially differ from the jealousy that threatens happy couples. In Racine,
there is only one desire, which is always identical to itself. Nero sees Junia's
love for Britannicus as a sign of her indifference toward him. In the same
way, Andromache's devotion to Hector's memory is indistinguishable from
her indifference to Pyrrhus. Though they lack autonomy on the material
level, on the spiritual level the autonomy of these two women is absolute.
This is in fact what wounds their magnificent lovers and turns them into
slaves of desire. Pyrrhus's flame is "servile," first of all because Andromache
is a simple captive, but second, and even more profoundly, because this
captive refuses to requite the desire of her lover, and in so doing, dispos-
sesses him of his glory.

Berenice and Narcissus mistake the Emperor's glory for a positive reality. They confuse the power to subjugate bodies wielded by a temporal
master with the power to subjugate souls. But this is the illusion of a soul
that is itself subjugated. No matter how meaningful in itself, the self-un-
derstanding of desire has no universal validity. For it is not based on an objective experience, but on a quasi-mystical revelation. The eyes of ordinary
mortals "open widely" (*dessille*) at the sight of the Emperor. But the Emperor himself hardly counts as an individual. This is not the apotheosis of a
man or even a god; it is the epiphany of adulation and desire. The only real
presence in the two tableaus is that of the "avid gazes" (*avides regardes*). It is
these gazes that engender and perpetuate glory. The light that is reflected
on the courtiers is itself but a reflection of their unanimous desire. If only
one gaze turned away, glory would lose its luster. It is this truth, of which
he is only vaguely aware, that is the cause of Nero's gloominess.

At first, Racinian glory appears to us as opportunist and even ma-
terialist. "Charms" (*appas*) are no less prized than high birth, wealth, or

an important position. But this eclecticism is superficial; nothing counts as much as desire itself. Glory finds its nourishment in desire and cannot survive without it. Desire is thus attached to glory, but glory is simply the object to which desire is attached. This circular process explains the elusive, capricious, and paradoxical character of human relations in Racine's dramas.

To desire someone is to recognize that person's superior glory; in other words, it means giving the person an excellent reason not to desire on his or her own account. Hermione attributes Andromache's success with Pyrrhus to "pride"; for her part, she regrets having responded so openly to her suitor's advances:

Alas! I trusted him to my undoing.
I did not hold back anything from him
And freely opened out to him my heart.
I did not shield my eyes with mock reserve;
As my love prompted, so I spoke to him. (*Andromache*, 2.1.456–60)

(Hélas ! Pour mon Malheur, je l'ai trop écouté.
Je n'ai point du silence affecté le mystère :
Je croyais sans péril pouvoir être sincère ;
Et sans armer mes yeux d'un moment de rigueur,
Je n'ai pour lui parler consulté que mon cœur.)

All desire is weakness—which is why only the desire that one inspires can redeem the shame of the desire one feels. Reciprocal relations are an exchange of glories, and managing them is as delicate as managing an alliance between two sovereign and equally prideful nations. With the slightest imbalance in their relations, the two partners fall into a hopeless dialectic. Only in the unhappiness of a relationship that is always asymmetrical and non-reciprocal will they find stability. One is doomed to be humiliated, that is, to suffer from a desire that goes perpetually unsatisfied; the other, the constant object of attentions that bore him to death, finds that there is nothing to maintain his glory in the devalued desire of his lover. These are two roles that one can play consecutively or simultaneously, because one can always participate in two or several systems of oppositions. In *Andromache*, for example, the four principal characters are divided into three almost identical systems. Hermione does not desire Orestes, who desires her;

Pyrrhus does not desire Hermione, who desires him; Andromache does not desire Pyrrhus, who desires her.

The intersubjectivity structured by glory irresistibly recalls its metaphorical definition in terms of "mastery" and "slavery." Given the historical and mythological background of the tragedies, there is an analogy here which reveals the extreme coherence and meaning—as rich as it is profound—of the synthesis effected at the level of glory. The constitutive elements of Racinian art define two very different forms of non-reciprocal relations: a third form emerges from their conjunction. Rhetorical non-reciprocity is purely formal; it derives from the codes of gallantry and even simple politeness. On the other hand, the historical relation between master and slave is a brutal reality. Racine has no particular concern for the constitutive elements of his art. He associates, assimilates, and combines these familiar elements in a thousand different ways in order to reveal the hidden dialectic of glory. The rhetoric of precocity "dematerializes" power relations, but the brutality of these very relations wrests rhetoric from its trivial neutrality, thereby imbuing it with the *spirit* of violence that is the defining feature of the world of subtle aggression engendered by glory. This synthesis defines a non-reciprocity that is more spiritual but no less real than the relation of servitude in ancient societies. The emancipated Narcissus, physically free but always a slave in spirit, furnishes, within a historical metaphor, a veritable symbol of a servitude freely chosen, the paradoxical result of the desire for glory.

The Hegelian dialectic of master and slave cannot assist us in isolating the dialectic of glory. Indeed, this dialectic is based on a systematic confusion between relations of power and relations of desire. The two types of relation are not identical, but analogous, and in order to reveal this analogy it is not enough to simply underline the similarities between relations of desire and relations of power; we must still bring out their differences. Eriphyle and Achilles, Berenice and Titus illustrate the first moment of this revelation; Andromache and Pyrrhus, Junia and Nero illustrate the second, which is more essential still, since it reveals glory's absolute dependence on desire, that is to say, its independence with respect to relations of power. Andromache is the master of her master, Pyrrhus, the slave of his slave. As long as relations based on desire appear as an exact copy of social relations, their immaterial essence remains partly concealed. To reveal them, the dialectic of desire must be opposed to the social dialectic. But in practice this exigency results in a certain dissociation of the elements that make up the synthesis. In short, the poet cannot reveal the essential without risking a destruction of the synthesis and a return to the level of heterogeneous elements. That we are sometimes amused by the image of the fierce Pyrrhus addressing his captive with a tone of *précieux* gallantry indicates that the elements of the tragic poem are perceived separately. The intention of the poet is no less clear. He wants to show relations of desire as triumphant rivals over relations of power. The two domains of metaphor cannot come together since they are separated by a negation, but they are on the same level, and their prescribed form must not be disturbed. We must play the game of Racinian glory and not rule out the essential meanings by treating them as hyperboles of preciosity. We must interpret Pyrrhus literally, which is confirmed by his actions when he exclaims:

I suffer all the pains I caused to Troy.
Vanquished and fettered, penitent I sit,
Seared by a greater flame than e'er I lit,
My restless tears and all my passion true . . .
Ah! was I ever so [cruel] as you [are now]? (*Andromache*, 1.4.318–22)

(Je souffre tous les maux que j'ai faits devant Troie :
Vaincu, chargé de fers, de regrets consumé,
Brûlé de plus de feux que je n'en allumai,
Tant de soins, tant de pleurs, tant d'ardeurs inquiètes . . .
Hélas ! fus-je jamais si cruel que vous l'êtes ?)

The negation that separates the two domains of metaphor does not, however, prevent their perpetual contamination. Racine always chooses the modalities of the master-slave relation which are the most apt to serve as a vehicle for the dialectic of glory. This is how the often-treated theme of the ravisher and the captive orients the relation of servitude toward a sexual meaning, by introducing into it an element of instability and mobility that already evokes non-reciprocal desire. The abduction belongs to the past, but it is a recent past. A queen yesterday, Andromache is a slave today; tomorrow she will perhaps be queen again. In the same way, Bajazet, of royal blood, is the slave of a crowned slave. The dialectic of desire makes him once again a master and Roxane a slave.

~

If the Roman woman that Titus is supposed to marry incarnates duty, Berenice, the foreigner he renounces, incarnates desire itself. There is a puritanism of glory in Racine that is fully revealed in the character of Titus. In maintaining his glory without faltering, the emperor succeeds where Pyrrhus and Nero fail. The radical divergence of these destinies necessarily presupposes a point of convergence, an obvious fact common to both, which is at once too conspicuous and too simple to be recognized. This obvious fact, which is based on *nothing* and decides everything, converts glory and desire into two incompatible things. Glory and desire engender and repel each other ceaselessly.

Here we find the source of the misunderstanding that leads to the complete misrecognition of Racinian glory. When a Racinian hero exclaims "It is a question of my glory," he or she is always speaking about desire. The honor of the Cornelian hero rests on ground that is too solid to be vulnerable to the play of desire. The difference between the two conceptions of glory is limited in principle but prodigious in its consequences; it is perfectly irrational, which is why it escapes rationalism, but it is not without reasons, which are primarily historical. The mutual recognition of social milieus in the Cornelian affirmation is also marked by a frenzy of chaotic action that announces their decline. Thirty years later, these same milieus will all be under the yoke of royal absolutism. The possibilities of concrete action will have completely disappeared. Corneille's early dramas always climax in one or more heroic actions. Rodrigo kills the count and destroys the Moors. This is very different from Racine, where the action occurs prior to or after the play; it is always either a memory or a project.

Even when deprived of concrete sustenance, the appetite for glory does not disappear: it transforms itself. One can see this in Saint-Simon. The courtiers avidly await the trifling rewards that the monarch dispenses with a calculated parsimoniousness. Saint-Simon gives us a thousand examples of this sterile competition. Competitions such as the King's bonnet provoke antagonisms that are all the more implacable the more trivial their object. Glory itself undergoes a metamorphosis; it is permeated with envy and jealousy; it acquires a vaguely sexual tinge.

The glory that Don Gomes and Rodrigo are vying for belongs entirely to the victorious combatant. Like Racinian glory, Cornelian glory is indivisible; it cannot be compromised or shared. However, the vanquished suffers neither envy nor humiliation, since he is dead. Everything changes when the duel disappears as a social institution. Don Diego and Chimena—characters in *Le Cid* who prefigure the Racinian problematic—are deprived of vengeance because of their sex or their age. Rodrigo can desire whomever he wishes, but Chimena cannot desire Rodrigo; already her glory forbids it. It is in the heroine, not the hero, that glory is opposed to desire in *Le Cid*. Nevertheless, Corneille's gesture in the direction of the Racinian drama of glory is sleight. Chimena, whose virility already announces the feminization of the Racinian hero, ends up by finding an avenger, and thereby joins the masculine world of Rodrigo. Without the somewhat artificial recourse to Don Sanche's symbolic sword, one can well imagine Chimena's love-esteem already becoming a humiliated and jealous desire for the glorious love-object.

Deprived of a worthy object, ambition is transformed into abstract competition, and this competition, deprived of any real consequences, perpetuates itself and becomes obsessive. Moreover, the spirit of rivalry sweeps over all of the domains still open to the privileged classes, the sexual domain in particular. As ambition is sexualized, sexuality becomes a form of ambition. It would seem that everything converges on this feminization that was noted above. Honor, a masculine concept, loses ground before the feminine idea of glory. Racinian subjectivity is completely dominated by the degradation and failure of Cornelian individualism. The two phenomena are interdependent and mutually reinforcing. Like every form of puritan one-upmanship, Racinian glory results in its contrary, that is, in a debacle in which even personal dignity succumbs. We can perhaps see in this process a transposition of the Jansenist theology of grace and its consequences.

It is understandable that violence in Racine never has the same positive and liberating role that it has in Corneille. Racinian tragedy takes place in an atmosphere of diffuse violence that, far from reflecting any real violence, signifies rather the privation of all violence in a society that no longer eliminates, or eliminates ineffectively, the poisons that it releases. The tragic conclusion is but the paroxysm of the sado-masochistic tensions produced by the dialectic of desire. In this dialectic one can thus recognize the ultimate consequence of the contradictions that define glory; the world that engenders it can tend only toward self-destruction.

Unlike Corneille, Racine cannot set his plays in worlds in which violence plays only a secondary role. He abandons classical subjects only to turn, in *Bajazet*, toward one of the rare modern societies in which slavery still exists. He looks to social forms untouched by Christianity to furnish metaphors for a spirit of violence that threatens Christian society at the very moment when, constrained by its internal logic, it abandons even the residual forms of violence.

Racine's works have a relation to history, but history opens these works to a truth that transcends the particular circumstances of its revelation. Descartes is blind to the problematic of the Other opened up by individualism. To pluralize the Self, as all classical philosophies do, is to mask, by its very elaboration, the radical negation of the Other by which these philosophies are defined. Individualism means nothing if, in the final analysis, it does not mean choosing oneself over the Other. Descartes and his successors do not reveal this consequence because they do not perceive it, and they do not perceive it because of the fundamental nature of their individualist choice.

As long as individualism does not structure intersubjective relations, as long as, in other words, it remains the affair of isolated individuals, the forgetting of the Other that it institutes does not—it is true—pose any problem. Triumphant glory is always a nascent glory. Descartes and Corneille describe this first stage. Only the first moment of the dialectic is perceived, which is why it is not recognized as a dialectic. In order to transcend triumphant glory in the direction of Racinian glory, one must get beyond this first moment, as Racine himself does. Glory should no longer be expected to produce the invariably happy outcomes that the early dramas of Corneille describe for us. To say that Racinian glory is purely rhetorical, as is sometimes asserted, or to say nothing about it, is to be a prisoner of a Cornelian—that is to say, Cartesian—definition of glory. The silence of traditional criticism is a reflection of the more fundamental silence of classical philosophy. In this instance one cannot choose between a philosophical and a non-philosophical critique; as always, one must choose between two philosophies. The critique of clear ideas and familiar concepts is not a critique purified of all "metaphysics"; it is a Cartesian critique that is unaware of itself.

Racine describes the first fallout from modern individualism. This is a phenomenon that recurs in various forms every time new social strata embrace individualism. When emptied of their humanity, intersubjective relations always tend toward a static and geometrical model, which is analogous to that which haunts Racine's tragedies. After Racine, it is in the novel that the intuition of non-reciprocity will be articulated. Thus, Roland Barthes can speak of a certain Dostoevskism in Racine. One could just as well invoke Proust: the Racinian theme of the ravisher and the captive, the harem and its capricious master—the theme of *Andromache, Britannicus, Bajazet,* and *Mithridate*—reappears in *The Prisoner,* though without historical or mythological garb. But the seamless tunic that is the Racinian "subject"—that far-reaching and singular metaphor—is fragmented in Proust into a multitude of historical, religious, or mythological images, as well as into literary and even specifically Racinian allusions. Racine reveals the dialectic of desire poetically; without the help of historical and mythological metaphors he would not perhaps have reached an understanding of this dialectic, which the nineteenth and twentieth centuries were gradually able to isolate.

No more than the novelists, Racine does not write in order to "refute Cartesianism"; he relies entirely on aesthetic intuition, which is why his works are foreign to the abstractions of classical philosophy. Starting with *Thebaide,* Racine resituates the individualist choice within its concrete— that is, intersubjective—framework. The affirmation of the self is inseparable from a challenge issued to the Other; thus it has as its immediate consequence the implacable rivalry of the *enemy brothers*:

Sovereign grandeur cannot be shared;
And it is not something one relinquishes and takes back again. (*Thebaide,* 1.5)

(On ne partage point la grandeur souveraine ;
Et ce n'est pas un bien qu'on quitte et qu'on reprenne.)

Precisely because one refuses to share it with the Other, sovereign grandeur cannot seek to embody itself at the essential level of desire without becoming, on the contrary, the possession that one perpetually relinquishes and takes back. The more completely the Other is forgotten in the egotistical decision, the more scandalous the foreign presence becomes. In *Thebaide* this truth is all but exclusively that of Eteocles and Polynices, that is, the truth of the myth; but it is already this truth that suggests the choice of such a subject; it is this truth which will soon guide Racine's dramatic intuition, drawing together and combining metaphorical domains in such a way as to gradually reveal itself as the truth of the entire work. The dialectic of glory is at first simply the synthetic and sometimes fugitive unity of the elements juxtaposed by the artist. If the structural unity that the artist was aiming for had been given with the first stroke, there would not be a work in the full sense of the term. *Phaedra* is the supreme expression of this slowly conquered truth. In this work the dialectical oppositions are more complete, more mobile, more extreme, and more meaningful than anywhere else. Thus, one should look to *Phaedra* for confirmation of the perspectives suggested by the other tragedies.

Phaedra descends from a race of gods. Like Titus's or Nero's empire, the divine part of her nature is inherited, but it is not an indestructible essence: it is a duty which, given her superhuman vocation, the heroine cannot shirk without falling into the subhuman.

And once again this duty is opposed to desire. Phaedra's desire for Hippolytus causes her to lose her divinity. This divinity is thus simply a more extreme form of glory; it thus considers itself *light*, and its source is the sun that Phaedra counts as one of her ancestors. Throughout the play one encounters a monotheism of the Ego that announces Nietzschean pride. The cult that the heroine wants to create around herself is incompatible with the cult that desire makes her create around Hippolytus. In this instance the sacred does not emanate from Christianity, but from what is most intractable in Racinian glory. Lucien Goldmann is right: in *Phaedra*, there are no gods, and there are no judgments exterior to the heroine; she alone brings against herself a condemnation—infinite and without appeal—worthy of her pride. Election and malediction are equally subjective. Metaphysical pride knows only extremes. Oenone, the lonely voice of humanist compromise, is not understood when she asserts:

Human weakness is only too natural. (*Phaedra*, 4.6.1301)

(La faiblesse aux humains n'est que trop naturelle.)

In this play there is a perpetual shift from god to monster that never stops at man. Because Hippolytus appears to her "like the depiction of our gods" (tel qu'on dépeint nos dieux [*Phaedra*, 2.5.640]), Phaedra is horrified. Later endeavoring to invert this relation in order to regain her divinity, she will tell Oenone:

I see him as a horrible monster in my eyes. (*Phaedra*, 3.3.884)

(Je le vois comme un monstre effroyable à mes yeux.)

The greater one's idea of one's own glory, the more it is compromised by desire. Here the pendulum swing that is already apparent in Pyrrhus and Nero attains its greatest amplitude. The masters and slaves of the historical tragedies have become the gods and monsters of *Phaedra*. This relationship, fully internalized for the first time, does not lose its external dimension. More clearly than the historical tragedies, it defines the twofold ambivalence of human relations that are radically alienated. This twofold ambivalence forms a dialectical totality, a structure that defines the world of glory and expresses *through myth* the truth of the individualist choice: to choose to be a god is to choose to see a monster in the other, but in the end it amounts to divinizing the Other and choosing to be a monster oneself.

In this instance the dialectic of desire reveals all its instability without ever betraying its totalitarian nature. The world that reveals itself to Phaedra in the form of her ancestors is the world of pride that is immediately overturned, becoming the world of humiliation. Though they are divine as long as Phaedra considers herself divine, the ancestors lose all of their glory when she loses hers:

Still Venus wills it, of this wretched blood
I die the last and most forlorn by far. (*Phaedra*, 1.3.257–58)

(Puisque Vénus le veut, de ce sang déplorable
Je péris la dernière et la plus misérable.)

Phaedra's mythical blood line also conveys the duality of the monster and the demigod. It is not a double heredity, in the passive and "scientific" sense, which condemns "the daughter of Minos and Pasiphae" (la fille de Minos et de Pasiphaé), it is a choice that perpetuates itself from generation to generation. Phaedra transmits to her children the prideful vocation that she herself inherited from her parents.

I only dread the name I leave behind.
How hideous a bequest for my poor children!
Their blood from Jupiter should swell their pride;
But howsoever much they vaunt this blood,
A mother's crime remains a crushing load. (*Phaedra*, 3.3.860–64)

(Je ne crains que le nom que je laisse après moi.
Pour mes tristes enfants quel affreux héritage !
Le sang de Jupiter doit enfler leur courage ;
Mais, quelque juste orgueil qu'inspire un sang si beau,
Le crime d'une mère est un pesant fardeau.)

By giving her name to her children, Phaedra condemns her descendants to the Pascalian double of the angel and the beast. This passage brings together pride and its contrary, shame, in such a way as to directly suggest their dialectical link.

~

The conflicts of Racinian drama that Roland Barthes defines under the term "tragic functions" resemble various moments of our dialectic of desire. If we accept Lucien Goldmann's terminology from *The Hidden God* (*Le Dieu caché*),[2] we would in this context be speaking about "dramatic" functions, reserving the term "tragic" for the attitude successively illustrated by Andromache, Junia, Berenice, and, in exemplary fashion, Phaedra. This attitude is that of the *tragic refusal* in the face of a world offering no possibility of authentic existence. Goldmann compares this world to the world of Marivaux. One must recognize this world as the world of non-reciprocal desire.

The question of tragic refusal is as far removed from Barthes' *Sur Racine* as it is from the first part of the present essay.[3] There is a radical incompatibility here, but it can be overcome. The tragic refusal would not constitute an effective refusal of the world if it were not *outside* this world. Since phenomenal descriptions are inside the world, the tragic refusal must therefore be exempt from them.

From the perspective of the world, the trans-phenomenal refusal necessarily leads to one of the intra-worldly attitudes. The principle of this reduction is not difficult to grasp. In all of these instances one is dealing with negative attitudes, which are very different in principle but very similar in their outward manifestations. Here we find an ambiguity of which there are numerous examples in Racine's works. Narcissus shows that one can take Junia's tragic refusal for coquetry:

And who knows if the wanton, from her cloister,
Did not contrive to trap the Emperor?
Too sure her beauty could not stay unsought,
Perhaps she fled in order to be caught,
To tempt the Emperor with the glorious sin
Of conquering [a pride] none else dared to win. (*Britannicus*, 3.7.947–52)

(Et qui sait si l'ingrate en sa longue retraite,
N'a point de l'empereur médité la défaite ?
Trop sûre que ses yeux ne pouvaient se cacher,
Peut-être elle fuyait pour se faire chercher,
Pour exciter Néron par la gloire pénible
De vaincre une fierté jusqu'alors invincible.)

Narcissus tries to trick Britannicus, but he does so cleverly; at the moment he is speaking, no objective criteria can distinguish authentic refusal from its tactical use. At once lure and trap, coquetry results from an intersubjectivity structured by glory. It is thus a possible attitude in the world of desire, whereas tragic refusal is impossible. It is not that the idea of such a refusal would be foreign to this world, but that this world would only see it as an instrument of dissimulation, a form of hypocrisy or "bad faith." And, it is not unimportant to note, this is how the young Racine interpreted the spectacular refusal of the Port-Royal group, as revealed in his *Lettres* on the *Imaginaires*.

Narcissus and phenomenology evince a mistrust toward noble attitudes that is a bit too absolute; but it is not unjustified, particularly from a tragic point of view. The malevolent power of the world should not be underestimated, since the legitimacy and seriousness of the question of refusal are contingent upon it. Phenomenal descriptions do not cohere with this question, but nor should they effectively contradict it. The synthesis of the two points of view—though always possible in principle—reveals itself to be quite difficult in practice. *Berenice* is a case in point. Roland Barthes' analysis of the play is clearly opposed to that of *The Hidden God.* Barthes avers that it is only "by habit" that Titus is bound to Berenice. Elsewhere he writes that it is not true that the emperor "must choose" between Rome and his mistress. The obstacles to a union of the two lovers are presented as external. Barthes wants to internalize them. One can easily understand why. *Berenice* is Racine's only tragedy where divided love plays a primary role. In the other tragedies, reciprocal relations are always subordinate to non-reciprocal desire. It is this reciprocity—maintained even in their separation—that is emphasized by the symmetry of Tacitus's *invitus invitam.*[4] For Roland Barthes, the needs of the State are only a pretext, put forward by a lover too weak to admit his weariness. The Titus of *Sur Racine* is Adolphe's distant relative. There is something other than an "original idea" here. There is an extreme Titus who is exalted by an extreme devotion to the idea of non-reciprocal desire. It is for eminently Racinian reasons that Barthes rejects the literal meaning of *Berenice.* The criticism of the *juste milieu* will reproach him for it. However, Barthes' rigor is useful and even necessary. It allows certain hitherto inaccessible problems to be posed.

This reading of Berenice calls the authenticity of the Racinian hero into question. To say that a hero is inauthentic is to say either that his creator intended this inauthenticity or that it reflects the inauthenticity of the creator himself. The first solution is hardly defendable. We must therefore examine the second, without deluding ourselves as to the risky nature of such an endeavor.

Literary creation is a human relation. It does not escape from the constraints and perils of such relations. If, as Goldmann believes, the tragic hero embodies the perspective of his or her creator, then it is tragedy itself that is against the world, and the poetic act represents a negative attitude with respect to a negative world. The ambiguity that characterizes negative attitudes is thus present at the level of the creative act. Writing a tragedy of refusal cannot be without consequence for the writer himself. The repudiated world can see its hold on the writer's existence weaken; it can also secretly triumph. The tragic hero is perhaps linked to a cathartic action of which he will be the trace or the instrument, or even both at the same time; but he may also be the result of a compensating illusion. Even if criticism is not able to resolve this problem, it will nonetheless have to consider it. The nature of the tragic refusal and its ambiguity calls irresistibly for an existential hermeneutics.

This hermeneutics is all the more desirable insofar as the structure of the first tragedies can be used to support the argument of the inauthenticity thesis. The tragic refusal transforms the slave into a master and vice versa. This could be seen as an abstract revenge of the weak on the strong, the perfect reflection of a dream of mastery that will not own up to itself.

As we have seen, there are no objective criteria that can distinguish authentic refusal from its simulacrum. But this uncertainty, which persists during the unfolding of the tragic action, ends, in a way, with the denouement. Junia takes refuge at the Vestals; Berenice goes away. The tragic denouement separates the true from the false, the authentic from the inauthentic. But why not look in the actual existence of the author for the tragic denouement's indisputable marker? Does not the aesthetic existence of Racine also have its denouement in the definitive abandonment of profane drama?

We must address the question of the silence that follows *Phaedra* from the perspective of internal criticism. To consider this question from a purely autobiographical viewpoint is already to lean toward an anecdotal explanation. But the biographical facts do not exclude a response that would link the tragedy of refusal to the refusal of tragedy—far from it. What happens in 1677 hardly resembles the stereotype of a "religious conversion." This is easily shown, but what is proved by showing it? What does Racine say in his letter to Mme de Maintenon? He does not describe a spectacular conversion; in this letter he speaks of his aunt from Port-Royal, "whom God used as his instrument to rescue me from fifteen years of distractions and miseries." He says nothing more and nothing less. It is certainly possible that he has "forgotten" events already long past. It is even possible that he lied in order to court Mme de Maintenon. But why look for such remote explanations? We have no important text that puts this letter into question. Should we reject this formal document, when we take so many biographical facts for granted that are based on our faith in evidence infinitely less authoritative than this letter?

The later Racine is not Rimbaud, but perhaps neither is he some sort of Tartuffe. To bring out the dual simplicity of these extreme visions one could appeal to the Kierkegaardian idea of spheres of existence. Like Kierkegaard's esthete, the young Racine, a rebel, a bachelor, and a Don Juan, believes that there is nothing higher than art. However, the bitter irony of the tragic vision already makes the call to ethics heard from within aesthetics itself. In 1677, Racine responds to this call. He renounces theater and starts a family; he takes on the responsibilities of a husband, a father, and a citizen with the utmost seriousness. Under Louis XIV, being a good citizen means being a good courtier. He rejects ancient wisdom and embraces the Old Testament. It has been remarked that Christ is almost completely absent from the religious tragedies. The predominance of the Law is perhaps revealing. Let us not forget that Kierkegaard places the Old Testament and Kantian morality in the sphere of ethics. For his part, Goldmann considers extremist Jansenism and this same Kantian morality as authentic expressions of the tragic vision. It is thus easy to shift back and forth between the two perspectives.

Barthes shows that in *Athalia* there is a pure and simple inversion of the earlier worldly categories. The ethical man never stops destroying what he loved. He makes truth into the ultimate—and perhaps the most dreaded—of all idols. This is tantamount to saying that ethics defines a new form of non-reciprocity; it represents nothing less than a real transcendence of aesthetics. Here we must appeal to Kierkegaard, who was able to recognize the superiority of ethics, though he long suffered from it in the figure of his father. We would perhaps hate ethics less if we could truly transcend it. We are in the time of disguised ethics, because we are in the time of ethics contested and gone mad. We should not allow the ethical being in each one of us to purely and simply negate Racine's ethics.

Is anchoring the tragic refusal in the silence that follows *Phaedra* not tantamount to marking the discourse that announces this refusal as radically inauthentic by cloaking aesthetics with a purely worldly nature? On the contrary, this means exorcizing once and for all the demon of inauthenticity by showing that authenticity is truly impossible within the world; one must not evaluate intra-mundane attitudes—and in particular the writing of tragedies—according to such a vain ideal.

The first and the most fundamental of the attitudes of failure in the world of non-reciprocity is desire itself. Escape, refusal, true or false renunciation, are, on the contrary, efficacious attitudes, perfectly adapted to the needs of the situation. The efficacy of negative attitudes does not depend on the intentions that animate them. These intentions are in some sense always pure, because the victim of desire can only wish for an end to his or her suffering. Orestes truly desires to renounce Hermione, and Hermione Pyrrhus and Pyrrhus Andromache. One desires all the more sincerely to escape from desire, insofar as this is the only way to satisfy it. The distance between the will to renunciation and the rejection of desire is never as great as one thinks. What does detachment mean in a world in which it alone can attach us to the other? From the very first scene of *Andromache*, we must recognize that the will to sovereign independence—in other words, glory—is inextricably tied to the "servile flame" (*flamme servile*). The ambiguity of negative attitudes is even more absolute on the inside than on the outside. Orestes teaches this to honest Pylades who, seeing his friend with Hermione again, cannot believe that Orestes' recent efforts to leave her are sincere.

Ashamed of all your fruitless prayers and moans,
You hated her, and mentioned her no more.
Friend, you deceived me.
—I deceived myself. (*Andromache*, 1.1.35–38)

(Honteux d'avoir poussé, tant de vœux superflus,
Vous l'abhorriez ; enfin, vous ne m'en parliez plus ;
Vous me trompiez, Seigneur.
—Je me trompais moi-même.)

---

To all, to me, my victory seemed complete;
I fancied all my ferment sprang from hate. (*Andromache*, 1.1.53–54)

(Je fis croire et je crus ma victoire certaine ;
Je pris tous mes transports pour des transports de haine.)

The will to renunciation belongs to the dialectic of desire. It exerts a force that is always approximately equal in strength and opposite in direction to the force of attraction exerted by the object; this is, of course, why desire can only describe a circular movement around the object. And in the end it is the will to renunciation—inseparable from desire—that imprisons Orestes in this circle. At every turn, the hero discovers his presence within the world of desire as a paradoxical consequence of his will to escape:

But marvel at the Fates whose dire pursuit
Holds out for me the very trap I shun. (*Andromache*, 1.1.65–66)

(Mais admire avec moi le sort dont la poursuite
Me fait courir alors au piège que j'évite.)

The will cannot break out of the circle of desire, because it is always in solidarity with it: it is the other half of the desire for glory. And, when one thinks about it, it must be thus if non-reciprocity is supposed to structure a *world* in the concrete sense of the term. The force that keeps us in this world cannot simply be defined as "bad faith." Bad faith is purely subjective, and the subjective significations are always modified at the intersubjective level. To practice renunciation is to multiply the temptations with one's every step. Indeed, Orestes only has to move away for Hermione to express a desire for his presence: "Sometimes she calls Orestes to her aid . . . " (Quelquefois elle appelle Oreste à son secours . . . [*Andromache*, 1.1]). Bad faith flows from negative attitudes. It speculates on an ambiguity for which it is not responsible and which no "authenticity" would be able to eliminate. It is the world itself—always permeated by solipsistic ideologies—that attaches an exaggerated importance to bad faith in order not to have to recognize the objective duplicity of its own structures.

All worldly acts are double. Considered from a temporal and static point of view, the double act always has the meaning of "bad faith." Considered from a dynamic point of view and from the perspective of its *end*, this same act is inscribed in a spiritual trajectory. It is one stage in the reconquest of unity. Worldly characters—around whom the circle of obsession closes ever tighter—will find their unity in madness, murder, or suicide. The figures of the first tragic refusal, those found in *Andromache*, *Britannicus*, and *Berenice*, are not double, in principle, since they are already outside the world. They will never penetrate into the world of desire. We cannot imagine them from a dynamic perspective because, in reality, they have no history. In taking refuge at the Vestals, Junia finds the same solitude that she has just left behind.

One could imagine a third kind of Racinian being. This being would be a victim of desire and a prisoner of the world; she would liberate herself and rediscover her unity in the renunciation not only of desire but of renunciation itself. This being would renounce the glory that puts all things in a false light. Phaedra—who discovers the dark side of glory on her deathbed—is such a being. It is thus necessary for her to be blinded in order to recover the meaning of the true light and to salute its inalienable rights in her final words. The farewell to light is also a farewell to blasphemous pride:

I now can see no more, save through a haze,
Heaven and my husband, whom my presence stains;
And Death, snuffing the luster from my eyes,
Repurifies the sunlight they defied. (*Phaedra*, 5.7.1641–45)

(Déjà je ne vois plus qu'à travers un nuage
Et le ciel et l'époux que ma présence outrage.
Et la mort, à mes yeux dérobant la clarté
Rend au jour qu'ils souillaient toute sa pureté.)

Phaedra embodies both the world and the refusal of the world; but she embodies these two values successively, and the terms of the opposition do not have the same meaning as in the early tragedies. The experience of desire becomes that of the descent into Hell: Greek fate and Christian redemption become one. Phaedra is as close to the pardoned sinners as to the victims of *hubris* who have been punished and reconciled. She is a bridge between the ancient and the Judeo-Christian world; she embodies the transcendence of aesthetics. To unite Racine's works and his existence into a single structure, one need only interpret everything in light of Phaedra's fate. The supreme work takes on the form of the spiritual adventure that it enacts. The weakening refusal of the first act, with its mixture of shame and pride, is a feature of the early tragedies, *Andromache, Britannicus,* and *Berenice,* those in which the tragic refusal is still tinged with idealism. The fall of Phaedra is about intra-worldly drama; in other words, it is about triumphant desire. The death of the heroine in *Phaedra* plays in the end the same role that this last tragedy plays in the existence of its author. It represents the death of the world of theater, which is seen as analogous to the Greek world of *hubris* or modern pride.

The first Racine already recognizes the radical worldliness of the theater. It is in the name of this worldliness that he defends his art in the quarrel of the *Imaginaires,* and it is in the name of this same worldliness that he will condemn it many years later. Theater is always entertainment; in the first case, it is inoffensive; in the second, it is culpable. Only the preface to *Phaedra* dissents from these two attitudes. Indeed, it suggests that one can turn this worldly art that is the theater back against the world. This point of view is more modern than Aristotelian; it is too divergent from the ideas of the period to have any lasting influence. But one can easily understand why it has an impact on Racine at the very moment when he is composing *Phaedra*. The poet is in a position to know that his heroine is exemplary—for she has been an example and a lesson to Racine himself. When read without presuppositions, the preface confirms the role of *Phaedra* in the spiritual evolution of its author. It says virtually the same thing about this heroine—this modern and sinful Beatrice—that Racine will say of Sainte-Thècle's mother in his letter to Mme de Maintenon: "She . . . is the one whom God used as his instrument to rescue me from fifteen years of distractions and miseries."

The preface to *Phaedra* is thus extremely significant. It states that one can effect an ethical transcendence of aesthetics *within aesthetics itself,* and this is asserted at the moment when Racine himself achieves this transcendence. The preface represents a very important transition, but it is only a transition. The poet cannot take another step without reaching a place from which this text will appear as a final attempt to elude the primordial choice, that between speech and silence. The point of view expressed in the preface will now only prevail in the tragedies derived from Scripture, that is, in the works whose worldly character is already contradicted and opposed at the level of the subject matter.

Compared to *Phaedra*, all of the previous works are worldly; that is to say, they are divided. Everything in them is derived from the world; but in another sense, everything is already derived from the silence to which the heroes of refusal aspire. In the first tragedies, this represents the "share" of silence which then secretly grows, flourishes in *Phaedra*, and finally triumphs over tragedy itself in the succeeding years.

But here again we are speaking in metaphors. One can no more speak of giving silence its share than one can the world. The Racine prior to *Phaedra* is himself divided. To speak here of inauthenticity would be to deny the creative dynamic. Every spiritual metamorphosis, unless it is instantaneous, presupposes the juxtaposition of a past and a future in conflict with each other. One must not choose between two opposed dimensions of the same tragedies; one must endeavor to hold them together in a single vision. In Titus, there is both an unacknowledged Adolphe and a potential Phaedra. It is the division of the work that divides criticism itself into two divergent tendencies: one, oriented toward *Bajazet*, is always attentive to the sinister dance of desire; the other, enamored with tragic values, leans toward *Berenice*. But these two tendencies are reconciled in *Phaedra*; for *Phaedra* synthesizes two attitudes that are too radically antithetical not to be secretly related. If it is true that the first tragic heroes prefigure Phaedra, it is no less true that they differ from her in one fundamental respect; their refusal is given at the outset; it emanates from a superior nature and a time-less essence. And if the characters that are hopelessly swallowed up by de-sire are in a sense the farthest removed from Phaedra, they are in another way the closest: indeed, it is her own experience of desire and shame that will drive Phaedra from the world.

There is thus in Racine a fundamental doubling of the imagination. And the double is subject before being object. It is not perceived, because it is the one that perceives. The ambiguity of the early tragedies, joined with the idealism of their tragic refusal, reflects the division of the Racinian soul. And this division, which is gradually overcome in his works, enrich-es the theme of the double. This theme is itself double: there is an inter-nal dimension which is inseparable from its external dimension. Nero is a hesitant and cyclical being, always divided between two contrary options. And he is also surrounded by doubles: Narcissus, his damned soul, and Britannicus, the *enemy brother*. The theme of the double is fundamental, and Racine, who is normally not very inventive, reinvents this theme if it is not already implied in his subject. One must not conclude that the *sub-ject* is unimportant. The subject matter of myth and Tacitus's histories are not infinitely malleable and as such susceptible to being shaped by an Ego that is always perfectly autonomous and exquisitely unique. This is clearly the case in *Iphigenia*, which is at the same time more Louis XIV and more scholastically Greek than *Phaedra*, for there is no real point of contact be-tween Racine the poet and the myth of the daughter sacrificed by her fa-ther. We must go beyond the radical subjectivism of thematic criticism without renouncing its rigor. Before being taken up by Racine, the theme of the double belonged to mythology. Beginning with *Thebaide*, the myth-ological double is at the center of Racinian drama. The subject furnishes the poet with possibilities of *objective* expression, which are gradually un-covered. This is how Racine is able to achieve the perfection of his art un-der the guise of a scrupulous respect for history and legend.

The two dimensions of the double, internal doubling and the double properly speaking, find their mythical expression in *Phaedra*: the first in the Racinian interpretation of the demigod; the second in the incestuous passion. Incest, the supreme expression of the prideful will to unity, is also the source of the most extreme doubling. The Same who becomes Other and the Other who becomes the Same cannot be separated by the slightest distance. The Racinian adaptation of the myth is far from being arbitrary. The demigod is a *hybrid* being; Phaedra is thus herself a spiritual child of *hubris*; she results from the violence that engenders monsters and the pride that engenders shame. The language itself of myth dissimulates a dialectic which is analogous to that of glory.

In every instant, *Phaedra* reveals the ability of myth to inform a spe-cifically Racinian content. The symbolism of light, whose significance was aesthetic and psychological in the earlier plays, achieves greater depth in *Phaedra* by becoming mythical. The desire for glory is united with the myth of Prometheus, who stole fire from the sky to make himself the equal of the gods. But Phaedra, recognizing the madness of this project, ends up, like Oedipus, by blinding herself *in order to improve her sight*. And thus she discovers Johnanic symbolism. Glory fails to be its own light. One must embrace this failure in order to reach the truth of Saint John the Baptist, that is, the truth of the Christian individual: "*Non erat lux, sed ut testimo-nium perhiberet de lumine*" (He was not the light, but was to give testimo-ny of the light [John 1.8]).

The articulations of myth fit perfectly with the play and paradoxes of non-reciprocal desire. The resulting attitudes never show themselves for what they are. These attitudes even go so far as to claim that they are in-spired by a concern for reciprocity. Theseus, for example, appeals to Nep-tune to avenge him against Hippolytus. The god is made to be responsible for reestablishing the justice of family relations by punishing the transgres-sor. Neptune hastens to satisfy a wish that in reality exacerbates the injus-tice of these relations. Theseus is guilty. He considers himself outraged as a father so as not to be aware that he is outraged as a husband. In this case divine irony consists in satisfying desire. It corresponds to the simplest dialectic: that of the all-powerful master who nonetheless rushes toward despair faster than the slave. The contradiction that engenders desire bears fruit quite immediately in this instance.

In *Phaedra*, we are no longer dealing with a simple mythological backdrop, but with the *form* itself of a dehumanized and mechanized existence. Myth raises to the level of the absolute an entire dialectic similar to that of glory. Evil shifts from one side to the other under the ironic gaze of the "gods" and with the implacable regularity of a law of nature. Here we find the expression of a calamity that we would not take seriously unless we were to find an equivalent in the world around us. Paradoxically, it is Marxism and psychoanalysis that can help us to understand the religious meaning of Racine's renunciation of profane tragedy. Psychoanalysis's fundamental intuition is the metaphorical relation it sees between myth and contemporary experience. This intuition is accompanied by a movement of revolt and refusal. The sexuality of Western man conforms to the Oedipal scheme because it unfolds in a climate of social mystification and family prevarications. In the same way, the mythical metaphor in Marx and the Marxists is used to stigmatize the non-reciprocity of human relationships—though in a less systematic manner. Finally, in Barthes this same metaphor denotes the magical saturation of everyday life in twentieth-century France.[5]

Under these circumstances, why should we be surprised that Racine cringed as he was writing *Phaedra*? Mythical existence is defined by an inability to distinguish the relative from the absolute. It is this impotence that all the great texts of the Old Testament tirelessly denounce under the name of *idolatry*. Racine turns away from the maleficent sacred of *Phaedra*, contrasting it with the beneficent sacred of the Judeo-Christian tradition. Desire redirects the language of the sacred to its advantage; Racine does not hesitate to accuse himself of idolatry, without, for that matter, realizing the scope of this term. But, as we have said, Racinian art consists in resituating metaphors in their concrete context in order to restore their full meaning. From the beginning to the end of *Phaedra*, Racine plays on the two meanings—one erotic and one religious—of the word "idolatry." And these two meanings reveal themselves to be identical. The parallelism between myth and human relationships based on idolatrous desire forces us to rethink the meaning of a term that seems insignificant by dint of being banalized. Common language goes from the sacred to the rhetorical, and Racine goes from the rhetorical to the sacred. He returns to the source; he goes in the opposite direction of the way that leads metaphors to their death.

The rupture of 1677 represents the logical endpoint of the discourse that preceded it. Racine's formal procedures gradually reveal the world as a theological figure of *evil*, placing him before a spiritual choice. The poetic game reveals the meaning of myth, and, as a result, it ceases to be a game. One would not be able to continue this game without opting against Christian redemption. From the perfection of aesthetics to its transcendence, a single process is inscribed within the very form of countless Racinian verses. Here is one that is seemingly insignificant in its preciosity:

[I love, why am I saying love,] I worship Junia. (*Britannicus*, 2.2.354–85)

(J'aime, que dis-je aimer, j'idolâtre Junie.)

The rhetorical contraction—the verse's double start—establishes a relation of gradation and succession, reflecting the duration of desire and its ever-increasing intensity. Behind the hyperbole of precocity, one can read the movement of a passionate being toward the object of his or her passion and the movement of the writer toward an ever more metaphorical mode of writing. Starting with a prideful affirmation: I, me, Nero, the verse ends with an affirmation of the Other that represents the radical negation of this Ego; it thus evokes the dialectic of desire that leads us beyond aesthetics. All the words in this verse are banal, but the alliterative sound of the consonants *j* and *d* confers on these words—when they are heard—some kind of exorbitant and obsessed feeling (*un je ne sais quoi d'exorbité et d'obsédé*), which is the very vibration of desire.

Only the criticism associated with Marxism and psychoanalysis is nowadays able to uncover the meaning of Racinian tragedy, for it is the only one that bases its assertions—at least implicitly—on the silence of late Racine. Humanist criticism does not want to hear of anything that lies outside poetic discourse itself. This is its strength as well as its weakness. Espousing the aesthetic attitude that was also Racine's during his theatrical career, this criticism endeavors to continue the debate at the literary level alone. But it is the denouement that gives the artwork its meaning— the denouement of *Phaedra* and the denouement of the aesthetic existence of Racine. Humanist criticism refuses to consider the denouement.

It celebrates the "harmony" of *Phaedra*, but it never wonders what the marvelous agreement between the mythical and the psychological could mean. Thus it always falls back to the level of heterogeneous elements. It makes and remakes the inventory of these elements, observing each time that poetry cannot be found at this level. The rhetoric of precocity is of little interest; history and mythology remain at the stage of an "ennobling" décor. The psychology is still waiting for concrete definitions. What remains is glory, the most sterile, it would seem, of all Racinian themes . . . The aesthetic unity of the work eludes the aesthetic perspective.

Giraudoux was right about Racine when he spoke of him in terms of the sacred, without recognizing, for that matter, the decisive meaning of what he was saying. He sees, in Racinian tragedy, "the Mass of worldly and atheistic centuries." This word "Mass" would have most probably amused the author of *Andromache*. It would have certainly displeased the Racine of 1677. One might say that it would have terrified him. But it did not take so much to keep Racine from writing a second *Phaedra*. Far from being paradoxical, our thesis, based on corroborating evidence from internal and biographical criticism, is in agreement with the views of Racine himself and those who knew him.

*—Translated by Robert Doran*

## Monsters and Demigods in Hugo
## [1965]

Gwynplaine, the hero of Victor Hugo's *The Man Who Laughs* (*L'homme qui rit*), is an artificial monster, a victim of the *comprachicos* (literally: buyers of children), the Spanish name Hugo gives to the makers of buffoons and dwarfs. Though they have disfigured Gwynplaine's face with a perpetual grin, the *comprachicos* have not disfigured his soul, which remains generous and good. Gwynplaine, the buffoon, is the living antithesis of Lord David and the Duchess Josiane, both of whom are elegant, wealthy, and beautiful as gods, but who are also cruel, indifferent, and immoral. The physically ugly and morally beautiful Gwynplaine is opposed to the physically beautiful and morally ugly Lord David and Josiane.

The association between the beautiful and the good and the evil and the ugly is so well ingrained that we speak of moral beauty and moral ugliness without realizing that we are appealing to an image. In *The Man Who Laughs*, this analogical relation is reversed: beauty is systematically associated with evil and ugliness with the good. Furthermore, one can easily see that this phenomenon of inversion is not limited to the theme of beauty and ugliness. The relation Hugo establishes between primal images and the fundamental antithesis of good and evil always contradicts the relation we are accustomed to, which is inscribed in language if not in the nature of things. This contradiction, which is directly linked to the message that the novelist wants to communicate, is even reflected in the proper names. The man who picks up Gwynplaine is called Ursus, and his pet wolf is called Homo. The animals in Hugo's late works are almost always more human than man, or at least less bestial. The antithesis light/obscurity is inverted as well. The only person who is able to *see* the true Gwynplaine is the blind Dea, who had been saved long ago by Gwynplaine: "With her shadowy eyes she contemplated on the zenith from the depth of her abyss the rich light of his goodness" (*The Man Who Laughs*, 2.2.3).[1]

The Hugo of *The Man Who Laughs* is sixty-seven years old; for over fifty years he has not tired in creating monsters. The first monster, the dwarf Habibrah from the novel *Bug-Jargal*, is a buffoon, like Gwynplaine; the second, Han of Iceland, has something of the vampire, the demon, and the beast about him.[2] In both cases, physical ugliness is associated with moral ugliness, and this twofold ugliness serves as a foil to the twofold beauty of the main character. The organization of these antitheses thus remains traditional and reassuring in these texts. Even so, there are two or three passages in which the monster plays a role that prefigures that of Gwynplaine. In *Han of Iceland* the traitor of the novel—the king of Norway's minister, and a dark soul if there ever was one—seeks to involve Han in his evil plots; in Han's presence he divulges some of his secrets. Struck by the hypocrisy of his interlocutor, Han looks him "straight in the eye," exclaiming: "If our two souls were to leave our bodies at this moment, I think that Satan would hesitate before deciding which soul is the monster." Han later boasts of his crimes before his judges: "I have committed more murders and set more fires than all of you together have pronounced iniquitous judgments."

The early Hugo does not yet rehabilitate the monster, but he opposes the clearly visible and—to put it frankly—honest monstrosity of the brute to the hidden monstrosity of the judges, priests, and government officials. This parallel contains the germs of an opposition which becomes clearer and more pronounced in *The Hunchback of Notre Dame*. Quasimodo is still a bit nasty, at least according to convention, but he is incapable of hypocrisy. He is the antithesis of Frollo, who is sinister and deceitful despite his magisterial appearance and the prestige associated with his rank.

Quasimodo's physical monstrosity still derives from nature, but his moral monstrosity is a product of society.

Malevolence was not, perhaps, innate in him. From his very first steps among men, he had felt himself, later on he had seen himself, spewed out, blasted, rejected. Human words were, for him, always a raillery or a malediction. As he grew up, he had found nothing but hatred around him. He had caught the general malevolence. He had picked up the weapon with which he had been wounded.[3]

Quasimodo was already victim of the moral *comprachicos*. The first time we see the deformed creature, on the square in front of the cathedral, he is surrounded by a pack of old bigots ready to pounce. The novelist is feeling his way toward the character of Gwynplaine, that is, toward a monstrosity that in no way involves the fundamental nature or freedom of the monster, a monstrosity completely *for* and *by others*, a monstrosity that is absolute innocence.

Quasimodo is the scapegoat of a cruel and superstitious society. Gwynplaine, for his part, has lost even the natural ugliness of the scapegoat that polarizes persecutions and prejudices. He is rather a sacrificial lamb, and his redemptive mission elevates him in the eyes of the reader. Gwynplaine discovers one day that he is the son of a great lord; called to sit in the House of Lords, he appears as a champion of the oppressed. He launches into a great speech on democracy, but it is his face, more than his ideas, which provokes catcalls from the nobles in the audience. Previously delivered to the *comprachicos* by royal order, now he succumbs a second time under the abuses of the aristocratic torturers. "What a prodigious denial of justice! Royalty, having had satisfaction of his father, had had satisfaction of him! The evil that had been done had served as pretext and as motive for the evil which remained to be done" (*The Man Who Laughs*, 2.9.2).

Not only does Gwynplaine remain innocent, but those who surround him are always the guilty ones. In the final pages of his book, Hugo convinces himself that his hero has no hand in the misfortunes that befall him. He evidently forgets what Gwynplaine did in a previous chapter. The man who laughs surreptitiously entered the room of the infernal Josiane, where he contemplated this nude beauty asleep in her bed. Hugo tells us that she resembles a monstrous spider at the center of her web. Gwynplaine was not thinking about democracy at this moment; he was succumbing to a rather indecent erotic fever, soon replaced by ambition, another impure sentiment.

Gwynplaine's first failure is caused by the *comprachicos*, but the second is the fruit of desire. In the first instance the hero is not responsible, but in the second case he is, and all the more so since the peaceful life with Ursus, the man, and Homo, the wolf, and above all the love of the blind woman Dea, have in a way canceled out the negative effects of his horrible disfigurement. The sudden revelation of Gwynplaine's high birth and the consequences of this revelation would not be able to destroy the humble happiness of the lovers if Gwynplaine were not abandoning his soul mate (who is perhaps a bit too ethereal) for the bewitching and alluring Josiane.

At the end of the novel, Hugo no longer makes any distinction between the affronts Gwynplaine suffers and the disfigurement originally inflicted by the *comprachicos*. Josiane and Lord David are like aristocratic *comprachicos* to him. The Duchess feels an unhealthy attraction toward Gwynplaine's fantastic ugliness. As for Lord David, he is passionate about boxing; he finds and trains future champions, that is, those who disfigure their opponents or are disfigured by them. The slap that Lord David administers to Gwynplaine constitutes a new disfigurement, and a new, more stinging humiliation than the first.

All human relationships in *The Man Who Laughs* are symbolized by disfigurement. And the rehabilitation of the monster is a process of identification: the failure in the House of Lords is also the bitter pain suffered by the moralist-prophet who wrote *Les châtiments*, taken for a simple man of letters, a public entertainer. The femme fatale who cleverly awakens a desire that she refuses to satisfy, Josiane incarnates the eroticism of the aging Hugo. It is Hugo himself who complains about his fellow man and who proclaims his innocence through the character of Gwynplaine. And here he tells us more than perhaps he himself believes. Josiane and Lord David represent all that Hugo cannot seduce or control; they are the insurmountable obstacle, perhaps the object of indignation, but they are even more an object of desire; they are desired for the very reason that they are an obstacle that cannot be overcome. Hugo's immense pride is always in need of being *tested*, and it is this need that makes the obstacle into the only truly desirable goal, the harsh stumbling block on which Gwynplaine, certainly a victim—but a consenting victim—never stops bruising himself.

The identification with Gwynplaine defines a "masochistic" moment in Hugo's consciousness, a moment of humanitarian and revolutionary feeling; it is most in evidence in *The Man Who Laughs* and the metaphysical poetry. But this masochistic moment is preceded by a "sadistic" moment which makes Gwynplaine into an outsider and defines him as a monster. This is a moment of proud exaltation and identification with Lord David, whose insolent taste for monsters bears a stunning resemblance to that expressed and displayed in Hugo's oeuvre:

Though handsome, he belonged to the Ugly Club. This club was dedicated to deformity. The members agreed to fight, not about a beautiful woman, but about an ugly man. The hall of the club was adorned by hideous portraits—Thersites, Triboulet, Duns, Hudibras, Scarron; over the chimney was Æsop, between two men, each blind of an eye, Cocles and Camoëns (Cocles being blind of the left, Camoëns of the right eye), so arranged that the two profiles without eyes were turned to each other. (*The Man Who Laughs*, 2.1.4)

Why does Hugo identify with the monster Gwynplaine? Because he first identified with the god Lord David. It is always a god's gaze that begets monsters. All that lies outside a god's perfection, all that a god cannot assimilate, appears as deformity. But Jupiter-Hugo quickly discovers the vanity of his thunder, the practical ineffectiveness of his excommunications: the monster refuses to be cast off into the outer darkness. If Hugo accepted limitations to his power, he would become a man like any other. But he refuses these limits. His pride does not accept compromise; he leaves to others the kingdom of form, light, and harmony, where he discovers he is not the only ruler. Instead, he rushes headlong toward the realm of formlessness, obscurity, and disorder. He takes refuge among the monsters and becomes one of them. Because pride refuses to surrender, failure becomes disfigurement, monstrosity, and the fall into darkness. The failed god must destroy himself with the lightning bolts with which he had wanted to destroy the others. He discovers that he is a monster, but he attempts to divinize this monster, because as a monster he does not stop wanting to be god.

The stages we have sketched in Hugo's rehabilitation of monsters coincides with his increasing gloominess during the 1840s and the beginning of the 1850s. And this parallel process becomes one in the evolution toward the so-called metaphysical poetry. This poetry too is defined by the identification with the monster and the fall into darkness, that is, by the inversion of primal images that we observed in *The Man Who Laughs*. One need only look at the following two verses from *Les contemplations* in order to recognize Dea, the visionary blind woman who sees the monster's secret beauty, as an allegory of the metaphysical poetry:

The blind man sees in the shadows a world of light,
When the eye of the body dims, the eye of the spirit becomes illuminated.[4]

We should not be surprised by the fact that the best part of *The End of Satan* (*La fin de Satan*) is the first, which describes the fall of the Accursed into the abyss. The vertiginous plunge into the depths, stars that dim, the metamorphoses of splendor into horror and the angel of light into the angel of darkness—what is all of this if not the very dynamism of Hugo's poetry, as affirmed in countless poems and revealed in Hugo's overall evolution, that is to say, the metamorphosis of the romantic into the metaphysical Hugo?

Satan's fall is poetic, but it is not theological, at least not intentionally; for Hugo cannot fathom Satan's guilt. Identification with the monster is in the end identification with Satan, the pariah par excellence, the prince of the deformed and the formless. Paul Zumthor has convincingly shown that there is no redemption of Satan in Hugo; there is a rehabilitation pure and simple. Hugo does not admit this to himself; he always tends to divinize Satan, in the same way that he tends to divinize Gwynplaine. In his speech to the lords, Gwynplaine says that his laugh would accuse God if it were Satan's laugh. In another passage, Hugo tells us that Gwynplaine is a rebel and that he is "Lucifer, a terrible killjoy"; not Satan, he insists, but Lucifer. Now Satan, as we know, is none other than the rebellious Lucifer. It is thus God who in the end takes on the figure of the accused.

The primal imagery of Western poetry has its origin in the troubadours. It derives from Christian mysticism; it is thus always turned toward God, at least implicitly, and one cannot invert it as Hugo does without turning it toward Satan. But why does Hugo feel the need to invert this imagery? Is it a matter of a purely literary discovery, a simple technical procedure that renews poetry? I do not believe so. *The Man Who Laughs* reveals the existential foundation of Hugo's Satanism. Pursued by the *comprachicos* like Orestes by the Eumenides, Gwynplaine is represented as the victim of an undeserved curse. The deformity ends up by resembling an original sin whose consequences are always getting worse and for which the deformed is the only one who is not responsible. The blossoming of monstrous imagery is linked to an appetite for domination that, refusing to give in to the obstacle and interrupt its march toward omnipotence while still in human territory, prefers to rush, verbally at least, headlong toward the lower realms. At the origin of this obsession with ugliness, we discover a combination of pride, failure, and desire analogous to the combination of pride, failure, and desire that defines the fall of Satan in traditional theology.

Hugo is incapable of conceiving Satan's error, because he commits this error himself. He justifies his own revolt and affirms his own innocence when he justifies Gwynplaine's revolt. Neither Hugo's critics nor his psychoanalysts have ever fully revealed this analogy between Satan's and Hugo's fall; nevertheless, this is what grounds the "authenticity" of the metaphysical poetry and constitutes its most sensational element. Hugo does not focus on Satan because he inverts traditional imagery; he inverts traditional imagery because he is focused on Satan.

Can we speak of this fixation on Satan without theological or metaphysical preconceptions, without condemning Hugo's poetry in the name of some orthodoxy or without exalting it in the name of some anti-orthodoxy? On the contrary, I believe that in order to avoid this double pitfall, we must fully grasp the existential basis of Hugo's Satanism.

How can we explain Gwynplaine's hidden moral flaw—in other words, Hugo's moral flaw—which is the source both of Hugo's poetic Satanism and of his monstrous imagery? We must look for this flaw in Gwynplaine's desire for the beautiful Josiane and in the fascination exercised by Lord David. If Gwynplaine-Hugo denounces Josiane and Lord David as violently as he does, it is not because he escapes their influence, but because he remains captive to it. And what do Josiane and Lord David represent if not tradition, authority, and the powers that be? Hugo remains closer than he believes to this ethical and aesthetic conformism which he ceaselessly stigmatizes. The properly Satanic element in Hugo must not be defined in terms of a break with traditions that have lost all of their fecundity, but in terms of the incomplete nature of this break. Hugo respects what he attacks and attacks what he respects; Satanism is linked

to rebellion, that is to say, to the ambiguity and duplicity that characterize rebellion.

Let us consider, for example, the case of the gothic. Hugo is passionate about this type of art, not because he appreciates it as we do, but
because he sees it as a powerful weapon against the neoclassical concept
of beauty. In short, the gothic is a part of this *ugliness* that the preface to
*Cromwell* tells us should be one of the ingredients of the artwork. The
gothic is the ugly-beautiful that is opposed to the beautiful-ugly of neo-
classicism, just as Gwynplaine is opposed to Lord David. The gothic is
Quasimodo, the grotesque gargoyle come down from its pillar, resembling
those "Barbary apes" (*magots*) that Louis XIV wanted to get rid of. For
Hugo, the true gothic is the flamboyant, and the gargoyle is the heart of
the flamboyant. Hugo's first monsters come right out of the English gothic
novel, whose aesthetics is revealed by the name. It is not God but the devil
that inhabits Hugo's cathedral; God will only make his entry into the gothic once the last spells of neoclassical form have been exorcised.

The treatment of the animal in Hugo's late poetry is no less significant in this context. The toad is another Gwynplaine, another Satan, another of the "cursed-elect":

Perhaps the cursed felt he was blessed . . .
For there is no sickly, cross-eyed, impure, sticky-eyed monster
Who does not have the immensity of the stars in his eyes.[5]

The toad is most probably sickly, but why would it be cross-eyed, and who
has ever seen sticky matter in the eyes of batrachians? The "impure monster" that Hugo describes is not a true toad; it is another gargoyle. Hugo
begins by condemning the innocent creature from the heights of a formal and exaggerated puritanism, after which he identifies with his victim
and rehabilitates him beyond measure. In the course of the poem, an old
priest, a young woman, and four schoolchildren torture the toad—that is,
they make it even uglier. The torturers all belong to human groups which,
for one reason or another, should be nearest to the angelic condition, according to the same hierarchical and conventional vision that makes the
animal into a creature that is repugnant, sinister, and a bit demonic. As in
*The Man Who Laughs*, Hugo opposes the bestial angels to the angelic beast.
The animals rehabilitated by Hugo are always those that are ostracized by

the wisdom of nations, fables, and academic aesthetics. Hugo would not have felt the need to contest this vision so violently if it did not continue to exercise a very strong influence over him. Significantly, Hugo indicates that he himself is one of the schoolchildren who torture the toad. Here again, he is both victim and torturer.

The poem of the toad could not end without the intervention of the donkey, the supreme cursed-elect of the animal world, which goes out of its way in order not to crush the agonizing insectivore. In this sublime instant, there are no longer any bounds to Hugo's enthusiasm:

Abject, dirty, bruised by the staff
This donkey is saintlier than Socrates and greater than Plato.[6]

Incapable of incarnating the animal, Hugo is even more incapable of incarnating man, except perhaps in works such as *Les misérables*, in which the dualism between monsters and demigods is attenuated. But Hugo's true genius is not found in the weakening of this dualism, but in its exasperation: black and white, abyss and summit, extreme obscurity and bedazzlement are all that remain. The monsters themselves do not survive in this rarefied atmosphere. It is at the level of primal images alone that the relative failure of "The Toad" ("Le crapeau") is transformed into complete success. Purged of what remains alive in it, the carbon metamorphoses into diamond.

Here, as elsewhere, the inversion of images remains haunted by the values it contests. Obscurity is not exalted as such, but as light; the praise of blindness is made in terms of vision, and the passion for ugliness always constitutes a secret homage to classical beauty. The darkness that thickens at the bottom of the abyss is another light, and it emanates from another sun; it emanates from the black Nervalian sun that dominates all of nineteenth-century poetry. In Hugo's "What the Shadow's Mouth Says" ("Ce que dit bouche d'ombre"), it appears after a plunge into the abyss. The last three lines of this poem sum up our argument:

And we see in the lowest depths when the eye dares to look down,
Beyond life and breath and noise
A terrible black sun from which the night shines forth![7]

*—Translated by Robert Doran*

## Bastards and the Antihero in Sartre
## [1965]

What does Sartre's *The Words* (*Les mots*, 1964) offer us? Impressions of childhood, the portrait of a grandfather, plenty of self-criticism, the beginnings of a more or less systematic autobiography . . . In short, it gives us literature, and even very good literature, but literature as we have always known it. We can enumerate the themes of the work; its genre holds no more secrets for us. We are thus reassured. *The Words* has nothing to teach us, nor can it any longer surprise us. Let us nonetheless be prudent: all the themes of the work are there, but their deep unity escapes us; this unity is not immediately graspable at the level of the anecdotal narrative.

Where do we look for this unity? Will Sartre's theoretical works, which are works of the past, deliver it to us on a silver platter? No, but we must nevertheless begin with them. *Being and Nothingness* (*L'être et le néant*) rejects static notions of character and personality in favor of a *project* that is dynamic and, in the last resort, revocable. From our earliest childhood, each one of us blindly activates a boundless freedom in a choice of being that determines a certain world. We will discover our desires' lack of reality only if we succeed in going through our entire personal history—ideally with the help of a psychoanalyst—all the way back to the original choice that makes us be what we are.

An autobiography that ignores the project does not get to the essential. Sartrean psychoanalysis does not condemn autobiographical inquiry;

it asks it to be more radical. One must go outside of oneself in order to conjure the world that one projects around oneself. An authentic resurrection of childhood is necessarily a matter for psychoanalysis, that is to say, for an exploration of oneself that is radical enough to modify individual being in a fundamental way. "I've changed," writes Sartre in *The Words*; "I will describe later what acids ate into the distorting transparencies which wrapped me around . . . "[1] In this quote we find the language of the project. Like the Freudian complex, the project is unfathomable, but this is due more to an excess than to a lack of transparency. The project escapes us in the way that language is spoken effortlessly by the illiterate. To gain access to the project, one must objectify one's whole consciousness; one must go outside of oneself and become other.

The total resurrection of the past called for by psychoanalysis will not be of the rough, fragmentary, and untidy quality that not long ago an aesthetics and a psychoanalysis far removed from Sartre demanded from "real-life." But the psychoanalytic autobiography is not the enemy of art. It originates in a more traditional and difficult aesthetics than that of "spontaneity" (*pris sur le vif*). Updated memories would all be variations on the same theme, modulations of the same fundamental pattern that is the original project. In order to fulfill the structural and totalitarian conception of the individual, the autobiography must rediscover the drive for harmony and organic unity that defines the patiently elaborated works—that is to say, the "classical" works. To speak of psychoanalysis is not to minimize the aesthetic aspect; it means justifying it by integrating it into a concrete questioning of the work.

In light of the new being that emerges from analysis, the past that is uncovered is a unified but also a mystified past. The self-criticism is so violent on certain pages of *The Words* that some have talked about denial. This takes us beyond the intentions of the author. The interview published in *Le Monde* shortly after the publication of *The Words* lends credence to this view. Here again the notion of an existential psychoanalysis will help us to situate *The Words*. Psychoanalytic inquiry is presented as an ordeal (*épreuve*); this ordeal is considered radical. It must therefore involve some disruptions, but the meaning and scope of the crisis are in some way defined in advance, guaranteed by the intimate nature of the instrument that triggers it. Is there anything more natural, or even more predictable, than a self-analyzing narrative in a thinker who claims he is founding a new psychoanalysis? Is Sartre not the inventor of the method used in *The Words*? Who better than Sartre would be able to make good use of it and control its effects? Once again, let us marvel at this existential psychoanalysis which reemerges from Sartre's past. It allows us to reestablish continuity in the midst of rupture, and even to skillfully reconcile these contraries in such a way as to meet the needs—a bit contradictory perhaps—of a hectic intellectual life and an ideological steadfastness in the face of any ordeal. Is to speak here of existential psychoanalysis not tantamount to rediscovering the perspective of an author who would like to change, who would like to change a great deal, but who would not like to change *too much*?

In following this path to its logical conclusion, we will, as one might guess, end up by completely conjuring away the meaning of psychoanalysis. No one can place limits on the psychoanalytic process, particularly not the patient. No one can boast of controlling the uncontrollable. Very quickly we realize in reading *The Words* that this work does not always fit with the theoretical frameworks laid out in *Being and Nothingness*. And when one thinks about it, this is the way it must be. These old theoretical frameworks, the creation of a Sartre who had not yet been analyzed, must reflect the illusions and ignorance of which analysis alone can rid us. If a blow has been dealt to Sartre's conception of psychoanalysis, and if, like every coherent philosophy, Sartrean thought is one, then the elements of the system have to be revised step by step. On cannot reinterpret *The Words* in light of the past, but one can no doubt reinterpret the past in light of *The Words*. This is the spirit of psychoanalysis, and the best passages of *The Words* remain faithful to it. If one needs to be convinced, one need only look at the brief but dazzling remarks on *Nausea* and *Being and Nothingness*. Sartre revisits his earlier works, critiquing them with a rigor and a profundity far superior to his enemies.

Here it is—groan—this awful psychoanalysis. It devours literary values; it deprives us of a lifetime consolation. The blind and forgetful *belles-lettres* are unable to recognize in the crime of lese-literature the very mark of Western literary genius. The artist is neither a politician nor a banker. He is free to reverse himself. Goethe and Chateaubriand reversed themselves. Great achievements are always built on the failure of the lesser great. Camus reversed himself in *The Fall* (*La chute*), his masterwork, misunderstood nowadays, which is curiously analogous to *The Words* in terms of its movement and its true meaning.

Today we accuse systematic thinking (*l'esprit de système*) of desecrating works that we were still deploring yesterday for being dominated by systematic thinking. Would true literature no longer be poking fun at literature? Who is showing their ideological rigidity in this debate? Who is succumbing to the magical power of anti-humanist jargon? Sartre obsesses over his past, we are told, in order to perpetuate his reputation as an *enfant terrible*. On the contrary, it seems that *The Words* keenly whets our appetite for meaning, only to leave us a bit unsatisfied. Sartre hesitates before the most extreme consequences of his own discoveries. These consequences must be drawn out. We must push the confrontation between the two Sartres farther than Sartre himself does. We must respond to the call of a thought that transcends its earlier works in order to reveal their structure. This is the challenge, it would appear, that *The Words* poses to criticism.

~

Everything starts with the grandfather; everything is organized around this old man who, from the very beginning, replaces the dead father in his grandson's life. *The Words* is closer to Freud than Sartre's *Baudelaire* or his *Genet*, for it recognizes in the Oedipus complex the foundational role that Freud had given it. In *Being and Nothingness*, the project of being is still conceived on the basis of a subject-object relation. The Other is absent from this model. The Oedipus complex cannot play a truly central role. One might object that in *Being and Nothingness*, as elsewhere, Sartre makes a glowing homage to Freud. This is true, but he does not see that Freud and psychoanalysis are incompatible with all philosophical thought that stems from the *cogito*. It is the implicit adherence to the Cartesian tradition that eliminates the Other from the project. If we want to formulate the Oedipus complex—such as Freud had conceived it—in Sartrean language, we would have to understand the project not as an original relation to the object, but as an original relation to the Other. The rapprochement with Freud brings out both the solipsism of classical philosophy, which Sartre had already denounced at the time of *Being and Nothingness*, and the solipsism of *Being and Nothingness* itself. How can Sartre transcend this solipsism, since he still attempts to "resolve" the problem specific to all solipsistic philosophies, which is otherwise admirably revealed in his work: that of the existence of the Other?

The Freudianism of *The Words* has nothing academic about it; it is a Freudianism of experience that is opposed to the solipsism of *Being and Nothingness*. It is not vain, however, to interpret the vision of *The Words* in terms of the project. The resulting formula purges a thought determined to make this formula its foundation from the residue of solipsism that haunts contemporary philosophy.

The ultimate meaning of the project, according to *Being and Nothingness*, is the desire to be god. Moreover, God is defined as a projection of the Other. If each individual's project is truly original, all projections are, by definition, based on the individual. We must thus conclude that the original project does not aim at the Other in general, at some abstraction or quintessence of otherness, but at an Other that is at once concrete and primary, this primordial Other that is the Oedipal father.

After having affirmed—rather fleetingly one might add—that the genesis of the divine is intersubjective, Sartre constructs this god that the project is aiming at according to a solipsistic model. This god that is the essence of the solipsistic project is itself necessarily solipsistic. If god does not belong to the world of human society, if it is not re-created by every individual out of his concrete relations with others, then this god, no matter how imaginary it remains, resides in some metaphysical empyrean. It is outside humanity and the world. In other words, it is Aristotle's god. *Being and Nothingness* asks us to believe that all men *desire* this academic and abstract god. Little children must thus completely master this image, no doubt through a study of neo-scholastic philosophy. Like Nietzsche's superman, the Sartro-Aristotelian project reflects the solitude of the Supreme Being. Through the influence of Descartes and medieval theology, Sartre, like Nietzsche before him, is here a victim of Greek philosophy.

To take up again the "project of being god" is not tantamount to a return to a Nietzscheanism or an anti-Nietzscheanism that have been equally outstripped. It does not mean falling back into the verbiage of "Promethean thought." The lofty nature of the debates provoked by the notion of the superman (*surhomme*) have their origin precisely in the theological influence from which Nietzsche was unable to escape and which has submerged most of his commentators. The Sartrean for-itself is a superman who fails; in other words, he remains a superman. The vulture brings Prometheus to completion; it does not destroy him. We must preserve what is essential in the Sartrean intuition by integrating it into an intersubjective problematic that will, moreover, alter its meaning, allowing us to understand the root cause of the failure of the "project of being god." This is what we believe Sartre is doing in *The Words*, at least at the level of aesthetic intuition. The project of being god, which had previously been abstract, bloodless, and skeletal, is transformed in *The Words* into something that is infinitely concrete, living, and rich in meaning. The god that I want to be is not some abstract and anonymous divinity, but the unique and only true god that I call my father. This means that the project of being Self coincides perfectly with the project of being Other, and that this rift is inscribed from the outset in all that one can call Ego. The essential frustration of the Ego must be founded on intersubjectivity. We can observe it on every page of *The Words*. The extraordinary prestige of the grandfather, his quasi supernatural authority, his omniscience, his sacred attributes, the ceremony with which he surrounds himself—all of this adds up to the concept of a man-god, a concept which is most often devoid of meaning in contemporary thinkers. What is new and invaluable in *The Words* is the concretely realized—though never made explicit—fusion between the Oedipal theme, the theme of the Other, and the "project of being god."

There are already numerous analyses in *Being and Nothingness* that achieve this fusion and contradict the solipsism of the project. Let us recall the analysis of the emotions. The suffering, joy, and sadness that are actually felt never conform to an intentional design:

The suffering of which we *speak* is never exactly that which we feel. What we call "noble" or "good" or "true" suffering and what moves us is the suffering which we read on the faces of others, better yet in portraits, in the face of a statue, in a tragic mask. It is the suffering which has *being*.[2]

The suffering that I desire—sacred suffering, divine suffering—is always the suffering of the Other. If, as Sartre suggests, the original project is entirely present in the least of our desires, we must extend the conclusions of the above-quoted text to the project itself. It is indeed true that I aspire to divinity, but this divinity is always that of the Other. Our mental states deceive us for the sole reason that they are ours. Phenomenological description always leads back to the Other, just as examination of the lines in a *trompe l'oeil* painting leads toward the vanishing point.

Each groan, each facial expression of the man who suffers aims at sculpting a stat-ue-in-itself of suffering. But this statue will never exist save through others and for others.[3]

In this passage, what we are dealing with—long before *The Words*—is a desire to be god that is also a desire to be the Other, a desire to be this god that is the Other. But Sartre does not draw any conclusion from this analysis. He will discuss desire or the project as such without ever men-tioning the Other. Desire then becomes again what it never should have ceased to be in a coherent solipsism: a mere object relation. The example that Sartre puts forward is that of thirst, and its pertinence cannot be de-nied. Thirst is indeed an object relation, and it is nothing more than that so long as it remains a simple need, in other words, so long as it remains at the animal level. As soon as need gives way to desire, thirst becomes a thirst for the Other by way of the object associated with him. Consider, for example, the whisky that is always consumed in preference to the au-tochthonous beverages that were desacrilized in the so-called "existential-ist novels" published immediately after the war. Since whisky was at this time as exotic (*autre*) as it was unavailable, the "objective" reasons that we give today for its vogue could not yet have accounted for it. The objective reasons obscure the phenomenon of sacralization. The project never rec-ognizes that it is aiming for the Other; it always claims to be aiming for this god that I already embody, the god that I *am* for all eternity. The phi-losopher who formulates the project in solipsistic terms succumbs to the philosophical tradition, and he succumbs to it because he suffers from a quasi universal illusion.

The synthesis of the project of being god and the theme of the Oth-er allows for a formalization—as coherent as it is economic—of the Oe-dipus complex and its consequences. The will to embodiment transforms the child's existence into a ritual imitation of the god. The child will thus appear in the guise of a little old man—a caricature of the pompous, bom-bastic, dramatic, and self-contented nature attributed to the grandfather. The child-god is the *double* of the divinized old man.

Imitation revolves around desire. The child desires to possess the object that his father desires and possesses. It is pointless to ask whether the desire to embody the father does or does not precede the desire for the object. Either way, the father will always be a god and a rival. We can thus bring the unity of a contradictory project back to this initial bifurcation of the libido, whose principle Freud finds himself obliged to posit. The more the father is venerated, the more the desire for the object he himself desires will intensify, and the more the relationship will be threatened by a hateful ambivalence. The Oedipal conflict is based on a rigorous logical necessity.

The father who always thwarts his son's desires personifies prohibition. The son attempts to create a new desire. Modern poetry is profoundly Oedipal in its will to renew desire. In *The Words* we can see this will as responsible for the first argument with the grandfather. The grandfather has his great men whom he admires, great French writers from Corneille to Hugo; their works adorn the shelves of the library; they are part of a familial cult in which the child is expected to participate. But the child is already attempting to assert his freedom against the affective and intellectual tyranny of the grandfather. He aspires to a happiness "with neither master nor collar." He will thus choose heroes that have nothing in common with those of his grandfather. Pardaillan, *Les pieds nickelés,* and the cowboys of Texas silently rival the official religion. The grandfather sees what is happening and shows his Olympian displeasure. He deplores the mediocrity of the books that his grandson devours more or less secretly with his mother's innocent complicity. The hostile reaction of the master whose mastery is threatened reveals the slave's obscure intentions.

The cult of the hero defines an initial negative attitude with respect to the Oedipal divinity. It is important to understand the nature and the failure of this negation. The child chooses against the god, but this is a new way of choosing to be this god himself. If he dreams of rescuing his mother from a crocodile-infested swamp, it is because he sees this as a way of proving his heroism and of forcing his grandfather to bow before his superiority. He is already dreaming, as he will later, of making himself the only true hero in place of the false heroes. In short, it is a matter of outdoing the grandfather in order to better impress him, and of impressing him in order to better outdo him—a twofold proposition that expresses the Oedipal ambivalence.

New models inject themselves between grandson and grandfather. The presence of these shifts enriches the structure with new dimensions; it complicates the dialectic, but it does not change the system's ultimate reference. It is a realization of Oedipal servitude—no doubt imperfect and limited, but real—that provoked the first crisis. This crisis does not result in the destruction of the original desire, as the child himself believes, but in its perpetuation, thanks to a displacement and reorganization which obscure the essential elements of the structure. Desire is only preserved if it is unaware of its own truth. The child is still oriented toward the grandfather, but he is no longer oriented toward him directly. He can believe himself governed by the hero and by the hero alone. There is neither a conversion nor an authentic transcendence, but a caricature of these two things. This is what Freud calls *sublimation*.

Like his grandfather before him, the grandson now only appears when surrounded by his heroes. He too immerses himself in the rites of a secretly egotistical cult. In other words, he becomes more than ever the caricatural *double* of his grandfather. Far from destroying imitation, this conflict develops and deepens it. This is the most generally misunderstood aspect of the situation. The negation of the grandfather does not distance us from him; on the contrary, it brings us closer to this subjectivity which is itself negative and Oedipal. It is no longer simply a matter of imitating the grandfather in a superficial manner, but of imitating him in what constitutes the very essence of his subjectivity—the grandfather's own imitation, his project of being god by way of the Other, the hero. This project thus becomes a *mise-en-abyme*: for it is indeed a new modality of this project that superimposes itself on the old one and takes center stage.

Oedipus took refuge in heroic passion. It is in this passion that, from this point forward, the dynamic element of the project will be embodied. Existence remains imitative at every level. If the child reenacts the exploits of his favorite heroes in his literary games, it is because he hopes, like Don Quixote, to live them out someday in reality. Reading is not a simple "pretext for dreaming." In *The Words* we do not find the myth of an autonomous and self-contained childhood where, since Romanticism, solipsistic intentions perpetually flouted by non-solipsistic desires have willingly taken refuge. Poetry is not an essence which would distil a forever solitary Ego serenely oriented toward its own private mysteries. Poetry is always outside itself, always avidly turned toward the Other and toward the act which would allow it to reunite with the Other. Literature is a prelude to the heroic act. In this "debate between the pen and the sword," Sartre is constantly on the side of the sword, like Don Quixote himself.

In order for the heroic passion to be a "project," it is doubtless unnecessary that it be completely unconscious; nevertheless, the passionate being must be incapable of following every consequence of this passion or of recognizing its presence in activities he finds alien. Such is the state of affairs that is described in *The Words*. Sartre speaks of the mystique of the hero in terms of possession and chronic sickness. He tells us that this sickness persisted well beyond the point at which its apparent goal had been achieved. He believes he has detected its influence in the first works that brought him fame, namely *Nausea* and *Being and Nothingness*. For in these books we can already find an implacable critique of the hero, a critique analogous, in a way, to that which we find in *The Words*. The heroic being is always a false being whose attentive gaze and lucid reflection reveals a void. From Garcin in *No Exit* (*Huit clos*) to Frantz in *The Condemned of Altona* (*Les séquestrés d'Altona*), Sartrean theater is replete with aspiring heroes who see their dreams of Corneillian glory destroyed. Heroic passion is always present, and it always results in shame and humiliation. This repudiated essentialism almost always presents itself under the guise of the heroic project, which, in the final analysis, is identical to that which Sartre will attribute to himself in *The Words*.

To speak here of a "paradox" would be to dull the point of the contradiction. We must sharpen this point in order to recognize it as the imperceptible yet central place where the drama of existential meanings unfolds. How can the antiheroic work originate in the mystique of the hero? This work is not a simple reflection; it is not a direct extension of the mystique that it negates. We must try to conceive of a different type of relation. The cult of the hero, such as the child experiences it, must result in disillusion. One fine day, the child discovered he was unable to attain the heroic ideal put forward by his Holy Scripture. Perhaps he never believed, in any formal way, that he was capable of this ideal, but he was living in a symbiotic relationship with his imaginary models in a world of magical mimetism. The date and the concrete modes of an experience that one can affirm *a priori* to have taken place matter little. No doubt *The Words* breaks off too abruptly to include a narrative of this event, but we can interpret one of the passages devoted to the Great War as an allusion to this decisive moment. The child feels dethroned and dispossessed by the *Poilius*: they are the true heroes:

I felt mystified; I was an impostor, I told stories that no one would believe . . . For the first time in my life I read what I had written. I was embarrassed. It was me; I was the one who was complicit with these puerile phantasms. It wouldn't have taken much for me to renounce literature.

The child could bend before the facts. Many infantile myths are lost in the sands of a weakly structured existence. This is not how the myth of Jean-Paul Sartre ended. The above-quoted passage helps us to reconstruct an essential experience. The Ego, suddenly deprived of the belief that exalts it, allows itself to be overcome by shame. It is through shame that self-consciousness deepens. A being too enamored of his individual difference, too full of pride, in short, to ever see himself as similar to others, can think of himself as incomparable in shame after having thought of himself as incomparable in glory. Shame is the other side of pride, and it is shame that provides the measure. If the shame is too intense, the being that suffers from it cannot ignore it, but neither can he accept it as shame. He takes the only path that remains open to him. Covered with shame, unable to escape from shame, he will thus assert his singular being at the degree of this shame: he will, in other words, endeavor to transform it into pride.

The child thinks that he does not share his disillusion with anyone else. This is what makes it daunting, but this is also what allows for the illusion's rebirth in a new form. The uniqueness of the hero's election threatens to be reversed into a curse that is just as unique. To discover that one is among the elect, one need only decree that shame, always singular *in fact*—always perceived as such, in other words—is universal *in law*. It is simply a matter of reconfiguring shame into a heroic vision of the true in a world entirely immersed in false heroism. From now on, those who ignore the disillusion will no longer enjoy the heroic being that has been denied to Jean-Paul Sartre, the accursed; they are immobilized at a stage of spiritual development which has been transcended by Jean-Paul Sartre, the elect.

Sartre has a name for these more or less consenting victims of the heroic illusion: he calls them *bastards* (*les salauds*).

Here we must imagine a spiritual operation analogous to that which Sartre himself discovered—and for a very good reason—in Genet, and analogous as well to the final stages of the *sickness unto death* described by Kierkegaard, which he reserves for *a few great poets*. But this schema should be assigned to the Other and no longer to God. Kierkegaard also speaks of metaphysical despair, and the expression should not shock us under the pretext that it brings with it a psychological content quite different from the serenity Sartre displayed—as he informs us—during the period when he was bemoaning the wretchedness of the human condition. Kierkegaardian despair is the motor of dialectical operations that are designed precisely to eliminate this psychological content. It is to avoid despair, in the ordinary sense of the term, that Jean-Paul Sartre divinizes his disillusion and inverts all of his earlier values. Rejecting the modalities that formerly applied to the heroic being, Sartre endeavors to conquer a new—completely ideal—one, which is defined by a negation and a renunciation of heroism itself. The major oppositions of the project reappear in an ideological context that is entirely new. At first it was a matter of triumphing over the Other by displaying a positive heroism; now it is a matter of proving the Other guilty of cowardly illusions in order to demonstrate one's own *heroic lucidity*. The inversion of the structure elucidates all of its elements. It reinforces the oppositions and, more generally, brings into relief the negative character of the structure as a whole.

The mystification of which Sartre sees himself the victim in *The Words* is quite real, and it is one with the will to demystify the Other—the constant inspiration and mainspring of his work. Sartrean discourse always remains impregnated with the illusions that it denounces. And these illusions are never so alive as at the very moment when the author is fighting against them, when he vilifies and ridicules them with all of the artistic means at his disposal.

∼

A psychoanalyst reportedly told Sartre that he had no Superego. The story is related by Sartre himself in *The Words*. But the content of *The Words* makes this proposition unacceptable. The Superego does not denote a mere "superstructure" of the psyche. It is farther removed from consciousness than the Ego, and it always remains in contact with the Id. Hidden behind the Superego or Ego ideal "one always finds the identification with the father from the early stages of childhood." The Superego appears at the moment when the libidinal attitude toward the original Oedipal object gives way to a narcissistic libido. However, as Freud writes, it is not

. . . simply a residue of the earliest object-choices of the Id; it also represents an energetic reaction-formation against those choices. Its relation to the Ego is not exhausted by the precept: "You *ought to be* like this (like your father)." It also comprises the prohibition: "You *may not be* like this" (like your father).[4]

Freud says that the formation of the Superego implies a renunciation of purely sexual goals; in other words, it implies this sublimation of which the cult of heroes so clearly bears the trace. One also finds in the cult of heroes all of the other characteristics that Freud attributes to the Superego or *Ego ideal*: religious imitation, rigid moralism, and, finally, this impression of impotence felt by the Ego vis-à-vis a model that always ends up by revealing itself to be inaccessible. If we identify the cult of the hero with the Freudian Superego, and if we compare Freud's description with the conclusions that *The Words* has allowed us to draw out, we must observe, once again, that the project of being this god that is the Other and the dialectic of the obstacle it engenders brings the Freudian dualism (be like your father—don't be like your father) back to the unity of a contradictory project. To translate Sartre in Freudian terms is to recognize in *The Words* perhaps the most appropriate, the most radiant, and the most exemplary of all the Superegos that literature has ever given us to contemplate.

If the writer who has renounced heroism still maintains, on the horizon of his desire, the heroic ideal in the form of the antihero, then the one who believes he has rid himself of his Superego is in fact the proud owner of an inverted Superego. It is in this manner that nowadays many believe that they are transcending ethics. The values previously affected by the plus sign will be affected by the minus sign and vice versa, but nothing essential will have changed; the old polarities will persist, and behind these polarities, the identifications that bring them to life. The idea of an anti-Superego is certainly not useless, for it defines a very advanced stage of sublimation in which anti-moral fanaticism represses the morality on which it is based. These distinctions are at any rate secondary. The anti-

Superego is a super-Superego that increases the demands of a Superego whose tyranny it claims to reject. It posits an ideal that is always more difficult to attain because it is always more exceptional, at least in principle. The anti-Superego thus exercises over the Ego an even more stringent supervision than the Superego it succeeds and whose authoritarianism offended it. We see this quite well in Sartre. It is the Superego that expressed itself in the literary games of the child, and it is a much more demanding anti-Superego that exercises control over every aspect of the antiheroic works of the adult.

The error of the psychoanalyst who imagined a Sartre without a Superego is obvious, and it can be explained. This doctor only knew Jean-Paul Sartre the public figure, the progeny of his literary oeuvre. He considered himself an insightful—though in reality docile—reader; he discovered not the real author behind *Nausea, The Flies,* and *Being and Nothingness,* as he had imagined, but the myth of this author, patiently elaborated in his works. In other words, he fell into the trap that Jean-Paul Sartre lays for his readers as well as for himself—the trap of the antihero. To be without a Superego, in a world that is constantly agitated and perturbed by the delirious Superegos of the rest of mankind, is to escape the common lot, to master the human condition. In this world where psychoanalytic truth reigns but does not govern, the authentic superman is the one who has no Superego.

~

Like the heroic project before it, the antiheroic project aims to establish an existence independent from the grandfather by establishing a new desire. It too is based on a realization of Oedipal servitude. This second realization is richer than the first, if only because it refers to a more complex structure: the one which emerged from the Oedipal crisis described above. In his shame the child discovers the naïveté of the spiritual efforts to which he had entrusted his salvation. At first he had rejected a certain type of hero; now he ferociously turns away from heroism itself. He repudiates his entire childhood. He radicalizes a negation that showed itself to be ineffective. But again he fails. The refusal of all mysticism defines a new mysticism. The Oedipal structures displaced in the first case are inverted in the second, and they are maintained in this inversion, more virulent than ever.

We are dealing with a second Oedipal crisis which is analogous to the first. Here again, it is the discovery of the true object of desire that leads to a reorganization of the structure. It is the subject's discovery of his Superego that leads to the formation of an anti-Superego. The object of desire is once again "lost" in the labyrinth of an ever more complex dialectic. The crisis perpetuates the servitude to which, each time, it claims to put an end.

The relations of analogy that unite the two crises lead us quite naturally to wonder if the experience from which *The Words* springs does not constitute a third crisis analogous to the first two. Psychoanalysis does not differ from the other realizations in any essential way. In its extreme richness, psychoanalysis is to the second realization what the second was to the first. Once again, it claims that it can reveal the truth of desire and eliminate the Oedipus complex. In psychoanalysis a new disillusion is observed, which is accompanied by a new, "definitive" renunciation of childhood illusions.

This *mise en abyme* of successive realizations, after the *mise en abyme* of the restructurings grafted onto them, allows us to incorporate everything into a single dynamic structure composed of perpetual breakdowns and reorganizations. The Sartrean continuity of existence is established beyond these ruptures. Sartre himself suggests this reading of *The Words*, in poking fun at his propensity for self-criticism and in making his penchant for "transcendence" into a virtual character trait. Judging from his interview with *Le Monde*, Sartre reconciles himself quite well, in fact, to this state of affairs. Self-criticism must not put certain fundamental positions into question. These claims of discontinuity, far from destroying the unity of the work, actually fulfill it; they infuse old themes with new vigor. Thus, the reemergence of the critique of the hero in the psychoanalytic autobiography appears very similar to what it was in the preceding works.

A suspicion now hangs over self-psychoanalysis; and Sartre is not always eager, it would seem, to dispel it. Does this mean that the light emanating from *The Words*, the light projected on the earliest works, is not a true light? The question is, in fact, hardly meaningful, for the darkness that haunts us would not exist apart from the light that seeks to penetrate it. And there is no other light. The truth that reveals itself in *The Words* confirms the truth of the hero, which the antihero already possesses; it also confirms the truth of Oedipal desire, which the hero already possesses. In contrast to the deceitful restructurings that reciprocally negate themselves each and every time, the final truth does not negate the earlier truths: it enriches them. This truth can be lost; perhaps it is already lost, like the preceding truths—but this also militates in its favor. What good are the superimposed veils of ever more complex dialectics if not to eliminate the brightness of an ever more intense light? There is a twofold process of alienation and disalienation that still persists, but the truth that slowly emerges is one, and the critic can champion it, in his domain, by bringing together and opposing texts of different periods in such a way as to extend and transcend the movement of self-criticism, instead of pointlessly denigrating it, as Sartre himself sometimes does. The judgment of *The Words* on the early writings must be put to the test using the texts themselves:

I pulled off this noble achievement at the age of thirty: describing in *Nausea*—most sincerely, I can assure you—the unjustified, brackish existence of my fellow-creatures and vindicating my own. I *was* Roquentin; in him I exposed, without self-satisfaction, the web of my life; at the same time I was *myself*, the elect, the chronicler of hells, and a photomicroscope of glass and steel bent over my own protoplasmic juices. Later on, I cheerfully demonstrated that man is impossible; impossible myself, I differed from others only in this one mandate: I had to illustrate this impossibility which, as a result, was transfigured and became my most intimate potentiality, the object of my mission and the springboard of my glory. I was a prisoner of these evidences, but I did not see them: I saw the world through them. Mystified and a fraud to my very bones, I cheerfully wrote about our wretched lot. In my dogmatism, I doubted everything except that I had been chosen by doubt; I was restoring with one hand what I destroyed with the other, and I took anxiety as the proof of my safety; I was happy.[5]

The creator of Roquentin hardly differs from the child who was dreaming, pen in hand, under the explorer's helmet or in Michel Strogoff's uniform. The dialectic of the antihero allows us to respond to the objection of the common sense perspective, which does not recognize the childhood heroes behind the lifeless protagonist of *Nausea*. We see in Roquentin the *contrary* of these heroes, and this contrary is a *same* that is unaware of itself. Roquentin does not believe in adventure or courage; he has renounced his ambition and the "great moments." He has renounced everything except his renunciation. Roquentin is a typical antihero. Sartre's language implies an antiheroic inversion at every turn. But this inversion is not really brought out into the open—which is indeed why the writer can play with it; he can make it sparkle in the form of antitheses, paradoxes, and other rhetorical figures. Our previous analyses allow us to clarify the situation. Sometimes one need only substitute one word for another, *hero* for *man*, for example, to make the antihero appear: "Later on, I cheerfully demonstrated that *the hero* is impossible; impossible myself, I differed from others only in this one mandate: I had to illustrate this impossibility . . . "

It is indeed about man, we should add, that the first Sartre is speaking. At the end of the day, the heroic illusion obsesses the writer to the point of enveloping the totality of individual and collective significations. This means that we are confirming in *Nausea* the existential value of the concept of the antihero. The most typical bastards are the conquering bourgeois of the nineteenth century, those whose portraits adorn the museum of Bouville: they ordered and gave meaning to all things; in some sense they gave birth to the city. English has a perfect expression for them: *the culture heroes*. The statue of Impetraz—the number one hero of the city—embellishes the square of Bouville. The people of Bouville never pass in front of their great man without lifting their heads and throwing back their shoulders. They make one think of those spectators whose air upon exiting the cinema reveals that they have just seen a war movie. This scene of exiting the cinema is found in Camus' *The Stranger*. And the theme reappears in *The Words*; but this time it is Sartre, of course, who accuses himself—due to heroic contagion—of having stuck out his torso.

In *Nausea* it is Roquentin who dies in the world of the culture heroes, to be reborn an antihero. Through Roquentin the author relives the experience that is the mainspring of the work. He will do this once again in *The Words*—from the standpoint of another experience and without the mediation of fiction. But why is *Nausea* necessary? Why should it be necessary to mime in the work the operation that inverts heroic values, giving the false, disenchanted hero the conviction that he has been chosen by the gods? This operation is self-sufficient only in appearance. As long as it rests on a unilateral decision, on a purely subjective *fiat*, it lacks reality. Only the consent of the Other can lend weight to what is still simply a dialectical sleight of hand. In order for my disillusion to become, in the fullest sense, good tidings reserved for me alone, I must spread far and wide the bad tidings of universal illusion.

The antiheroic being's conquest is achieved through the destruction of the heroic pretensions—real or supposed—of a multitude of Others. The work is a mirror in which the genesis of the antihero is reflected; but it is also, and still more essentially, this genesis itself—or its failure—for it contains the essential message; and the antihero depends, in his being, on how this message will be received. Hiding behind the characters of the novels, as behind the logical arguments of philosophy, are the antagonists of the creative psyche: the grandfather and his grandson, the hero and the traitor, the antihero and the bastards, the writer and his readers. *Nausea* is a psychodrama.

But we are told that in *Nausea* the primary characters are the inert objects. Are the literary merit and the influence of the work on the contemporary novel not attributable to its original treatment of objects? This is no doubt true, but before leaving this point we must define the object. How does Sartre himself define it? The object is a meaning that masks the brute existent, that hides the in-itself. And it is the bastards—the culture heroes—who confer meaning. The object, insofar as it contains a meaning, that is, insofar as it is truly an object, always refers to the Other; it belongs to the Other. Impetraz's statue symbolizes the "petrification" of bourgeois values, but the contrary movement, from man to stone, is also present, and it is no less essential. In its material reality, the statue asserts the bastards' stranglehold on the real—the cloaking of the stone and of other inert substances with an enemy meaning.

This union between the Other and meaning, this obsessive presence of the Other in the object and of the object in the Other, is the synthesis of the in-itself and the for-itself. This synthesis has a name in *Being and Nothingness*: it is called God. The metaphors that denote the bastard, in *Nausea*, do not express the viscosity—that is, the failure—of the synthesis, but the synthesis itself, always figured in Sartre by the impenetrable density of granite. We have already encountered these metaphors in *Being and Nothingness* in reference to the suffering of others. Here is another example. The suffering of Others

. . . is presented to us as a compact, objective whole which did not await our coming in order to be and which overflows the consciousness which we have of it; it is there in the midst of the world, impenetrable and dense, like this tree or this stone; it endures; finally it is what it is.[6]

In *Being and Nothingness*, the desired Other is a tree, a stone, a statue, a tragic mask. In *Nausea*, the scorned bastard is a tree, a stone, a statue, a grotesque mask. The metaphors which, in the philosophical essay, describe the Other as the divinely desirable synthesis of the in-itself and the for-itself, can be exactly superimposed on the themes of *Nausea*, that is, on the countless variations on the theme of the bastard. What should we conclude? The hatred that floats around the bastard is mixed with desire. It is the Oedipal ambivalence that one finds in *Nausea*, and this ambivalence, in our formulation, reveals the presence of the divine obstacle, this obstacle that always opposes the desire of the religiously imitated Other to my own desire.

How can the bastard constitute an obstacle, since Roquentin turns away from him? But Roquentin only turns away from the bastard in order to better convey his message to him, that is, in order to convince him, the bastard, of his own shamefulness. There are two possibilities: either the bastard accepts this message or he refuses it. Either he renounces his heroic aspirations and adopts the mysticism of the last prophet, like a Saint John the Baptist of nothingness, or he does not allow himself to be "demystified" and instead reaffirms his own values. The two attitudes reveal themselves to be equally disappointing to the antihero: the first attitude, that of the disciple, abolishes the difference that must separate the superman from all other men; the second attitude, that of the skeptic, maintains this difference, but it also maintains and even reinforces its problematic character. The writer can never see his antiheroic being reflected in the admiring gaze of his readers. He will never truly enjoy this being.

The realization that is the mainspring of the antiheroic project is quite far-reaching. The imitative character of the previous desires is clearly recognized. The antihero wants to be his own model. Like M. Teste, he claims to derive everything from himself. In divinizing his own failure, he thus seeks to establish a desire that will not be mediated by the Other. The antiheroic vocation is the first modality of the Oedipal project that fully realizes the "project of being god." But it does not invent this project; it reveals an aspect of the structure which was always implicit in the earlier stages. That is why the antiheroic vocation is necessary for the revelation of this project. To describe the grandfather as a god, which is what Sartre does in *The Words*, is to describe him in light of the adult project, but this is not at all a betrayal of the sacred that is specific to childhood; on the contrary, it is the only way to resituate the sacred in the language of the adult.

Each modality of the project is at once more ambitious than the preceding and a retreat from it, because it internalizes, in the name of lucidity, an always aggravated form of impotence. The Oedipal subject wants first to embody his father; he then wants to embody the hero; and he finishes by wanting to be god. He resembles the gambler who, despite his losses, continues to up the ante . . .

In the eyes of the man who thus projects being god without the mediation of the Other, the earlier projects—all of which divinize the Other—are rooted in an infinitely culpable, though almost universal weakness. This is the "Jansenism" of the antihero. Just as there is really only one evil in the Old Testament—idolatry—there is really only one sin in this theology of the Ego, but it is everywhere: it consists in bowing before the Other's superiority. But the Other, this Other that the antihero accuses of rushing headlong into metaphysical servitude—the bastard resolutely "mystified" and proud of it—now reveals himself to be autonomous and independent with respect to the antihero himself. Through his indifference, his invulnerability, through the incomprehension that he opposes to the dazzling dialectical games that continue under his gaze and for his benefit, through his blindness to the signs and prodigies that multiply around him—he threatens at any moment to realize for himself this divine, autonomous being that the antihero thought was already his. So long as he opposes himself to the antihero's desire for recognition, the bastard now embodies the insurmountable obstacle. After having discovered the obstacle in the god, the Oedipal subject discovers a god in all the obstacles that present themselves on his way. The passive resistance of the inert object and the Other's consciousness always tend toward the synthesis that Sartre declares impossible, but which haunts him, in *Nausea,* in the person of the bastard.

Because the emergence of the god and the obstacle happen simultaneously, a sacred aura is linked to the obstacle from the very start. From crisis to crisis, the subject turns away from this or that particular obstacle, but it is only in order to run up against new obstacles. All desire is, in fact, a desire for the obstacle, since it is a desire for the sacred. This is precisely what the antihero's desire so strikingly demonstrates. The antihero appears to be in search of a desire without obstacle, since he divinizes his failure.

But no divinity is in more need of models than the divinity of failure. And it is at the level of a recognition that is claimed and refused that the object reappears, indefinitely multiplied by the project's ambition itself.

Impetraz and the culture heroes are symbols of paternity. They incarnate the Oedipal god. How could we doubt that this is the case, since they resemble the grandfather and his grandson in *The Words*. In his autobiography, Sartre rediscovers the tone he used in his early works to describe the "bastards." Here we find the same observations, the same satirical procedures, which had been perfected elsewhere. This is why certain readers reject the authenticity of this twofold portrait; they find it too literary—particularly for a writer who violently attacks literature. But these readers misconstrue the circular character of the experience that is the mainspring of *The Words*. The image of the primordial Other reappears under the guise of the hated bastard, and this Other is always the caricatural double of the Ego.

If, despite himself, the antihero divinizes the obstacle, he has not forgotten the lessons of the past; he knows that he is incapable of incarnating this divinity, and he no longer seeks to embody it. He tries to prove to himself that the divine apparition is a mirage, and if the mirage persists, he endeavors to annihilate it. This effort results in the disassociation between meaning and the in-itself; that is, it results in the revelation of the "brute existent." Roquentin's trajectory is toward a loss of meaning, a regression toward chaos. But this horrible experience is also a kind of deliverance. It announces the defeat of the false heroes and the triumph of the antihero.

From the bastard to the object, from the object to Roquentin, and from Roquentin to the brute existent, *Nausea* describes a counterpoint in which we can perceive the truth of a desire now destined to satisfy itself only through the fantasy of the destruction of its object. The world of the bastards is chipped and cracked; it is destined to be destroyed. The myriad ways in which objects are corrupted and broken in *Nausea* announce and symbolize the disintegration of the fascinating synthesis that structures this world. Hence Roquentin's predilection for the torn up and stained papers, and for all of the dirty things that are rotting. The attempt at embodiment that characterized the earlier desires gives way to an attempt at disembodiment. Roquentin takes a long look at the statue of Impetraz; he discovers with joy a greenish leprosy, barely visible, which gnaws at the seemingly incorruptible material of the great man's statue. The stone is sick; it vomits the heroic values that it has been asked to embody. The disorder of the material already proclaims the inanity of meaning and the emptiness of the Oedipal divinity. It proclaims the bad tidings of our collective illusion to all. We do not need to underline the masochistic nature of this illusory triumph. Let the world collapse on my head, the antihero tells himself in short, so that it will collapse on the heads of the bastards as well.

The desire to take refuge in the elementary, the frolics in the organic or the pure inorganic, the many "dialectics of matter," always hide the desire to escape from the Other. But desire is deceived once again with respect to its object. What attracts and repels desire in the in-itself is its analogy with the Oedipal obstacle of which it is the supreme metaphor. Desire is thus always the desire for the Other. The part of being that appears the most devoid of intersubjective meanings is no less permeated with them, in the last analysis, than is the rest of the world.

The experience of *Nausea* does not result in an authentic transcendence; it radicalizes the Oedipal oppositions and universalizes them in order to better "reify" them. The absolute separation of the in-itself from the for-itself and the dualism of being and nothingness are the very expression of the Oedipal structure such as the antihero endeavors to live it. One might add that, as such, this separation possesses in our time a truth and a generality which is far superior to that of many philosophical systems.

The in-itself is the Oedipal father; it is a god without spirit and in theory fallen, but in reality it is more a god than ever, because the spiritual mutilation inflicted on it can only reinforce the characteristics it already possesses and which make it a god. The in-itself is the silence, the impenetrability, and the definitive indifference of the absolute obstacle. The for-itself is, on the contrary, the antihero who feels like a nothing, a zero, an emptiness, before the Oedipal obstacle, and who endeavors to divinize his own impotence by calling it lucidity.

We can now define the role of the inert object in *Nausea*. It furnishes the seemingly neutral terrain on which Roquentin conducts his war against the Others. This detour through things is not only tactical. It allows the

Ego, both the Ego of the reader and of the author, to ignore the war that is raging. It preserves the illusion of absolute autonomy and indifference required by the antihero's mystique. Roquentin resembles the sulking child who takes out his anger on his toys in order not to openly take it out on his father. But this ruse cannot fool us. It is the bastard and the bastard alone that Roquentin is aiming at. And he openly turns toward the bastard in the decisive moments. For example: he sizes up doctor Rogé. This fake tough guy, "built like the side of a house," takes up the challenge. A duel of icy stares ensues between the two café tables. Very quickly, the champion of the Bouville elite backs down. He closes his eyes, leaving the world to the vengeful passion of his conqueror . . . Roquentin takes a walk, aiming his ocular machine gun at all of the suspects of this inexpiable crime: self-confidence or confidence in others. Terror reigns over Bouville.

The synthesis of the in-itself and the for-itself always shimmers in the eyes of the antihero. To prove to oneself that this synthesis is not real or, if it persists, to cause it to unravel—such is the task of the antihero, and it is up to the *gaze* to accomplish it. This gaze does better than to simply reveal the first effects of the illness that infects the world. It accelerates the fatal process. It deflates the wimps, exposes the always deceitful reputations, and unmasks all the impostures. Men or things—nothing can withstand him. His offensive power is literally fabulous. He gnaws on, corrodes, bites, slices, slashes, penetrates, pierces, and finally disintegrates everything before him. No obstacle can stop him. It is the antihero's secret weapon, the *ultimate weapon* that the generals dream about nowadays. It is the death ray, the neutron bomb. Silent and invisible, it never misses its target; and it never forgives. What progress has been made since the cane-sword that Tartarin convulsively clutched during his nightly rounds through a sleeping Tarascon!

The sexual meaning does not lie behind the existential meaning; it is one with it, and it is useless to explicate them separately. But nothing better reveals the epic and military origins of the antihero than this perpetually provocative and combative gaze. Whatever else one might say, it is the sense of sight that dominates in *Nausea*, just as it dominates in modern authors as different from one another as the naturalists and Paul Valéry.

From his theater box, M. Teste reduces to nothingness the spectators quietly arrayed at his feet. With the spectators neutralized, this man who can do nothing and does nothing, but "who does not think any less of it"—as Sartre will himself say in his text on Nizan—enjoys a superiority just as illusory as that of Roquentin. Valéry still feels comfortable in the infinitely narrow and rigid framework defined by the dialectic of the antihero. It is not the same with Sartre. *Nausea* is the late, decadent, and morose expression of a structure of which M. Teste is the classic, satisfied, and coquettish example. The structure is in the midst of self-dissolution, which is why the hatred of the Other is even more visible in Sartre than in Valéry. *Nausea* anticipates the will to transcendence of Sartre's later works. As a writer of remarkable vigor caught in an extremely difficult historical and literary situation, Sartre erects a veritable compensating myth around the gaze. The destructive power that Sartre confers on his hero's gaze shows that a purely visual existence has not transcended the intersubjective struggle. It simply chooses to continue this struggle on the only terrain it considers favorable.

But the world in which this epic of the gaze unfolds cannot be the true one. The flip side of this illusion is the for-itself of *Being and Nothingness* overpowered by the Other's gaze and suddenly dispossessed of the real. The author does not identify with this for-itself like he identified with Roquentin. The structures that manifest "the impossibility of man" are those of the Other. The in-itself of *Being and Nothingness* polarizes all that contradicts the myth of the antihero in Sartre's experience, all that Sartre cannot recognize as his own. And we must resituate this missing half of an experience always split between the Ego and the Other, in order to understand Roquentin's quotidian reflections. As we noted above, if the world did not so much or even essentially belong to the Other, if it were not the property of the bastards and the culture heroes, Roquentin would have no reason to oppose it so fiercely.

The role of the bastards in Sartre's early works is analogous to the role of the bourgeois in Flaubert. Flaubert believes that he has transcended the romantic project of the hero. But the mysticism of art is really the mysticism of the hero in disguise. Flaubert is a false hero. Sartre tells us this, and he is right; but Flaubert is a false hero because he already is, like Sartre himself, an antihero. Whether he is referring to Flaubert, Baudelaire, or Genet, Sartre is always talking about the antihero: the truth of the antihero reveals itself as the truth of the Other before becoming Sartre's truth.

The curses that Oedipus lays at the feet of his father's murderer—this indubitable Other—are slowly turned against himself. But in a time and in a society made up of abstract oppositions, there is no living criticism that is not a criticism of the *doubles*, that is, a criticism that results in self-criticism. Rare, however, are the writers who discover the circularity of their own thought, and this discovery is generally underappreciated.

Sartre is closer to Flaubert than he ever thought. He speaks about his literary past in *The Words* in virtually the same way that he spoke about Flaubert's oeuvre not long before.[7] The only difference being that he says "Flaubert wrote against all his readers," when it doubtless would be no less exact, but more to the point to say: "Sartre wrote for and against his grandfather." In *The Words*, we do not find the whole truth of *Nausea*, but its rough-shape. To complete this truth, we must bring out the *double figure* of the antihero and the bastard, that is to say, the Ego and the Other, always opposed to and identified with each other in a structural opposition underlying all of the themes of the work. This opposition alone can allow us to grasp the work as a "signifying totality." A critical approach that remains closed to the intersubjective problem will tell us that what is essential in *Nausea* is what occurs between Roquentin, on one side, and the pebbles, sticky paper, and walnut roots, on the other. This approach will limit itself to glorifying the myth of the antihero, which is the dominant myth of contemporary intellectuals; but it will not grasp any kind of unity, not even an "aesthetic" one, for it will not know what to do with the theme of the bastard. There is unity only at the level of the intersubjective drama. And we cannot see this drama as a simple reflection of the original Oedipal drama. On the contrary, we must see in the Oedipal drama the germ of the intersubjective drama that succeeds it and which alone fully embodies *the project of being this god that is the Other*. To discover the interweaving and peripeties of these two dramas in the works that most often claim to be speaking to us about something else completely is not tantamount to a hostile attitude toward literature, as has sometimes been remarked. Literature has long preceded criticism and even psychoanalysis in this endeavor. And judging from *The Words*, this is still the case. Sartrean self-criticism claims to be inspired by Marx and Freud, but it is also linked to Kierkegaardian meditations on the ethical meaning of aesthetics and to the great quixotic interrogation of writing.

The true defenders of literature are perhaps not those who would want it to be incapable of lying, for this would also make it incapable of telling the truth, in the strong sense of the term. It is indeed necessary for certain works to deceive us if there are others to tell us the truth, not of such and such an author—not *a* truth among so many others, but, simply, *the truth*.

—*Translated by Robert Doran*

# Critical Reflections on Literary
# Studies [1966]

We hesitate to bring up the quarrel M. Picard is waging against the *nouvelle critique*. It has to be done, though, since *MLN* is somewhat involved in the affair. It was in these very pages, it will be remembered, that the article appeared (before it figured in the *Essais critiques*) which drew M. Picard's wrath against M. Barthes.[1] On a page of *Le Monde*, which I do not have in front of me, M. Picard accused M. Barthes of craftily slipping his anti-Sorbonnic propaganda into the place where it was most likely to be believed: foreign journals with "ill-informed" readers. I cannot guarantee the literal exactness of his other assertions, but I was struck by that phrase "ill-informed," and I believe I make no mistake in attributing it to M. Picard.[2]

We were the accomplices, albeit involuntary, of a vast, encircling conspiracy threatening M. Picard and the Sorbonne, which he embodies. We were cat's paws without knowing it. Fortunately there was M. Picard to enlighten us. The news was reaching us. It remained only for us to make honorable amends to the professor himself and to the Sorbonne, who had been jointly "defamed" (the word is there—I am not inventing it) by M. Barthes' article.

Let M. Picard be reassured; we have not been used. Roland Barthes has not taken advantage of our good faith. He has not forced our hand. However ill informed we may be, neither M. Barthes nor M. Picard himself was altogether unknown to us when we asked M. Barthes to give us his "Deux Critiques."

It seemed superfluous to us at the time to review the facts. Since then, M. Picard has renewed and broadened his attacks against M. Barthes and other critics in a pamphlet which is attracting a certain amount of attention: *Nouvelle critique, nouvelle imposture.*[3]

Controversy is not always bad. On both sides of the Atlantic we need some stimulation. But, still, the debate should have a real object. The plots M. Picard sees surrounding him have only the most remote connection with current intellectual life. On the one hand, there is the reasonable, docile criticism of sensible people, the principles of which seem so natural that it needs no definition; and on the other, there is the subversive, perverse, one is tempted to say *deviationist,* criticism, the very existence of which *defames* the Sorbonne and all decent people.

In this system, M. Jean-Paul Weber represents and perhaps even embodies psychoanalysis, just as M. Picard embodies the Sorbonne. Sartre would speak here of a world of essences. I would have thought M. Weber as different, say, from the Lacanians, as M. Picard himself is different from M. Weber. In the same way, between the criticism which sees in the work the emanation of a subjectivity always identical with itself, always susceptible of apprehension in an immediate intuition, the criticism of M. Poulet, for example—between this and the criticism which, at the heart of the work and in our relationships with it, gives the place of primary importance to intersubjective relationships, I would have believed the distance to be as great as between M. Picard and the *Traité du Sublime.*[4] Such fine nuances doubtless carry no weight in the face of the almost planetary encirclement now threatening the Sorbonne.

The most ill informed of our readers or editors would, I believe, recognize within criticism differences which are strangely manhandled, if not even obliterated, in M. Picard's critical Western. The *nouvelle critique* has its weaknesses and even its ridiculous points. It is contradictory, tumultuous, sometimes unfair. It is wide open to contemporary thought, to all sorts of influences. It is, in a word, *alive.* That is hard to forgive.

In a hundred years, ours will probably look like the period of a metamorphosis in the very concept of literature, a revolution comparable, in a sense, to that of Mme de Staël and her time. Mme de Staël did not simply add to the discourse on literature the *theme* of history. She was the first to grasp *all* themes historically. Her theory of history was perhaps inadequate; her ideas doubtless lacked originality. Her importance lies elsewhere. For since Mme de Staël, one can no longer speak of literature in the same way as before; or rather, one may, but anything one may say about it without taking her into account is marked by sterility.

Today it is not a question of history, at least not in its nineteenth-century sense, but perhaps of *anthropology*, in a sense as yet not easy to define. One can reject this or that critic on the basis of his particular opinions, but this is an evasion of the main issue. The *nouvelle critique* is no more existentialist than it is Freudian or Marxist or structuralist. It must, however, take into account Hegel, Marx, Sartre, Freud, and, today, Lévi-Strauss and Lacan. The "sciences of man" besiege us. Despite appearances, despite differences M. Picard seems not to suspect, this broadening of the context does not contradict, but rather confirms the concern with the creative experience which is also characteristic of the twentieth century.

Mme de Staël and her group were accused of a dreadful abuse of jargon. They, too, quoted at every turn rebarbative thinkers. They seemed sometimes more at ease in a misty, romantic Germany than in classical, reasonable France. Every revolution takes place in confusion and disorder and leaves behind much dross. Depriving men of their habitual points of reference, it seems to them to be destroying what in fact it is transforming.

The revolution in criticism is already accomplished. One might say that M. Picard's pamphlet confirms it to the very degree that its author embodies—this is important to him and must be true—an authority and a continuity necessarily opposed, in the intellectual order, to freedom and to life. Without going back to Rabelais and Port-Royal (a little heavy for all our shoulders), one can fit M. Picard into an already venerable tradition, that of Brunetière excommunicating naturalism. We should note that it was for literature itself that the academic dogmatism of yesteryear saved its thunderbolts—already a bit damp. The fact that they are brandished today against a criticism which is constantly expanding its domain affords one more argument for those who call ours an essentially hermeneutic period and see as its task "an inventory of significations." More than ever before, the best of our writers are critics. It is they, and not the recipients of showy literary prizes, who today are the stewards of our literary heritage; it is they who are renewing it. M. Picard may embody the Sorbonne, but Roland Barthes is creating the literary works of our age.

One may wonder, moreover, whether the Sorbonne's opposition, not to mention its approval, can any longer confirm anything whatsoever. But who gives a thought to the Sorbonne nowadays? Not a single idea of this half-century is associated with it in even a negative way. One could not call the Sorbonne hostile; it does not recognize contemporary thought, and is not recognized by it. Not that the Sorbonne cannot claim eminent men, as it always has, but their presence there is always exceptional. One is astonished to find them there and always forgets that they are there as soon as they get involved in the real issues of their day. Even in academic circles in France, it is no longer toward the Sorbonne that the intellectual community turns its attention. It is always elsewhere, it seems, that *things are happening.*

The revolution in criticism is accomplished; it even dates back to the beginning of the postwar period. But one could hardly say that it has triumphed; it remains strangely marginal. It might yet even prove abortive. We were already aware of this; the fact is now confirmed by the truly extraordinary delight occasioned by M. Picard in quarters at times quite opposed to his real values. M. Picard is a true historian. One can disagree with him on many points without showing any lack of respect for the scope of his work, for the thoroughness of his documentation, for the discretion of his focus on this or that detail. M. Picard believes today that he is serving the cause of literary history. He is mistaken. He is encouraging a phenomenon which is particularly widespread in our day and which we must call by name: academic anti-intellectualism, flourishing everywhere but taking on different forms in different places. What is the ubiquitous obstacle to living thought in the United States as in France? Mme de Staël had only Napoleon to contend with. Our tyranny is better disguised, but universal; it is identical with the bureaucratic organization of literary studies.

The vertiginous growth of literary studies has its good side, of course, for which we are ever grateful, but it sometimes resembles a malignant proliferation. Our libraries, ever more numerous, buy an ever-growing number of books published by more and more university presses. Our system of academic publishing functions as a closed circuit. No longer does any external sanction control our intellectual life. We have become our own signifying totality, and it is perhaps time to ask ourselves what indeed it signifies. Who will distinguish in our studies, on the one hand, what springs from a true desire for knowledge, from free intellectual activity, and on the other, what exists only as a function of the insatiable bureaucratic machine, demanding servile conformity to its requirements, having no other aim than to insure its own indefinite expansion? The more neutral, colorless, and repetitious the results of our sacrosanct *research*, the better they answer our administrative demands. This situation would seem to call for extreme vigilance, and yet the *nouvelle critique* alone provokes any anxiety in us. Could it be that anti-intellectualism has already triumphed in places claiming to be impregnable fortresses of intelligence and culture?

The so-called *nouvelle critique*, however aberrant at times, and perhaps in its very aberrations, is always implicitly calling into question the very system that produces it. It is always the protestation of an individual. In its best proponents, it is more, but if it were never more than that, it would still deserve our sympathy. The so-called *nouvelle critique* stubbornly insists on seeing in art, in thought, in literature, something more than one of the cogs (and one of the least) in the machinery of the academy. It is unorthodox criticism, criticism which defies administrative pigeonholes, demanding and pretentious criticism, criticism which requires "interdisciplinary" training. It is the spoilsport of the academic publication game.

One can understand that Picard would be welcomed as a savior. The most "Picardian" among us are not always the most learned. Between genuine literary history and living criticism there should be no quarrel. In its truly dynamic period, literary history did not claim to be an end in itself. It saw itself as the basis and the instrument for a richer and deeper interpretation. If certain works are as *definitive* as we are told, we must not be asked to redo them. The greatest homage one can render to literary history is not to repeat its work indefinitely but to use its results.

Living thought is always more dynamic than ready-made thought; it asserts itself, believes in itself; it is dogmatic and has an obligation to be so. To pretend that this dogmatism is *dangerous*, that it is a threat to our intellectual freedom, is a joke. This freedom cannot be exercised without the clash of contradictory beliefs. Today there is no conflict, no debate, no dialogue, no real life outside of the *nouvelle critique*.

We have in America a dominant aesthetic. It claims to be eclectic, devoted to beauty, infinitely broad-minded. Its anti-dogmatism sometimes reaches the point of intolerance vis-à-vis living thought. What is the derivation of this aesthetic? It curiously combines somewhat emasculated fragments of New Criticism with European academic conformism. It proclaims the autonomy of art in order to defend the autonomy of departments of literature, ever threatened by the conquering disciplines, the "truly scientific" disciplines. An essentially bureaucratic credo, *l'art pour l'art* tempered by bibliography is also a defeatist credo. The scientism which challenges our role is not itself challenged. Feeling incapable of impugning it, we impugn philosophy in general. But we become so suspicious, so narrow, that we can no longer see the difference between the "social sciences" and the "sciences of man." In the latter we see a new enemy, and not the opportunity they offer to renew literary studies, to emerge finally from the crisis which engulfs us.

Our slogans—all of which are defensive and negative—are aimed at preserving the insularity of a discipline which grows day by day more desiccated. They can all be related to a holy horror of what is called reductive or even reductionist criticism. Barthes uses the language of psychoanalysis and is therefore reductionist. Actually he is not, and he explains himself on this point with great clarity, but to no avail. The only reduction to which psychoanalysis leads is, obviously, a reduction to the author himself, to the author's psyche. Now the author Racine in Barthes' *Sur Racine* is hardly mentioned. And that is precisely the surprising point; that is what we should talk about. On the first page of the introduction, anyone may read:

The language is somewhat psychoanalytical, but the treatment is hardly so. . . . The analysis here presented does not concern Racine at all, but only the Racinian hero: it avoids inferring anything about the author from the work or about the work from the author. It is a deliberately circumscribed analysis.[5]

If we are correcting the error of which Barthes is the victim, it is not because we, too, feel the enormity of the crime of which he stands accused; it is because this error appears to us to be symptomatic in its absurdity. It is enough simply to utter the word "reductionist" to strike us dumb. Our critical faculties abandon us, and it does not even occur to us to ask the simplest of questions: "He is reductionist, and why shouldn't he be?"

Any vigorous thought is sooner or later bound to arrive at its own foundation; it will end, then, in reduction. We can, of course, remain ignorant of our first principles, believing ourselves to be alone in having none, even glorying in this vacuum; but none of this does credit to our thought.

The word "reductionist" is, in fact, rather tiresome. It is surprising to find it used so much by those who claim a devotion to beauty. The truth is that the word reeks of punitive bureaucracy from a mile away. It plays the same role in our ever-so-slightly sclerotic universe as "Trotskyite" did in Stalinist Russia. It tells more about those who brandish it on every occasion than about those whose instant damnation it proclaims in a perpetual verbal exorcism.

It is not the fact of reduction that matters to the critic, but what precedes it. The Hegel of the *Phenomenology* reduces everything to mind. So we are spared the trouble of reading him. A pity. What a formidable reduction might we not witness, *Antigone* to *Rameau's Nephew*, if we were to moderate slightly our dogmatic anti-dogmatism. The reductive thought of Hegel embraces a prodigious amount of material; the least reductive criticism imaginable might very well embrace nothing at all, might never overcome a pathetic emptiness.

The reduction phobia threatens to emasculate all critical thought. There are those who reject contemporary criticism *in toto*, on the pretext that it is "philosophical." There is, in our period as in any other, philosophical criticism, but it is not always the criticism which appears philosophical. The Cartesianism, or the positivism, of traditional criticism is not recognized as philosophical by our anti-philosophers. The criticism that offends them, on the contrary, is the criticism which is so much more wary of philosophy than ever before that it can speak *all* the languages of philosophy. One cannot say that it reduces art to philosophy without by the same token saying that it reduces philosophy to art. A clever and shrewd aestheticism like Valéry's could "reduce" to pure aesthetics any will to systematize. Sartre maintains that every work of art contains a latent philosophy, but one can turn his proposition around: a philosophical system is an unconscious work of art. The philosophical, in the traditional meaning of the term, enjoys no privileges in contemporary criticism.

It would take only a little humor, perhaps, and a little true faith in literature to apply Valéry's reduction-in-reverse to structuralism. In Lévi-Strauss there is at least as much literature as in many a place where it is today feverishly being sought. The concept of *model,* put forward by structuralism and extended by it to cultural phenomena, is perhaps only a metaphor rich enough and accurate enough to be systematized, a metaphor with multiple dimensions, whose existence, moreover, poses many problems. The recourse to models has diverse implications, but, from an admittedly schematic point of view, it represents, with regard to the science of the past, something analogous to preciosity in the literary realm. Instead of appealing, for the description of an object, to conflicting and multiple metaphors, to fugitive images whose choice depends on no conscious system, one adopts a single metaphor—as all-inclusive as possible—and pushes it to its furthest limits, prolonging its usage even beyond previously tolerated limits, beyond a now dated "good taste." That was the way preciosity proceeded. And it is precisely an impression of preciosity that Lévi-Strauss first makes on new readers. To say this is not to attack either science or literature, but rather to observe their closeness. Literary preciosity fails, no doubt, from an inability to communicate intuitions which are essential but too subtle for the sloth and vulgarity of its readers; despairing, then, it falls into paradox and pure vanity. Structuralism, however, may succeed precisely because of its will to systematize, because of the scientific precisions to which it resorts, the rigorous methods with which it arms itself in order to formulate, to preserve, and to transcend intuitions which are at times quite analogous, at least fundamentally, to those of the past.

Those who cannot penetrate structuralism, those who remain closed in a more general way to all dialectical thought, see in the contemporary effort only a will to paradox, a desire to surprise, a gratuitous attack on common sense. And yet, thought which intends to be thought about literature cannot be based on common sense. It cannot reject structuralism, among other things, without rejecting a mode of knowledge which is much closer to the best literature than the positivism of yesteryear. Structuralism brings out, between the parts and the whole and between the whole and the parts, homologous relationships whose existence is affirmed by an aesthetic criticism which can neither reveal nor demonstrate them. Far from being hostile to authentic aesthetic understanding, structuralist knowledge is perhaps only its extension and development. This is perhaps why structuralism cannot recognize aesthetics as a separate domain, any more than the truly religious can see any distinction between the sacred and the profane.

We ought to claim structuralism as being naturally our own. It would permit us to join the contemporary desire for cultural interpretation without betraying (as did the old sociologism and psychologism) the privileged place which we accord and which must always be accorded to the great works. The criticism which thus draws close to the sciences of man, in the broadening of its interpretive function, is not the least *literary* in the best sense of that word. But it probably should not answer to the name of "literary criticism," which is too limited by its traditional usage and too liable to misunderstandings. This broadened interpretation may constitute, alongside literary history, a true academic discipline. This discipline, it will be said, does not exist. That is exactly what we mean; we must create it.

There are today hundreds, perhaps thousands of us devoting ourselves to literary studies. We are not giving away any secret if we admit that our books and journals are not always the most original or essential to knowledge. When veritable armies are competing as laborers in the same literary vineyard, duplications are inevitable. Perhaps it is better to republish the same books than to publish nothing at all. It is perhaps inevitable that these repetitious works should almost always receive favorable reviews. But we must not exceed certain limits. We must not erect this system into a standard for the human spirit. We do just that when we show our claws only before the great talent of a Goldmann or a Barthes and pull them back, predictably, when we encounter the imitative and the banal. We do just that when we deplore the time "wasted" in examining the malaise in literary studies. We do just that when we send our colleagues back to urgent but ill-defined tasks which await them, it seems, from time immemorial. Whatever the pretext, let us not exhort each other to maintain the status quo.

Must we really, faced with any work of some difficulty, call the author back to the demands of clarity and nontechnicality imposed on him, it seems, by his role as intermediary between the work and that now mythical creature, the "common reader"? These perpetual recalls to an order which is no more (and perhaps never was) hide from us the real conditions of our academic pursuits. Sainte-Beuve, we all agree, was addressing himself to non-specialists. But there was only one Sainte-Beuve and he had an audience. The Modern Language Association numbers more than twenty thousand Sainte-Beuves and no audience whatsoever. This is no catastrophe—far from it; we talk to each other and we are, all by ourselves, more numerous than the audience of Sainte-Beuve, Molière, or Shakespeare. We provide our own audience, and that should be enough. The myth of the enlightened common reader has not the least foundation in our intellectual and sociological situation. We can be and we must be as technical and as philosophical as the actual level of our academic audience will allow. Our intellectual autarchy presents certain dangers but also some advantages.

The common reader proves singularly ungrateful. He does not want us, it seems, to condescend to his level. Our solicitude leaves him cold. The only criticism that interests him at all is that of Goldmann and Barthes, the unreadable *nouvelle critique*.

The "urgent" tasks can wait. What we need is truth. We owe it to ourselves and to the prodigious system of higher education with which America has provided itself. Everything demands of us a real leap forward. The "publish or perish" system is no less destructive of the research it claims to honor than of teaching. It creates a "mediocracy" of researchers desperately attached to stock ideas. Genuine talent gets lost in a mob dominated by a timorous ultra-conservatism. A system as vast as ours is necessarily conservative. We are not asking it to be revolutionary. What worries us is its feeble capacity to respond to new ideas, the time it takes to assimilate recent acquisitions. It is a bit demagogical to suggest to our flocks that aside from these black sheep, the "new critics," all is for the best in the best of all possible academies.

The intellectual enlargement that the times demand is no easy feat. We must face up to the problem. In trying to avoid it we must not—even with the Sorbonne's approval—construct a critical dogma all the more narrow and intolerant as it claims to be liberating. This dogma always comes down to the absolute and insurmountable separation of, on the one hand, the aesthetic (elusive, ineffable, nebulous, misty, exquisite, reassuring) and, on the other hand, intelligence (tedious, systematic, forbidding, destructive of all beauty). If we examine this distinction thoroughly, we still find the basic defeatism which we demonstrate vis-à-vis the exact sciences—a defeatism which today has no further reason to exist.

We must be initiated into complex thought, into difficult methods we have been taught to neglect. But our universities, precisely, dispose of resources which would make it possible to make up for lost time. If the spirit of bureaucracy does not triumph, we shall certainly undertake, and on a grand scale, thanks to postdoctoral fellowships, thanks to the literally staggering means to which we all have access, what certain groups are already trying to do at the Ecole des Hautes Etudes.[6] The crisis of the "humanities," the student problem, all of this is linked to our intellectual timidity and calls for an effort on our part to rethink all of our themes with today's intellectual resources.

Literary studies are in crisis; no one, I think, would dream of denying it. In literary historian Gustave Lanson's day, everyone could believe he was playing his little role in the vast workshop of advancing knowledge. Knowledge, founded thenceforward on truth itself, had only to pursue its imperturbable march forward. No one believes this any more. At the end of the war, the crisis could still be seen as transitory. Peace would bring back the old order. This hope is gone. The atomic age is not a return to the *belle époque.*

To observe this is not to kneel before some historical idol; it is rather to draw the consequences from the impasse in which traditional criticism finds itself. To escape this impasse, more and more we are avoiding the great problems. In Lanson's day no subject was taboo. Lanson himself tells us that he wants to *explicate* works. He fears neither the psychological nor the sociological. His concept of "influences," moreover, is not so simplistic as the one attributed to him. Henri Peyre points this out, rightfully, in his introduction to the *Essais,* which he had the good idea of republishing.[7] Lanson anticipates many contemporary themes. Peyre is at times closer to those who attack him than to those who claim to carry on his work.

The divergences are no less real. At the beginning of the century we still dreamed of being able to define once and for all the great terms of literary history—Classicism, Romanticism, realism, etc. A segment of literary reality was to come and take its place under each of these words. It was always a question of cutting out this segment with *exactness.* With Lanson, the idea of scientific precision does not refer solely to the establishment of facts—the domain in which it is still intact today—but remains linked to the principle of a division of the literary substance around certain key words, certain chapter headings. This is what we no longer believe in. The undertaking demands a concept of language which is no longer ours.

Then we sought the frontiers of Classicism or Romanticism, in the way a Bismarck or the diplomats of Versailles sought natural frontiers on ordnance survey maps. We believed that words had a real substratum which we tried to determine. Words, it seemed, were like watertight receptacles, placed in literature for all eternity; they were jars, duly labeled, awaiting their definitive *contents.* At that period, to re-pose the grand problems meant to propose a new distribution of the literary jam among these eternal jars. The more time passed, the more the shifts from one jar to another multiplied and accelerated. Some thought to stop this interminable shuffling by adding new jars. Jars of all sizes and shapes jostled each other in growing confusion.

The honor of having upset all these jars goes to our Professor Lovejoy of Hopkins. He showed that the word "Romanticism," for example, had a multiplicity of meanings, sometimes contradictory. So the jars were not watertight; in fact they were full of holes. That is all fine and good, but where will this criticism stop? Does Romanticism mean nothing, or does it on the contrary mean too much? If we give up this word, why should we trust the rest? Historians of literature are certainly not the only ones to play the role of the fabled knight eying to fill the enchanted, unfillable keg. What becomes of literature itself, that mistress of ambiguity, if we reject equivocal terms?

This criticism of language leads straight to logical positivism and its sequellae. We shall next try to base all knowledge on a verbal reduction in which things adhere to words. But literature enjoys no privileged status here. And so we stand convicted of radical *irrelevance.* Contemporary aestheticism does not answer this criticism but embraces it, submits to it body and soul, and thereby renounces our claim to a share of truth.

This criticism is nonetheless necessary. The categories of our literary history depend on certain words and on their history. Classicism, for example, makes a very late entrance, at first more acrimonious than majestic. *Littré* puts a wary little cross beside this word rejected by the French Academy. A neologism, it designates a literary ideology, invented after the fact, in the period of ideologies, to correspond to "Romanticism" (*à "romantisme," ou même à "romanticisme"*). A veritable abyss separates this modern Classicism from the old *classicus* from which it derives and which it imbues with its ideological effluvia. Classic will henceforth be opposed to romantic, and it is within a system of oppositions that all these terms signify.

Current criticism, we should point out here, is continually reproached for looking at the past through twentieth-century glasses. But this is no worse, perhaps, than looking at it through nineteenth-century glasses. Boileau does not talk about existentialism or structuralism. But he does not talk about Classicism either. I fail to see why Classicism should survive if we must banish jargon.

In the middle of the nineteenth century, the opposition between Classicism and Romanticism is blurred. The past appears thenceforth as a national treasure to be catalogued. The concepts which existed shortly before only in their reciprocal opposition are now to be added together. Perhaps that is what Lanson means when he says that criticism divides and literary history unifies. This latter verb is not quite exact. True unity is not a sum but a dialectical totality. The very idea of totality is foreign to literary history. That is precisely its weakness; today we have to choose between an outmoded positivism and one form or another of dialectical thought. Literary history does not unify; it can only add up. And what it adds is not really addable. The sum has no stability. Every modification of detail echoes throughout the system. It is not a matter of correcting a detail here or there, as they tell us, of tightening some bolt, of replacing a worn-out part with a new one. A whole *worldview* is in question, as Lucien Goldmann would say. The learning of 1900 today reflects the world of 1900 no less than the *Memoires d'outre-tombe* reflects the first quarter of the nineteenth century—the spiritual universe of Chateaubriand, Mme de Staël, Benjamin Constant; with the difference that Benjamin Constant, Chateaubriand, and Mme de Staël, much more than the petits-bourgeois professors of the triumphant Third Republic, are aware of *being immersed in* a particular historical period. They seem in many ways closer to our own cosmopolitan values.

The vision which fifty years ago sustained the overall plan of our literary history has vanished. If Nerval is entitled to only a footnote in Lanson's manual—a footnote shared, moreover, with Maurice and Eugénie de Guérin—it is not because of an easily rectifiable error. Nerval cannot figure in the French romantic school as called for by this overall plan. This romantic school must be the counterpart of Classicism as it is then conceived, just as Second Empire sculpture is made for the Classical Paris that surrounds it. Nerval does not measure up. He lacks a certain elegant stance, a monumental quality, a Classicism-of-the-romantics to balance the Romanticism-of-the-classics. Indeed, that is just why we like him so much today. He rises among the ruins of a certain handbook Romanticism. That Romanticism served as a buttress to the vaulting of Classicism. Everything has crumbled at once. Classicism survives, but within a new opposition to a newcomer: the baroque, whose presence upsets all previous designations.

We must control systems of opposition and not allow ourselves to be controlled by them. Lanson, it will be said, foresaw the dialectical nature of certain oppositions. His formulas always have subtle shadings. He states, for example, that a certain author is influenced by another *although* he differs from him on numerous points. He will show us that Romanticism and realism, *in spite of* their antagonism, have many common traits. Lanson demonstrates great *flexibility*. Frequently, he sees clearly even against his own principles; he rides roughshod over obstacles which ought to stop him. It is when he gives in to his intuitions that he interests us. And his scientific pretensions surprise us more and more; they are at best barely visible outside his methodological writings. Does this mean we must give up all rigor, all intellectual rules in literary studies? That would be tantamount to giving up knowledge itself. Of course, it is absurd to criticize Lanson's scientism. But neither, perhaps, should we justify Lanson in the name of an intuitionism and an impressionism which lead nowhere. We must recover the demand for rigor and surpass it. If we look closely, we find that these nuances and this flexibility we admire so much in Lanson have no air of ineffability. These intuitions can be systematized. It is because realism and Romanticism share the same literary project that they can be opposed to each other. Every opposition rests on a ground of identity. One may say of Lanson what Proust says of M. de Norpois, the diplomat of

*Remembrance of Things Past*: his *althoughs* and *notwithstandings* are *becauses* unrecognized as such. But we have to recognize that oppositions and "influences" are dialectically linked, that the positive and the negative are inseparable from one another. In literary history one can proceed neither by positivist addition, nor by those absolute and quickly outmoded negations that living literature needs in order to survive. Whether we like it or not, we cannot ignore the problem of dialectical thought; it presents itself even on the most technical level, prior to any ideology.

We cannot ignore the controversies surrounding language. The renaissance of dialectics is quite significant for us. For we are devoured by a secret scorn for our own language, forever irreducible to that of the exact sciences. Merleau-Ponty, structural linguists, and yet other thinkers show us that any language which is not equivocal ceases to have meaning. If there is any privileged language, it is not the poorest but the richest in ambiguities, in associations and resonances, both convergent and divergent. Ought we not examine the bodies of thought which claim to be able to restore literary studies to their full dignity?

As professionals in the field of language, we must look squarely at the sickness afflicting language. There are those among us who are ready to believe, along with society as a whole, that non-quantifiable speech is essentially vain and empty speech, tolerable only if recognized as pure gratuity or simple diversion. Our faith in the object of our study has weakened. Perhaps this faith cannot be reconciled with a serene adherence to the values of contemporary society. But this adherence appears today as all the more appealing since, by a curious ricochet effect, we profit from the very thing that demeans our endeavors in the eyes of the world: the idea that there is no knowledge, in the strict sense of the word, except in the exact sciences and in tangible—and preferably explosive—results.

To reject without examination the kinds of thought that run counter to the dogma from which we are suffocating is to push intellectual paralysis to the point of a death wish. Are we to scorn minds that restore to us both our literature and our discourse on literature?[8]

*—Translated by Catherine and Richard Macksey*

# 14

## Narcissism: The Freudian Myth
## Demythified by Proust [1978]

In his *On Narcissism: An Introduction*, Freud defines this notion as the attitude of a person who treats himself as an object of sexual love. He can also detect, he believes, an "object narcissism" in which the subject turns his libido not directly toward himself but toward love objects that "resemble" this subject too much to qualify as "real" objects. These objects must be viewed as mere appendages of the subject. Narcissism, in other words, is the condition of a subject who prefers never to get out of himself, even when he appears to do so.[1]

Freud likes to think in terms of a fixed quantity of libidinal energy that can be directed either toward the self, or a substitute of the self, on the one hand, or toward a "real" object, different enough from the subject, on the other. In the first case—narcissism—the libidinal energy goes in a circle, so to speak; it stays with the subject or returns to it. As a result, this subject may be said to be self-contained or self-sufficient, whereas in the second case—"true object-love"—the libidinal energy is discharged outside. The self is "diminished," "impoverished."

Still according to *Narcissism*, it is normal for children to be highly narcissistic; even adults should retain a certain degree of narcissism, but not too much. An excessively narcissistic adult can be said to be "immature." Freud considers women and artists as especially prone to excessive narcissism. The notion of narcissism plays a major role in Freud's theory of art and the artist. In the nineteenth century and in the first half of the twentieth, there is a large amount of philosophical and literary theory that corresponds rather closely to Freud's views on the affinity between artists and the self-sufficiency that he labels narcissism. A major difference, however, is that in many pronouncements by artists and writers, the condition described by psychoanalysis as excessively and pathologically narcissistic is presented as a positive asset, even as an ideal toward which the artist must strive if he has not yet truly achieved it. Between philosophers such as Fichte or Stirner, some major romantic and symbolist poets, and a prose writer like André Gide in twentieth-century France, we find many differences, of course, but we also find a common element; it could be summed up as a deliberate embrace and celebration of some or all features of "excessive narcissism." We often hear from these writers that loved objects are desirable and poetic only insofar as they become reflections of the poet's self. As soon as it is no longer suffused with subjective passion and imagination, reality becomes banal, vulgar, disappointing.

When Marcel Proust expresses himself directly in regard to desire, as if he were a psychologist rather than through his fiction, he shares the narcissistic or individualistic ideology that was still widespread among intellectuals and artists during his lifetime. People, he writes, love primarily themselves, and they seek themselves in the objects of their desire. They endow the desired object with a mystery and beauty that really flows from themselves. The superior self radiates enough energy to transfigure commonplace reality into its own image, turning it into poetry. Only when the genuine *otherness* of outside reality breaks through to us does disenchantment occur. Reality does not come up to the high expectations of the self; it is less beautiful, less rich, less authentic, less substantial than the self's own private projections.

In his first novel, *Jean Santeuil*, which he never published, Proust portrays a young man who is intensely preoccupied with himself; the effect he produces on other people is almost invariably good. Jean Santeuil experiences desire—it is not an experience a brilliant young man would like to do without—but his desire never takes him beyond the boundaries of his own beautiful world. He is in love with a girl who has the same refined taste and leads the same beautiful life as himself; she frequents the same people; her aspirations run parallel to his.[2]

If we read the theoretical pronouncements on the nature of the self and of desire in *Remembrance of Things Past*, the great masterpiece Proust wrote and published in the last ten years of his life, we find that they often remain very much as before. As long, therefore, as we base our judgment on Proust's theoretical pronouncements, wherever they may come from, or on his actual practice as a novelist in *Jean Santeuil*, we will only find material that appears to confirm Freud's conception of narcissism and its privileged application to both the artist and the work of art.

The only place where things are different is also the one that counts most from a literary standpoint—Proust's practice as a novelist in his great masterpiece. There, the fictional substance is quite new as far as desire is concerned; it no longer corresponds to the narcissistic model. It is the desire of a self that feels extremely "impoverished," even destitute. The word "impoverishment" is actually used by Proust, just as it is used by Freud in *Narcissism*, in connection with "anaclytic" or object-love. We may suppose, therefore, that between the two novels, Proust has shifted from "narcissism" to "object-love." This fact, after all, should not surprise us, since the Proust of the later novel is older than the Proust of the earlier one. "Object-love" is constantly described by Freud as "more mature" than "narcissistic love."

This idea seems strengthened at first by the type of object that fascinates the narrator as well as the other characters in *Remembrance of Things Past*. Love objects always give an impression of "blissful autonomy" or "self-sufficiency." They correspond to Freud's idea of "intact narcissism." It is no longer the subject of desire that is narcissistic, as in the earlier novel, but its object. This sounds like a paradox, but if we turn back to *Narcissism* we will see that the same paradox is also present in Freud, and that it is a paradox of "anaclytic" or object-desire.

It seems very evident that one person's narcissism has a great attraction for those others who have renounced part of their own narcissism and are seeking after object-love; the charm of a child lies to a great extent in his narcissism, his self-sufficiency and inaccessibility, just as does the charm of certain animals which seem not to concern themselves about us, such as cats and the large beasts of prey. In literature, indeed, even the great criminal and the humorist compel our interest by the narcissistic self-importance with which they manage to keep at arm's length everything which would diminish the importance of their ego. It is as if we envied them their power of retaining a blissful state of mind—an unassailable libido-position which we ourselves have since abandoned. The great charm of the narcissistic woman has, however, its reverse side; a large part of the dissatisfaction of the lover, of his doubts of the woman's love, of his complaints of her enigmatic nature, have their root in this incongruity between the types of object-choice.[3]

If we go to the great descriptions of desire in *Remembrance of Things Past*, Proust is going to look even more "mature" and Freud even more astute than the one and the other did up to this point. Down to almost every detail, it seems, everything corresponds to that "great attraction" that "one person's narcissism" exerts upon those "who have renounced part of their own narcissism and are seeking after object-love."

Let us turn to a famous passage in *Within a Budding Grove*: the first encounter by Marcel, the narrator, with a group of girls he calls *la petite bande*. The scene is in the resort town of Balbec-Cabourg—in Normandy. Marcel's attention becomes immediately attracted by the adolescents, because of the tightly knit appearance they give and their contemptuous indifference toward anyone but each other.

Though they were now separately identifiable, still the mutual response which they gave one another with eyes animated by self-sufficiency and the spirit of comradeship, in which were kindled at every moment now the interest now the insolent indifference with which each of them sparkled according as her glance fell on one of her friends or on passing strangers, that consciousness, moreover, of knowing one another intimately enough always to go about together, by making them a "band apart" established between their independent and separate bodies, as slowly they advanced, a single atmosphere making of them a whole as homogenous in its parts as it was different from the crowd through which their procession gradually wound.

For an instant, as I passed the dark one with the fat cheeks who was wheeling a bicycle, I caught her smiling, sidelong glance, aimed from the center of that inhuman world which enclosed the life of his little tribe, an inaccessible, unknown world to which the idea of what I was could certainly never attain nor find a place in it.[4]

Words like "autonomy and "self-sufficiency" recur several times in the course of the description, which extends in the novel over ten pages. There is not one feature in one writer which does not have its counterpart in the other. The girls, of course, are neither "great criminals" nor "humorists," but their behavior verges, at times, on juvenile delinquency, and Marcel immediately assumes that they are not "virtuous." They must have many love affairs, he speculates, in which they always play the commanding role; they are never the ones who get hurt. He also supposes they must be of a sharply satirical mind, and he is afraid they would make fun of him if they noticed his existence, something he both terribly fears and desires.

At one point, one of the girls climbs on the bandstand in the shade of which an old banker is sitting and she jumps over him, frightening her senile victim, who is made more impotent still by the brief absence of his wife: she has left him to make him believe he can still manage by himself. Marcel, too, has been temporarily freed from the surveillance and protection of his grandmother, and he visibly identifies with the old man. Fear is an indispensable ingredient in his desire, which is greatly inflamed by such a mixture of youthful arrogance and innocent cruelty. He imagines the adolescents as the very antithesis of what he himself is: invulnerable to the vicissitudes of existence, just as invincible in everything they undertake as he feels vulnerable and ungainly, unsuccessful and sickly.

Throughout the description the accent lies on the youthful inhumanity of the tightly knit little group. Just as in the case of Freud, the beloved narcissist is compared to animals that are not only graceful and cruel, but above all completely indifferent to human beings. In Freud, the animals are "cats and large birds of prey." In Proust, they are seagulls, as befits an episode that takes place on a beach. The metaphor is more elaborate, but the significance remains exactly the same:

I saw coming towards me five or six young girls, as different in appearance and manner from all the people whom one was accustomed to see at Balbec as could have been, landed there none knew whence, a flight of gulls which performed with measured steps upon the sands—the dawdlers using their wings to overtake the rest—a movement the purpose of which seems as obscure to the human bathers, whom they do not appear to see, as it is clearly determined to their own birdish minds.[5]

The similarities between Proust and Freud are striking. And yet, a careful observer will note a difference which a little reflection will reveal to be crucial. Freud clearly implies that the people who have renounced part of their narcissism did so as a matter of choice, not because it is pleasurable, to be sure, but out of a sense of obligation. They have decided to become "mature" and "virile." They are the good people, in other words, they choose the path of duty.

With Proust, there is no such thing as a voluntary renunciation. "Blissful autonomy" and "self-sufficiency" are things the narrator never freely renounced, because they were not his to renounce in the first place. As far as he can remember, his lot has always been an "impoverishment" so extreme as to amount to complete destitution, too painful certainly to be freely assumed.

Of what possession does the narrator feel deprived? Of the "blissful autonomy," of course, that the desired *other* seems to possess. It is quite clear in the case of *la petite bande*. The narrator does not desire any of the girls in particular but all simultaneously, at least most of the time. The very coherence of the group, its "tightly knit" character, gives it the appearance of self-sufficiency that the narrator would like to appropriate, that awakens his desire, in other words.

What Freud calls "intact narcissism" is the main, even the sole object of desire in the novel of Proust. Since "intact narcissism" is defined as perfect self-sufficiency, and since self-sufficiency is what the subject of desire does not have and would like to have, there is nothing "incongruous" in the choice of "intact narcissism" as an object of desire.

With Proust, in other words, desire can be both self-oriented and other-oriented at the same time, because the main "business" of the impoverished or even nonexistent self is to acquire the richer self that it lacks, or, if you prefer, to become "self-sufficient" at the expense or after the pattern of the self it desires, a self that already is, or appears, "self-sufficient."

Nothing is more logical, therefore, than the superficially paradoxical conjunction of self-centeredness and other-centeredness. Freud does not perceive that logic, or he refuses it because he insists on viewing what he calls "object-desire" as a selfless gesture, a deliberate and virtuous sacrifice of "self-sufficiency" rather than a fascination for an alien "self-sufficiency" forced upon us by a state of severe and involuntary deprivation in which human beings might generally find themselves in regard to that commodity. And yet, the possibility of that solution cannot be far from his mind, since he observes "the great attraction" that "one person's narcissism has . . . for those others who have renounced . . . " etc. The Proustian solution is almost visible, and yet Freud must not really see it, because, if he saw it, he could not view the "great attraction" as an incongruity.

Could it be that Proustian desire is really "narcissistic" in Freudian terms, in other words that it focuses on objects "too similar" to the subject, too much like mirror images to deserve the badge of "true object-love." The following lines certainly do not support this narcissistic hypothesis:

The fact that we had, these girls and I, not one habit—as we had not one idea—in common, was to make it more difficult for me to make friends with them and to please them. But perhaps, also, it was thanks to those differences, to my consciousness that there did not enter into the composition of the nature and actions of these girls a single element that I knew or possessed, that there came in place of my satiety a thirst—like that with which a dry land burns—for a life which my soul, because it had never until now received one drop of it, would absorb all the more greedily in long draughts with a more perfect imbibition.[6]

This desire has nothing to do with the so-called narcissistic desire of Freud, since it is not resemblance but an absolute difference that it seeks. And this absolute difference is the same thing, in the last analysis, as the self-sufficiency the other always seems to possess and the Ego never possesses. This grim vision of desire is as far from narcissism à la Freud as from the reassuring clichés of literary and philosophical individualism in the nineteenth and twentieth century, and yet, I repeat, Proust tends to revert to these clichés and, as a result, to something very much like "narcissism," when he speaks about desire in the abstract.

There is another difference between Proust and Freud that we have not yet observed. In Proust, the "blissful autonomy" and the "self-sufficiency" of the desired object are not real. They are never experienced by anybody. They are a mirage of desire, which confers them wrongly upon the desired object.

Not long after his first encounter with *la petite bande*, Marcel becomes acquainted with the girls and their superhuman prestige evaporates. They no longer look like the superbly indifferent demigods he first imagined. Not even Albertine. If his infatuation with this one girl becomes lasting and obsessive, the reason lies in her presumptive unfaithfulness. A treacherous Albertine is crowned once more with the halo of inaccessible independence that, at the outset, radiated from the entire group. Marcel's thirst for the mirage of *being* reawakens. He becomes indifferent again if he can persuade himself that Albertine is loyal. Unfortunately, there are always new or old reasons to suspect foul play, and whenever one of these turns up, painful desire is resurrected, even though there is no more faith in the "blissful autonomy" and "self-sufficiency" of Albertine. In other words, there is no such thing as a "real," objective narcissism for Proust. Narcissism, especially intact narcissism, is a projection of desire. No one can really be a self-conscious narcissist, a narcissist for himself.

To say that no one is a narcissist for oneself and that everyone wants to be one, is to say that the self does not exist in the substantial sense that Freud gives to that term in *Narcissism*. But everybody is trying to acquire such a substantial self; everybody believes, more or less as Freud does, in the existence of the substantial self.

If the substantial self does not really exist, how can everybody believe in its existence? We already know the Proustian answer to that question. Everybody believes that someone else possesses the self he wants to acquire. That is why everybody experiences desire.

Snobbery in Proust operates exactly like erotic desire; as a matter of fact it can hardly be distinguished from it. A salon can become desirable only if it appears blissfully self-sufficient. And it will so appear only if it is sufficiently *exclusive*, if it excludes enough potential candidates whose very eagerness is interpreted as unworthiness. A salon is like a collective self, at least for the outsiders who desire to appropriate that self. It would be wrong, however, to conclude that the self is a purely subjective illusion. It is an illusion in which everybody, ultimately, collaborates and shares. Since even desire seeks self-sufficiency, no one really possesses it, and an open display of desire amounts to a confession of non-being. Such an admission of failure places the imprudent and candid person making it in a position of inferiority. He finds himself unable to attract other people's desires, exposed to their contemptuous indifference, and, as a result, vulnerable to their own power of attraction.

Desire in the Proustian world is a one-way street that runs not from an objectively poorer to an objectively richer self, but from whichever self, having first betrayed its own fundamental nothingness, enables the other self to maintain his show of indifference a little longer, and the show, as a result, will become a reality in regard to that first self.

Almost any encounter, therefore, presents itself as a kind of antagonistic parade. When people like Charles meet other people like themselves they look a little like two male birds displaying their feathers trying to look as impressively attractive as possible; each wants to awaken in the other the painful desire which as a result he himself will he spared.

It would be wrong to believe that the deceivers at this game are sharply separated from the deceived, that the world is neatly divided between the cold calculators and the innocent dupes. Everybody is a little of both; you must be a dupe of your own comedy to play it with conviction. The romantic and satanic vision of the cold calculator, of the totally lucid manipulator of other people's desires, is a more sophisticated version of the narcissistic illusion.

The preceding remarks place us in a position to give a Proustian reading of the road traveled by Proust from *Jean Santeuil* to *Remembrance of Things Past*. In the first novel, we recall, the hero seems to possess the "blissful autonomy" that would make him a narcissist in the eyes of Freud. This hero manages to see himself much of the time as if he had already reached the goal of his desire, as if the beautiful self-sufficiency toward which he aspires were already achieved.

This hero is also a successful rendition of the various models that were popular at the time. *Jean Santeuil* is much more of a period piece than *Remembrance of Things Past*. The historical interest it arouses, as well as its apparently healthy and well-adjusted hero, made it quite popular when it was first published in the fifties. Some critics have suggested that it might be the better of the two novels written by Proust. This view, however, did not prevail. The earlier novel fails miserably, much of the time, in the area where the second most strikingly succeeds—the description of desire. *Jean Santeuil* simply does not convey the subjective experience of desire.

The reason for this failure obviously lies with the self-sufficiency of the hero. Wherever there is self-sufficiency, there is no desire; the notion of a narcissistic or self-sufficient desire is a contradiction in terms. The weakness of *Jean Santeuil* in regard to the evocation of desire suggests that the only conception of desire that really works, aesthetically, is the opposite one, the one that underlies *Remembrance of Things Past*.

Does it mean that the author of *Jean Santeuil* was unacquainted with the type of desire that the later Proust so successfully portrays?

If we adopt the conception of the later Proust, we will realize that the reverse must be true; it means that the author was still too much under the grip of his desire, even when he wrote his novel, to abandon the half-strategic, half-sincere pose of self-sufficiency demanded by that desire. He had to represent himself "on top" of every situation, already enjoying the commanding position that we always feel we are about to acquire through the success of our desires, but that in reality belongs only to the desired object.

Thus, in the case of *Jean Santeuil*, narcissism appears like a valid concept only because the novel is false, because it is a strategic extension of desire, a mere reflection rather than a revelation of that desire.

In both novels there is a great theater scene in which the main focus of interest is not the stage but the box in which the aristocrats and other prestigious people are seated. The two scenes are similar enough to be recognized as one and the same, and yet they are strikingly different. The difference will make my point clear.

In *Jean Santeuil*, the hero, Jean, is with the "beautiful people" inside the box; he is the center of flattering attention, an ex- but still very famous king helps him straighten his necktie; all the ladies crowd admiringly around him just as in a television advertisement for an aftershave lotion. In *Remembrance of Things Past*, the narrator is outside the box, looking at the Duchess of Guermantes with desperate desire, feeling a thousand light years away from the divinity. The enclosure of the box symbolizes an autonomy and self-sufficiency that now belong exclusively to the object of desire, insofar as that object remains inaccessible. The difference between the novel that does and the novel that does not represent desire convincingly becomes manifest in these two perspectives. To regard it as a difference in narrative technique only, as most critics would now do, is to miss the point entirely. In the great novel, the novelist places his narrator, that is, himself, in the position of the rejected outsider; he assumes humiliation and exclusion; this is what the author of *Jean Santeuil* is unable to do; the truth hurts too much to be faced.

What we have in *Jean Santeuil* is only one of the countless manners, of course, in which the mediocre writer can escape the knowledge of his own desire, the practical knowledge that Proust achieves only later and that nourishes the greatness not only of *Remembrance of Things Past* but also of the few literary works that can be called its equals in regard to the description of desire.

Thus, the inferiority of *Jean Santeuil* relative to *Remembrance of Things Past* is revealed as an inability of its author to realize that the "blissful autonomy" exists nowhere, not even in the desired object. What prevents the first Proust from reaching its own genius is very close if not identical to the belief of Freud in something he calls "intact narcissism."

This suggests that, from the perspective of the last Proust, the critique of *Jean Santeuil* should extend to *Narcissism*. If we go back to the passage quoted above, we will see that it calls for some kind of analysis. There is something defensive and self-righteous about it. Freud obviously counts himself among the high-minded people who have "renounced part of their narcissism" in order to "seek after object-love." This renunciation was necessary, we are given to understand, to make the invention of psychoanalysis possible. It had to be performed for the benefit of all mankind, but there was nothing pleasurable about it.

Freud must be one of these people, therefore, who feel an attraction for the "intact narcissism" of the coquette. He speaks of this attraction as an "incongruity," something a little odd, no doubt, which he is too observant to pass up, but which is not important enough to deserve a full investigation. He does not say why this attraction should occur, except perhaps for the striking sentence: "It is as if we envied . . . "

This envy is presented as something that cannot be real, because Freud's renunciation of the narcissistic position is deliberate. The question is: how does one go about freely renouncing the unassailable libido position of narcissism? Freud does not say. If the renunciation were not deliberate, if the lack of "blissful autonomy" were the major predicament of the psyche, the same terrible ordeal that it is in Proust, we would understand that desire must be a perpetual effort on our part to escape from that predicament, and we would not find "incongruous" at all the choice of objects that seem to enjoy that blissful state of being. We would understand with Proust that it is the universal law of desire.

The dutiful man who freely renounces narcissism is a mask. The blissfully decorous playboy of *Jean Santeuil* is also a mask. The two masks are different. The man who passionately embraces narcissism is not the man who virtuously rejects it, but the difference is not so important as it always seems, since the narcissism embraced in one case and renounced in the other does not really exist. The Freud who invents narcissism as something of which he himself is deprived reaches deeper into the essential *abjection* of desire than the Proust who was still a *mondain*, but not as deep, I am afraid, as the Proust who had renounced his *mondanité*—and is not the same thing at all as renouncing a narcissism that never was ours in the first place for us to renounce. Freud, it seems, never gave up his belief in the narcissism of others, in an objective narcissism that the naughty and seductive people who do not heed the voice of duty must tremendously enjoy.

Behind the seething puritanism of our passage, a desire analogous to the desire generated in the narrator by the first encounter of *la petite bande* cannot fail to be at work. And the concept of narcissism is a projection of that desire. The "blissful self-sufficiency" of *intact narcissism* is perceived by Freud not as his own experience, no doubt, but as the real experience of other people: flighty women, bohemian artists, and so on. Whereas the narrator understands after a while that the self-sufficiency of *la petite bande* is the same old mirage of desire that a prolonged acquaintance will dispel, Freud is really taken in, and the mythical nature of the object to which he feels so greatly attracted remains hidden from him. The result of that continued delusion is *narcissism*, a theoretical construct for which psychoanalysis claims scientific status but which is really mythical. I personally believe that the descriptions of desire in *Remembrance of Things Past* and a few other literary works amount to a critique of narcissism which is really decisive and much more "scientific" than anything psychoanalysis has to offer on the same and related topics. It is unfortunate, to be sure, that this critique remains implicit and that the writers who achieve it regress to conceptions more literary but really equivalent to the theory of narcissism when they try to become their own theoreticians. That is the reason why we must not remain content with their theoretical pronouncements on the matter, and why we must go to the real substance of their work.

The reader will perhaps object that the juxtaposition of self- and other-centeredness that we find in Proust is not only possible with Freud, but that it is also the rule, since no one can be one hundred percent narcissistic and addicted to self-love, or altruistic and addicted to object-love. Even the "normal" personality must retain a certain amount of narcissism. Thus, there will be a certain amount of infantile narcissism even in the man who successfully graduates to object-love and vice versa.

This is true, indeed, but Freud nevertheless ends up with something quite different from Proust, because his models remain mechanistic. The libidinal energy can be allocated in different proportions between the self and the other, but it remains a fixed quantity; as a result, you cannot increase the share of the one without diminishing the share of the other and vice versa. This conception leaves no room for the fundamental paradox of human desire, which is, I repeat, that the more morbidly self-centered an individual becomes, the more morbidly other-centered he also becomes.

The substantial self and the quantitative conception of the libido are great obstacles to the understanding of desire. They turn it into meaningless paradoxes and therefore compel us to disregard aspects which the Proustian conception makes perfectly intelligible. The deficiencies of Freud's models are widely suspected; what is not realized, however, is that the choice of such models must be forced upon Proust by his continued belief in the reality of *self*-sufficiency, which is really the same as his belief in a substantial self. On the whole, these various beliefs function like the primitive conception of *mana*, or sacred energy. The substantial self is crystallized *mana*. That is why any discharge of libidinal energy that is really "spent" outside and does not return to the self, as in the circular pattern of narcissism, constitutes for that self a material "impoverishment."

We have exactly the same thing in many Polynesian religions. If you spend too much of your *mana* you may exhaust your supply. In such a system, the person with an "intact narcissism" is the one who, for some reason or other, manages to hoard the stuff of which the gods are made in greater quantities than anyone else. No wonder he appears more desirable than anyone else. He is more like a god than anyone else. That is why the man with an "impoverished narcissism," as Freud says, would like very much to be among them, to be one of them, but he feels they are too divine not to be inaccessible. The divinity of the primitive god is the same thing as the "blissful self-sufficiency" of Freudian narcissism or the *schöne Totalität* of German idealism:

. . . the supposition that I might some day be the friend of one or other of these girls, that their eyes, whose incomprehensible gaze struck me now and again, playing upon me unawares, like the play of sunlight upon a wall, might ever, by a miraculous alchemy, allow to interpenetrate among their ineffable particles the idea of my existence, some affection for my person, that I myself might some day take my place among them in the evolution of their course by the seas edge—that supposition appeared to me to contain within it a contradiction as insoluble as if, standing before some classical frieze or a fresco representing a procession I had believed it possible for me, the spectator, to take my place, beloved of them, among the godlike hierophants.[7]

Behind its scientific appearances, the energetic model of Freud really means exactly the same thing as the literary metaphors. The only difference is that the novelist does not believe his metaphors; they reveal a process of transfiguration akin to the primitive sacred and understood as such by the novelist, whereas it remains hidden in *Narcissism* behind the myth of a truly self-sufficient narcissism.

Freud is obviously a greater poet and Proust a greater analyst of desire than the "specialists" in the respective fields of poetry and analysis have ever realized. The most characteristic aspect of a "poetic" talent is that it reaches farther and deeper with such devices as metaphors and other figures of speech than with conceptual thought. Proust is certainly closer than Freud, here, to the conceptual truth of his own metaphors. The metaphors are really the same in both writers, and they often murmur, in the text of Freud, the truth that Proust certainly makes explicit, at least up to a point, the truth or rather the untruth of narcissism, the impossibility of a self-conscious narcissism that would remain "blissfully autonomous."

All the living creatures Freud associates with "intact narcissism," small infants and animals, are deprived of a full human consciousness. These metaphors really suggest between narcissism and human consciousness an incompatibility amounting to an impossibility.

If narcissism reflects a desire still too intense to acknowledge its own projections, the popularity of this theoretical concept in modern psychology, sociology, and literary criticism should not surprise us. Freud himself says that only mystified concepts that buttress the illusions of our desires are readily acceptable to vast throngs of people.

It is not the ineffable nature of the work of art that makes narcissism useless as a critical tool; it is its mythical nature. How could the concept of narcissism help us understand *Remembrance of Things Past,* since the level of understanding that generates the concept is lower than the best passages in the novel?

The modern mind is easily seduced by the prestige of terms that sound technical. Even with those readers who know both Proust and Freud and whose mind is not prejudiced against literature, the scales will remain weighted in favor of Freud. He, alone, provides us with the labels around which our incipient and still formless intuitions can crystallize. As soon as the word "narcissism" comes to our mind, we perceive that it corresponds to certain elements that are really present in the text of the novel, and we almost inevitably feel that the right solution has been reached. How could Freud be wrong about narcissism since we, ourselves, can diagnose narcissistic aspects in the text of Proust?

In reality, the concept of narcissism acts as an obstacle, it arrests our thinking at the point where Freud arrested his; it confirms our natural tendency, the tendency of all desire to consider "self-centeredness" and "other-centeredness" as separate poles that can become dominant in separate individuals. Our intuition will remain not only incomplete and partial, but grossly misleading. The superiority of the great novelist, which lies in the perfect identity of self-centeredness and other-centeredness, will remain invisible, or it will be perceived only as the "paradoxical" but ultimately unimportant and "rhetorical" nature of literary talent.

Freud claims somewhere—and he is right—that he was the first to attempt a systematic investigation of relationships that, before him, were the monopoly of creative writers. Thus, we cannot exclude *a priori* the possibility that some writers did at least as well or even better than Freud. To consider this a possibility has nothing to do with the mystical cult of literature per se or with a blind rejection of psychoanalysis. It does not mean that Freud was not a great man. As we said earlier, Proust tends to regress to a lower level of intuition, much lower than Freud, as soon as he tries to become his own theoretician.

Strangely enough, the literary critics do not seem very interested in the possibility I am trying to explore. A little reflection will show that this lack of interest is almost inevitable. The literary critics, since Freud, have either been Freudian or against Freud. If they are Freudian, they will never place the literary text on the same level with that of Freud. Even the most sophisticated among them, the ones who now carefully refrain from practicing a *psychoanalyse sauvage* of literary texts, have not yet reached the point where they could regard those texts as a possible source of theoretical insights.

If the critics are against Freud, they perceive the failure of psychoanalysis in its literary applications, but they usually ascribe it to some divine or inane *littérarité* that would lie beyond the more or less "sordid truths" exhibited by their Freudian colleagues. In practical terms, it really means that they have tacitly surrendered the theme of desire, in literary texts, to their adversaries. For years, they have tried to convince themselves that the area of common interest between Proust and Freud is of little or no relevance to their pure essence of literature, and they have now succeeded. Most critics of Proust will embrace any topic and work it literally to death rather than even allude to the one subject that occupies Proust most of the time: desire. The dresses of Mme de Guermantes, the texture of Albertine's skin, the Platonic essence of the hawthorne bud, pure consciousness, the "undecidable" nature of the sign, the frequency of the imperfect subjunctive, the divorce between words and things—anything will do as long as they can get away from that implacable and rigorous mechanic of desire that remains at all times the principal affair of the novelist.

All the other topics are interesting, of course, but their real significance is subordinated to desire and can be understood only in its context. It is not the "ineffable" or, at the opposite end, the purely "rhetorical" nature of the work of art that makes narcissism useless as a critical tool; it is the faulty and misleading nature of the concept. The bluntness of this one-sided instrument ratifies our natural propensity to cancel out the genius we do not possess, the paradoxical understanding that shocks our own desire.

An unwritten law divides all texts in two categories, the ones that do the interpreting and the ones that are there mostly to be interpreted, like *Remembrance of Things Past.* Our great critical revolutions have not yet succeeded in overturning that law, or even in questioning it seriously, probably because our identity as literary critics depends on its perpetuation.

Far from questioning that ultimate taboo that justifies our professional existence, our most recent critical fads and fashions have emphasized the alleged specificity of literary language, its difference with the language of "real" knowledge.

I personally feel that the language of both literature and the social sciences tends to become more specific as it becomes mediocre. Weak creative writers no less than weak researchers must resort to visible signs of "specificity" as they become less and less sure of their own competence within their own chosen field of endeavor. In other words: the less we have to say, the more jargon we tend to use.

This is not the case with such writers as Proust and Freud. The text of *Narcissism* shows that Freud is no less literary than Proust, and Proust is certainly no less psychoanalytical than Freud. There is a difference, however: Proust did not coin the specialized vocabulary that would have been out of place in a "novel," and Freud did not resort, most of the time, to the sort of transposition that frees the novelist from the constraints of straight autobiography.

Between the institutions and limitations of psychoanalytical theory, on the one hand, and of great literature on the other, there is a gap that we must bridge. Literature and psychoanalysis in the best sense need *each other*. My intention is not to build up Proust against Freud, or even less "literature" against "psychoanalysis," but to facilitate a dialogue between the two, a dialogue of equals that has never occurred so far, and through the fault of literary critics, really, as much as psychoanalysts. Most critics do not have enough confidence even in the greatest literary texts to hear the theoretical voice behind them and to make it explicit.

The relationship between texts, the role of active interpreters or passive "interpretees" which they must play in regard to each other, should be decided on the basis not of some *a priori* decision that labels the one "theoretical" and the other "literary," but of that dialogue of equals I have just mentioned; only a fair encounter will reveal the relative power of each text in regard to the other.

It seems to me that a fair enough encounter between *Narcissism* and *Remembrance of Things Past* must reveal that the whole theory of narcissism is one of the most questionable points in psychoanalysis. We were irresistibly drawn, I believe, to adopt the vision of the last Proust, if not his theoretical views. This vision alone makes the itinerary of the writer intelligible, from the relative mediocrity of the first novel to the genius of the second. A writer's career can be an intellectual experience of major dimensions, a genuine conquest of the mind to which even the most sympathetic Freudian readings remain invariably blind.

We found that this Proustian vision gives, to one text of Freud at least, the same privileged access that psychoanalysis promises in the case of the literary work but fails to deliver. Thus, after countless Freudian readings of Proust, we can propose, for a change, a Proustian reading Freud. The idea at first sounds whimsical, but it can be shown, I believe, that *Remembrance of Things Past* is not the only literary work that provides the basis for a critique of narcissism. Comparable results could be obtained with the work of Cervantes, Shakespeare, Dostoevsky, and also Virginia Woolf, to name one other novelist among the contemporaries of both Freud and Proust.

We have no time for these works, but Proust is more than enough, I trust, to show the ease with which a great writer can see through defense mechanisms still visibly at work behind the slightly sanctimonious tone of the man who, curiously enough, discovered defense mechanisms in the first place.

Quite reminiscent of our *Narcissism* passage is the attitude of Swann toward the "cocotte" Odette de Crécy, his constant rationalization of jealousy as a "mature commitment to object-love." Swann is one of those people who can be surprised to see the nicest human beings fall in love with the most disreputable characters. Like Freud, he finds his own irresistible attraction to Odette an inexplicable "incongruity." And he does not investigate the matter too searchingly. He is too well bred for such a course, too genteel, and secretly afraid, perhaps, of what he might discover.

The irony of Proust is evident in all this, as well as in the exclamation that concludes the volume on *Swann in Love*, the magnificent *cri du coeur* of the man who remains deluded to the end and still defines the love-object in terms of a narcissism quite alien, he feels, to his temperament and even to his erotic inclinations: "To think that I have wasted years of my life, that I have longed for death, that the greatest love I have ever known has been for a woman I did not really like, who was not in my style!" (*une femme qui ne me plaisait pas, qui n'était pas mon genre!*).[8]

As a fictional personality, Swann is quite remote from Freud, of course, and from the flavor that gives our text on *Narcissism* its charm as literature, a rather Herr-Professorish charm in a slightly *Blue Angel* sort of way. We are not dealing, therefore, with mere character similarities. What Proust derides, with gentle humor, is an extremely widespread delusion, the same, evidently to which the mythical psychic entity known as *narcissism* owes both its existence and its persistent popularity.

# Theory and Its Terrors[1] [1989]

Writing about literary criticism is not something I do very often. It is difficult not to offend some people when you speak about criticism. In a short text, I cannot mention every trend, and I may well offend the trends I will mention even more than the trends I will not. It is impossible not to be a little polemical on such a subject. Let me be polemical right from the start and proclaim that I am polemical openly and explicitly, instead of deviously and underhandedly, as is often the fashion nowadays.

You should take what I say with a grain of salt. I am not really as one-sided as I will seem, but to make at least a few points one must inevitably be a little schematic and one-sided. Everything I say can also be turned against me, and you are welcome to play the game if you enjoy it.

Most of us here belong to departments of modern literature. We take the existence of these departments for granted, but in the life of universities they do not go back very far; they are relatively recent creations.

The Middle Ages had nothing of the sort. As in the ancient world, rhetoric was taught, but not "literature" as we understand it. Fiction was generally regarded as mediocre escapism, and it shared in the general contempt of the learned for whatever was written in the vulgar dialects, the forerunner of the national European languages. The only language of culture was Latin. At the time of the Renaissance, interest in classical culture became intense. The humanists studied and edited Greek and Roman texts. Greek and Latin literature became a legitimate object of study.

This was not true of "literature" in our sense. It was too lively and productive to become an academic subject. It was left to the creative writers themselves and to their readers. Departments of literature were created rather late in the nineteenth century, at a time when the study of ancient culture was on the decline. As the role of Greek and Latin shrank in the education of gentlemen, the role of the modern national literatures increased. Another factor was Romanticism and the rise of European nationalism. In each country, the national literature became a national heritage, the preservation and cultivation of which was entrusted to the professors of literature, just as the aesthetic heritage was entrusted to museum curators.

With nationalism on the rise, history, and especially the national history of each country, became the dominant discipline of the humanities, and literary studies were first conceived as adjuncts to the study of that national history. Until World War II, the professors of literature who dedicated their careers either to critical editions or to literary history were in the majority. "Criticism" or "literary interpretation" in our sense did not exist.

The literary historians and the authors of critical editions were greatly influenced by the positivistic and scientistic temper of the time. They came under the sway of the greatest cultural force of the modern centuries, which is the secularization of intelligence, the decline of religion.

The force that was supposed to displace religion was science, and whatever passed for science at any given moment was embraced with blind passion. The historians of literature fancied themselves scientists dispelling the myths of sacred origins. The sun of objective knowledge was dissolving the fogs of an obscurantist past, replacing poetic legends and transcendental nonsense with the hard facts of the national and bourgeois struggle for a place in the sun.

In the early twentieth century, these positivistic professors of literature remained impervious to the living literature of the time, which was turning against positivism. As early as Romanticism, of course, artists and writers had felt uncomfortable with scientism. The early manifestations of the modern industrial and bureaucratic society were uncongenial to most "intellectuals."

To those whose aspirations were not satisfied by the matter-of-fact world in which they lived, the teaching of literature in universities appeared to be a kind of haven. Inevitably, a more romantic, intuitive, and irrational trend began to challenge the ascendancy of scientistic ideology in literary studies. It was the same evolution as in the literary world itself, with naturalism giving way to symbolism and its sequels, but in the universities it occurred later because of the institutional entrenchment of the positivistic ideology. The organization of academic studies, and the small number of chairs, turned universities into well-defended fortresses against the forces of change.

And yet, in the end, the myth of literary history as a science of literature failed. One reason, of course, was the ambiguous nature of the beast. One cannot talk about literature without becoming at least minimally involved with literary interpretation in the wider sense. One cannot discuss a novel or a play without touching upon the "psychology" of the characters. One cannot present Balzac or Dickens and say nothing of their views of modern society or of the relationships between rich and poor in nineteenth-century Europe. One cannot be a literary historian, in other words, without being a little bit of everything. And this is what a good literary historian really is—an interdisciplinary scholar *avant la lettre*.

The notion of literary history as a well-circumscribed field is an illusion that did not have to be denounced to affect its practitioners negatively and undermine their rather naïve conception of literary studies.

At the time when literary history triumphed, the social sciences were in a dynamic and expansive mood. They, too, were "positivistic" in the old sense and genuinely convinced that they could elaborate truly scientific ways of accounting for man and his various activities.

Even if they wanted to, literary people would have been unable to criticize this illusion, and most literary historians did not want to. They shared the scientistic optimism of their colleagues in the social sciences.

As a result, they felt more and more amateurish and impressionistic. They did not possess the formal training needed to turn them into the professional psychologists, sociologists, and anthropologists that they should have been to speak competently about the various themes of many literary works.

Thus, students of literature were increasingly ill at ease when discussing the content of literary works. They began to wonder whether their discipline could do more than provide useful but peripheral information about literature, supplemented with some amiable chatter about its content.

If professional psychologists alone are competent to deal with the psychological aspects of literature, professional sociologists with the sociological aspects, anthropologists with the mythical or ritual aspects, and so on, the specialist of literature is left empty-handed.

Everything that had anything to do with the *content* of literature came to be regarded with suspicion by literary people, who felt uncomfortable with it—and even with the dreams of a writer, since there was a Sigmund Freud by that time to claim that he had turned our dreams into a genuine science.

The scientific aspirations of literary studies were undermined not only by the growing influence of the neo-romantics but by the field's own conceptual weakness, by its inability to define an object that would be unambiguously its own.

As a result, there was a good deal of pressure, from the early twentieth century on, for literary studies to discover its own specificity. To be protected against the encroachment of imperialistic disciplines that were not literary, literary studies needed to define some pure essence of literature, something that would justify its existence as an autonomous academic enterprise.

This pressure was intense in Russia after the revolution, when one could still hope to protect intellectual life from simplistic Marxism through intellectual means, and this resulted in Russian formalism.

Pressure was felt in America, too, especially after World War II, when the prestige of science was at its peak and departmental organization generated a competition for funds between the social sciences and the humanities.

The most precious aspect of literature, the one most worthy of being studied, had to be whatever is left of a work of art when it has been emptied of its content. At this point, it was natural for literary studies to rediscover the old opposition of form and content, which seemed the perfect vehicle for hard-pressed literary critics in their effort to find something in the literary work that no one could steal from them.

The avant-garde of the time proclaimed that the real purpose of literary studies was the examination of form. Content was declared more or less irrelevant and rather lowly stuff anyway, dreadfully unpoetical and materialistic, and worthy only of the social scientists who made it their business to soil their hands with it.

The beauty of a work was in its form exclusively. Form was exalted in terms reminiscent of the plastic arts or of shipbuilding. The great drawback, except in the case of poems that exhibited the same formalistic and idealistic bias held by critics themselves, was that this celebration of form was not conducive to concrete emphasis on the work itself, which was supposed to be the goal of the whole enterprise.

Formalistic studies were becoming more and more unsubstantial. This background is necessary to understand why the new European methodologies of structuralism and deconstruction as represented by such figures as Barthes, Lévi-Strauss, Foucault, and Derrida were so successful in this country. The emphasis was on structural linguistics in the Saussurian and Jakobsonian manner. For both Ferdinand de Saussure and Roman Jakobson, language is a system of diacritical signs that signify in opposition to one another, rather than in immediate and unchangeable relationship to the things they signify.

Saussurian linguistics became a means to confirm and reinforce the expulsion of "content." The "signifier" corresponds to "form," the hierarchically inferior "signified" becomes the new word for "content," and the despised "referent" the new word for reality.

More than ever, the humanities were eager to declare their independence from the mundane university, which was busy with the "real world." At the same time, structural linguistics was privileged because one part of it, phonemics, was built on a finite set of variables, unlike the older social sciences, which used ordinary language. Was it legitimate for the literary "applications" of structuralism to claim a scientific status on this basis? No one believes this anymore, but for a time many people did.

Structuralism seemed able to reconcile the scientific impulse, on the one hand, and the romantic feeling of a literary transcendence, on the other. This was a very powerful and potent combination, which explains the fascination that structuralism and even post-structuralism have exerted on literary studies.

Structuralism was developed in the context of the social sciences, but it was successful primarily in literary and philosophical circles. This movement has enabled literary circles to conduct a kind of counter-at-tack against the imperialism of the social sciences. The precise form of this counterattack came from the fact that the social sciences use ordinary lan-guage in a non-critical way. At the beginning of the twentieth century, a French writer named Paul Valéry was already suggesting that the social sci-ences are little more than mediocre literature, meaning fiction. They are a form of literature unaware that it consists of language. The good thing about creative writers is their awareness of language. They know that lan-guage is treacherous, and they deliberately use rhetorical means to achieve certain effects. Social scientists are doing the same thing but with no real awareness of it—a dreadful *esprit de sérieux.* They have a naïve faith in facts, as if they could reach the facts directly, whereas in reality they reach only their own words. They mistake words for things, and this is the real meaning of the title of Michel Foucault's *Les mots et les choses.*[2]

The movement was launched in earnest by Claude Lévi-Strauss, who was the first social scientist to criticize the social sciences of his time from the point of view of their language. But Lévi-Strauss immediately turned around and tried to establish structural linguistics as the model for a new type of social science, structural anthropology. In my opinion, this attempt has completely failed. Post-structuralism continued to rely on structural linguistics to discredit the referentiality of all texts.

In his most characteristic works, Jacques Derrida joins Lévi-Strauss and Foucault in insisting that we can and must undermine all philosophi-cal systems, all philosophical texts, with the help of structural linguistics. But he goes on to argue that the reverse is also true: we must undermine any scheme that would base itself on structural linguistics, with the help of philosophical language and philosophical texts. The truth is that there is no truth in any text, except perhaps for the truth of an absence of truth, and even that is not quite certain. Even the most prudently acrobatic and Derridian uses of language remain prisoners of the fundamental concep-tual illusion of Western metaphysics—namely, our instinctive trust in the substantiality and stability of language. This instinctive trust in language is characteristic of a younger culture whose faith in reality is inseparable from its faith in itself. In contrast, deconstruction and its attitudes are the prod-uct of an aging and terribly disenchanted culture. Deconstruction tries to show that, if handled correctly, any system of thought will ultimately self-destruct.

True or false, this bleak nihilism appeals to people who feel that they are at the bottom of the ladder, on the last rung, and that if the ladder itself collapses everybody on it will fall down, they have nothing to lose. But literature will come out on top because, at its best, it does not take itself seriously. Literature is aware that it turns language into play, instead of being the involuntary plaything of a language in which it believes. Deconstruction is a weapon turned against the idea of truth.

Deconstruction originates in a spirit of mimetic rivalry with the social sciences. This spirit always turns the rivals into identical twins, and this paradoxical effect can be observed in our present situation. Even though the social sciences and deconstruction are poles apart philosophically, their ultimate impact on intellectual life and on the academic world is strikingly similar. This, I think, is one of the most curious consequences of the present situation.

Blind faith in deconstructive methodologies and the extreme seriousness with which they are taken in the United States have resulted in the neglect of our great cultural tradition in favor of the latest research. Too much respect for the latest research is dangerous, because statistically there are not that many geniuses at any given moment in the history of any culture, and a bit of sifting is needed to separate the wheat from the chaff. The social sciences believe, or pretend to believe, that the latest research is necessarily superior to what came before simply because it comes later. So do the media. They all believe that knowledge is progressive and cumulative. This belief is extremely convenient. Even if we are not very good ourselves, we enjoy all the benefits of past research, plus the benefits of our own. We may be dwarfs, but we stand on the shoulders of giants, and ultimately we are greater than these giants. This is a dangerously complacent illusion. If such things as experience, personal insight, talent, and hard knocks are important in our ability to acquire any kind of knowledge, especially in human affairs, this belief in progress is disastrous for the transmission of the highest culture. It never considers the possibility that the most recent research might turn out to be no more than the ephemeral product of fad and fashion—cultural garbage that, fifty years later, no one will read. Yet experience shows us that this has already happened to a large extent, and it is probable that it will happen again in the future.

Radical theory and deconstructive theory do not believe in cumulative knowledge. They criticize this myth, sometimes too harshly, because in certain areas there really is such a thing as cumulative knowledge. According to a strange paradox, however, they end up behaving in exactly the same way as the social sciences. Knowledge is not cumulative, but deconstruction and its projected disintegration of Western illusions are, at least up to a point. Deconstruction is a long and arduous task that demands the allegiance of many workers. Deconstructionists do not believe in progress in the old sense, but they believe in progress in the battle against Western metaphysics, and their concrete position is a mirror image of the belief in progress. Every ten years or so, we have a new batch of deconstructive literature that claims to render the previous batch outmoded. The latest research is supposed to be so much more radical and so much more revolutionary than the previous research that it is completely unnecessary to read the old fogies. If one wanted to be really polemical, one could say that faith in the progress of knowledge has been replaced by faith in the progress of ignorance. Let us hope that this second faith will prove to be as unfounded as the first one was.

Deconstruction is to the false knowledge it deconstructs a little like the antimatter of the physicist in its relationship to matter: they behave in exactly the same way, so that it is difficult to distinguish one from the other. A century ago, the belief in cumulative and progressive knowledge destroyed the role that Greek and Latin culture had long played in our education. Today, the belief in an anti-progress is destroying the role that modern and classical literature played in our education only a few years ago. This, however, may be too pessimistic a view. I exaggerate to make my point clear. It must be observed, in all fairness, that the original leaders of the movement try to react against the anti-intellectual consequences of some of their doctrines. They insist that, even though philosophical discourse possesses an inherently illogical foundation, it must be studied because it is the strongest discourse available and cannot be dispensed with.

With many epigones, however, no such precautions are taken. I recall, for instance, an incident a few years ago at a great East Coast university that had become a kind of revolving door for the fiercest theorists of all stripes. When I was teaching there, the students were in a state of almost catatonic apathy, which was briefly interrupted by fits of frenzied activity. They felt that they were under permanent attack, that there were plots against deconstruction as a whole, and that both the rest of the university and many deconstructionists as well were their enemies. They were divided into slightly different versions of the same ideology, completely indistinguishable from one another to the uninitiated, but to them as different as night and day. They felt that the fate of the world depended on the redemptive value of the particular brand of nihilism they were promoting in literary studies.

One day, one of the students, a charming young woman, was going through some rhapsody of her own composition; we were all swimming laboriously in a murky ocean of Anglo-Franco-Teutonic jargon when suddenly I caught her saying something about a prophet of the school that was absolutely false—I knew it for a fact because I had been a witness of the event. I did not want to waste my one and only chance to say something relevant to her talk, and I interrupted her with alacrity. After listening to what I had to say, she put on a gentle but slightly condescending smile and said, "But you don't understand. You are too old. We are already third-generation deconstructionists, and we read only the second generation. We don't have to read Derrida himself, who has been deconstructed quite a few years ago. We can completely dispense with that sort of thing." It is nice to see that American optimism will reassert itself even in the most desperate circumstances, but the cultural results can be a little weird, to say the least.

Deconstructionism is not, of course, entirely responsible for the situation we have today. The mechanics of an academic career in the United States has a lot to do with the worst features of "criticism" today. There are very good aspects to literary studies in this country, but there are also aspects that are not so good, and they should be debated openly, for if we remain silent we will go from bad to worse.

Assistant professors at American universities are extremely interested in a strange institution called academic tenure. The path to tenure is publication, and in all my years of teaching, the law of "publish or perish" is the only one that has survived every cultural revolution. To publish, you must have something to write about. This "something" is supposed to be at least slightly different from what other people have already published. It is difficult to say something genuinely new and original. It is relatively easy, however, to simulate originality by saying the opposite of what your immediate predecessors have said, especially if they are the only people you have read and studied.

The danger today is that people who do genuinely brilliant work will be overshadowed by the ebb and flow of fads and fashions that have little substance and that are hardly more than a collective form of *esprit de contradiction*: the shift from one abstract extreme to another. This is not only true of literary criticism. If we look at all fields, ranging from sociology to ethology to dietetics, we find hordes of hungry researchers trying to overturn the theories of their predecessors every ten years. They embrace these theories in reverse form to gain tenure at little intellectual cost. The top becomes the bottom and the bottom becomes the top. Ten years ago, for instance, when ethology was very much in fashion, we heard that animals are much sweeter creatures than man and that they never resort to murder. This was the optimistic spirit of 1968. In 1988, animals do commit murder after all.

Every day, new examples appear that contradict the literature of ten years ago. In the strange world of contemporary studies, it is often hard to distinguish how much of the strangeness results from the creative genius of so-called radical theory, and how much from the social and organizational conditions of academic life today.

Let us consider two major principles of deconstructive criticism in the light of requirements for tenure. The deconstructionists have been saying, quite eloquently and at great length, that interpretation is infinite. There is no limit to the number of interpretations that can legitimately be made of the same texts, even of non-literary texts, whatever that means. The same is true of the interpretations one could give of these first interpretations. Each time I reread a text, whether I like it or not, I produce an interpretation that is different from my previous interpretations. Each one of these can and should be published. This is good news indeed in an academic system that demands that each assistant professor publish at least one book-length essay in his field of specialization as a requirement for tenure, regardless of how inflated the literature in that field already is. The good news is that it is impossible to interpret any text to death.

We live in a world where plagiarism has become a philosophical impossibility. It simply cannot exist. If a dean tells you that there can be such a thing, she must belong to some benighted field like computer science. This is very good news indeed. It is so good that literary critics should be discreet about it for fear of appearing a little self-serving.

A few years ago, I remember listening to a great pontiff of deconstruction from the East Coast. Speaking as an academic critic, he loudly congratulated himself as he beheld an eternal future in which the entire world would be regarded as a text interpreting itself—everybody interpreting everybody else—until the end of the world. When you consider that any respectable English department in this country must have at least one Milton specialist, it is wonderful to know that Saudi Arabian oil will run out before we exhaust possible interpretations of *Paradise Lost.* Before the advent of radical theory, Milton specialists could not help but feel vaguely uncomfortable with the thought that, perhaps after the ten-thousandth book on Milton, the most respected scholars would decide to declare a moratorium on all future Milton publications. Thanks to recent advances in critical theory, even that remote danger has been eliminated once and for all. We can look forward to a brave new world in which even ten million books on Milton will not begin to make a dent in the material available for interpretation.

A second principle of deconstructive criticism, which flows from the first, is that no interpretation can be said to be better or worse than any other. All are equally good. I even heard someone say once at a symposium that all interpretations are equally *indispensable.* When you remember that our interpretations are absolutely infinite in number, the idea that they are all indispensable becomes as scary as science fiction stories in which mutants invade the whole planet.

In this new context, the idea that certain publications might not be good enough to be counted toward tenure no longer makes any philosophical sense. The belief that writing can be good or bad is a "metaphysical" prejudice to which academic deans tend to cling because they usually come from the sciences and from the stodgiest fields of the humanities; they cannot understand or appreciate the brave new world that the avant-garde is bringing about.

These are, I realize, cheap shots, and I apologize for my self-indulgence. If there is any relevance to what I say, it does not pertain to the best of deconstruction, but to something called the sociology of literature, a concrete sociology of literature that takes the university into account as a social institution. Many critics over the last fifty years have tried to reduce great works of art to the social circumstances of their creation. In my view, they have not been successful. I am not a Marxist, and I am not suggesting that this type of reductionism should be practiced. But it does seem that, if there is a historical period that is particularly amenable to Marxist criticism, it must be our own. Within our period, I would say, there is one literary genre that is particularly amenable to Marxist criticism: literary criticism itself.

Because of tenure requirements, literary criticism has become a kind of minor industry. It is also the only economic activity that escapes the kind of fiercely suspicious criticism to which all other literary genres are now subjected by this same criticism. Hence I would suggest that all radical theories, including Marxist theory, turn their attention on themselves and concentrate on their own mechanisms of production. These mechanisms, in my view, verify the principles of Marxist theory more strikingly than any phenomenon of the past. Our critical theories are wonderfully true because they are self-fulfilling prophecies. If the world about which they speak did not exist at the moment these theories were elaborated, we need not worry. Give them a little time and their very popularity will generate the world whose existence they postulate. The world in which Western humanistic and ethical values have become meaningless is really upon us, and, of course, it is the world of deconstructive theory.

Thus, deconstruction tends to function in exactly the same way as the social sciences it attempts to rival. Today, in fact, this counterattack is remarkably successful. The area where deconstructive criticism is truly on the march is no longer literature, where it has probably reached its zenith, but in departments of history and other social sciences, which no doubt have good reasons to feel a little dubious about themselves and their own methods. Deconstructive criticism could not have the influence it does on these disciplines were it not for its tendency to divorce itself from our cultural tradition in a manner quite reminiscent of the social sciences themselves. Deconstruction may yet bring back to the social sciences that self-confidence and intolerance they once had, which seem to be on the decline at the present time.

Despite what I have said, I do not really believe that deconstruction and the other radical theories are the principal cause of our crisis. They are more a symptom than a cause. There are other causes, and some of them are so vast that they cannot be considered in the framework of a brief essay. I do think, however, that others are specific to the academic world, and that we should examine them just as critically as we examine the social context of nonacademic phenomena. The increase in the academic population over the last thirty years, the broadening of the base of higher education, plus the great wealth of American universities, where teachers have ten or fifteen students, have led to an enormous multiplication of the number of professors. This has transformed our world into one so different from the nineteenth- and even from the early twentieth-century university that the use of the same word to designate the two is probably misleading.

If you consider our numbers in the abstract, you might think we are about the right size for a harmonious and productive intellectual life. How many of us are there in the humanities? How *many* members does the Modern Language Association have? There must be at least twenty thousand active people. We complain about the indifference of the outside world. The public pays no attention to us; it is not interested in criticism; yet our numbers correspond, more or less, to the actual audiences of Shakespeare or Racine at the time they were writing. Our sector of the academic world is as large as the entire cultivated public of Elizabethan England or the France of Louis XIV.

And yet our cultural world is a far cry from Elizabethan England or *la cour et la ville* in seventeenth-century France. There is a reason for this, so simple and so obvious that no one ever mentions it. At the time of Elizabeth and Louis, one percent, perhaps, of the educated people were producers, and ninety-nine percent were consumers. The ninety-nine percent were truly interested in what was produced. With us, the proportion is curiously reversed. We are supposed to live in a world of consumerism, but in the university there are only producers. We are under a strict obligation to write, and therefore we hardly have the time to read one another's work. It is very nice, when you give a lecture, to encounter someone who is not publishing, because perhaps that person has not only enough curiosity but enough time to read your books.

I myself feel guilty because I do not spend enough time reading my contemporaries. In many universities today it has been decided that, to be promoted to associate professor with tenure, you must write two books. I hear that, in some instances, the tenure guidelines specify that these books be important enough to "revolutionize" the field. If an assistant professor must revolutionize his field twice before he can get tenure, he can read absolutely nothing outside that field. He has to cheat all along the line. He is totally unable to keep up with neighboring disciplines.

These requirements are absurd. The situation is a disaster. The demands of an academic career are incompatible with the requirements of a meaningful intellectual life, and this fact should be faced openly. No wonder such phenomena as mass guruism and the fanatical embrace of pseudo-radicalism occur. Many people do not even read the gurus' books, but they do exchange gossip about these teachers and make jokes about their sexual escapades as though they were movie stars or famous athletes. The same people who do this also create subsections of a subsection of a subsection at MLA meetings, devoted to an analysis of, for instance, feminism in northern Albania between 1922 and 1923. Their real desire is to reconstruct the community that they are deprived of, which the university can no longer provide.

The tendency of graduate students today to apply for admission to comparative literature or to so-called interdisciplinary programs, and their fascination with all theories that still talk about the global picture, even if negatively, is basically a healthy one. It stems from a need to re-create an intellectual life that is real. The situation is especially discouraging to the best people because, even though there is a romantic myth that we all write for our own pleasure and do not need readers, the truth of the matter is quite different. If you really have ideas, you want them to be tested against the ideas of other people. The present system is creating vast reservoirs of resentment—reservoirs of legitimate resentment, because those who have ideas receive no echoes from their colleagues.

We live in a world where the very ease of communication has become the greatest barrier to meaningful communication. Instead of improving the situation, knowledge retrieval schemes and computerized monstrosities can only make it worse.

The truth is that only the individual human being can give us the recognition we all seek, and the capacity of this individual mind to read and assimilate books is finite. If you create a world in which production is as excessive as it is today, everything in it tends to appear equally insignificant from an intellectual point of view. Even the best material is likely to go unnoticed and remain forever unread. The very size and organization of our intellectual life creates a reserve army for our current and future nihilistic enterprises. I would be surprised if the future did not have fads and fashions in store for us that will make the present ones look quite tame in comparison. Ours still have a few redeeming features, if you make allowances for the context in which they have appeared. The truth is that a certain complacent humanism has collapsed—the humanism of the "great books" courses—which is associated with a belief in the automatic carryover of technical advances into the intellectual field.

My view, however, is that the great texts of our literature are intact. They are totally unaffected by what has happened during the last fifty years. Earlier, I suggested that the radical methodologies of the present are rebellious children of a New Criticism and of a formalism that has emptied literature of its content. We have to go back to that content.

To give an example of what I mean, I will first go back to *esprit de contradiction*. Why and when does contradiction become an *esprit?* When it spreads like the plague to dominate and distort every argument. The life of the mind needs contradiction as a stimulus, but too much of it kills genuine creativity.

Intellectual movements can die of not enough contradiction, and they can also die of an overdose, especially in France. The fatal disease begins deceptively enough. It produces an excitement that seems to be the height of "creativity" and "innovation." Like a malignant fever, it flushes the cheeks of those it is about to devour.

Many instances of this process have been recorded but, significantly, by playwrights and novelists rather than philosophers, in works that philosophy would never regard as valid descriptions of its own processes.

Molière's Alceste is marvelously French but also non-French, a valid portrait of the modern intellectual that remains pertinent to this day. Molière did immortalize our type in highly favorable circumstances: a certain mode of intellectual life was beginning to disintegrate—call it "French classicism," the "salon," or whatever. Negative thinking was on the march, and Alceste was leading that march.

To understand the man, you must go beyond his arguments in favor of ecology and old-fashioned virtue. This first Alceste is for the birds, or rather for Philinte and Rousseau, who were made for each other, as well as for the petits marquis and the traditional critics. The real Alceste, the profound Alceste, is the one portrayed by Célimène. She alone is his equal, and she alone understands him. If you are as gifted as Alceste and Célimène are, in a university as well as in a salon, success will make you a coquette, and failure a misanthrope. Is it purely a question of language? Almost but not quite, like everything in human affairs.

Classical genius reduced Alceste to a single but supremely relevant feature—*esprit de contradiction*, the inevitable correlative of his famous "Je veux qu'on me distingue" and the sign of his power, and impotence, in a world exclusively dedicated to language, like our own, and just as competitive.

Et ne faut-il pas bien que Monsieur contredise?
A la commune voix veut-on qu'il se réduise,
Et qu'il ne fasse pas éclater en tous lieux
L'esprit contrariant qu'il a reçu des cieux?
Le sentiment d'autrui n'est jamais pour plaire;
Il prend toujours en main l'opinion contraire,
Et penserait paraître un homme du commun,
Si l'on voyait qu'il fut de l'avis de quelqu'un.
L'honneur de contredire a pour lui tant de charmes,
Qu'il prend contre lui-même assez souvent des armes;
Et ses vrais sentiments sont combattus par lui,
Aussitôt qu'il les voit dans la bouche d'autrui. (*Le misanthrope*, 2.4.669–80)

(And is not this gentleman bound to contradict? Would you have him subscribe to the general opinion; and must he not everywhere display the spirit of contradiction with which Heaven has endowed him? Other people's thoughts can never please him. He always supports a contrary idea, and he would think himself too much of the common herd, were he observed to be of anyone's opinion but his own. The honor of gainsaying has so many charms for him that he very often takes up the cudgels against himself; he combats his own sentiments as soon as he hears them from other people's lips.)

This portrait is really the key to everything Alceste says and does, from his ridiculous controversy with Oronte to his unforgivable behavior when he tries to court Eliante just to spite Célimène. *Esprit de contradiction* is a more elegant, powerful, and even courteous interpretation of his conduct than the *hypocrisy* with which he perpetually clubs everybody over the head, even though he is the one who most deserves to be clubbed.

The difference between a university and a salon is that you cannot have a salon unless you remain on speaking terms with the people in it. Even though Alceste prefigures our own bad manners in his fits of silent pouting, he occasionally comes out of them to vituperate Célimène and her flatterers. Not so with us. We speak only to our own schools of thought.

Our intellectual machines have become so efficient that, at the very instant a potential opponent begins to speak, he disqualifies himself. By opening his uninitiated mouth, he reveals that he still partakes of that grossly naïve and ancestral confidence in language of which twentieth-century philosophies liberate their devotees.

Long before the military, we have invented the Star Wars of intellectual life. We can shoot down enemy missiles at the very instant they leave their silos. The only problem, of course, is that we bring intellectual life to a standstill.

One can distinguish two main phases in postwar French intellectual life, characterized by an increasingly virulent and self-destructive *esprit de contradiction*.

The first phase was Hegelian and relatively optimistic. Countless errors had to be crushed through generous applications of stern demystification; but beyond the carnage a faint hope glimmered. Like the happy ending of old movies, universal *synthesis* was always around the corner.

Orthodox Sartrism belongs to this phase, but it also represents a strategic retreat into the self. Negative thinking concentrates its poisons to use them more efficiently against all comers. Sartre's faith in the possibility of *having a philosophy* looks startlingly naïve, however, from the deconstructive point of view.

At its paroxysm, the *esprit de contradiction* turns against itself and destroys its own crystal palaces in order to forestall their possible destruction by others. It denounces philosophy as a huge contradiction of which it is a part, even though it is also heroically fighting a patient battle against the universal illusion.

This is the deconstructive phase, when the negative spirit becomes so clever that it disappears as such. It can always stay a step ahead of everyone, so it becomes impregnable. Molière captured the dynamics of this escalation; Célimène's last lines are dedicated to self-contradiction.

Célimène herself is an even better example than Alceste. She is the arch-deconstructionist. She contradicts herself as much as he does, but she no longer tries to hide it. She turns it into a novel kind of superiority. When convenient, she does not hesitate to discard the ancient ideal of self-consistency.

The assault on truth always comes at the end of a competitive escalation about truth. All such escalations divide into two main phases. The first is a positive phase in which everyone tries to reach a certain type of "truth." It ends in a deadlock, with everyone advocating his own "truth" against all the other "truths." At some point, everyone gives up the search simultaneously, mimetically, and the rivalry shifts to the demonstration of how impossible it is to reach any kind of truth.

Formalism already belonged to that phase, but discreetly, through its minimization of *content*. Structuralism is the same, with a vengeance—it is a more radical way to evacuate "content," and post-structuralism is an even more radical one. To exalt the signified at the expense of the referent, and the signifier at the expense of the signified, is always to dismantle the still positive something that had survived until then. Structuralism is an excellent analysis of what happens to culture when *esprit de contradiction* takes over.

Our only mistake is to believe that this process is everything, that there is nothing beyond it. Oppositions are not all that matter. Structuralism is *esprit de contradiction* shooting itself in the foot. Post-structuralism is that wounded foot grabbing the pistol and shooting back at the entire body.

In one essential respect, our deconstructive stage of German idealism resembles language analysis in its heyday. The two schools belong to the negative phase of two philosophical escalations that take language and truth as their objects and end up regarding both as annihilated once and for all by their own negative process, the force of which they grossly exaggerate, just as Célimène, intelligent though she is, exaggerates the importance of her salon. How awesome is the power of critical thinking once you no longer believe in words—except, of course, if they happen to be your own!

Molière could not imagine our world, but he shows us one in which the comic and tragic outline of our own is retroactively visible. Only the playwright or novelist treats the comedy of the intellect as the human interaction that it always is, even and especially when it refuses to recognize itself as such.

To me, the content of the *Misanthrope,* or its referent, or what you will, is Célimène on *esprit de contradiction.* Whichever way you call it, this is the sort of thing our literary criticism has systematically neglected, and it begs to be studied. This content is about ourselves *together*—not about society as a whole, and not about myself as an individual, a solitary *Dasein,* a Freudian unconscious, or anything else.

This *content* is specific to Western dramas and novels at their best. Our real motivation for eluding it is not that the psychoanalysts or the sociologists are more competent to deal with it than we are. The competence of literary critics is a negative one. They do not have to pay allegiance to some pseudo-science. They have the greatest texts. If literary critics, too, keep eluding the content of these texts, they must have some other reason, which may well be truth itself. Especially in human affairs, nothing is as unpopular as truth.

If we look at deconstruction as the child of New Criticism, we will understand that it entered a literary world from which content had already been expelled. I think we must return to content. We must not be intimidated by linguistic terrorism. Linguistic terrorism makes all reference impossible to reach. My own work has convinced me that the most perspicacious texts from the standpoint of human relations are the great texts of Western literature. They do not have to be studied from a Marxist or a Freudian point of view to yield what they have to yield; indeed, they must counterattack. We must counter with literature as a whole, instead of attacking the social sciences with an impoverished notion of what literature is.

Radical theory tells us today that the notion of the masterpiece is completely outdated, and that the so-called best works were chosen arbitrarily or as a way of manipulating power. I do not believe this at all. Go to writings that have not been sanctioned by posterity and you will quickly discover that in literature we have a tremendous advantage. We have the greatest texts in the world. When a social scientist writes a great book, which does happen from time to time, it must be discarded ten years later because new research takes its place. What happens to that text? Sooner or later the literary people inherit it. Literature is the repository of all great texts that exist outside of fashion. Therefore we must not become the victims of fashion. I believe that the canon of great texts is meaningful. I feel we can rejuvenate our studies from the inside. When we reconquer the content of our literary works, we will reconquer the ground lost to the social sciences without resorting to the terrorist methods of what the French call *la politique du pire*: the policy of choosing the worst option to destroy your enemy, even though you are destroyed at the same time. That is terrorism. We have no right to feel demoralized, discouraged, resentful, and underprivileged. We are sitting on a great treasure whose value far too many of us underestimate. If we learn to make that treasure fructify, the future belongs to us.

# Love and Hate in Chrétien de Troyes' *Yvain* [1990]

The following observations might be entitled: "Impressions in a Vacuum."[1] I am not as well read as I should be, and I may be saying things that have become banal. Rereading *Yvain*, I was struck by something very banal indeed, the importance of fame.

Knightly fame, in Chrétien, is not a static value, but something mobile and unstable because eminently competitive, as competitive as the public image of politicians today, or prestigious businessmen, artists, basketball players, etc. The ultimate question is always: "Who is the best knight?" The answer does not depend on the king, or some other infallible authority; it depends on all the other knights. Each knight tries to impress his fellow knights so much that they will be forced to admire him more than they admire themselves.

We have many indications of hysterical competitiveness in *Yvain*. At the beginning, Arthur's seneschal, Keu, derides Yvain in front of the queen and accuses him of bragging. This is as potentially deadly as plagiarism in the academic world. It is the reason why Yvain rushes to Esclados le Roux ahead of the expedition Arthur is preparing against this mysterious knight. Yvain is jumping the gun on his fellow knights, and his initiative is ethically questionable; he is cheating his peers of their share in an affair that interests their reputation as well as his own. He is guilty of unfair competition.

A knight fighting in a distant land had a problem of information with the people back home. Nowadays, many cameras would be following him; in the Middle Ages, his stories of monsters and giants exterminated with the greatest of ease encountered the kind of skepticism that has disappeared from our world as a result of television.

After killing Esclados, Yvain hides inside his victim's castle, but, in spite of the danger, he does not want to leave; in addition to his love for Laudine, he has a "professional" reason to stay: his efforts would be wasted if he returned to court without some fragment of his opponent's body, a relic of Esclados, convincing proof of his own victory. He must validate his claim with his peers, who are suspicious by definition, being also his rivals. Only his peers can give an ambitious knight the fame that he seeks, and we can well understand why they would give it most reluctantly.

To a conventionally "modern" critic, a value as explicit as this one, the competition for fame, must be a critical dead end; it must be discredited, therefore, and replaced by hidden motivations, Freud's sexual unconscious, for instance.

Chrétien puts chivalry at the top and subordinates everything to it, including sex. In his world, fame is not sex in disguise; more often than not, the reverse is true. Sex has not yet become the instrument of fame that it will become later, but it always surrenders to fame, whereas fame never surrenders to sex; it does not have to; sex makes itself the humble servant of fame.

When a Freudian sees this hierarchy, he automatically assumes that it must be deceptive, not because it is intrinsically unbelievable—we only have to look around us—but because it contradicts the number one Freudian dogma.

The idea that the competition for fame could influence libidinal desires more than it is influenced by them does not seem like a serious proposition. Wherever sex is not the dominant force, we have been taught to conclude that repression is at work. The predominance of fame must be a cover for a sexual desire that cannot express itself directly; fame seems too high-minded not to be a form of sublimation.

The problem with this view is that sexual desire is far from hidden in Chrétien. Its expressions are symbolic, no doubt, but of a kind so transparent that they cannot seriously qualify as symptoms of repression; they sound more like humor.

You all remember the young lady-in-waiting who finds Yvain lying unconscious in the wilderness, entirely naked. After scrutinizing him at great length—an undressed hero is hard to identify—in a state of great agitation she goes back to her mistress, who hears her story with interest and gives her a box full of very strong medicine. The patient should be rubbed with it, the mistress says, but very sparingly, and his forehead only because his illness is obviously in the head.

The lady tackles her job with such zeal that she forgets these wise recommendations; she rubs the whole content of the box over the entire body of Yvain who, not surprisingly, is most successfully revived.

The critic venturing into this kind of text with heavy Freudian artillery reminds me of Tartarin de Tarascon hunting for lions on the outskirts of modern suburbia . . . What about the famous fountain at the entrance of Esclados's domain? Whenever a strange knight presumes to meddle with it, the fountain goes wild. Esclados shows up and defeats the intruder. After Esclados himself is defeated and killed, his beautiful wife, Laudine, worries greatly about the magical fountain, which is now revealed as her own: "With my husband dead," she keeps repeating, "who is going to defend my fountain?"

Chrétien plays with sex quite wittily and freely, and yet it is true that sex does not come first in his work. He has enough of it to make his demystificators seem more naïve than himself, but not enough to satisfy their pansexualist creed. Sex plays second fiddle to chivalry in his work, but for reasons that no psychoanalyst will ever demystify; they are beyond his grasp, more profound than any psychoanalysis, in my view.

After marrying Enide, Erec feels so comfortable at home that this promising young knight stretches his honeymoon beyond the permissible. Enide is not pleased by this extreme devotion to her. She tells her husband that a knight with a beautiful wife or lady friend cannot afford to be lazy. A well-born woman will cease to admire the man in her life, and therefore to admire herself, if, because of her, he becomes a worse rather than a better knight.

There is a veiled threat in these words. In order to keep her own desire alive, Enide needs a famous husband. If she cannot be proud of Erec, her love for him will starve to death.

It is just as wrong to interpret Enide in terms of Freudian repression as it was to interpret her in terms of noble-minded devotion to duty. She should be interpreted literally; she is not one of these wives whose real happiness lies in keeping their husbands at home and who sacrifice their own feminine goals to a purely masculine ambition.

Admiration for the most successful knight is so ingrained in Chrétien's women that it governs sexual desire. We must not ritually oppose duty and pleasure as if the two necessarily contradicted each other. In our world, success in business or politics can be as erotic as good looks; so can an Olympic medal or a Nobel prize; why not chivalry?

Enide is the ambitious wife of those times when prestigious careers were closed to women. She competes vicariously; she makes the best of a bad situation. Her husband is her one trump card, and she does not want to waste it.

This feminine involvement in the competitive aspect of chivalry reappears in *Yvain,* and in a more extreme, even caricatural fashion. The novel shows us a husband who does something even worse than staying away from the battlefield; he suffers a defeat so complete that he dies as a result. What can a wife do when her lord and master lets her down in this fashion?

According to the logic of mimetic and chivalrous desire, she must fall in love with his murderer. Women always fall in love with a winner in Chrétien. If you think that I exaggerate, just listen to a slightly abbreviated version of the conversation between Laudine and Lunete:

Lunete: You must defend your magic spring. (1499)[2]
Laudine: I won't find one as brave as he!
Lunete: Oh, yes you will, if you'll agree! (1490–91)

Laudine keeps silent for a little while; Lunete continues:

Lunete: Dear lady, please do not delay . . . (1501)
[ . . . ]
Oh, you have cowards, and to spare,
but no one brave enough to dare

to ride a horse, and so the king
will easily seize everything
unchallenged, such a host has he! (1508–11)

Laudine becomes angry, but Lunete is the voice of the entire culture:

Lunete: Now you must overcome your sorrow . . . (1545–46)
  [ . . . ]
  Now, do you believe
  all valor has died with your husband?
  But men as good as he ever was, and
  some better men are still on earth! (1550–53)
Laudine: Name one man who's shown
  such valor as my lord was known. (1555–56)
Lunete: You won't be grateful,
  my lady, you'll become so hateful,
  you'll start to threaten me again! (1557–59)
Laudine: No, no, I promise. Please explain! (1560)
Lunete: But I may say, it seems to me,
  when two knights meet, both equally
  well armed for war, and test their might
  whom do you think the better knight?
  when one man beats the other one?
  Now I think that the knight who won
  should have the prize. What would you do? (1567–73)
Laudine: I think that you are trying to
  use my own words to capture me. (1574–75)
Lunete: The man who is the better knight
  than your lord is the man who's shown
  that he could conquer him alone,
  and then was brave enough to chase
  and shut him in his dwelling place! (1578–82)

After a sleepless night, Laudine decides that Lunete is right; she wants to meet the victorious Yvain. For the sake of decency, Lunete had planned that five days should elapse before a first amorous rendezvous could take place between the grief-stricken widow and her husband's murderer, but now Laudine is becoming impatient, and she forces Lunete to hurry things up.

Chrétien develops with amazing audacity the logic of a competitive desire much more scandalous, "radical," and amusing than anything Freud or Lacan can put in its place—and much more realistic as well. Those who portray this novelist as a cold rationalist and a light-hearted man do not understand him. I see him as a satirist unraveling what he regards as the logic of devouring ambition in the feudal aristocracy of his time.

The political expediency of Laudine's actions is unquestionable, but if we rashly embraced a socio-political interpretation of her behavior, we would fall into a trap that parallels the one in which our psychoanalytical friend is already entangled. The two traps lie on opposite sides of the straight and narrow path which consists in sticking to the text of Chrétien and understanding what he is really saying to us. His own story is much more interesting, really, than the perpetually rehashed message of our tired old master thinkers.

The true reason for the precipitous marriage of Laudine with Yvain is a desire of the same type as we already found exemplified in Enide, a mimetic desire, but this time it arises in circumstances that make it seem less respectable than in the other novel. Laudine needs an excuse to justify her falling in love not even at first sight but at no sight at all and with such a man as Yvain, the murderer of her husband, and at such a time as she does, immediately after the murderous deed. As an excuse for her new infatuation, the only pose she can strike is that of the coldly rational politician. The dreadful truth is that she falls in love not in spite of what Yvain did to her husband, but because of it. She falls in love with the champion.

After Yvain and Laudine have decided to get married, Lunete organizes an assembly of her vassals; it will be more honorable to remarry, the two women surmise, if these vassals beg Laudine to do it. It goes without saying that they all find Yvain the best possible choice, for reasons not very different from hers. The only difference is that she likes him as a lover even more than they like him as a lord and a military protector.

This unanimity is foreordained, and we can easily see why; the criteria of choice are the same in the political field as they are in the erotic field. Yvain's victory makes him most desirable in the eyes of men and women alike. All desires follow the same path, contagiously, mimetically. That is why the agreement is complete between Laudine and her vassals.

In our cultural world, and probably in quite a few others, competition is the soul of sex, not the Freudian libido. We understand nothing if we imagine that Laudine did not really love Esclados, or that she was beginning perhaps to be a little tired of him. Not at all; as long as no one could defeat him and he looked like the best knight in the world, she loved him as much as she knew how, in the only way she knew how to love, and now she loves Yvain for the very same reason.

Everybody is a spectator at the same tournament; a beautiful heiress, or a widow, will applaud the winner as enthusiastically as everybody else, so enthusiastically that they want to marry him; they all want to marry the winner; when they finally marry him, if they ever do, they feel at one with the crowd, and this is what they want. I cannot put it better than Chrétien himself in the concluding lines of the episode:

The lord Yvain
is master now. The dead man's been
forgotten since the moment when
the very knight who took his life
had courted and had wed his wife.
They sleep together. All adore
and prize the living man far more
than their dead lord. (2014–21)

~

The most climactic and puzzling text in *Yvain* is the description of the fight between the two best knights, Yvain and Gauvain. Everything I have said so far was an effort to establish the proper context for this remarkable text. The proper context, I believe, is the enormous role of mimetic competitiveness among the knights and in feudal culture generally.

The ostensible reason for the fight of Yvain and Gauvain is a sisters' quarrel concerning their inheritance. Without investigating the case, Gauvain accepts to champion the older sister, in a typically chivalrous and most literally *quixotic* fashion. He is such a champion that no other knight, now, dare take up the cause that happens to be the just one, the cause of the younger sister.

At long last, a fully armed knight answers the challenge without giving his name. He is Yvain, of course, but Gauvain, too, is already fully
armed, and:

The knights,
Who are going to fight, don't recognize
each other, though throughout their lives
they've loved each other like a brother!
Do they no longer love each other?
Yes, I would answer you, and no;
and I will prove that this is so.
Each answer's right. The lord Gawain
sincerely loves the lord Yvain,
fights by his side in war and game;
and Sir Yvain has done the same
for Sir Gawain, when there was need.
If Sir Yvain had realized, he'd
have greeted Sir Gawain instead;
he would be glad to have his head
for him before he'd strike one blow.
His friend would do the same, I know.
Is that not perfect Love and true?
Of course! But Hate is present too,
and so you must make no mistake,
because the knights intend to break
each other's heads, and do great damage
and all the harm that they can manage. (5728–50)

Chrétien gives a credible enough excuse for the fight of these two excellent friends. Their medieval helmets cover their faces entirely. A modern
equivalent would be two fighter planes trying to shoot each other down
at two or three times the speed of sound. Even if the two pilots had been
friends at an earlier time, they cannot identify each other's features and
there is no hate in their hearts. If a writer told us that they both love and
hate each other in a modern transposition of Chrétien's text, we would find
the point a little puzzling. There seems to be no valid justification for the
elaborate parallel between love and hate.

Chrétien, as a rule, is not long-winded and yet, here, he goes on forever:

Hate's in the saddle and will spur
Ahead of Love, who cannot stir.
Oh, Love, what has become of you?
Come, see what they're about to do! (5769–72)

Would this be what medieval scholars call an allegory? The English translator must think so; otherwise he would not capitalize Love and Hate as much as he does. Yvain and Gauvain fight one another and so do Love and Hate. The cause of Yvain is just, whereas Gauvain's is unjust. Hate is compared to a knight in the saddle, spurring his mount and pricking it forward.

Can we conclude from all these apparently converging signals that each knight corresponds to one of the two allegorized sentiments and to this one only? Not at all. Neither knight personifies anything. If Love and Hate could be quantified, there would be the same amount of each inside each knight. Instead of one single battle of Love against Hate, we really have two, and they take place not between the two knights but inside each one. Both men are divided against themselves.

This text does not fit any of the traditional conceptions of medieval allegory. Should we, therefore, regard it as a meaningless assemblage of words? Chrétien is "playing with words," no doubt, but we have no right to say that he is *merely* playing, as the current fashion demands. This text is highly *literary*, but it is not an example of the narcissistic self-indulgence that Roland Barthes called *littérarité*; its interest is of a kind that the linguistic school is unable to explicate. It makes marvelous sense in terms of the competition for fame, the mimetic rivalry of the two knights.

In order to see this, we must take everything into account, beginning with the fact that our two knights are the two highest embodiments of the chivalric ideal at Arthur's court. Gauvain "illuminates chivalry just as the morning sun illuminates with its light all the places on the earth"; so does Yvain. Seeing eye to eye on every subject, our two knights have excellent reasons to be excellent friends. Their friendship is not a matter of chance, a historical accident, but a direct consequence of what both of them *are*.

Each one, in his humility, ranks himself lower than the other and sees the other as the perfect illustration of what he himself should be. To each, therefore, the other is a revered model. This emulation is the quintessence of chivalry.

Who, therefore, is in a position to make the star of Yvain shine less brightly in the firmament of chivalry? Gauvain, of course. Who can overshadow the glory of Gauvain, if not Yvain? The mutual imitation cannot fail to generate a tension that will remain invisible most of the time because both knights do their best to hide it, even from themselves, for the sake of their beautiful friendship.

Two identical desires that converge toward the same goal necessarily interfere with one another. If all knights are rivals for the same fame, the two greatest rivals must be Yvain and Gauvain, for the simple reason that they are the best—the same reason that motivates their friendship. On the ladder of prestige, they occupy the highest rung together; each wants to occupy it alone. Their two loves and their two hates are really the two sides of the same coin.

Gauvain, we are told, was so well treated by Lady Laudine that, according to obviously ill-intentioned people, she must have fallen in love with her husband's best friend. If this is mere gossip, as Chrétien suggests, why does he mention it? He is really very sly, and he understands this type of rivalry very well; the possibility of an erotic component in the relationship means no more and no less than the socio-political component in the marriage of Yvain and Laudine.

The principle of rivalry stands above all possible fields of application, and, as soon as it appears somewhere, it can stir up trouble everywhere. This principle is what our text is about; the love of each knight for the other goes to the admired model, and the hate goes to the obstacle and rival that the two also are to each other. We found earlier that Laudine hates Yvain, then loves him for one and the same reason. This is true as well in the case of Yvain and Gauvain. Hate and love are always one and the same in this hypermimetic world.

Chrétien expresses the ceaseless reinforcement of the two roles, the beloved model and the hated obstacle/rival. If we understand this, we can see exactly what his language is doing and why:

Look at the armies of your foes,
and learn the men who strike the blows
are the same men we're speaking of,

who love with such a sacred love.
A Love which is not feigned or vile
is rare and holy. All this while
Love has been blind, and Hate can't see,
for if Love saw these two men, she
would have forbidden either knight
to harm his friend or start to fight.
So Love is blind, filled with dismay,
confused, beguiled, and led astray.
She's seen these men, but hasn't known
she ought to claim them as her own,
and even though Hate cannot say
why the two knights should fight that day
or hate each other; as we've stated,
he fills them full of mortal hatred. (5773–90)

Since the knights acquire fame at each other's expense, and since this fame is supremely competitive, their relations must inevitably lead to this climactic encounter. It is logical that, after defeating countless strangers and outsiders, the victorious knights, those with the greatest reputation, would dream only of defeating one another in fair combat, in front of all their peers. When no potential opponents remain outside the group, the most prestigious insiders cannot acquire any more prestige. The logic is the logic of world championship.

Indications that this logic dominates our text are everywhere. The timing is no less significant than the location. The combat occurs at the very end of the novel, and its real purpose is to answer the ultimate question: "Who is the best knight?" or rather to show that it cannot be answered. The combat occurs at court, in front of everybody, and thus the problem of information that I mentioned earlier cannot arise.

Each knight is fighting for the purpose of becoming the sole object of admiration and desire for everybody else, and above all for his opponent. The duel is a tournament not in the sense that it is not a fight to the death—it certainly is, even if it does not result in death—but in the sense of taking place at home and being watched by all those whose judgment counts and who can express a competent opinion on the fighters and on their fight; the presence of many spectators is mentioned before anything else, at the outset of the battle:

Everyone
went out too, as is always done,
to see blows fall in battles, fights,
and fencing matches . . . (5725–28)

The two knights are so well matched that no decision can be
reached:

the valiant knights were tied,
and no one watching could decide
who was the better knight. They bought
renown with anguish as they fought.
Both were amazed and both despaired
that they were so exactly paired.
Each warrior wondered who could stand
his onslaught with such courage . . . (5917–24)

[ . . . ]

So it is no wonder
the two knights, who were so hard pressed,
were wishing they could take some rest.
And so the warring knights withdrew
to rest again, and each knight knew,
despite his triumphs in the past,
that he had met his match at last. (5932–38)

The two sisters are forgotten at this point, except perhaps for the fact
of their sisterliness, which should remind us of the brotherly symmetry between their two champions: moral, physical, spiritual, psychological, etc.

When they finally identify each other, each knight proclaims the victory of his friend with such somber energy that they seem close to ex-
changing blows once again over this paradoxical matter. They both want
to prove not their superiority this time, but their inferiority; this is the
modern sense of *courtoisie* in French: neither one will yield to the other the
privilege of yielding to the other. As in the primitive rituals of the *potlatch*
type, conflictual symmetry reappears in the symmetrical efforts that the rivals make to exorcise it once and for all.

The perfect match of the two knights is really the key to the significance of the entire text. If Yvain and Gauvain are equal in strength, equal

in courage, equal in fighting skills, equal in endurance, then they can only go on fighting until they have annihilated the best soldiers of their King for no good purpose, or rather for a purpose that is simultaneously nothing and everything in this competitive world. It resembles the definition of Being in the philosophy of Martin Heidegger, or rather the impossibility of defining Being.

The circular relationship of attraction and repulsion turns the two knights into a graphic illustration of the biblical stumbling block (*skandalon*), physically represented by their ever renewed assaults against each other and their ever repeated failures, by the equal severity and sterility of the damage that they inflict on one another.

The interminable and undecidable nature of the fight is hyperbolic praise of both knights, of course; it is a happy ending in the sense that neither champion is killed or even humiliated, but it has sinister connotations as well.

When things come to the point at which the better knights fight one another instead of outsiders, the very same force that protects the culture against hostile outsiders turns against itself and threatens to destroy the system from the inside.

The presence of the two *doubles* and their unending fight suggests that the novel should be defined as a mimetic and sacrificial crisis after the tragic and mythical pattern. Even the names, Yvain and Gauvain, are almost the same, hardly differentiated, like those of Romulus and Remus, Fafner and Fasolt, and many other mythical embodiments of mimetic rivalry at its most destructive. This fight has something to do with that quintessential drama during which differences violently suppress each other and turn back into that warring confusion from which they formerly emerged—and they may or may not reemerge in the future.

All our observations so far can be defined in terms of undifferentiation, between sex and fame, men and women, inside and outside, Mars and Eros, etc. We first witnessed how hysterical competitiveness destabilized the institution of marriage and distorted sexuality; then we witnessed the destruction of something even more essential to the preservation of feudal institutions, its fundamental cement: mutual loyalty, friendship between the best knights.

The paradox of this society is that the more harmony there is between its highest value and the actual behavior of its members, the greater the danger of self-destruction becomes. It simply means that, in the eyes of Chrétien, feudalism is what many historians have always seen in it, barely institutionalized anarchy. The king's authority is purely honorific and nominal.

This is the worm in the apple, the enemy at the heart of the system. The life-giving principle is also a principle of death. This most beautiful thing, chivalry, is a self-devouring monster. The same force, *mimesis*, that generates and perpetuates cultural differences dissolves its own creation as soon as, losing its transcendental quality, it turns into mimetic rivalry. The battle of Yvain and Gauvain comes close to showing this process explicitly, and yet it never really does; the truth hides behind the conventional veil of the two opponents' ignorance of their respective identities.

The real message behind our text is so disturbing that its full impact must be eluded. Chrétien is not the only one who eludes it; the theme of the two best fighters who would not be fighting if each could recognize his best friend is a popular one, and it must always signify more or less the same kind of mimetic paroxysm as in *Yvain*.

The medieval tournament was carefully regulated not because it is an inherently playful affair, but for the opposite reason: it satisfies that dangerous urge that the best knights have to fight it out among themselves. The tournament is the most dangerous fight not only for those directly involved but for the entire society, which it may deprive of its best fighters.

The theme of the unidentified knight can be interpreted as a paradoxical symbol of desymbolization, another clue to the total crisis of identity brought about by the leveling effects of mimetic rivalry.

This crisis is not some individual pathology, but a collective affair, a crisis of symbolicity itself, which can never be expressed directly, and it remains beyond the grasp of all the schools, structuralist and post-structuralist, that place language and differentiation above the vicissitudes of history.

Our text tells us how the two knights, and all those whom we might choose to substitute for them—all competitive elites in the Western world—never really apprehend the substance of their own experience; they never recognize themselves in the perpetual metamorphosis of "love" into "hate," and vice versa. They see a mere conjunction of "opposites" that literary playfulness alone can juxtapose because it is rationally meaningless.

Our text points to the psychological mechanism of this misprision in a few lines that were located before my last quotations, but I have postponed reading them until now:

I wonder how a love so great
can coexist with mortal Hate?
How can two things so opposite
be lodged in the same house? For it
appears to me that they could not
be found together in one spot,
or even spend a single night
without quarrel or a fight,
as soon as Love or Hate could sense
the other one in residence.
Still, in a building, there may be
many a hall and balcony
and bedroom found throughout the place.
I think that this must be the case.
Love's in one of the hidden nooks;
Hate's on the balcony, and looks
out on the road, and wants to try
to be seen by all passers-by. (5751–68)

The inner life of the two knights is hopelessly fragmented. The various rooms do not communicate. This metaphor evokes the idea of something unconscious, but in a sense different from Freud. Both Hate and Love are fully conscious of each other's presence, but they manage never to meet; each one separately dominates the entire psyche in turn; they try not to be conscious of their relatedness; they hardly realize that they are the divided unity of the same consciousness.

This schizophrenic division also prevents Yvain and Gauvain from seeing that their hate is their love and vice versa, or, in other words, that there is no real love in them, no real love in the sense of John's first letter:

He who says he is in the light and hates his brother is in the darkness still. He who loves his brother abides in the light, and in him there is no cause for stumbling. (1 John 2:9–10)

Thanks to the trick of the two helmets, Chrétien feigns to cut off the umbilical cord that ties his text to the novel as a whole; he enables us to see this page as a purely decorative addition to his novel, a useless supplement, the verbal game of oxymora that rhetoricians and critics always describe as literary artifice. Literary theories are often recipes for perpetuating the mental compartments that Chrétien is talking about. Like the feudal lords and ladies, we convince ourselves that we have nothing to learn from this.

If you examine this text, you can see that little or nothing would have to be changed if its object were erotic desire. The same text could be used in the case of two, three, four lords and ladies playing with each other as in the physical combat of Yvain and Gauvain.

There is a universal applicability of this language to all desires, regardless of their object, which is tempting to interpret in purely libidinal terms, once again. The root of it all, many people invariably surmise, must be homosexual or bisexual desire. All types of sexuality may indeed show up in the context of mimetic rivalry, as well as social problems of all types, but the one and the other are only aspects of mimetic configurations that remain the same regardless of the content which they inform.

In all major writers, I believe, the rhetoric of oxymora significantly alludes to the vicissitudes of some mimetic interplay and obscurely reenacts the fundamental human drama of the mimetic stumbling block, the *skandalon* of the Gospels, which no psychoanalytical, no social, no purely linguistic interpretation can ever apprehend.

# Innovation and Repetition [1991]

"Innovation," from the Latin *innovare, innovatio*, should signify renewal, rejuvenation from inside, rather than novelty, which is its modern meaning in both English and French. Judging from the examples in the *Oxford English Dictionary* and the *Littré*, the word came into widespread use only in the sixteenth century and, until the eighteenth century, its connotations were almost uniformly unfavorable.

In the vulgar tongues, as well as in medieval Latin, the word is used primarily in theology, and it means a departure from what by definition should not change—religious dogma. In many instances, innovation is practically synonymous with heresy.

Orthodoxy is unbroken continuity and, therefore, the absence of innovation. This is how Bossuet defines the orthodoxy of the great ecumenical councils: "On n'innovait rien à Constantinople," he writes, "mais on n'avait pas plus innové à Nicée" (Nothing was innovated at Constantinople, but nothing was innovated at Nicea either).

All uses of the word are patterned on the theological. Good things are stable by definition and therefore untainted with innovation, which is always presented as *dangerous* or *suspicious*. In politics, innovation is almost tantamount to rebellion and revolution. As we might expect, Hobbes loathes innovation. In *Government and Society* (1651), he writes:

There are many who supposing themselves wiser than others, endeavor to innovate, and divers innovators innovate in various ways.

Besides theology and politics, language and literature seem threatened by unwanted innovation, especially in "classical" France. The seventeenth-century French grammarians and literary theoreticians are against innovation, of course. Here are two mediocre lines of Ménage:

N'innovez ni ne faites rien
En la langue et vous ferez bien.

(Don't innovate or do anything
to the language, and you will do well.)

Hostility to innovation is what we expect from conservative thinkers, but we are surprised to find it under the pen of authors whom we regard as innovators. When Calvin denounces "l'appétit et convoitise de tout innover, changer et remuer" (the appetite and desire to innovate, change, and stir up everything), he sounds just like Bossuet. So does Cromwell in 1658, when he attacks what he calls "Designs . . . laid to innovate upon the Civil Rights of Nations, and to innovate in matters of religion."

The reformers see the Reformation not as *innovation* but as a *restoration* of original Christianity. They profess to return to the authentic imitation of Christ, uncorrupted by Catholic innovation.

*Mutatis mutandis*—the humanists feel just like the Protestants. They, too, hate innovation. More than ever, they look back to the ancient models that the Middle Ages revered. They indict their medieval predecessors not on the grounds that they selected the wrong models but that they did not imitate the right ones properly. The humanists differ from the Protestants, of course, in that, instead of being religious, their models are the philosophers, writers, and artists of classical antiquity.

Montaigne hates innovation. "Rien ne presse un estat," he writes, "que l'innovation; le changement donne seul forme à l'injustice et à la tyrannie" (Nothing harries a state except innovation; change alone gives form to injustice and tyranny). In the *Essays*, innovation is synonymous with "nouvelleté," a word which the author also uses disparagingly.

A social and political component is present in all this fear of the new, but something else lies behind it, something religious that is more archaic and pagan than specifically Christian. The negative view of innovation reflects what I call *external mediation*, a world in which the need for and the identity of all cultural models is taken for granted. This is so true that, in the Middle Ages, the concept of innovation is hardly needed. Its use is usually confined to technical discussions of heresy in Latin. In the vulgar tongues, the need for the word appears only in the last phase of external mediation, which I roughly identify with the sixteenth and seventeenth centuries.

People mutually accuse each other of being bad imitators, unfaithful to the true essence of the models. Not until a little later, with the great *Querelle des anciens et des modernes*, does the battle shift to the question of which models are best, the traditional ones or their modern rivals? The idea that *there must be models* still remains common to both camps. The principle of stable imitation is the foundation of the system, and is the last to be questioned.

The world of external mediation genuinely fears the loss of its transcendental models. Society is felt to be inherently fragile. Any tampering with things as they are could unleash the primordial mob and bring about a regression to original chaos. What is feared is a collapse of religion and society as a whole, through a mimetic contagion that would turn the people into a mob.

We have many echoes of this in Shakespeare. In *Henry IV, Part I*, the King speaks of

Poor discontents
Which gape and rub the elbow at the news
Of hurly-burly innovation (5.1.78–80)

"Hurly burly" means tumult, confusion, storm, violent upheaval. In 1639, Webster mentions: "The Hydra-headed multitude that only gape for innovation." On the subject of the English revolution, Bossuet speaks a similar language and reflects a similar mentality:

Quelque chose de plus violent se remuait dans le fond des cœurs; c'était un dégoût secret de tout ce qui a de l'autorité, et une démangeaison d'innover sans fin dès qu'on en a vu le premier exemple.

(Something very violent stirred in the bottom of their hearts; it was a secret disgust of everything having authority, and an urge to innovate incessantly from the moment of seeing a first example of it.)

A taste for innovation is supposed to denote a perverse and even a deranged mind. The unfavorable implications of the word were so well established that we still find them under the pen of a thinker as radical as Diderot: "Toute innovation est à craindre dans un gouvernement" (In a government, every innovation is to be feared). There is an apocalyptic ring to this old use of innovation that contrasts sharply with the modern flavor of the term.

The Jacobin Terror was such, it seems, as to keep this fear alive, but only the most eloquent traditionalists can play the old tune successfully—Xavier de Maistre, and, on occasion, Edmund Burke. He calls the French Revolution "a revolt of innovation; and thereby the very elements of society have been confounded and dissipated."

Paradoxically, the Revolution did not reinforce the ancient fear of *innovation*, but instead greatly contributed to its demise. The guillotine terrified many people, of course, but it was "political" terror in the modern sense and no longer something mysterious and uncanny. What disappeared at that time is the feeling that any deliberate tinkering with the social order is not only sacrilegious but intrinsically perilous, likely to trigger an apocalyptic disaster.

Even if the bad connotations of our word occasionally resurfaced in the eighteenth century, the story of the hour was not the perpetuation of the past, but its overthrow. It is not the core *meaning* of "innovation" that changed, but its affective "aura."

The reason, of course, was the shift away from theology, and even philosophy, toward science and technology. The word was interpreted in a new context which caused examples of brilliant and useful inventions to spring to the mind. The good impression automatically spilled over into areas and disciplines unrelated to science and technology. This process exactly reversed the earlier one, when the bad connotations rooted in theology extended to the non-theological uses of the word.

In his *Histoire philosophique* (1770), Abbé Raynal rehabilitated innovation through the contextual change just defined. In typical *philosophe* style, he discarded the theological background with alacrity. Addressing his reader directly, the abbé writes:

Tu entendras murmurer autour de toi: cela ne se peut, et quand cela se pourrait, ce sont des innovations; des innovations! Soit, mais tant de découvertes dans les sciences et dans les arts n'en ont-elles pas été?

(You will hear murmured all around, that's not possible, and when that would be possible, it's innovations, innovations! Right, but so many discoveries in the sciences and in the arts, haven't they been innovations?)

All it takes to nip intelligent reforms in the bud is to brandish this old scarecrow, "innovation." The very sound of the word has been so unpleasant, traditionally, that no further argument is needed. Since inventions in the arts and the sciences are also innovations, the bad connotations are unfounded, and should be replaced by good ones.

At the time Raynal was writing, the change he advocated was occurring. The foul smell of heresy finally dissipated and was instantly replaced by the inebriating vapors of scientific and technical progress.

From then on, in all walks of life, would-be innovators leaned upon the prestige of science in order to promote their views. This is especially true in the political and social sphere. Social organization is now perceived as the creation of mere human beings, and other human beings have the right to redesign it in part or even *in toto*.

As early as the beginning of the nineteenth century, innovation became the god that we are still worshipping today. In 1817, for instance, Bentham characterized an idea as "a proposition so daring, so innovational . . . !" (Someone must have found innovative too short a word, and forged the longer "innovational." That someone must have been Bentham himself. Innovation to him is like candy to a child—the bigger the piece, the more slowly and voluptuously it will dissolve in your mouth.)

The new cult meant that a new scourge had descended upon the world—"stagnation." Before the eighteenth century, "stagnation" was unknown; suddenly, it spread its gloom far and wide. The more innovative the capitals of the modern spirit became, the more "stagnant" and "boring" the surrounding countryside appeared. In *La rabouilleuse*, a supposedly conservative Balzac deplores the retrograde ways of the French provinces: "Hélas! Faire comme faisaient nos pères, ne rien innover, telle est la loi du pays" (Alas! To do things as our fathers did, to innovate nothing, such is the law of the countryside).

In an amazingly short time, a systematically positive view of innovation replaced the systematically negative one. Everything was reversed, and even the least innovative people found themselves celebrating innovation.

## Innovation and Imitation

As in most semantic revolutions, rhetoric plays a role, but more than rhetoric is involved. The world that reviled innovation was changing very fast, faster, no doubt, than at any previous time in its history, but the world that exalts innovation has been changing even faster.

Our little revolution coincides with two big ones that have not yet completed their course: the democratic revolution and the industrial revolution. The latter is rooted in a third, the scientific revolution, which started earlier, no doubt, but whose pace greatly accelerated when the other two also picked up steam.

As I said before, the negative view of innovation is inseparable from a conception of the spiritual and intellectual life dominated by stable imitation. Being the source of eternal truth, of eternal beauty, of eternal goodness, the models should never change. Only when these transcendental models are toppled can innovation acquire a positive meaning. *External mediation* gives way to a world in which, at least in principle, individuals and communities are free to adopt whichever models they prefer and, better still, no model at all.

This seems to go without saying. Our world has always believed that "to be innovative" and "to be imitative" are two incompatible attitudes. This was already true when innovation was feared; now that it is desired, it is truer than ever.

The following sentence is a good example. Michelet deplores the influence of moderate elements on the French Revolution: "Ils la firent réformatrice, l'empêchèrent d'être fondatrice, d'innover et de créer" (They made it reformatory, prevented it from being a new foundation, from innovating and creating). The romantic historian puts innovation on a par with foundation and creation itself, the creation *ex nihilo*, no doubt, that, up to that time, had been the exclusive monopoly of the biblical God.

During the nineteenth and much of the twentieth centuries, as the passion for innovation intensified, the definition of it becomes more and more radical, less and less tolerant of tradition, that is, of imitation. As it spread from painting to music and to literature, the radical view of innovation triggered the successive upheavals that we call "modern art." A complete break with the past is viewed as the sole achievement worthy of a "creator."

At least in principle, this innovation mania affects all aspects of human existence. This is true not only of such movements as surrealism, but of writers who, at first sight, seem to continue more traditional trends.

Consider, for instance, the implications of the following sentence in Raymond Radiguet's *Le diable au corps*: "Tous les amants, même les plus médiocres, s'imaginent qu'ils innovent" (All lovers, even the most mediocre, believe that they innovate). If the novelist finds it necessary to say that the innovation of mediocre lovers is imaginary, he must also believe that it can be real, when it proceeds from genuinely talented lovers.

Just as the measure of a painter's talent is now his capacity to innovate in painting, the measure of a lover's love is his or her capacity to innovate in the field of love-making. To be "with it" in the France of 1920, one had to be "innovative" even in the privacy of the boudoir. What a burden on all lovers' shoulders! Far from exorcising the urge to mimic famous lovers in literature and history, compulsory innovation can only inflame it further.

Even philosophy succumbed to the "terrorism" of innovation. When French philosophers began to look for an insurance policy against the greatest possible ill—fidelity to the past, the repetition of *dépassé* philosophies—one of their inventions was *la rupture épistémologique*. This miraculous concept made it possible for the communist Althusser to be an old style *aparatchik* on the one hand and, on the other, one hundred percent innovational, almost as much so as Marx himself, since Althusser was the first to take the full measure of the prophet's innovative genius.

The psychoanalyst Lacan pulled exactly the same trick with Freud. Very quickly, however, one single *rupture épistémologique* for all times and for all people seemed paltry. Each thinker had to have his own, and then the really chic thinkers had several in a row. In the end, everybody turned oneself into a continuous and monstrous *rupture*, not primarily with others—that goes without saying—but with one's own past.

This is how *inconsistency* has become the major intellectual virtue of the avant-garde. But the real credit for the *tabula rasa* school of innovation should go to Nietzsche, who was tired of repeating with everybody else that a great thinker should have no model. He went one better, as always, and made the refusal to *be* a model the mark of genius. This is still a sensation that is being piously repeated everyday. Nietzsche is our supreme model of model repudiation, our revered guru of guru-renunciation.

The emphasis on *ruptures, fragments,* and *discontinuities* is still all the rage in our universities. Michel Foucault has taught us to cut up the history of ideas in separate segments with no communication between them. Even the history of science has developed its own counterpart of Foucault's *épistémé.* In the *Structure of Scientific Revolution,* Thomas Kuhn tells us more or less that the only scientists worth their salt are those who make themselves completely unintelligible to their colleagues by inventing an entirely new *paradigm.*

This extreme view of innovation has been dominant for so long that even our dictionaries take it for granted. *Innovation* is supposed to exclude *imitation* as completely as imitation excludes it. Examples of how the word should be used are of this type: "It is easier to imitate than to innovate."

This conception is false, I believe, but its falsity is easier to show in some domains than in others. The easiest illustration is to be seen in contemporary market economies. This is certainly a domain in which innovation occurs on a massive, even a frightening scale, at least in the so-called developed countries. It is not difficult to observe the type of behavior that fosters economic innovation. In economics, innovation has a precise definition; it is sometimes the bringing of a technical invention into widespread practical use, but it can be many other things, such as improvements in production technique, or in management. It is anything yet untried that gives a business an edge over its competitors. That is why innovation is often regarded as the principal, even the sole source, of profits.

Business people can speak lyrically about their mystical faith in innovation and the brave new world it is creating, but the driving force behind their constant innovation is far from utopian. In a vigorous economy, it is a matter of survival, pure and simple. Business firms must innovate in order to remain competitive.

Competition, from two Latin words, *cum* and *petere*, means to "seek together." What all businessmen seek is profits; they seek them together with their competitors in the paradoxical relationship that we call "competitive."

When a business loses money it must innovate very fast, and it cannot do so without forethought. Usually there is neither the money nor the time for this. In this predicament, business people with a strong survival instinct will usually reason as follows: "If our competitors are more successful than we are, they must be doing something right. We must do it ourselves, and the only practical way to go about it is to imitate them as exactly as we can."

Most people will agree that there is a role for imitation in economic recovery, but only in the first phase of the healing process. By imitating its successful competitors, an endangered firm can innovate in relation to itself; it will thus catch up with its rivals, but it will invent nothing really new.

This common sense makes less sense than it seems. To begin with, is there such a thing as "absolute innovation"? In a first phase, no doubt, imitation will be rigid and myopic. It will have the ritual quality of external mediation. After a while, however, the element of novelty in the competitor's practice will be mastered, and imitation will become bolder. At that moment, it may—or may not—generate some additional improvement, which will seem insignificant at first, because it is not suggested by the model, but which really is the genuine innovation that will turn things around.

I am not denying the specificity of innovation. I am simply observing that, concretely, in a truly innovative process, it is often so continuous with imitation that its presence can be discovered only after the fact, through a process of abstraction that isolates aspects which are inseparable from one another.

Not so long ago, in Europe, the Americans were portrayed as primarily imitators, good technicians, no doubt, but the real brain power was in Germany or in England. Then, in very few years, the Americans became great innovators.

Public opinion is always surprised when it sees the modest imitators of one generation turn into the daring innovators of the next. The constant recurrence of this phenomenon must have something to teach us.

Until quite recently, the Japanese were dismissed as mere copiers of Western ways, incapable of real leadership in any field. They are now the driving force behind innovation in more and more technical fields. When did they acquire that inventive spark which, supposedly, they lacked? At this very moment, imitators of the Japanese—the Koreans, the Taiwanese—are repeating the same process. They, too, are fast turning into innovators. Had not something similar already occurred in the nineteenth century, when Germany first rivaled and then surpassed England in industrial might? The metamorphosis of imitators into innovators occurs repeatedly, but we always react to it with amazement. Perhaps we do not want to know about the role of imitation in innovation.

"It is easier to imitate than to innovate." This is what the dictionaries tell us. But it is true that the only shortcut to innovation is imitation. And here is another sentence that illustrates the meaning of innovation: "Many people imitate when they think that they innovate." This cannot be denied, but it should be added that *many people innovate when they think that they imitate.*

## Innovation and Competition

In economic life, imitation and innovation are not only compatible but almost inseparable.[1] This conclusion runs counter to the modern ideology of *absolute innovation.* Does it mean that this precious commodity comes in two varieties, one that relies on imitation and one that does not, a lower type reserved for business and a "higher" type reserved for "higher" culture?

This is what many intellectuals want to believe. If we agreed with them, we would nullify the one great insight of Marx—that the *same* competitive pattern dominates *all* aspects of modern culture, being the most visible in economic life. On this particular point, Marx is our best guide.

The radical view of innovation is obviously false. But why does our culture so stubbornly cling to it? Why are modern intellectuals and artists so hostile to imitation?

In order to answer this question, we must go back to our example of mimetic inventiveness—business competition. The very fact that those who compete are models and imitators shows two things: imitation survives the collapse of external mediation; and a crucial change has occurred in its *modus operandi.*

In "external mediation" either the models have the advantage of being long dead or of standing so far above their imitators that they cannot become their rivals. This is not the case in the modern world. Since competitors stand next to each other, in the same world, they must all compete for the things that they desire in common, with resulting reciprocal imitation. This is the great difference between "external" and "internal" mediation.

All imitators select models whom they regard as superior. In "internal mediation," models and imitators are equal in every respect except one: the superior achievement of the one, which motivates the imitation of the other. This means, of course, that the models are successful *at their imitators' expense.*

Defeat in any kind of competition is disagreeable for reasons that go beyond the material losses that may be incurred. When we imitate successful rivals, we explicitly acknowledge what we would prefer to deny—their superiority. The urge to imitate is very strong, since it opens up possibilities of bettering the competition. But the urge *not* to imitate is also very strong. The only thing that the losers can deny the winners is the homage of their imitation.

Unlike external mediation, the internal variety is a reluctant *mimesis* that generally goes unrecognized because it hides behind a bewildering diversity of masks. The mimetic urge can never be repressed entirely, but it can turn into counter-imitation. The losers try to demonstrate their independence by systematically taking the course opposite to that of the winners. Thus, they may act in a way detrimental to their own self-interest. Their pride turns self-destructive. No political or Freudian "unconscious" is necessary to account for that.

Even in economic life, where the material incentives to imitate are strongest, the urge *not* to imitate may prove even stronger, especially in international trade, which is affected by questions of "national pride." When a nation cannot successfully compete, it is tempted to blame its failure on unfair competition, thus paving the way for protectionist measures that put an end to peaceful competition.

## Innovation in the Arts

The rules of the game may be objectively unfair, of course, but they never seem so to the winners and they always seem so to the losers. Nations greatly dislike the image of themselves projected by any kind of defeat, and they will try to efface it by all possible means. If they feel that it cannot be done through fair competition, they may resort to violence or retreat into the sterile isolation of *autarkie*.

It is not a deficit but an *excess* of competitive spirit that makes productive competition impossible. If this occasionally happens in economic life, where the incentive to compete is greatest, what about more subtle and hidden but even more intense forms of competition, like in the sciences, the arts, and philosophy, where universally acknowledged means of evaluation are lacking?

In my opinion, the tendency to define "innovation" in more and more "radical" and anti-mimetic terms—the mad escalation that I briefly sketched earlier—reflects a vast surrender of modern intelligence to this mimetic pressure, a collective embrace of self-deception which Marx himself, for all his insights, remarkably exemplifies.

Like many nineteenth- and twentieth-century intellectuals, Marx sees competitiveness as an unmitigated evil that can and should be abolished, together with the free market, the only economic system that, for all its faults, channels the competitive spirit into constructive efforts instead of exacerbating it to the level of physical violence or discouraging it entirely. Marx's purely historical thinking misses the complex anthropological consequences of democratic equality which Tocqueville perceived. Marx did not detect the change from one modality of imitation to another; he was unable to define the mimetic rivalry unleashed by the abandonment of transcendental models, by the collapse of hierarchical thinking.

In spite of many glorious exceptions, our recent intellectual climate has been determined not by a lucid analysis of these phenomena, but by their repression, which produces the type of effects described by Nietzsche as *ressentiment*. Most intellectuals take the path of least intellectual resistance vis-à-vis internal mediation, and their obsessive concern with their own mimetic rivals is always accompanied by a fierce denial of participation in mimetic rivalry and a determination to crush this abomination through the means of political and cultural revolution.

As a result, most theories fashionable in Europe in the nineteenth and twentieth centuries have been philosophical and aesthetic equivalents of the economic *autarkie* that preceded World War II, and their consequences have been no less disastrous. The urge to imitate successful rivals is so abhorrent that all forms of mimesis must be discredited. Instead of re-examining imitation and discovering its conflictual dimension, the eternal avant-garde has waged a purely defensive and ultimately self-destructive war against it.

When the *humility* of discipleship is experienced as *humiliating*, the transmission of the past becomes difficult, even impossible. The so-called counter-culture of the sixties was a climactic moment in this strange rebellion, a revolt not merely against the competitiveness of modern life in all its forms, but against the very principle of education. Avant-garde culture has disfigured innovation so badly that we have to look to economic life to see why our world of internal mediation is so innovative.

Economic life is an example of an *internal mediation* that produces an enormous, even a frightening amount of innovation, since it ritualizes and institutionalizes mimetic rivalry, the rules of which are willingly obeyed. Economic agents *openly* imitate their successful rivals instead of pretending otherwise.

False as they are, the theories that dominate our cultural life are "true" in that they truly influence the cultural environment. In the arts, the scorched-earth policies of the recent past have led to a world in which radical innovation is so free to flourish that there is little difference between having it everywhere and having it nowhere at all.

The dazzling achievements of modern art and modern literature seem to give the lie to what I have just said. And it is true, indeed, that, in these domains, spiritual *autarkie* has a fecundity which has no parallel in science, technology, or economic life. Romantic and post-romantic literature thrive for a while on a diet of antiheroes and on critical or naïve portrayals of individual reactions to the pressures of internal mediation—the retreat of the modern "consciousness" into "itself."

Rousseau was the first great explorer of a territory that already had a large population when he began to write. In no time at all, he became immensely popular and had countless imitators. He ruled over the *under-ground* realm whose most lucid master is probably Dostoevsky. The Russian novelist's greatest work is a prodigious satire of self-pity, a luxury that much of the world cannot afford. From Rousseau to Kafka and beyond, the best of modern literature focused on the *fausse conscience* to which intellectuals are more prone than other people because of their preoccupation with those purely individual pursuits—books and works of art—that become the principal yardsticks of their being. The private question of *being* seems entirely separate from another and supposedly minor one—the question of where these artists and thinkers stand in relation to each other. However, in reality, the two questions are one.

## Conclusion

After providing a great deal of genuinely innovative material, and postponing for more than a century the day of reckoning with our solipsistic ideologies, the rich vein of failed spiritual *autarkie* has finally run out, and the future of art and literature is in doubt.

Most people still try to convince themselves that our "arts and humanities" will remain forever "creative" and "innovative," fueled by "individualism," but even the most enthusiastic espousers of recent trends are beginning to wonder. Innovation is still around, they say, but its pace is slackening.

This pessimism, which I share, is a subjective judgment—but, in such matters, can there be any other? It seems obvious to me that the still genuinely innovative areas of our culture are those in which innovation is acknowledged in modest and prudent terms, whereas those areas in which "innovation" is absolute and arrogant hide their disarray behind meaningless agitation.

I do not say this because I believe in an intrinsic *superiority* of the still innovative areas in our culture—science, technology, and the economy. But I think that our cultural activities are vulnerable in direct proportion to the spiritual greatness that should be theirs. The old scholastic adage always applies: *Corruptio optimi pessima*—the corruption of the best is the worst.

The true Romantics believed that if we gave up imitation entirely, deep in our selves an inexhaustible source of "creativity" would spring up, and we would produce masterpieces without having to learn anything. Mistaking the end of transcendental models for an end of *all* imitation, the Romantics and their modern successors have turned the "creative process" into a veritable theology of the self—with roots in the distant past, as we have seen. In the old dispensation, innovation was reserved for God and therefore forbidden to man. When man took upon himself the attributes of God, he became the absolute innovator.

The Latin word *in-novare* implies limited change rather than total revolution—a combination of continuity and discontinuity. We have seen that, from the beginning, in the West, *innovation* departed from its Latin meaning in favor of the more "radical" view demanded by the extremes of execration and adulation alternately triggered by the idea of change.

The mimetic model of innovation is valid not only for our economic life, but for all cultural activities whose innovative potential depends on the kind of passionate imitation that derives from religious ritual and still partakes of its spirit.

Real change can only take root when it springs from the type of co-herence that tradition alone provides. Tradition can only be successfully challenged from the inside. The main prerequisite for real innovation is a minimal respect for the past and a mastery of its achievements, that is, *mimesis*. To expect novelty to cleanse itself of imitation is to expect a plant to grow with its roots up in the air. In the long run, the obligation always to rebel may be more destructive of novelty than the obligation never to rebel.

But is not all this ancient history? Has not the modern theology of the self been fully discredited and discarded along with the rest of "Western metaphysics"? As the deconstruction of our philosophical tradition proceeds, shall we not be "liberated" at long last, and will not a new culture automatically flourish?

The blurring of all aesthetic and intellectual criteria of judgment underlies what is now called the "post-modern" aesthetics. This blurring parallels the elimination of truth in post-Heideggerian philosophy. Our age tries to overcome the modern obsession with the "new" through an orgy of casual imitation, an indiscriminate adoption of all models. There is no such thing anymore as a mediocre lover, in the sense of Radiguet. Pierre Menard's perfect copy of Don Quixote is just as great as the novel of Cervantes. Imitation has lost its stigma.

Does it mean that concrete innovation is back? Before we become too hopeful, we must observe that *mimesis* returns to us in a parodic and derisive mode that is a far cry from the patient, pious, and single-minded imitation of the past. The imitation that produced miracles of innovation was still obscurely related to the *mimesis* of religious ritual.

The real purpose of post-modern thinking may well be to silence, once and for all, the question that has never ceased to bedevil "creators" in our democratic world—the question of "Who is innovative and who is not?" If such is the case, post-modernism is only the latest modality of our romantic "false consciousness," one more twist of the old serpent. There will be more.

## Mimetic Desire in the
## Underground: Feodor Dostoevsky
## [1997]

Mimetic desire is often regarded as an artificial construct, a "reductionist" device that impoverishes the literary works to which it is "applied." During my entire career, the "reductionist" objection has dogged my books with the regularity of a Pavlovian reflex, and if there is a chance to escape unscathed for a change, why spoil it?[1]

Mimetic desire is "reductionist," no doubt, but so is the very process of abstraction, and, unless we renounce thinking altogether, we cannot give up abstracting. Even if it were a viable option, a non-reductionist interpretation would merely paraphrase Dostoevsky; it would be of no interest to me. The only concrete choice, I feel, is between good and bad reductionism.

Since our starting point is mimetic desire, we must begin with its definition. To say that our desires are imitative or mimetic is to root them neither in their objects nor in ourselves, but in a third party, the *model* or *mediator*, whose desire we imitate in the hope of resembling him or her, in the hope that our two beings will be "fused," as some Dostoevskyan characters love to say.

The psychologists interested in *role models* tell us that young people, when they grow up, must imitate the best possible models. These should be older persons who have made a place for themselves in the community.

If the growing youngsters imitate these good people, presumably they will not go astray.

What I like about the idea of role model is the paramount function that, at least implicitly, it attributes to imitation. Most psychologists believe, mistakenly in my view, that imitation affects only our superficial attitudes and manners. If it did not influence our very *desires*, even the best role models could have no significant influence on their imitators.

Why do peers, as a rule, even if not intrinsically bad, make bad role models? As I borrow the desire of a model from whom nothing separates me, neither time and space, nor prestige and social hierarchy, we both inevitably desire the same object and, unless this object can be shared and we are willing to share it, we will compete for it. Instead of uniting us, our shared desire will turn us into rivals and potential enemies.

This *mimetic rivalry* is most obvious in small children. When two of them are left to play together, even and especially on a mountain of toys, the togetherness does not last. As soon as one child selects a toy, the other tries to take it away from him.

The second child imitates the first. And the first child does his utmost to retain possession of the toy, not because this one, at least, "knows what he or she wants," but for the opposite reason. The first child does not know any better than the second, and the latter's interference reinforces the original choice. Conflicts of desire keep occurring not because strongly individualized desires strongly oppose one another, but for the opposite reason. Each child takes the other as the model and guide of a desire that must be fundamentally free-floating and unattached, since it attaches itself most stubbornly to the object of its rival, not only in children but in adults as well.

Because of their mimetic nature, the rivalries of desires keep escalating, and the disputed objects acquire more and more value in the eyes of both rivals, even if the initial choice had no significance whatever, even if it was more or less random.

We hate to think that adults behave like children in matters of desire, especially in an "individualistic" world such as ours, but we do. We all protest that our desires are strictly our own, and we despise imitation, but we imitate one another more fiercely than children. The only difference is that, unlike children, we are ashamed, and we try to hide our imitation.

When we borrow the desires of those we admire, we must play the deadly serious game of mimetic rivalry with them. Whenever we lose, our models successfully thwart our desires and, because we admire them, we feel rejected and humiliated. But since their victory over us confirms their superiority, we admire them more than ever and our desire becomes more intense.

As our confidence in our models increases, our self-confidence decreases. When this frustration occurs too often, and we turn too many models into rivals and obstacles, our perversely logical mind tends to speed up the process and automatically turn obstacles into models. We become *obstacle addicts*, so to speak, unable to desire in the absence of an obstacle-who-is-also-a-model, a beloved enemy who has, as Shakespeare writes in *A Midsummer Night's Dream*, "turned a heaven into a hell" (1.1.207).

What does all this have to do with Dostoevsky? Everything. Take the "hero" of *Notes from Underground*: this puny little man, this "acutely conscious mouse," entirely devoid of charisma, always finds himself in the most grotesque situations. One day, in a billiard room, he stands in the way of some arrogant petty officer who, most unceremoniously, lifts him from one spot and puts him down in another.

Because the officer treats him as an insignificant obstacle, our hero sees him as an enormous, monstrous obstacle that must be overturned at all cost. This we can well understand. What seems inexplicable, however, is that, simultaneously, he sees the officer as a fascinating idol with whom he would like to be "fused."

The officer is automatically transformed into a model simply because he is an infuriating obstacle. The underground man spends long hours trying to fulfill his twofold desire—overturning the obstacle and becoming "fused" with it—into an appropriate revenge, which finally consists in—what else?—mimicking his insultor and treating him as an insignificant obstacle himself, jostling him off the sidewalk on the famous Nevsky Prospekt, the elegant promenade of St. Petersburg.

Childish rivalries are quickly extinguished and forgotten . . . Adult rivalries go on forever and have a lasting influence. When physical violence is suppressed, as normally happens in modern civilized life, all frustrated rivalries go underground and show up as "psychopathological symptoms," the very symptoms exhibited by underground characters in Dostoevsky's masterpieces.

One goes "underground" as a result of frustrated mimetic desire. All underground people carefully hide their imitations, even from themselves, so as not to give their models the psychic reward of seeing themselves imitated, not to humiliate themselves by being revealed as imitators.

Dostoevsky grants a quasi-technical value to the word "underground." He used it again in *The Eternal Husband*, in connection with the "apishness" of his central character, who is another, slightly different type of underground "antihero."

For many years, his wife was having love affairs on a regular basis. After her premature death, the widower leaves his provincial town for Petersburg, in search of her former lovers, and he keeps circling around one of these who is also the narrator of our story. For many a day this behavior remains enigmatic.

Our culture is so steeped in psychoanalytical lore that most of us, when asked to solve this enigma, suggest that the eternal husband must be "unconsciously" in love with his rival. This is Freud's "latent homosexuality" hypothesis. In our particular case, it was proposed by the master himself in his article on Dostoevsky. The difficulty with it is that it leaves ninety-five percent of the story out of account.

Mimetic desire works better. Quite understandably, the eternal husband feels deficient in the art of seduction. To remedy his inferiority, he seeks the best possible model and, from his own personal standpoint, it has to be the man who supplanted him in the heart of his wife, demonstrating *ipso facto* his superior expertise in the erotic field. This choice is startling not because it is irrational, but because it is based on an unimpeachable logic.

The true nature of the relationship becomes obvious when the eternal husband decides to marry again and invites his former rival to come along for a visit to his prospective bride.

He pictures himself as a modern man, an "individualist," and he has chosen his future wife independently from his model, but then he cannot go ahead with his project unless the eternal lover approves of his choice. The young woman must be stamped with the latter's official seal, so to speak.

The eternal husband expects and even hopes, yes, he hopes that the eternal lover will find his prospective wife desirable, that he will actually desire her. Without this guarantee of quality, she would not seem worth marrying and the eternal husband would look for a better prospect, more to the liking of his model.

At first, the eternal lover is scandalized at the idea of meeting the girl, but the invitation is repeated and he feels a mysterious compulsion to accept. She is ludicrously young, but as soon as he is introduced to her, the eternal lover starts acting as if he, too, were interested in her and, very quickly, between the two, a semi-erotic complicity is established against her ridiculous suitor, the eternal husband.

At first, we believe that the latter has willfully engineered this new humiliation, but, on closer examination, we can see that he is looking forward to more mimetic rivalry with the eternal lover, which he hopes to win this time. The eternal lover responds in kind; his competitive urge is aroused. The two men behave like two children fighting over the same toy.

The eternal husband is in love not with his rival but with his rival's *success as a lover*. Like a bold gambler, he wants to recoup his losses at a single stroke. The only triumph that really interests him is the one he would achieve at the expense of his rival . . . He will never achieve it. Being less elegant and handsome than the eternal lover, he will always come out second best. His frantic desire for *revanche* exposes him to endless defeats. The eternal lover's successes and the eternal husband's failures are two sides of the same coin.

And yet the relationship is less one-sided than it seems. The two men interchange their roles in the one case of poor little Liza, the adulterous wife's daughter, who may also be the eternal lover's daughter . . . The eternal husband cruelly uses her to blackmail his revered enemy. And yet Liza dearly loves and pities the man whom she regards as her real father, rightly surmising that he has been greatly wronged and that he greatly suffers. When the eternal lover takes her away from the eternal husband, she becomes ill and dies.

Since the objects of our desires are infinitely diverse and forever changing, when we try to understand desire in general, we must avoid the mistake of Marx, Freud, and others, and we must privilege no particular category of objects. Desire can be understood neither through its objects nor through its subjects. We must interpret many phenomena through the human subject, such as appetites and needs on the one hand, disinterested affection on the other, and all these things can get mixed with desire, no doubt, but desire as such is something else. What we must stress is the convergence of two or several desires on the same object, which may increase enormously the value of literally any object. Mimetic desire is a realistic theory of why human beings cannot be realists.

∼

In the first and more theoretical part of *Notes from Underground*, the hero's "lifestyle" is contrasted to the theories of some English philosophers who were highly fashionable in Dostoevsky's day and who, once again, are fashionable in ours, the "pragmatists" and the "utilitarians," those who think that the human predicament can be solved through sheer neglect or pure laissez-faire, the original free market devotees.

According to these thinkers, human beings must first be freed from religious faith. And then, if nothing else is done, if we are all left to our own devices, we will all spontaneously engage in productive activities beneficial both to ourselves and to our communities. The natural law of human behavior is *enlightened self-interest*. If it is allowed to prevail, economic, social, and political problems will all miraculously be solved.

The underground man regards all this as nonsense and, at the end of this first part, he announces that, in the second part, which is more like a novel, he will refute utilitarianism through the sheer demonstrative force of his own life, which squarely contradicts his own self-interest. He manages to live in such a way that his interaction with other people generates the maximum amount of failure, unpleasantness, anger, humiliation, and despair for all those involved, especially himself.

And yet, the underground man fulfills all the conditions that, according to the English philosophers, should automatically lead him to seek his "enlightened self-interest." He has no religious faith; he disdains conventional morality and other "superstitions." He despises the starry-eyed idealism and altruistic benevolence that, still according to these philosophers, have always impeded the smooth functioning of "enlightened self-interest."

The underground hero is as selfish as he can possibly be, and this is precisely where his trouble lies: he cannot be sufficiently selfish. His intense mimetic desire compels him to gravitate around human obstacles of the pettiest kind. His motivation is strictly egotistical, but he is so disgusted with himself that his would-be egotism constantly turns into its own opposite and delivers him, body and soul, into the hands of petty tyrants, such as the arrogant officer on the Nevsky Prospekt or his fellow alumni from the mediocre engineering school where Dostoevsky himself had been a student. Our hero treats these people as fearsome divinities, even though, simultaneously, he sees them as complete nonentities, vastly inferior to himself in intelligence and cultural finesse.

The dramatic part of *Notes* shows us how "enlightened self-interest," at the very moment when it should triumph, is likely to be replaced by its exact opposite, a most bizarre law of "unenlightened self-enslavement," we might say, or "obscurantist *other-interest.*"

Is not this underground law irrelevant to the vast majority of us who pride ourselves on being normal, the solid citizens of this world who have no affinities, we feel, for the antics of such mimetic freaks as Dostoevsky's grotesque creations?

The novelist anticipates this objection, and he has the underground man, his mouthpiece at this point, reject it as hypocritical. The underground is a caricature, of course, but its inmates are only taking to logical extremes tendencies and propensities present in all human beings. Out of sheer timidity, and also for the purpose of keeping our own underground under control, most of us keep everything carefully hidden, even from ourselves, if not always from others. The caricatural dimension of Dostoevsky's art is also demanded by the exigencies of coherent expression; his ironic genius responds to the need for clarity by reinforcing all contrasts, by making the picture even more grotesque than it really is.

What are these tendencies and propensities which are present in all of us? Dostoevsky does not say. He cannot reach a sufficiently high level of abstraction to round up his own demonstration. He cannot put the underground in a nutshell, but we can do all this for him.

We can formulate the law of the underground in terms of mimetic desire, as a relatively benign illness, no doubt, unless it is pushed to what Dostoevsky calls its logical extremes, and then it turns into what I called the obstacle addiction. What this addiction really entails is clear: underground people are irresistibly attracted to those who spurn them, and they irresistibly spurn those who are attracted to them, or even those who do no more than treat them kindly.

The second part of *Notes* consists in three separate little dramas all equally grotesque, except for the third which is heart-rending as well. The first two are the story of the arrogant officer and the story of the dismal school reunion. The third is the story of the kind prostitute who tries to befriend the underground man and who is brutally rejected by him.

The first two dramas illustrate the first half of the underground law; they show that the underground man is irresistibly attracted to those who spurn him. The third drama illustrates the second half of that same law; it shows that the underground man irresistibly spurns those who are attracted to him.

Thus, exasperated mimetic desire insures a maximum amount of misfortune to those who surrender to it. When pushed far enough, the mimetic obstacle addiction compels human beings to behave in a manner diametrically opposed to anything even remotely reminiscent of their "enlightened self-interest." This, I believe, is what Dostoevsky is trying to prove.

The underground goes beyond this first demonstration. What it shows really, again and again, is that hell truly exists. Hell is not a figment of a human imagination still imprisoned in archaic thinking. Dostoevsky's interplay of obstacles and models is a terrestrial version of hell with a religious significance that still awaits definition.

We can round up Dostoevsky's demonstration by being even more reductionist than he is, with the help of mimetic desire. The theory of mimetic desire is reductionist in the extreme; its critics are right: it is reductionist with a vengeance. That is why some literary people regard it as too "systematic"; it can only imprison the fictional characters into a straitjacket, they say, a straitjacket of my own making. The function of a literary critic, these people also say, is to recapture the uniquely ineffable and inexhaustible *je ne sais quoi* with which great novelists endow the lives of their characters; he must suggest the infinite richness of a pure and noble work of art . . .

There is something true in this objection, and it is the straitjacket. The word is a good one to express not what I myself am doing to the underground man but what he is doing himself. He is in a straitjacket, to be sure, but not one of my own making. He got into it himself, and he made it himself, or rather Dostoevsky made it for him. In this story, Dostoevsky is not yearning for some ineffable and inexhaustible *je ne sais quoi*. He seeks to convey a much starker reality, a psychological life so impoverished that it generates an incredible amount of repetitive and mechanical behavior.

Exacerbated mimetic desire is not about the richness of life, to be sure, but about the same impoverishment Dostoevsky is talking about. Much of the best twentieth-century fiction follows Dostoevsky's lead and is even more impoverished—Samuel Beckett, for instance. Fiction itself becomes "reductionist," I say, and the trend begins with *Notes from Underground*. Mimetic desire and the obstacle/model obsession finally enable us, I believe, to formulate rigorously the law of this self-impoverishment when it is realistically portrayed, as in Dostoevsky.

Even though the underground hero occasionally talks about his freedom—and he is free, indeed, in the sense that no one can prevent him from impoverishing his own life—he is very much aware that he always reacts to the stimulus of other people in exactly the same predictable way. He behaves like an automaton. As a result, his life, in spite of its constant upheavals, is ultimately monotonous and repetitive. The real question is whether or not the principle of *repetition* at work in the underground is captured by the mimetic theory.

What Dostoevsky says to the laissez-faire philosophers is that, in a world as empty of transcendence as ours now is, if people are left to their own devices, many of them will choose the underground. If the novelist is right, the tepid blandness of English utilitarianism, even at its most enlightened, cannot compete with the underground, because, crazy as it seems, the underground often is *the law of our own desire*.

∿

The refutation of enlightened self-interest is inseparable from the social, historical, and religious preoccupations of Dostoevsky. When religious faith recedes in the modern world, human beings no longer look up to the transcendental causes that had heretofore dominated their lives. Human beings feel that they have become more rational, and, in many respects, they are right. Scientific and technical progress depends wholly on the precise and patient observation made possible by the shift of our attention from the heavenly to the earthly.

Once we are deprived of transcendental guideposts, we must trust our subjective experience. Whether we like it or not, we are little Cartesian gods with no fixed point of reference and no certainty outside of ourselves.

Since modern man has no way of knowing what is going on beyond himself, since he cannot know everything, he would become lost in a world as vast and technically complex as ours, if he had really no one to guide him. He no longer relies on priests and philosophers, of course, but he must rely on many other people nevertheless, more people than ever, as a matter of fact. They are the *experts*, the people more competent than we are in innumerable fields of endeavor.

The role of our subjective experience, therefore, is more restricted than it seems. All it can hope to do, really, when we are in trouble, is to direct us to the right *experts*.

The modern world is one of experts. They alone know what is to be done. Everything boils down to choosing the right expert. In the eyes of the eternal husband, the eternal lover is one such expert, however strange it may seem at first. It should seem less strange now than a hundred years ago. Nowadays, indeed, we have experts even in sentimental life and love-making.

I observed before that the hero's choice of his wife's lover as the model of his own erotic life is supremely rational in the Cartesian and modern sense of an exclusive reliance on an individual's purely subjective experience. Our man has learned the hard way who, in matters erotic, the real expert is. It is not he, obviously; it is the eternal lover, and he behaves accordingly. He does not conform to social decorum and conventional morality; he does not follow any religious precepts. To the bitter end, he sticks to the lessons of his own subjective experience.

A rationality torn from its religious moorings surrenders its total but incompetent liberty into the hands of experts so competent that their expertise must prevail. Our attention is focused so narrowly on our immediate surroundings that we lose all sense of the wider context, of the broader picture. Our balance becomes precarious and our gait seems unsteady, a little like Frankenstein's monster. That is why we must cling to experts.

Our cult of experts is really one with the underground fascination for the obstacle/model of mimetic rivalry. It verges on archaic man's magical faith in terrifying idols. Having repudiated religion in order to be more rational, modern man comes full circle and, in the name of a superior rationality, embraces a rational and technical form of irrationality.

If we envisage all human behavior from a great distance, we will observe that the strange evolutions of the eternal husband can be subsumed under the label of primitive religion just as well as under the label of subjective rationality. He treats the eternal lover like a ferocious sexual idol that must be propitiated and occasionally blackmailed into dispensing some favors. To that end, he sacrifices all the women in his life. From the perspective of this demonic religiosity, the death of Liza is most significant. If I had to rewrite my own long essay on Dostoevsky, I would emphasize this extremely important event.

As a result of giving up transcendence, individual pride increases, and the higher it rises, the less willing it is to humble itself, to yield any particle of its self-sovereignty. Sooner or later, this pride must encounter the tiny little stone, the puny obstacle that it will turn into a major stumbling block. This idea of an obstacle toward which we are constantly drawn, however much it hurts, is present in the Gospels. Jesus's own word, *skandalon*, or stumbling block, designates the very same mechanism as the model/obstacle of mimetic rivalry.

The more our ego-centeredness increases, the more likely it is to turn into an underground "other-centeredness" that is not "altruistic" in the slightest, even though it often masquerades as altruism. Mimetic desire is failed selfishness, impotent pride that generates the worshipful imitation of idols unrecognized as such because they are hated as much as they are revered. The modern world insidiously brings back forms of self-enslavement from which Western society had largely escaped during the Christian centuries.

The more Dostoevsky explores the underground, the more aware he becomes of this dark and "satanic" dimension of modern life. In *The*

*Demons* and *Brothers Karamazov* he explicitly interprets the fascination for obstacle/models as demonic possession, and the psychology of the underground turns into demonology. This is no surrender to irrationality, but a denunciation of it.

Social norms and restraints exist for the purpose of suppressing and moderating mimetic rivalry. The revolutionary spirit arises in an already half-disintegrated social order, one in which these norms and restraints are being relaxed and mimetic rivalries are very much on the increase. The revolutionary mystique originates in the victims of this situation, the obstacle addicts, who blame their own discomfort on the restrictions which the social order traditionally imposed upon individual behavior. The revolutionists pursue the complete destruction of this order with a passionate intensity of purpose.

Far from alleviating mimetic rivalries, the gradual loosening of the social order exasperates them. This is the reason why revolutionists never find any personal relief in the social and political "permissiveness" of pre-revolutionary periods. Their desire for revolution redoubles and becomes "radicalized."

If we project our own mimetic tangles upon society as a whole, the more entangled we are, the more rigid and tyrannical the social order will appear to us, even if, in reality, it is collapsing. To revolutionists of the Dostoevskyan type, the more feeble society becomes, the more oppressive and repressive it seems.

This whole paradoxical process is the real subject of *The Demons*. To those who do not believe that the paradox is real, Dostoevsky's critique of the revolutionary mystique appears unfair, excessive, and far-fetched. Shigalyov, a minor character in *The Demons*, seems a good example of this supposed Dostoevskyan heavy-handedness. This radical theorist thinks that the only effective road to total freedom is total despotism. Whatever the revolution may do to insure total freedom, it will end up with its opposite. This is what Shigalyov discovers, and, instead of prudently minimizing his embarrassing discovery, he embraces it wholeheartedly; he boldly makes it the centerpiece of his own program! As Richard Pevear observes: "Here we have the voice of the demonic idea in its pure state."[2]

Does not Shigalyov confirm those critics who dismiss *The Demons* as an unfair caricature of the sincere revolutionists with whom the author was associated in his youth? The character is certainly alien to factual observation. No nineteenth-century revolutionist has ever advocated despotism. Shigalyov is a slanderous creation invented for purely polemical purposes.

This character is fictional, no doubt, but what kind of a fiction is he? Obviously not the pure and gratuitous kind in which our literary critics so passionately believe. As fiction, he must be regarded as impure, since he alludes to something quite real, but not to revolutionary theory, which he distorts. He really alludes to something that even our most sublime theorists can no longer entirely disregard at the end of a century with so many revolutions in it: revolutionary *reality*.

Almost in the wink of an eye, after the Russian Revolution, the total freedom proclaimed by the Bolsheviks was metamorphosed into total servitude. This unexpected metamorphosis also occurred not merely in some of the countries which were unfortunate enough to have Communist regimes thrust upon them, but in all of them without a single exception. In light of this fact, of these many facts rather, Shigalyov acquires a prophetic dimension which is unquestionable. There are very few unambiguous examples of fulfilled historical prophecy anywhere in human history. Shigalyov is one.

Dostoevsky was writing quite a few years before the events that would confirm his pessimistic view of the forthcoming Russian Revolution. How could he convey his misgivings in a work of fiction? Since theorizing was the main revolutionary activity going on at the time, he had to distort revolutionary theory just enough to make what he regarded as its real implications obvious. He had to invent Shigalyov.

Genuine prophecy always sounds a little indecent to those whose minds are closed to its truth. A real prophet has to make do with the material provided by his own historical period, the very same material that leads all his contemporaries to conclusions completely opposed to his own. Was it not indecent, in 1871, to suggest that the sincere and politically correct Russian revolutionists would end up with Stalin and Beria?

Shigalyov is a revolutionist more honestly deluded than most, and armed with the implacable logic of an eternal husband. We can well imagine that such a man might have stumbled upon the real consequences of his own principles and naïvely spelled them out for the benefit of fellow activists. Like many comic creations, Shigalyov is a little implausible, to be sure, but very little really, and, in view of the great prophetic truth he enables his creator to express, even a much higher degree of implausibility, in this character, would still deserve our unstinted admiration.

Professional historians do not like to acknowledge prophecy. They keep warning each other against the prophetic temptation. And I can well understand why. If we cannot recognize our own prophets even after they have been proved right, we are well advised, no doubt, to abstain from prophecy altogether.

Why did it take so little time for freedom to disappear after the Russian and other twentieth-century revolutions? The truth is that, as a rule, the original revolutionists and their successors did not merely resign themselves to the Shigalyovian paradox. In the name of liberty, they actively planned and organized the suppression of all liberties. They had not foreseen this particular kind of "historical necessity," but, when it came, they adjusted to it with the greatest of ease. All along, they must have been more Shigalyovian than anyone, except for Dostoevsky, ever realized.

As long as the Soviet Union had not collapsed, it was such a formidable historical reality that, even though discredited as an ideology, it retained the prestige of a great power, of a superpower as we love to say, pursing our lips with sensuous relish. (The people primarily interested in politics are rarely as indifferent to power as they claim to be.) To "specialists" and "experts," Communism was a mistake all right, but so gigantic that even its severest critics handled it with respect. There was still a vague fear or, in some quarters, a vague hope that the historical "necessity" of Marxism had not been disproved. A leftist version of the Thousand Year Reich was still floating in the air.

Dostoevsky would not have been impressed. He foresaw the tremendous destructiveness of the forthcoming revolution, but he never took it seriously from a spiritual or intellectual standpoint. To him it was an avatar of the underground, more ridiculous than authentically tragic. The final demise of the superpower proved him right once again. It was not the grandiose apocalypse which respectful Western historians would have expected, no doubt, had they been able to predict this collapse if only a few years before it actually occurred; it was something that, except for some wild Russians such as Dostoevsky, neither friends nor foes had anticipated. And it happened in the same furtive and rapid manner as underground obsessions when they finally go away, not with a bang but with a whimper. Communism fizzled out in no time at all. Suddenly everybody was thinking about something else.

~

Should we disregard Dostoevsky because of his reactionary opinions? Contrary to what many people realize, he was a very "modern" man, deeply influenced by the spirit of his age until very late in his life. He was highly susceptible to the scientistic and materialistic case against religion. He lived in the period when "scientific materialism" was triumphant, and even though, in his later life, he badly wanted to be a real Christian, genuine religious faith kept eluding him. This was the worst, perhaps, of his many thorns in the flesh.

Since he fully understood the negative usefulness of religion as a social prop against anarchy and chaos but was personally unable to believe, his was the mood, obviously, which makes reactionary politics a real temptation.

In his great period, his embrace of the Russian Slavophils and traditionalists was as uncritical, in some respects, as his former embrace of their opponents. He was far from immune to the oscillation between extremes that characterizes the modern psyche. He was almost as mimetic as his underground characters.

Like some Russians writers of our own time, notably Solzhenitsyn, Dostoevsky did not respect the democratic spirit as much as it deserves, and he did not realize that, in spite of their anti-Christian tendencies, the Western democracies are deeply rooted in the Christian tradition.

Just as many Russians and Europeans nowadays deplore the servile imitation of everything American in their own countries, Dostoevsky deeply resented the servile imitation of everything Western that dominated the Russia of his time. His reactionary leanings were reinforced by the smugness of the West, already boasting of its great "advance" over the rest of humanity, which was then called "progress." The West was almost as vulgar as it is today, already confusing its very real material prosperity with a moral and spiritual superiority that it did not possess.

In his satire of the West and of a Westernized Russia, Dostoevsky can be hilariously funny, but he can also be excessive and unjust. Had he been a Westerner and a political scientist, this flaw in his thinking might have been fatal, but he was a Russian, and his bias, when it influences his work, is not difficult to spot.

Dostoevsky at his best is not reactionary. He perfectly understood that Russia was in desperate need of reforms, and that tsarist autocracy plus the ultra-nationalistic Orthodox Church could not provide lasting answers to the problems of his day.

Before we dismiss Dostoevsky for political reasons, we must never forget that, even though his ferocity against those we still call revolutionists was exemplary, he was not gentle either with those who now call themselves conservatives, the original free-marketeers, the true founders of laissez-faire economics.

The resiliency of Western democracies in the past, their ability until now to resist the totalitarian threats that engulfed Russia for so long, are no guarantee for the future. The current wave of underground symptoms in our society is amazingly reminiscent of Dostoevsky.

When we compare our two worlds, his and ours, the striking thing is not how much more clever, modern, "advanced," and "complex" we are compared to late nineteenth-century Russia, but how stupefyingly similar. What would Dostoevsky say about our "multicultural" universities, our dismal sexual "liberations," our radical feminists forcing their "all-inclusive" versions of the Bible down the throat of meekly submissive Christian churches? We do not have to ask; we only have to read *The Demons*. We are living a permanent remake of Dostoevsky's most prophetic novel, down to the silent complicity of our elites and the universal appetite for scandals, so richly fed by our media.

When Western humanists first encountered Dostoevsky, they mistook him for a relic from the days of Ivan the Terrible. "He is too Russian for us," they complained. Little did they know that, one century later, this "superlatively bad writer," as someone said—no, it was not Nabokov, it was Lenin—would be superlatively relevant to the interpretation of a post-Communist world.

The prophetic genius of Dostoevsky is not sufficiently acknowledged and studied. Ours is not a Dostoevskyan period in the sense of being hungry for the kind of warning his novels should be for us. The real reason why this warning is not heard may well be its striking relevance. When I reread *The Demons*, I cannot help wonder if our time does not turn away from Dostoevsky because it is Dostoevskyan in the underground sense, the hysterically mimetic sense.

Dostoevsky undermines our contemporary illusions not only by satirizing them mercilessly, but more simply by showing that many supposedly brilliant innovations of ours, stupendously original creations, are really warmed-over nineteenth-century ideas, just a little more shrill and impudent with each passing decade.

Dostoevsky's flaws are real, to be sure, but they should not be turned into a test of political correctness. Such tests are terroristic devices really, the true purpose of which is to shunt aside a work most rewardingly alien to the conformity of our intellectual milieu. We need Dostoevsky badly, and we must resist all attempts at censoring him. His work is more alive than the cultural morticians who would like to bury him.

## Conversion in Literature and
## Christianity[1] [1999]

As far as I am concerned, the subject of literature and Christianity is literally the story of my whole intellectual and spiritual existence. Many years ago, I started with literature and myth and then moved to the study of the Bible and Christian Scripture. Great literature literally led me to Christianity. This itinerary is not original. It still happens every day and has been happening since the beginning of Christianity. It happened to Saint Augustine, of course. It happened to many great saints such as Saint Francis of Assisi and Saint Theresa of Avila who, like Don Quixote, were fascinated by novels of chivalry.

One of the greatest examples of literature leading to Christianity is Dante. The experience is expressed symbolically by the role of Virgil in Dante's *Divine Comedy*. There are many reasons why Dante chose Virgil. In the *Aeneid*, Virgil makes his hero Aeneas visit hell. More important was the fact that in the Middle Ages, Virgil was regarded as a prophet of Christ, and most important of all was the fact that Virgil was greatly appreciated by Dante and had really played a role, I believe, in leading the author to Christianity.

What role? In order to understand, you have to take literally the idea of guiding someone through hell. The world of the *Aeneid* is really a world of hellish violence and, according to Dante, the function of profane literature is to guide us through Hell and Purgatory. This is what Virgil did for

Dante, and it was a great help to Dante because hell is not a very nice place to live. It is not even a nice place to visit. If you still have even two cents worth of common sense when you are in hell, you will want to get out, for very selfish reasons.

Common sense and selfishness can be good things up to a point. This fact is acknowledged in the parable of the prodigal son. Why does the prodigal son return to his father? Not because of some great mystical reason, not even because he is sorry. He decides to go back to his father when he realizes that even the lowest servant in his father's house is better off than he is now that he has left that house. He still has enough common sense and selfishness to recognize hell when he finds himself in it, and he wants to escape.

In my case, it was not Virgil or even Dante who guided me through hell, but the five novelists I discussed in my first book: Cervantes, Stendhal, Flaubert, Dostoevsky, and Proust. The more modern the novel becomes, the more you descend down the circles of a hell which can still be defined in theological terms as it is in Dante, but can also now be de-fined in non-religious terms—in terms of what happens to us when our relations with others are dominated exclusively by our desires and theirs, and their relationships dominated by their desires and ours. Because our desires are always mimetic or imitative, even and especially when we dream of being completely autonomous and self-sufficient, they always make us into rivals of our models and then the models of our rivals, thus turning our relations into an inextricable entanglement of identical and antagonis-tic desires which result in endless frustration.

Frustration is the law of the genre, but it can be of two kinds. If we are prevented by our model from acquiring the object we both desire, our desire keeps intensifying painfully as a result of the deprivation. If, on the contrary, we acquire the object we desire, the prestige of our model collaps-es and our desire weakens and dies as a result of being fulfilled. This is the second kind of frustration and it is worse than the first. When it happens, we look for another model for our desire, but the moment may come, after many such experiences, when we are totally disenchanted and cannot find any new model. This is the worst kind of frustration, the one the experts call post-modern or post-Christian desire; perhaps one could even call it post-mimetic desire.

The mortality of desire, its finitude, is the real problem in our world, since it destabilizes even the most fundamental institutions, beginning with the family. Our psychological and psychoanalytical theories do not even acknowledge the reality of this problem. Desire according to Freud is immortal and eternal, since human beings desire only substitutes for their parents and cannot cease to desire them. Freud is silent about the death of desire. Only great literature has a great deal to say about that subject.

The individualism of our time is really an effort to deny the failure of desire. Those who claim to be governed by the pleasure principle are, as a rule, enslaved to models and rivals who make their lives a constant frustration. But they are too vain to acknowledge their own enslavement. Mimetic desire makes us believe we are always on the verge of becoming self-sufficient through our own transformation into someone else. Our would-be transformation into a god turns us, as Shakespeare says, into an ass. In Pascal's terms, it becomes "Qui veut faire l'ange fait la bête" (Whoever tries to act like an angel turns into a beast).

Understanding the real failure of desire leads to wisdom and ultimately to religion. Many philosophies and all religions share in that wisdom which modern trendiness denies. Great literature shares in that wisdom because it does not cheat with desire. It shows the necessary failure of undisciplined desire. The greatest literature shows the impossibility of self-fulfillment through desire. Mimetic obsessions are dreadful because they cannot vanquish their own circularity, even when they know about it. They are the mother of all addictions, such as drugs, alcohol, obsessive sexuality, etc. One cannot get out of the circle even as its radius becomes smaller and smaller and our world becomes more narrowly obsessive.

Unlike most philosophies which are fundamentally Stoic or Epicurean, Judaism and Christianity preach no kind of self-fulfillment or self-absorption. Nor do they preach self-annihilation, in the manner of Oriental mysticism. Christianity acknowledges the ultimate goodness of imitation as well as the goodness and reality of the human person. It teaches that instead of surrendering to mimetic desire, by following the newest fashion and worshipping the latest idol, we should imitate only Christ or Christlike noncompetitive models.

If one is badly caught up in this circularity and wants to get out of it, one must undergo an experience of radical change which religious people call a *conversion*. In the classical view of conversion, it is not something of our own doing but the personal intervention of God in our lives. The greatest experience for Christians is the experience of becoming religious under a compulsion that they feel cannot come from themselves but from God alone. What makes conversion fascinating to those who have this experience (but also to those who do not) is the feeling that at no time in the lives of human beings is God closer to us and actually intervening in our lives.

This experience is not necessarily identical with the Christian experience. Many good Christians never experience it, either because, as far back as they can remember, they have always believed, or because even though they became Christians in their adult life, they never experienced anything dramatic enough to be labeled a conversion. The religious experience of these people is not necessarily less profound or even less intense than the experience of those who benefited from a dramatic conversion.

Nevertheless, the idea of conversion enjoys great prestige with all people religiously inclined because there is no doubt that the Gospels emphasize conversion. The Pauline idea of the new man, and Paul's theme of salvation through faith, can be interpreted in terms of radical conversion. Almost everything in Paul can be so interpreted.

There is a problem with the word we use to describe that experience, the word "conversion" itself, or the Greek word *metanoia*. According to my dictionaries, the Latin word *conversio* was used for the first time in the Christian sense by Augustine. But Augustine, curiously, did not use it in his *Confessions,* which is the story of his own conversion. He used it for the first and last time in *The City of God* (VII, 33) in a phrase which refers to Satan's efforts to prevent us from achieving our conversion to the true God.

The problem with the Latin word *conversio* is that it does not really mean what we all mean by a Christian conversion and what Augustine himself undoubtedly meant. It means turning around in a circle; it refers to a full circular revolution that ultimately brings you back to your point of departure. This is not what a Christian conversion is. A Christian conversion is not circular; it never returns to its point of origin. It is open-ended; it is moving toward a totally unpredictable future. It seems to me that the real Latin significance of the word is characteristically pagan, in the sense that it reflects the pagan conception of history and time itself, which is circular and repetitive. This conception is always reminiscent of that Eternal Return which can be found in the Puranas and elsewhere in the East. Various versions of it are also present in some of the pre-Socratic philosophers in Greece, especially Anaximander, Heraclitus, and Empedocles.

The Latin word *conversio* refers to reversible actions and processes, such as the translation of a text into another language, and also to mythical metamorphoses. When Christians adopt the word, they change its connotation from a circular to a linear phenomenon which is open-ended. It now means a change that takes place once and for all, with no conceivable return to the starting point. Therefore, it should be irreversible.

The Greek *metanoia* was first used in Greek-language churches to designate a certain type of penance. It does not designate a circular motion, but it is not very good either at signifying Christian conversion. It is too weak a word.

*Meta-noeo* means to change one's mind about something; to have second thoughts regarding something that seemed settled; to perceive a mistake too late, when it can no longer be changed. It can mean, therefore, regret, but nothing as strong as Christian repentance when the convert hears the question that Paul heard on the road to Damascus, "Why do you persecute me?"

Christian conversion is a transformation that reaches so deep it changes us once and for all and gives us a new being, so to speak. The result is so superior that it is not possible to cancel that change, either by moving back or going around in a circle. To us Westerners, moving in a circle is a fate worse than death. It is hell. The idea of conversion is much more than reform, repentance, re-energizing, repair, regeneration, revolution, or any other word beginning with "re" which suggests a return to something that was there before and which therefore limits us to a circular view of life and experience. In Christian conversion, a positive change is connoted which is not caught inside a circle.

Christians give the notion of conversion a depth and a seriousness that must be recognized in order to appreciate the significance of an important episode in the history of early Christianity, the Donatist heresy. The Donatists were fourth-century Christians in North Africa who took Christian conversion so seriously that, after periods of persecution, they refused to reintegrate into the church those people who had not been heroic enough to accept martyrdom and who had recanted. They regarded Christian conversion as something so momentous that it could occur only once in a lifetime. One didn't have a second chance. The Donatists felt that people who did not have enough courage to face the lions in the Roman circus and die gladly for their faith were not good enough to be Christians at all.

These people had such an exalted view of the Christian conversion that the idea of its happening twice was blasphemous. In their eyes, it debased the whole process and made a mockery of the Christian faith. The Donatists were condemned by the Church and were certainly wrong from an evangelical viewpoint. If their absolutist principle had applied to Peter on the night of Jesus's arrest, after his triple denial of Christ, he would not have been reintegrated. He would never have become the leader of the Church. The Donatists were wrong. To condemn their intransigence was certainly the right thing to do for the early Church, but their appeal to such great Christians as Tertullian gives us a clue as to how seriously the notion of conversion was taken in early Christianity.

The aspect of literature that corresponds to that view, to that absolute view of conversion, is the belief which I hold, that the most outstanding forms of literary creation are not, as a rule, the product merely of native talent, the pure gift of literary creation, even though that gift exists. Nor are they the product of an acquired skill or technique, even though no writer can be really good unless he has sufficient skill as a writer.

The writers that seem the greatest to me do not consider what we call their genius a natural gift with which they were born. They view it as a belated acquisition, the result of a personal transformation not of their own doing, which resembles a conversion. As far as the relationship between literature and Christianity is concerned, my main interest has been the relatedness of a certain form of creation to this notion of religious and especially Christian conversion.

The novelist who made me interested in this relationship was Marcel Proust. In Proust, of course, the hero and the writer are one, but not simultaneously. The hero comes first, and then the writer takes over at the end of the novel. Thanks to a break, a rupture which the novelist experiences, the hero becomes the novelist. But it is not the novelist's achievement. He feels he had little to do with the event that turned him into a novelist.

When I was writing about Proust, it was already fashionable to say that Marcel the narrator is a pure invention of the novelist, that the art of a writer has nothing to do with his life. This is not true, of course. The novel, even though it is not Christian at all, is, in its beliefs, morals, and metaphysics, an aesthetic and even spiritual autobiography which claims to be rooted in a personal experience, a personal transformation structured exactly like the experience Christians call a conversion.

At the beginning of the last volume, *Time Recaptured,* the hero suffers a great illness and finds himself in a state of profound depression. He no longer hopes that, someday, he will become a great writer. Then, at the moment of complete discouragement, even depression, some trivial incidents happen to him, like walking on the uneven pavement of the Guermanteses' courtyard and being reminded of the same experience in the past. This kind of remembrance triggers in him an aesthetic and spiritual illumination that transforms him completely. This tiny event provides him with his whole subject matter, the dedication needed to write the book and, above all, the right perspective, a perspective totally free for the first time of the compulsion of desire, of the hope of fulfilling himself through desire.

The titles chosen by Proust for the novel as a whole and for the last volume of his novel, which is the first, of course, in the sense that it recounts the creative experience, are highly significant. The whole novel is entitled *A la recherche du temps perdu,* which literally means "searching for lost time," for the time the hero has wasted and frittered away until the moment of conversion. The title of the last volume, which was truly the first to be conceived and written, at least in its main outline, is *Time Recaptured.* It is the story of that spiritual death and rebirth to which I just alluded. It is really the beginning of the great creative period in Proust's life.

Thus, we have two perspectives in Proust and other great novels of novelistic conversion. The first perspective is the deceptive perspective of desire, which is full of illusions regarding the possibility of the hero to fulfill himself through desire. It is the perspective that imprisoned him in a sterile process of jumping from one frustrated desire to the next over a period of many years. Everything the narrator could not acquire, he desired;

everything he acquired, he immediately ceased to desire, until he fell into a state of ennui that could be called a state of post-mimetic desire.

The second perspective is one that comes from the end of the novel, from the omega point of conversion, which is a liberation from desire. This perspective enables the novelist to rectify the illusions of the hero and provides him with the creative energy he needs to write his novel. The second perspective is highly critical of the first, but it is not resentful. Even though Proust never resorts to the vocabulary of sin, the reality of sin is present. The exploration of the past very much resembles a discovery of one's own sinfulness in Christianity. The time wasted away is full of idolatry, jealousy, envy, and snobbery; it all ends in a feeling of complete futility.

The word "conversion" is indispensable because Proust is describing, on the whole truthfully, the personal upheaval in his life and the great surge of creativity that enabled him to become the great novelist he could not have been earlier. Everything in the life and legend of Marcel Proust fits the conversion pattern. He enters great literature just as, earlier, he might have entered the religious life. There is something quasi-monastic about the partly mythical but nevertheless authentic account of his spending the rest of his life isolated from the world, in his cork-lined bedroom, waking up in the middle of the night to write his novel, just as monks wake up to sing their prayers.

There are many indications of a great change in Proust. The people who have worked in the Proustian archives say that one can distinguish at a single glance the post-conversion writing from the pre-conversion writing. His great novel is entirely written in the converted handwriting. The interpretation of the great Proustian creation as conversion was propounded by some of the first interpreters of his work, especially Jacques Rivière. All I did was go back to that theory armed with more biographical facts, with *Jean Santeuil* and, of course, with the mass of writing Proust produced at that time and then discarded. The major difference between *Jean Santeuil* and the later masterpiece is the author's unawareness of his own mimetic desire.

I do not claim that Proust became a saint after his conversion or even that he had a religious conversion. He did not. It is unquestionable, however, that at that time, and for the only time in his life, he became interested in Christianity. He felt it could be relevant to his transformation. He sought some advice, and being totally ignorant about the subject, he had the curious idea of consulting, of all people, André Gide, a lapsed Protestant. André Gide discouraged him from investigating the matter any further.

What I really claim is that the creative experience of Proust is truly comparable in most respects to a religious conversion which cannot be said to have failed, but which bore only aesthetic fruit and never resulted in a religious conversion. It functions like a religious conversion, and certainly there is no reason to disregard the voice of the novelist himself, especially in the mass of now published manuscripts which he wrote during the *Time Recaptured* period.

Before his great change, Proust was a talented amateur. His conversion turned him into a genius. When André Gide read the manuscript of Proust's first volume for his publishing house, he rejected it out of hand. The author, in his eyes, was an intellectually insignificant social butterfly, who had not turned into a major writer overnight. This sort of metamorphosis is very rare indeed, and Gide was statistically correct in choosing not to believe it. He was a busy editor; but in this case he was wrong.

My insistence on the word "conversion" is like a red flag to a bull. In my first book, I did not wave one red flag at the bull, but five, since I applied this notion not only to Proust but to the four other novelists I was studying, Cervantes, Stendhal, Flaubert, and Dostoevsky. Take Don Quixote, for instance. On his deathbed, he repents and says he wishes he had time to read good books instead of the novels of chivalry that had turned him into a lunatic, a puppet whose strings were pulled by a puppeteer who did not even exist, Amadis of Gaul. Take Julien Sorel, about to be guillotined in *The Red and the Black*. Take Madame Bovary when she eats the arsenic which is about to kill her. Flaubert is already Proustian enough not only to say: "Madame Bovary, c'est moi," but to add that during the creation of the death of his heroine, he had the taste of arsenic in his mouth. In other words, he shared the creative death of his heroine. It is the same thing with the Siberian exile of Raskolnikov in Dostoevsky's *Crime and Punishment*.

In all these writers, I felt, there was a central work, which is the conversion novel, *The Red and the Black* for Stendhal, *Madame Bovary* for Flaubert, *Crime and Punishment* for Dostoevsky. In all these writers, I found the same two perspectives as in the great Proust, the pre-conversion and the post-conversion perspective that rectifies the pre-conversion perspective which is always some kind of self-deception.

I was guided by Proust when I coined the notion of a novelistic conversion. In the great mass of manuscripts associated with *Time Recaptured*, there is a text which compares the still-to-be-written last and first volume of the great novel to the conclusions of many great novels in the past, and of some works that are not novels. Cervantes is there, and Stendhal, Flaubert as well. There are also other novelists I have not mentioned, such as George Eliot.

The notion of conversion provides the work with a past and a future, with its "human time," its temporal depth that unconverted novels do not have. The second perspective distances the writer from the experience he recounts. Great novels are written from both ends at the same time. We might say there is, first, the perspective of the unenlightened hero, and then the omega perspective, the all-knowing perspective that comes from the end.

When I published my first book, my good friend, John Freccero, now chairman of Italian Studies at New York University, was quick to point out that my last chapter did not mention the most important work in connection with its thesis, the work that invented the spiritual autobiography and is based on a great experience of conversion: Augustine's *Confessions*. This work is the first and greatest example of the dual perspective in a work. It must be regarded as the first great literary autobiography in a sense that the ancient world did not really know.

Before all these examples and their ultimate model come the Gospels themselves, and if we look at them closely, we will see that we have the dual perspective in them also. In the three synoptic Gospels, but especially in Mark, the disciples are represented as unable to understand the teaching of Jesus at the time they hear it from his own mouth. They are not really converted—not even Peter—though he is able to recognize Jesus as the Messiah.

The apostles do not understand much while they are listening to Jesus. They misunderstand everything. They believe in the triumphant Messiah after the Davidic model rather than the suffering Messiah after the Servant of Yahweh in Second Isaiah. Only after the death and resurrection

of Jesus are they able to understand what they first heard without understanding. The resurrection to them is a conversion experience, which is the
same as the descent of the Holy Spirit at Pentecost when they were filled
with a grace which was not theirs when Jesus was still alive. The real definition of grace is that Jesus died for us, and even though his own people,
as a people, did not receive him, he made those who did receive him able
to become children of God.

# The Passionate Oxymoron in Shakespeare's *Romeo and Juliet* [2005]

In the comedies of Shakespeare, all characters infatuated with one another see themselves as perfect embodiments of "true love." Love is true to the extent that the two partners are interested in each other exclusively and are indifferent to intermediaries, go-betweens, and third parties in general. "True love" is the Elizabethan equivalent of what we would call a great or authentic passion. It insists on its independence from the entire world and from other people in general. The concept is suffused with the spirit of modern individualism.

If this "true love" were as independent as it claims, the two lovers would be satisfied with each other's company and would never become entangled with anyone else. In the comedies of Shakespeare, the opposite happens. True love constantly runs into trouble. This is what Lysander explains to his beloved Hermia at the beginning of *A Midsummer Night's Dream*:

Ay me, for aught that ever I could read
Could ever hear by tale or history,
The course of true love never did run smooth . . .
(*A Midsummer Night's Dream*, 1.1.137–40)

The lovers do not feel responsible for the misfortunes of true love. They see themselves as innocent victims of tyrannical parents, jealous friends, and other unwanted meddlers. *A Midsummer Night's Dream* is both the apotheosis of that myth and its humorous deconstruction. That is why four lovers are needed instead of two. Their unseemly entanglements during the long and hot midsummer night are blamed on the most preposterous, charming, and traditional excuse imaginable. Under the pretense of helping the lovers solve their various problems, some mischievous fairies have been squeezing a potent love potion into the eyes of the wrong lovers . . .

Behind the self-deceit of "true love," the truth is mimetic desire. Far from being rooted deep in the lovers themselves, their adolescent infatuations result from their perpetual imitations both of the books they read and of one another. The four predictably end up fighting over the same object, the two boys over the same girl, the two girls over the same boy. These spoiled adolescents, just like our own, have too much time on their hands and too little to worry about. The more true love is exalted in theory, the more it is betrayed in practice. This fairy tale is the ballet of mimetic disharmony, so harmonious in its symmetries that this miraculous masterpiece is most often mistaken for an insignificant fantasy, not quite worthy of its creator's genius.

My book on Shakespeare suggests that true love is nowhere to be found in the early Shakespeare.[1] This conclusion has been challenged on the grounds that it takes no account of the one play that contradicts it most spectacularly: *Romeo and Juliet.*

One could argue that the love affair in this play is too short to be tested for its durability, but that would be piddling. It is true that Romeo and Juliet are fiercely loyal and honest with one another. One obvious indication of Juliet's "truth" or "authenticity" is her refusal to "act coy" with her lover, unless specifically requested by him to do so:

O gentle Romeo
If thou dost love, pronounce it faithfully;
Or if thou thinkest I am too quickly won,
I'll frown and be perverse, and say thee nay . . . (*Romeo and Juliet*, 2.2.942–45)

In order to see what is at stake here, one must compare Juliet with another Shakespearean heroine more similar to her than is generally realized, Cressida. Just like Juliet, Cressida surrenders too quickly and impetuously to her first lover, Troilus. Just like Juliet, she perceives the danger but, just like Juliet again, she cannot dissemble, and she throws all caution to the winds. Just like Juliet, Cressida gambles on her first lover, *but with entirely different results.*

On the morning after she becomes his mistress, Troilus unwittingly reveals to Cressida his masculine vanity, his mediocrity, his selfishness, his arrogance, and his profound indifference. Those who turn Cressida into a symbol of unprovoked feminine infidelity must be just as sexist as Troilus, I am afraid, since they remain blind to the young man's faults. Far from being a victim, Troilus is twice the corruptor of Cressida. On top of his other faults, he is so naïvely jealous that he himself suggests to his quick-witted mistress the only vengeance available to her.

## The Special Problem Posed by Romeo and Juliet

Romeo and Juliet are just the opposite, so incapable of treachery that nothing really tragic, nothing dramatically exciting can happen to their relationship. In such plays as *Troilus and Cressida* and *A Midsummer Night's Dream*, the relations between the characters are treacherous enough to provide the incidents that will keep the public entertained. Not so in *Romeo and Juliet.*

However wonderful and admirable this is in real life, in the theater it is an unmitigated disaster unless the playwright takes underhanded measures to hide the dramatic inadequacy of "true love."

Shakespeare did not need André Gide to teach him that "good sentiments do not add up to good literature." In *Romeo and Juliet*, he imports all dramatic effects from outside the love affair. The solution is the Verona blood feud. This is the reason why, from the first to the last line, the mutual hatred of the Montagues and the Capulets plays an enormous role in this play. Shakespeare constantly resorts to it to literally spice up the rather tasteless love affair. He does this in several ways: the simplest and most obvious is conspicuously exemplified in the balcony scene.

In such scenes, the suspense, as a rule, is generated, at least in part, by the offended young lady who threatens to shut her window, even to call her father for help. In Juliet's case, this resource is unavailable. She has made it quite clear that Romeo is welcome in her bedroom. Romeo knows it, we know it too, and we know that everybody knows. In the absence of the traditional suspense, Shakespeare can only resort to the blood feud, in the shape of Juliet's ferocious kinsmen who might be hiding in the bushes. Even for a lesser offense than climbing Juliet's balcony, they would gladly massacre a dozen Montagues before breakfast:

Juliet: If they do see thee, they will murder thee.
Romeo: Alack, there lies more peril in thine eye
    Than twenty of their swords! Look thou but sweet,
    And I am proof against their enmity.
Juliet: I would not for the world they saw thee here.
Romeo: I have night's cloak to hide me from their eyes,
    And but thou love me, let them find me here;
    My life were better ended by their hate,
    Than death prorogued, wanting of thy love. (*Romeo and Juliet*, 2.2.70–78)

Shakespeare makes his reliance on the blood feud almost comically obvious. The ferocious kinsmen are not there, however. On that particular night, they must have obviously had some time off. Even as a subject of conversation, the Capulet kinsmen are sorely needed. Like all young lovers, Romeo and Juliet have very little to talk about on their own. Romeo tries to pretend that the greatest danger is Juliet's possible indifference to his love, more threatening in his eyes than the entire Capulet military, but it is manifestly untrue. It must be the young man's delicate sense of courtesy that makes him speak in this manner.

It is quite normal for a blood feud to spread fear and violence in the vicinity. What is more remarkable, in *Romeo and Juliet*, is the extent to which the blood feud affects something essential in this play, which is the language of passion, especially Juliet's expression of her love for Romeo. The blood feud becomes a kind of literary device, and that is an amazing role for a blood feud, which is nothing, after all, but an endless chain of vengeance.

~

In order to elucidate this aspect, I must first recall a problem that was much discussed fifty or a hundred years ago: the inappropriateness of the rather flamboyant rhetoric in *Romeo and Juliet*. The most noticeable figure of speech is the *oxymoron*, of course. It consists in juxtaposing two emotional opposites, joy and madness, pleasure and pain, above all, love and hatred. In the love poetry of early modern Europe, there is a strong impulse to associate words of passionate affection with words of intense hostility, even hatred and horror. Early twentieth-century critics felt uncomfortable with the oxymoron in general, because of the inner contradiction that it implies. Opposites are by definition incompatible and to bring them together in a single figure of speech seems to go against reason itself. A work with too many oxymora was regarded as inevitably alien to genuine greatness.

The old humanistic critics regarded oxymora as a sign of self-indulgence on the author's part, and, with regard to *Romeo and Juliet*, perhaps of a youthful weakness. Is the oxymoron fever bad enough in this play to require its exclusion from the list of Shakespeare's "unquestioned masterpieces"? There were different answers, of course, but no one disputed the legitimacy of the debate.

One of the reasons why this debate seemed important, in the case of *Romeo and Juliet*, was the prominence of "true love" in that play. These humanists had a truly romantic soul, always a little at odds with their sense of responsibility as "serious critics." They regarded authentic passion as the greatest emotion of the human heart. Since there is precious little of it in Shakespeare, *Romeo and Juliet* assumed a great importance in their eyes. Is it not fitting that the supreme playwright in the English language should have devoted at least one of his "unquestioned masterpieces" to the exaltation of true love? *Romeo and Juliet* seems to be the best candidate for the role. Hence the eagerness to rank this play with "the bard's unquestioned masterpieces." The numerous *oxymora* gave these critics pause. Do they not suggest that the author failed to regard his own play with all the seriousness an unquestioned masterpiece deserves?

This hesitation is understandable. The most prominent congregation of oxymora in the whole play is Juliet's reaction to the news that Romeo has killed her cousin and childhood friend Tybalt:

O serpent heart hid with a flow'ring face!
Did ever dragon keep so fair a cave?
Beautiful tyrant! Fiend angelical!
Dove-feathered raven! Wolfish ravening lamb!
Despised substance of divinest show!
Just opposite to what thou justly seem'st.
A damned saint, an honorable villain!
O nature, what hadst thou to do in hell
When thou didst bower the spirit of a fiend
In mortal paradise of such sweet flesh?
Was ever book containing such vile matter
So fairly bound? O that deceit should dwell
In such gorgeous palace! (*Romeo and Juliet*, 3.3.76–85)

When considered in and by themselves, these oxymora do not seem to make much sense. A "fiend" and "angel" are poles apart and to associate them seems absurd. If Juliet regards Romeo as a fiend, she should say so and leave it at that. If she regards him as an angel, she should call him an angel and nothing else. To fuse the two together and call Romeo a "fiend angelical" is a contradiction that should be avoided.

Such is the traditional reasoning against oxymora. It fails to take into account the fact that even in the most quiet lives, enormously upsetting events with opposite impacts may occur in such quick succession that they impinge on one another and chaos results. This is precisely what is happening to Juliet. She has fallen in love with a man she should regard as a murderer, now more than ever, since he has killed Tybalt. The old hatred is fighting with her new love in such a way as to turn her heart into a jumble of opposites endlessly clashing together.

The real question is not the intrinsic reasonableness of the oxymora, but how appropriate they are to the situation of the character who resorts to them. Juliet is a living oxymoron: as a lover, she blesses Romeo; as Tybalt's cousin, she curses him.

This explication of the oxymora is unavoidable, since the plot itself demands it. But the plot, here, is not the whole story. It does not really account for the impression made by Juliet's tirade. The oxymora are simply too numerous, too spectacular, and too stereotyped as well—most of them appear elsewhere in Shakespeare and other writers of the period—not to make us suspect some irony on the author's part, some deliberate parody.

Is Shakespeare simply trying to break the world record of oxymora? Is he trying to portray Juliet, or rather himself, as a compulsive producer of oxymora? He must have had something more interesting in mind, something more relevant to the nature of this particular play. What is there to be ironic about?

It is remarkable that, in the entire tirade, there is not even one reference to the violent death of Tybalt, or even to Tybalt himself, not one allusion to the supposed cause of this amazing assemblage of oxymora.

It we read this text as a separate poem in an anthology, a reading that the author himself officially rejects but underhandedly seems to invite, what impression would it make on us? We would never suspect that this great rhetorical outburst was triggered by the violent death of a close relative. It would sound to us like the speech of a woman whose reasons to grieve come from her lover, no doubt, but they seem directly rooted in the love affair itself, not in the death of a relative. We would surmise that this woman has some reason to distrust the man with whom she is madly in love. She fears that, in return for her love, he does not love her half as much as he should. She suspects something more dreadful, from the standpoint of her passion, than the death of a dozen cousins—some infidelity no doubt . . .

The worst aspect of the situation is that, far from being diminished by the ingrate's probable betrayal, her passion is increased and she is ashamed of herself. She should return the culprit's indifference with an even stonier indifference. She should serve him a dose of his own medicine, but she cannot do it. She feels utterly defeated. She cannot forget the angel behind the fiend that her lover has become: he really fits the "fiend angelical" formula.

Before learning about Tybalt's death, Juliet might have compared Romeo to an "angel" but not to "a fiend." In the oxymoron "fiend angelical," the angel is still with us, but it is associated with something much less attractive, even repulsive, a "fiend." The language of "true love," in principle, should be entirely positive; it should be composed only of words of affection, praise, admiration, and tenderness . . . The oxymora associate these words with others that mean the very opposite, words that suggest dislike, blame, abhorrence, fear, etc.—here, the word "fiend." This addition, it would seem, should result in an overall weakening of the passion that Juliet feels for Romeo. When hatred is added to some already existing love, the result should be a subtraction, a diminution, and therefore a weakening of erotic tension rather than an increase. A mixture of hot and cold should produce a lukewarm desire.

The oxymoron does not work that way at all. Instead of lowering the temperature of the passion, it raises it. The mixture of love and hatred suggests a love much stronger than the one conveyed by a mere accumulation of loving and positive words.

This is how all the hysterical oxymora operate in poems of the sixteenth and seventeenth centuries; they all convey the exasperated despair of a spurned lover. The oxymoron is the language of erotic jealousy, not the language of mourning. Shakespeare is aware, I feel, of the real impression conveyed by Juliet's tirade, and far from emphasizing the mistake that it is according to the plot, he reinforces, underhandedly, at least, our spontaneous reaction to the oxymora. The great tirade conveys the impression of a woman madly in love, completely obsessed with Romeo. Juliet has no objective reason to be jealous, but Shakespeare is too skillful a writer not to know that the stronger desire lies with the frustrated rather than the happily fulfilled love affair.

~

This is the paradox of the oxymoron: in the right context, a "fiend angelical" will sound more desirable than a mere angel. Why should that be? Logically, the negative feelings that should extinguish passion—jealousy, anger, or resentment—in reality make them seem stronger. Even though the love of Romeo and Juliet has been defined as innocent and sweet, it obviously obeys that law. Without the oxymora, Juliet's love for Romeo would sound less hysterical, less impressive therefore. How is this possible?

In order to explain this magic, one must situate the oxymoron in the context of mimetic desire, the type of desire I briefly discussed à propos of *A Midsummer Night's Dream*. Whenever we desire mimetically, I said, we imitate the desire of someone we admire and we turn it into our own, with the almost inevitable result that we desire the same object as our model, the same woman for instance, like the two boys in *A Midsummer Night's Dream*. They both love Hermia at the beginning of the play, then, later into the night, they both love Helena. They both shift from one girl to the other and always at the same time, since they are under each other's influence. This mimetic agreement is really the worst possible disagreement. The same is true of the two girls. The one invariant in the whole system is universal rivalry, which can only breed universal frustration.

The law of mimetic desire is universal frustration. If you believe that this law is defeated each time one of the rivals decisively triumphs over the other, you are mistaken. The victor appropriates the disputed object, but his resulting happiness does not last. A safely possessed object is an object that no powerful model and rival designates to us, and it quickly loses its mimetic allure. The only objects that remain permanently desirable are inaccessible objects, the ones designated by models too powerful to be vanquished.

In a world full of hypermimetic individuals, such as the Elizabethan court, or our own consumer society, the principle of frustration is inexorable. The real reason why the course of true love never did and never does run smooth is that this so-called true love is really a mimetic desire unable and unwilling to acknowledge its own mimetic nature, a desire that becomes truly intense and durable only when it is frustrated by a victorious model and rival.

All mimetic addicts, both males and females, are really addicted to indifference and rejection. This is not masochism in the sense of modern psychoanalysis; it is not a "love of suffering." It is the mimetic mechanism that creates its own nemesis, by always preferring the mediated to the unmediated, the inaccessible, therefore, to the accessible.

Mimetic addicts cannot permanently desire someone who responds positively to their own desire, and they cannot remain permanently indifferent to someone who is really indifferent to them. The inaccessible woman often combines the roles of object and model, or mediator. She knows how to keep her lover at bay in order to insure his continued enslavement to her. This is how the "dark lady" in the *Sonnets* acts with the poet. She plays the mimetic game with consummate skill, and makes the poet jealous. She knows how to exploit the laws of mimetic desire to her own advantage.

All possible combinations of mimetic desire always obey the law just defined: there is an inverse relationship between the intensity of a desire and its prospects of fulfillment. Mimetic desire is the infallible recipe for a life of endless frustration, perfectly exemplified by Duke Orsino in *Twelfth Night*. Since intense love is always unrewarded, it always coincides with an intense resentment of the beloved.

It is this combination of passion and resentment that the oxymoron perfectly expresses. There is no love that does not entail some hatred, and, reciprocally, no hatred that cannot suddenly convert to intense passion, if only for an instant, as in the case of Aufidius and Coriolanus. Far from being an "artificial" figure of speech, therefore, as bourgeois optimism suggested, the oxymoron made perfect sense for the type of mimetic relations that love affairs become when they are constantly blocked by mimetic rivalry, real or imagined.

The widespread use and abuse of the oxymoron in the still aristocratic world of early modern literature is not quite the artificial fashion that is often portrayed. It is rooted in the way erotic relations really were in that world, subject to the same type of frustrations and dysfunctionalities that dominate our own cultural world as well, and in an even more conspicuous and brutal manner.

In such a world, the educated public becomes accustomed to associate the stronger passion with the figure of speech that brings opposites together: love and hatred, sentiment and resentment, sympathy and antipathy. It corresponds to the endless impasse of courtly or salon life.

Thanks to the blood feud, Shakespeare can bring back into *Romeo and Juliet* these conjunctions of opposites that should not be there in the case of these two lovers, since their relationship is supposed to be perfect. Shakespeare knows that his public is unable to conceive of passionate desire except in terms of oxymora, in other words, in terms of extreme frustration. Thanks to the murder of Tybalt, thanks to the blood feud, Shakespeare can bring the oxymoron back into the picture under false pretenses. The death of Tybalt, in a duel that Romeo had done everything to avoid, is not really a criminal offense since Romeo did everything he could to avoid it. It is a mere pretext for the deluge of oxymora that follows.

If Shakespeare had played the game of true love with complete honesty, he would have renounced the oxymoron altogether, at the risk of disappointing his contemporary audiences. The love of Romeo and Juliet should be free by definition from all violence, since it is supposed to be authentically "true." In order to make it seem intense enough, Shakespeare had to buttress it with imagery more appropriate to the infidelities and other dirty tricks that mimetic lovers play on one another than to Romeo and Juliet. And to make this violence seem legitimate, instead of rooting it where it really belongs—in the erotic relations themselves—he systematically projected it onto the blood feud.

True love is supposed to be the most intense desire, but, in reality, it is too perfect and peaceful a relationship to really satisfy Shakespeare's original audience, and all subsequent audiences as well. It lacks the spice that only a little violence between the lovers can bring into their relationship. Shakespeare needs the mimetic disturbances that the oxymora suggest, but he cannot give Juliet the usual reasons lovers have to be angry at each other without tarnishing their true love, without destroying the myth he is trying to erect. In order to keep his "true love" both sufficiently true and sufficiently intense, the only way is to resort to the blood feud, underhandedly, and this is what he did, systematically.

Thanks to the murder of Tybalt, Juliet can be furious at Romeo and sound insanely jealous without having any real cause for jealousy. Shakespeare does everything he has to do under the mask of the blood feud. He has Juliet unleash a veritable torrent of oxymora without making her sound like the dark lady in the *Sonnets*.

The true love of Romeo and Juliet should exclude all the cruel mimetic tricks lovers play on one another; however, if Shakespeare followed that rule to the letter, the result would doubtless be a sentimentally correct but rather insipid drama. In order to conjure up the feeling of intense passion that his public expects, without paying the price that this decision entails, he must resort to some contraband violence, and this is precisely what the blood feud is there to provide.

Tybalt's death really replaces the infidelity that Romeo should commit in order to justify the sentiments implied in Juliet's oxymora. Thanks to the blood feud, Shakespeare can give the impression of intense jealousy without any unwanted consequences for the purity of the true love between Romeo and Juliet.

~

In order to verify our "mimetic" interpretation of the violence in the language of *Romeo and Juliet*, all we need is to read, after the great tirade, the brief exchange between the heroine and her old nurse, the only other character on stage during the tirade, and therefore Juliet's only audience.

The nurse is a very simple woman as well as a loyal member of the Capulet clan. Quite understandably, she wishes that Juliet would forget her passion for Romeo. When she hears words of intense hatred for this young man, she takes them at face value and she is overjoyed. Juliet seems to be talking once again like a loyal Capulet and the nurse welcomes the change. In order to encourage this evolution, she loudly exclaims: "Shame to Romeo!"

This simple old woman does not understand the peculiar logic of the oxymoron. She applies her common sense to the great tirade, and she misunderstands it. Seeing that words of hatred are added to Juliet's usual praise of Romeo, she automatically assumes that the hatred should be subtracted from the love. She falls into the trap that all people hysterically in love set for those around them. She assumes that Juliet means what she says and says what she means.

When Juliet hears Romeo insulted by the nurse, she flies into a rage:

Blister'd be thy tongue
For such a wish! He was not born to shame:
Upon his brow shame is asham'd to sit;
For 'tis a throne where honor may be crown'd
Sole monarch of the universal earth,
O, what a beast was I to chide at him! (*Romeo and Juliet*, 3.2.90–95)

Juliet perfectly understands the nurse's mistake, and the proof is that she couches her reply in an unambiguously positive language just to make sure that, this time, the nurse will not misunderstand her. Something a bit similar happens between Friar Laurence and Romeo. When the priest begs his pupil to renounce his unintelligible jargon, Romeo immediately explains very clearly why he left Rosaline for Juliet. The first girl did not respond to his advances, whereas Juliet does.

Juliet's anger against the nurse is characteristic of poets and artists when an uneducated public misunderstands their finer points. The nurse did not realize that Juliet's great tirade signifies an increase, not a decrease in the temperature of her passion for Romeo.

Thanks to the blood feud, Shakespeare can have his cake and eat it too; he can blame the blood feud for a violence that, in reality, plays a positive role in the language of the two lovers. It is this violence that makes the love of Romeo and Juliet sound like real passion.

Like all great styles with a long history behind them, the oxymoronic style of *Romeo and Juliet* is less artificial than it seems. It is a realistic representation of how lovers related to each other in a hypermimetic world, more realistic than our contemporary critics are willing to acknowledge. As a matter of fact, it is this realism of the oxymoron that our anti-realistic critics do not see, because they do not see the mimetic nature of our desires and its consequences. The oxymoron may be regarded, I believe, as the literary forerunner of the deluge of violence and pornography that is nowadays submerging much of what is left of our culture.

Thanks to Tybalt's death, Juliet sounds as painfully divided against herself as a passionate lover should be, while still appearing serenely united with Romeo. Far from being a hindrance, the blood feud is indispensable to the impression of intense passion conveyed by a relationship that, left to itself, could not generate the conflictual intensity required by the public.

The Tybalt tirade is somewhat caricatural, not because Shakespeare is unable to achieve a fuller integration of all the elements involved in his literary game, but because, in that particular passage, his purpose is, I believe, humorously didactic. He wants his more perceptive spectators to detect the game he is playing. This passage has a parodic quality that, inevitably, makes it less successful aesthetically. In order to make his intention obvious, Shakespeare goes a little too far with his oxymora. In other passages of the same play, the various elements in the total mixture are so smoothly integrated with one another that, when we hear the text, its harmonious quality is such that we are not tempted to separate its component parts and analyze them. The fusion of the words that apply to the love affair with the words that apply to the blood feud is convincing enough for the whole thing to sound like the splendid expression of a love whose depth and intensity are such that to question anything would seem sacrilegious.

Here is but one example: four simple lines of Juliet once again, at the end of her first encounter with Romeo. She has just learned that the young man with whom, one minute before, she has fallen in love is sole heir to the Montague family. Here is how she reacts to the news:

My only love sprung from my only hate!
Too early seen unknown and known too late!
Prodigious birth of love it is to me
That I must love a loathed enemy. (*Romeo and Juliet*, 1.5.138–41)

It would be impossible for Juliet to be more straightforward and factual about the situation than she is in these four lines. It is really with a loathed enemy that she is in love. Just as in the case of Tybalt's death, she cannot say anything about the situation in which she finds herself without reinventing the oxymoron. These four lines are based on exactly the same principle as Juliet's great tirade. Each statement looks like an oxymoron, sounds like an oxymoron, and yet is really not an oxymoron, since it is not a metaphor at all; it is a purely factual statement, rooted in the real historical and political background of the situation. It does not really allude to some kind of internal battle that would rage in the heart of Juliet; and yet it cannot be denied that, thanks to the blood feud and the quasi-oxymora that it provides, the whole text sounds more passionate than it would without this added ingredient. If the word "love" in the first line were not balanced with the word "hate," it would sound quite different. The same is true of the last line. If the word "love" were not followed first by "hate" and then by "loathed enemy," Juliet would not sound as mysteriously carried away as she does. The halo of archaic sacredness that seems to be there is rooted in the violence of the blood feud, and if we eliminated the blood feud, it would disappear.

In spite of all the violence in Juliet's language, her relationship with Romeo always looks as fresh as pure snow. And that is really the purpose of the whole rhetorical legerdemain. The "oxymoronic style" of *Romeo and Juliet* is a mutual contamination of the love affair and the blood feud that produces some poetic miracles as well as some more or less deliberately ludicrous effects.

Romeo is really Juliet's loathed enemy, not as a lover, but as a member of the Montague family. And yet we feel that Juliet's love is not only intensified but "deepened" by the addition of "hate" and by "loath'd ene-my" in the following line. The blood feud plays an essential role in the love discourse. The interpenetration of the blood feud and the love affair is sup-posed to occur *accidentally* but, in reality, it is the doing of the playwright who is completely aware that he must import some violence into his play, but in such discreet fashion so as to leave the love affair unaffected.

Our four lines are more successful aesthetically than Juliet's great ti-rade because everything in them is factually as well as poetically justified and their "rhetorical" dimension is less visible. In the great tirade, Shake-speare makes himself less skillful on purpose, like an expert who shows some students or friends how to proceed with some delicate manipulation by making himself deliberately less adroit than he normally is, and there-fore easier to imitate.

Recently, a French critic, Olivier Maurel, has pointed out that the "star-crossed lovers" are just as mimetic as the characters in the comedies.[2] If Shakespeare really interpreted his own play in the habitual "romantic" fashion, would he not have shown, at the beginning, a Romeo already madly enamored of a Capulet girl, but not the right one, a certain Rosaline whom he showers with the poetic clichés he will redirect at Juliet a little later? If Shakespeare intended Romeo and Juliet to be genuine paragons of true love, would he have represented them as little mimetic snobs? This is certainly what he does at the beginning of the play. After Romeo kisses Ju-liet for the first time, she exclaims: "You kiss by the book," not to blame his lack of spontaneity, but to applaud his perfect obedience to fashion. Lady Capulet is so aware of Juliet's snobbish literariness that, to predispose her in favor of the man she and her husband want her to marry, this mother literally woos her daughter and recites to her an extremely contrived little poem about Count Paris, such as Juliet herself might write for Romeo.

Olivier Maurel is right: Romeo and Juliet resemble all the classical figures of mimetic desire in Western literature, and Shakespeare artificially immunized their relationship from the disruptive consequences of that de-sire. He wants Romeo and Juliet to pass the test of "true love" with flying colors, and he sees to it that they do. All the make-believe that goes into the myth of *Romeo and Juliet* Shakespeare explicitly mocks, a little later, in *A Midsummer Night's Dream*, including the artificiality of the double sui-cide at the end, borrowed from *Pyramus and Thisby* and turned into the hi-larious satire of the play-within-the-play in the later comedy.

If Shakespeare had not manipulated our mimetic desire a little, he could never have turned the story of Romeo and Juliet into the rather formidable myth that it has become. There is something clandestine about the exploitation of violence in this play, because Shakespeare insists at the same time that the violence of the blood feud is totally alien to Romeo and Juliet, who, both in the prologue and in the conclusion, are defined as innocent victims of the blood feud, and the blood feud itself is identified with the old generation.

In *Romeo and Juliet,* the hate inside the love plays a role equivalent to that of the *pharmakon* ritual in the Dionysiac cult of ancient Greece. This violence is good and bad at the same time, violent and peaceful more or less simultaneously. It may be observed that Friar Laurence, the man who tries and fails to manipulate everything in the play, may well be a humorous symbol of the author and director that Shakespeare was. The first thing he does when he first appears on the stage is to give a fascinating speech on the subject of the pharmaceutical *pharmakon,* which can be read as an allegory of *Romeo and Juliet* in its entirety. It suggests that Shakespeare was aware of the sacrificial compromises with the truth that the rhetorical technique of this play entailed, and he warns his more knowledgeable readers about the "sacrificial" role played by violence in it:

Oh! mickle is the powerful grace that lies
In herbs, plants, stones and their true qualities;
For nought so vile that on the earth doth live
But to the earth some special good doth give,
Nor aught so good that strain'd for that fair use
Revolts from true birth, stumbling on abuse:
Virtue itself turns vice, being misapplied
And vice sometime's by action dignified
Within the infant rind of this weak flower
Poison hath residence and medicine power;
For this, being smelt, with that part cheers each part;
Being tasted, slays all senses with the heart.
Two such opposed foes encamp them still
In man as well as herbs, grace and rude will;
And where the worser is predominant,
Full soon the canker death eats up that plant. (*Romeo and Juliet,* 2.3.15–30)

# Sources

1. "History in Saint-John Perse," translated by Robert Doran, appeared under the title "L'histoire dans l'œuvre de Saint-John Perse" in *Romanic Review* 44 (1953): 47–55. [Reprinted with permission from the Romanic Review 44 (1953).]

2. "Valéry and Stendhal," translated by Robert Doran, appeared under the title "Valéry et Stendhal," in *PMLA* 59 (1954): 347–57. [Reprinted by permission of the Modern Language Association.]

3. "Classicism and Voltaire's Historiography" appeared in *The American Magazine of the French Legion of Honor* 29, no. 3 (1958): 151–60.

4. "Pride and Passion in the Contemporary Novel" appeared in *Yale French Studies* 24 (1959): 3–10.

5. "Stendhal and Tocqueville" appeared in *The American Magazine of the French Legion of Honor* 31, no. 2 (1960): 73–83.

6. "Memoirs of a Dutiful Existentialist: Simone de Beauvoir" appeared under the title "Memoirs of a Dutiful Existentialist" in *Yale French Studies* 27 (1961): 41–47.

7. "Marcel Proust" appeared as the editor's introduction to *Proust: A Collection of Critical Essays*, ed. René Girard (Englewood Cliffs: Prentice Hall, 1962), 1–12.

8. "Marivaudage, Hypocrisy, and Bad Faith" appeared under the title "Marivaudage and Hypocrisy" in *The American Magazine of the French Legion of Honor* 34, no. 3 (1963): 163–74.

9. "Formalism and Structuralism in Literature and the Human Sciences," translated by Robert Doran, appeared under the title "Des formes aux structures, en littérature et ailleurs" in *Modern Language Notes* 78, no. 5 (1963): 504–19. [Girard, René. "Des formes aux structures, en littérature et ailleurs," *Modern Language Notes* 78, no. 5 (1963): 504–19. © The Johns Hopkins University Press. Reprinted with permission of The Johns Hopkins University Press.]

10. "Racine, Poet of Glory," translated by Robert Doran, appeared under the title "Racine, poète de la gloire" in *Critique* 205 (1964): 484–506.

11. "Monsters and Demigods in Hugo," translated by Robert Doran, appeared under the title "Monstres et demi-dieux dans l'œuvre de Hugo" in *Symposium* 29, no. 1 (1965): 50–57. [Reprinted with permission of the Helen Dwight Reid Edu-

cational Foundation. Published by Heldref Publications, 1319 18th Street, NW, Washington, DC 20036–1802. www.heldref.org. Copyright (c) 1965.]

12. "Bastards and the Antihero in Sartre," translated by Robert Doran, appeared under the title "L'anti-héros et les salauds" in *Mercure de France* 353 (1965): 422–49.

13. "Critical Reflections on Literary Studies," translated by Catherine and Richard Macksey, appeared in *Velocities of Change: Critical Essays*, ed. Richard Macksey (Baltimore: Johns Hopkins University Press, 1974), 72–88 [reprinted with permission of The Johns Hopkins University Press (copyright holder)]. This essay originally appeared under the title "Réflexions critiques sur les recherches littéraires" in *Modern Language Notes* 81, no. 3 (1966): 307–24.

14. "Narcissism: The Freudian Myth Demythified by Proust" appeared in *Psychoanalysis, Creativity, and Literature*, ed. Alan Roland (New York: Columbia University Press, 1978), 293–311. [Copyright (c) 1978 Columbia University Press. Reprinted with permission of the publisher.]

15. "Theory and Its Terrors" appeared in *The Limits of Theory*, ed. Thomas M. Kavanagh (Stanford, CA: Stanford University Press, 1989), 225–54.

16. "Love and Hate in Chrétien de Troyes' *Yvain*" appeared under the title "Love and Hate in *Yvain*" in *Modernité au Moyen Age: Le défi du passé*, ed. Brigitte Cazelles and Charles Méla (Recherches and Rencontres series) (Geneva: Droz, 1990), 249–62.

17. "Innovation and Repetition" appeared in *SubStance* 62–63 (1990): 7–20.

18. "Mimetic Desire in the Underground: Feodor Dostoevsky," under the title "Mimetic Desire in the Underground," appeared as the postface to *Resurrection from the Underground: Feodor Dostoevsky*, by René Girard, ed. and trans. James G. Williams (New York: Crossroad Publishing, 1997), 143–65. The postface was written in English.

19. "Conversion in Literature and Christianity" appeared under the title "Literature and Christianity: A Personal View" in *Philosophy and Literature* 23, no. 1 (1999): 32–43.

20. "The Passionate Oxymoron in Shakespeare's *Romeo and Juliet*" appeared in *Passions in Economy, Politics, and the Media*, ed., Wolfgang Palaver and Petra Steinmair-Posel (Vienna: Lit, 2005), 17–37.

# Notes

EDITOR'S INTRODUCTION

1. From the group's website: "The Colloquium on Violence and Religion (COV&R) . . . is dedicated to the exploration, criticism, and development of René Girard's mimetic model of the relationship between violence and religion in the genesis and maintenance of culture" (http://theol.uibk.ac.at/cover). The group has also created an important scholarly journal, *Contagion: Journal of Violence, Mimesis, and Culture*, which, as the journal's editor notes, "has followed the research agenda of The Colloquium on Violence and Religion, which draws its inspiration from René Girard's mimetic hypothesis" ("From the Editor . . . ," *Contagion* 12–13 [2006]).

2. Johns Hopkins University Press has recently published a new, 40th anniversary edition of the seminal anthology based on this conference (see *The Structuralist Controversy: The Languages of Criticism and the Sciences of Man*, 40th anniversary edition, ed. Richard Macksey and Eugenio Donato [Baltimore: Johns Hopkins University Press, 2007]). Girard's paper was entitled "Tiresias and the Critic." The "Concluding Remarks" were co-authored by Richard Macksey, Girard, and Jean Hyppolite.

3. Nearly all of Girard's early articles, written from 1953 to 1966, were devoted to the analysis of literary texts. Toward the end of this period, just as structuralism was starting to take hold, Girard began to write essays on anthropological topics, such as the Oedipus myth and the cult of Dionysus. See "De l'expérience romanesque au mythe oedipien," *Critique* 222 (1965): 899–924; "Symétrie et dissymétrie dans le mythe d'Œdipe," *Critique* 249 (1968): 99–135; and "Dionysos et la genèse violente du sacré," *Poétique* 3 (1970): 266–81. (The first two articles have been translated and collected in René Girard, *Oedipus Unbound: Selected Writings on Rivalry and Desire*, ed. Mark Anspach [Stanford, CA: Stanford University Press, 2004]). Though Girard would continue to publish occasional essays on modern literature, much of his production in the 1970s and 1980s would be oriented toward religious anthropology. An exception is his work on Shakespeare, which culminated in the publication of *A Theater of Envy: William Shakespeare* (Oxford

University Press, 1991). This title has recently been re-released by Saint Augustine's Press (2004).

4. It would not be until the publication of his next book, *Things Hidden since the Foundation of the World* (originally published in French in 1978; English translation by S. Bann and M. Metteer [Stanford, CA: Stanford University Press, 1988]), that Girard would become a major figure in France. Girard's writings on modern literature have in general been more influential in France than in the United States.

5. An excerpt from *Violence and the Sacred* was included in the massive anthology *Critical Theory since 1965*, edited by Hazard Adams and Leroy Searle (Tallahassee: University Press of Florida, 1986), a popular textbook for courses in literary theory.

6. The best overall introduction to Girard's work is certainly the recent monograph by Chris Fleming, *René Girard: Violence and Mimesis* (Cambridge: Polity Press, 2004).

7. Girard often refers to imitative desire as *acquisitive mimesis*, which he opposes to the good, non-acquisitive form of mimesis, of which the paradigmatic example is the *imitatio Christi*—the imitation of Christ. See "Violence Renounced: A Response by René Girard," in *Violence Renounced: René Girard, Biblical Studies, and Peacemaking*, ed. Willard M. Swartley (Telford: Pandora Press, 2000), chapter 14.

8. In his exposition of mimetic desire, Girard often focuses on concrete examples that involve interpersonal, triangular relationships within a restricted group of characters. However, the "third party" can just as well be the social itself, particularly when a social ideal is embodied in a particular character.

9. One can read a similar dialectic in the Heideggerian notion of authentic subjectivity, which is opposed to the "they" self (*das Man*). These are supposedly two dimensions or levels of a single being, rather than an opposition between an exalted self and the inauthentic others. But as Samuel Moyn notes in a recent book, "Heidegger's solipsism is reinforced by the older English translation of Heidegger's term 'das Man' as 'the They'—the third-person crowd from which the first-person *Dasein* must secede. More recently, sympathetic readers of Heidegger have translated it [*das Man*] as 'the one' and emphasize the self's inclusion in the syndrome of social meaning. While doctrinally correct, this view ignores Heidegger's consistently derogatory rhetoric when speaking of the one" (*Origins of the Other: Emmanuel Levinas between Revelation and Ethics*, [Ithaca: Cornell University Press, 2005], 67–68 n. 25).

10. Girard related to me that "At that time, if one dipped one's little finger into psychoanalysis one was thought to be drowning in it" (personal conversation). However, Girard added a footnote on Freud to the English translation of *Men-*

*songe romantique et verité romanesque* (see *Deceit, Desire, and the Novel* [Baltimore: Johns Hopkins University Press, 1965], 186–87 n. 1).

11. Girard sees Freud's notion of "identification" as a proto-mimetic theory the consequences of which are never explored. As Girard observes in his chapter on Freud in *Violence and the Sacred*: "We are presented, therefore, with a rivalry devoid of preliminary identification (the Oedipus complex) followed by an identification without rivalry (the superego)" (*Violence and the Sacred*, trans. Patrick Gregory [Baltimore: Johns Hopkins University Press, 1976], 185). Putting the two halves of the equation together would have naturally led Freud to mimetic theory.

12. "Bastards and the Antihero in Sartre" (chapter 12 in this volume).

13. A similar example can be found in the essay "Formalism and Structuralism in Literature and the Human Sciences" (included in this volume), in which Girard compares Lévi-Strauss's ethnographic insights to Proust's evocation of Combray in *Swann's Way*.

14. In his well-known essay on Albert Camus, "The Stranger Retried," Girard argues that Camus the author of *The Fall* (*La chute*) is a critic of Camus the author of *The Stranger* (see *To Double Business Bound: Essays on Literature, Mimesis, and Anthropology* [Baltimore: Johns Hopkins University Press, 1978]: 9–35; the essay has been reprinted in several anthologies).

15. However, the mere understanding of mimetic structures is not alone sufficient to trigger a conversion. As Eric Gans observes: "In the dialectic of desire, knowing is not transcending" ("Pour une esthétique triangulaire," *Esprit* 429 [1973]: 581). Mimetic theory is heuristic, not curative.

16. For a systematic comparison between Girard and the early Derrida, see Andrew McKenna, *Violence and Difference: Girard, Derrida, and Deconstruction* (Urbana: University of Illinois Press, 1991). See also Jean-Pierre Dupuy, "Deconstructing Deconstruction: Supplement and Hierarchy," *Stanford Literature Review* 7 (1990): 101–21.

17. This often-cited phrase, which appeared in Derrida's *Of Grammatology* (trans. Gayatri Spivak [Baltimore: Johns Hopkins University Press, 1976], 158), had originally been translated as "There is nothing outside the text," which seemed to imply that there were no physical objects. A corrected edition was published by Johns Hopkins University Press in 1997.

18. This is not to say that Derrida was responsible for the cultural form that deconstruction took in the United States. Girard objected more to the way in which Derrida was used than to Derrida's thought in itself. In fact, Girard taught some of Derrida's texts in his courses at Stanford.

19. The terms "literary" and "literature" are, of course, anachronistic in this context, since these concepts did not come into widespread use until the nineteenth century. Ancient critical texts speak of "poets and prose writers."

20. It is because of this polyvalence that *katharsis* is taken to be an ambiguous or even dubious concept in literary studies. See Girard's discussion of *katharsis* in chapter 11 of *Violence and the Sacred.*

CHAPTER I

1. Paul Valéry, *Variété* (Paris: Gallimard, 1924), 189.

2. "'I am proud to have known him so early on' . . . Saint Léger, Saint-John Perse, is virtually the only contemporary whom Paul Valéry—who admired so rarely—spoke of in this way" (Herbert Steiner, "Amitié du Prince," *Les Cahiers de la Pléiade,* Summer-Autumn [1950]: 31); as for Breton, see his essay, "Le Donateur," in the same issue of the *Cahiers de la Pléiade:* 68–70; this issue, completely dedicated to Perse's oeuvre, will henceforth be referred to as *Cahiers.*

3. Denis de Rougemont, "Saint-John Perse et l'Amérique," *Cahiers,* 136.

4. Saint-John Perse, *Collected Poems,* Complete Edition with Corrections, translations by W. H. Auden, Hugh Chisholm, Denis Devlin, T. S. Eliot, Robert Fitzgerald, Wallace Fowlie, Richard Howard, Louise Varese (Princeton: Princeton University Press, 1983), 205–7.

5. *Exile, suivi de poèmes à l'Etrangère, Pluie, Neiges* (Paris, 1946), (*Neiges,* 3).

6. Perse, *Collected Poems,* 179 (*Pluies,* 3).

7. A. Rolland de Renéville, "D'une chronique miraculeuse," *Cahiers,* 76.

8. Perse, *Collected Poems,* 193 (*Pluies,* 8).

9. Ibid., 203 (*Neiges,* 2).

10. André Malraux, *Les noyers de l'Altenburg* (Paris: Gallimard, 1948), 141–42. [Editor's translation.]

11. Jules Monnerot, *La poésie moderne et le sacré* (Paris: Gallimard, 1945), 152.

12. André Gide, "Don d'un arbre," *Cahiers,* 24.

13. Perse, *Collected Poems,* 171 (*Exil,* 7).

14. Roger Caillois, "Une poésie encyclopédique," *Cahiers,* 98.

15. Perse, *Collected Poems,* 175 (*Pluies,* 1).

16. Ibid., 191 (*Pluies,* 7).

17. Caillois, "Une poésie encyclopédique," *Cahiers,* 98.

18. Perse, *Collected Poems,* 135 (*Anabase,* 10).

19. Ibid., 137 (*Anabase,* 10).

20. Pierre Jean Jouve, "Exil," *Cahiers,* 57.

21. Caillois, "Une poésie encyclopédique," *Cahiers,* 98.

22. Perse, *Collected Poems,* 147 (*Exil,* 2).

23. Perse, *Collected Poems,* 298 (*Vents,* 3.2).

24. Ibid., 311 (*Vents,* 3.5).

25. Ibid., 155 (*Exil,* 4).

CHAPTER 2

1. Paul Valéry, "Stendhal," in *Masters and Friends*, trans. Martin Turnell (Princeton, NJ: Princeton University Press, 1968), 176–212.

2. I am not unaware of the article by G. Turguet-Milnes, "Valéry and Stendhal," *French Studies* 4 (1951): 45–49. Since the methodology and goals of the two articles are quite different, I did not judge it necessary to modify a title that does not intend in the least to cast doubt on the conclusions of Turguet-Milnes.

3. Valéry, "Stendhal," 188–89.

4. Ibid., 191.

5. Ibid., 196.

6. Paul Valéry, *Monsieur Teste*, trans. Jackson Mathews (Princeton, NJ: Princeton University Press, 1973), 10.

7. Ibid., 50.

8. Ibid., 51.

9. Ibid., 36.

10. Valéry, "Stendhal," 211.

11. Ibid., 179.

12. Ibid., 178.

13. Stendhal, *Vie de Henri Brulard*, in vol. 1 of *Oeuvres completes de Stendhal* (Paris: Champion, 1914–34), 34. [Editor's translation.]

14. [Valéry writes: "I had hardly written down the words 'vaudeville' and 'operetta' (a little earlier on) when I had the feeling that the reader would be shocked. He probably does not care for this mixing of the literary castes; he is astonished to find Stendhal, who was praised by Taine and Nietzsche, and who was almost a philosopher, placed so close to mere men of wit. But truth and life add up to disorder; connections and relationships which are not surprising are not real" (Valéry, "Stendhal," 178).]

15. Ibid., 178.

16. Ibid., 198.

17. Ibid., 177.

18. [The first words of "An Evening with Monsieur Teste" read: "Stupidity is not my strong point" (Valéry, *Monsieur Teste*, 8).]

19. Valéry, "Stendhal," 211.

20. Claude-Edmond Magny, *Histoire du roman français depuis 1918* (Paris: Sueil, 1950), vol. 1, 175.

CHAPTER 3

1. Letter of June 10, 1752.

CHAPTER 4

1. [This essay originally appeared in a special issue of *Yale French Studies* entitled "Midnight Novelists and Others."]

CHAPTER 5

1. Article anonymously published in *Le National*, March 10, 1830, and reproduced in Stendhal, *Mélanges de Littérature*, ed. Henri Martineau (Paris: Le Divan, 1933), vol. 3, 317–28.

2. Stendhal, *Romans et nouvelles* (Paris: Gallimard [Pléiade], 1952), vol. 1, 825, for the text; vol. 1, 1500, for the marginal note.

3. Alexis de Tocqueville, *The Old Régime and the Revolution* (New York: Harper, 1856), 213.

4. Alexis de Tocqueville, *Democracy in America* (New York: Colonial Press, 1900), vol. 2, 147.

5. Tocqueville, *Democracy in America*, vol. 2, 219.

6. Stendhal, *Mémoires d'un touriste* (Paris: Crès, 1927), vol. 2, Geneva article.

7. Tocqueville, *Democracy in America*, vol. 2, 220.

8. Ibid., vol. 2, 146.

9. Ibid., vol. 2, 255.

10. *Mémoires d'un touriste*, vol. 1, 44.

CHAPTER 6

1. [This essay originally appeared in a special issue of *Yale French Studies* entitled "Women Writers."]

CHAPTER 7

1. [This essay was originally published as René Girard's introduction to *Proust: A Collection of Critical Essays* (Englewood Cliffs: Prentice Hall, 1962): 1–12. In his introduction, Girard refers to the texts of the various contributors to the volume, which will henceforth be referred to as *Proust*.]

2. [Robert Champigny, "Proust, Bergson, and Other Philosophers," in *Proust*, 122–31.]

3. [Ramon Fernandez, "In Search of the Self," in *Proust*, 136–49.]

4. [Richard Macksey, "Architecture of Time: Dialectics and Structure," in *Proust*, 104–21.]

5. Translated by Sylvia Townsend Warner under the title *On Art and Literature* (Meridian, 1958).

6. [Robert Vigneron, "Creative Agony," in *Proust*, 13–27.]

7. [Georges Poulet, "Proust and Human Time," in *Proust*, 150–78.]

8. [Georges Cattaui, "Images as Instruments," in *Proust,* 88–91; Elliott Coleman, "Religious Imagery," in *Proust,* 92–96.]

9. [Albert Thibaudet, "Faces of Proust," in *Proust,* 47–52; Charles Du Bos, "The Profundity of Proust," in *Proust,* 132–35.]

10. [Henri Peyre, "The Legacy of Proust," in *Proust,* 28–41; Jacques Rivière, "Analytic Tradition," in *Proust,* 42–46.]

CHAPTER 8

1. Paul Gazagne, *Marivaux par lui-même* (Paris: Seuil, 1955).

2. "Que fait votre main? / Je tâte votre habit : l'étoffe en est moelleuse."

CHAPTER 9

1. René Wellek and Austin Warren, *Theory of Literature,* 3rd ed. (New York: Harcourt Brace, 1956), 127.

2. Louis Hjelmslev, *Acta Linguistica* 4 (1944): 5. [Editor's translation.]

3. Nikolai Trubetzkoy, "La Phonologie actuelle," in *Psychologie du langage* (Paris: Alcan, 1933), 227–46, quoted in Emile Benveniste, "'Structure' en linguistique," in *Sens et usages du terme 'structure' dans les sciences humaines et sociales,* ed. Roger Bastide (The Hague: Mouton, 1962), 34. [Editor's translation.]

4. "Il n'est pas de serpent, pas de monstre odieux ; / Qui par l'art imité ne sache plaire aux yeux" (Boileau, *Art poétique,* 3.1–2). [Editor's translation.]

5. Roland Barthes, "L'homme racinian," in *Sur Racine* (Paris: Seuil, 1963), 15–132.

6. "L'instance de la lettre dans l'inconscient ou la raison depuis Freud," *La Psychanalyse* 3: *Psychanalyse et sciences de l'homme* (1957): 70. [Editor's translation.]

7. Claude Lévi-Strauss, *The Savage Mind* (Chicago: University of Chicago Press, 1966), 89–90.

8. Lévi-Strauss, "La notion de structure en ethnologie," in *Sens et usage du terme 'structure,'* 44. [Editor's translation.]

9. Claude Lévi-Strauss, *Introduction to the Work of Marcel Mauss,* trans. Felicity Baker (London: Routledge & Kegan Paul, 1987), 35–36.

CHAPTER 10

1. [All English translations of Racine's plays are from the following edition, and will henceforth be referred to by act, scene, and line number: Jean Racine, *Complete Plays,* trans. Samuel Solomon (New York: Random House, 1967), 2 vols.]

2. Lucien Goldmann, *Le Dieu caché* (Paris: Gallimard, 1955); *The Hidden God: A Study of Tragic Vision in the "Pensées" of Pascal and the Tragedies of Racine,* trans. Philip Thody (London: Routledge, 1964).

3. Roland Barthes, *Sur Racine* (Paris: Seuil, 1963); *On Racine*, trans. Richard Howard (Berkeley: University of California Press, 1992).

4. ["Titus reginam Berenicem, demisit invitus invitam" (Titus dismissed the queen Bérénice both against her and his own will).]

5. [Girard is referring to Barthes' journalistic essays written between 1954 and 1956, and later collected in Roland Barthes, *Mythologies* (Paris: Seuil, 1970).]

CHAPTER 11

1. [All English quotations from *The Man Who Laughs* are taken from the following online source, and will be referenced by book and chapter number: http://www.gutenberg.org/files/12587/12587-12587-h.htm (accessed May 20, 2007).]

2. [Though published after *Han of Iceland* (1823), *Bug-Jargal* (1826) was begun in 1818, two years before *Han of Iceland*, and therefore Habibrah can be said to be Hugo's *first* monster.]

3. Victor Hugo, *The Hunchback of Notre Dame*, trans. Isabel F. Hapgood, http://www.gutenberg.org/dirs/etext01/hback10.txt (accessed May 20, 2007).

4. "L'aveugle voit dans l'ombre un monde de clartés, / Quand l'œil du corps s'éteint, l'œil de l'esprit s'allume" ("A un poète aveugle," *Les contemplations*, 1.20). [Editor's translation.]

5. "Peut-être le maudit se sentait-il béni, [ . . . ] / Pas de monstre chétif, louche, impur, chassieux, / Qui n'ait l'immensité des astres dans les yeux" ("Le crapaud," *La légende des siècles*, vol. 2). [Editor's translation.]

6. "Cet âne abject, souillé, meurtri sous le bâton, / Est plus saint que Socrate et plus grand que Platon" ("Le crapaud"). [Editor's translation.]

7. "Et l'on voit tout au fond, quand l'œil ose y descendre, / Au delà de la vie, et du souffle et du bruit, / Un affreux soleil noir d'où rayonne la nuit !" ("Ce que dit bouche d'ombre II," *Les contemplations*, 6.26). [Editor's translation.]

CHAPTER 12

1. Jean-Paul Sartre, *Words*, trans. Irene Clephane (New York: Penguin Books, 1967), 156.

2. Jean-Paul Sartre, *Being and Nothingness*, trans. Hazel E. Barnes (New York: Washington Square Press, 1956), 141–42.

3. Ibid., 142.

4. Sigmund Freud, *The Ego and the Id*, trans. Joan Riviere, rev. and ed. James Strachey (New York: W.W. Norton, 1960), 30 [Freud's emphasis].

5. Sartre, *Words*, 156 [translation slightly modified].

6. Sartre, *Being and Nothingness*, 142.

7. [Sartre wrote a multivolume work on Flaubert entitled *L'idiot de la famille* (Paris: Gallimard, 1971–72); *The Family Idiot*, trans. Carol Cosman, 5 vols. (Chicago: University of Chicago Press, 1981–93).]

CHAPTER 13

1. "Les Deux Critiques," which first appeared in *MLN* 78 (1963): 447–52, was reprinted in *Essais critiques* (Paris: Editions du Seuil, 1964), 246–51. [An English translation appears in *Velocities of Change*, ed. Richard Macksey (Baltimore: Johns Hopkins University Press, 1974).]

2. *Le Monde*, March 14, 1964.

3. [Raymond Picard, *Nouvelle critique, nouvelle imposture* (Paris: Jean-Jacques Pauvert, 1965).]

4. [First-century rhetorical treatise attributed to Longinus, known in English as *On the Sublime*. In 1674, Nicholas Boileau published the first French translation of Longinus's treatise, which he entitled *Traité du Sublime de Longin*.]

5. Roland Barthes, *Sur Racine* (Paris: Editions du Seuil, 1963), 9.

6. [Girard is referring to the Ecole des Hautes Etudes en Sciences Sociales (EHESS), in Paris, France, which is a school devoted to graduate studies outside of the traditional university system. Jacques Derrida taught there for most of his career.]

7. Gustave Lanson, *Essais de méthode, de critique et d'histoire littéraire*, ed. Henri Peyre (Paris: Hachette, 1965).

8. [I have eliminated the concluding paragraphs on the critic Lanson (less than two pages), which would not have made much sense to contemporary readers.]

CHAPTER 14

1. Sigmund Freud, "On Narcissism: An Introduction," in *General Psychological Theory* (New York: Collier Books, 1963), 56–82.

2. Marcel Proust, *Jean Santeuil* (Paris: Gallimard, 1952), 3 vols.

3. Freud, "On Narcissism," 70.

4. Marcel Proust, *Within a Budding Grove*, trans. C. K. Scott-Moncrieff (New York: Vintage Books, 1970), 271.

5. Ibid., 267.

6. Ibid., 272.

7. Ibid.

8. Marcel Proust, *Swann's Way* (New York: Vintage Books, 1970), 292. The theoretician of narcissism is still, like Swann but unlike Proust, in the position of the desiring subject, *because he does not know it*. In order to confirm this point, I will quote, from *Narcissism*, the lines that come immediately before and after the passage discussed above. They speak for themselves:

> A different course followed the type most frequently met with in women, which is probably the purest and truest feminine type. With the development of puberty, the maturing of the female sexual organs, which up till then have been in condition of latency, seems to bring about an intensification for the original narcissism, and this is un-

favorable to the development of a true object-love with its accompanying sexual overestimation; there arises in the woman a certain self-sufficiency (especially when there is a ripening into beauty), which compensates her for the social restrictions upon her object-choice. Strictly speaking, such women love only themselves with an intensity comparable to that of the man's love for them. Nor does their need lie in the direction of loving, but of being loved; and that man finds favor with them who fulfils this condition. The importance of this type of woman for the erotic life of mankind must be recognized as very great. Such women have the greatest fascination for men, not only for aesthetic reasons, since as a rule they are the most beautiful, but also because of certain interesting psychological constellations . . .

Perhaps it is not superfluous to give an assurance that, in this description of the feminine form of erotic life, no tendency to depreciate woman has any part. Apart from the fact that tendentiousness is alien to me, I also know that these different lines of development correspond to the differentiation of functions in a highly complicated biological connection; further, I am ready to admit that there are countless women who love according to the masculine type and who develop the over-estimation of the sexual object so characteristic of that type. (Freud, "On Narcissism," 69–71)

It is on such texts, rather than on the more exotic and harmless myth of *Penisneid* (penis envy), that the critique of Freud from a woman's standpoint should focus. The position of Freud toward women is basically the same as the sadomasochistic position of the homosexual object in Proust. The only difference, once more, is that Proust knows it and Freud does not.

CHAPTER 15

1. [This essay was originally given as part of a series of lectures organized by Thomas M. Kavanagh at the University of Colorado, Boulder, during 1986 and 1987, and later collected by him in a volume entitled *The Limits of Theory* (Stanford, CA: Stanford University Press, 1989).]

2. [Literally: *Words and Things*, but translated as *The Order of Things: An Archaeology of the Human Sciences* (New York: Random House, 1970).]

CHAPTER 16

1. [This essay was originally presented at a colloquium organized by Brigitte Cazelles, who was a Professor of French at Stanford University specializing in medieval literature. Girard began his talk with these words: "To a fallen away medievalist like myself, this great company is intimidating. It reminds me of my yearly examinations at the Ecole des Chartes. After a forty-year absence from the field, I may be a little rusty. If it shows too much, please, blame Brigitte; she was extremely generous when she asked me to speak, but she may have been unwise."]

2. [All quotations from *Yvain* are from the following English translation, and will be referred to by line number: Chrétien de Troyes, *Yvain, or The Knight with the Lion*, trans. Ruth Harwood Cline (Athens: University of Georgia Press, 1975).]

CHAPTER 17

1. For a discussion concerning problems of economic life and mimetic desire, see Paul Dumouchel and Jean-Pierre Dupuy, *L'enfer des choses: René Girard et la logique de l'économie* (Paris: Seuil, 1979). [Another collection devoted at least in part to this problematic in Girard's thought is *Passions in Economy, Politics, and the Media*, ed. Wolfgang Palaver and Petra Steinmair-Posel (Vienna: Lit, 2005).]

CHAPTER 18

1. [This essay originally appeared as the postface to the English translation of Girard's book on Dostoevsky entitled *Resurrection from the Underground: Feodor Dostoevsky* (New York: Crossroad, 1997), 143–65. The postface began with these words: "I am grateful to my good friend James Williams for translating and editing with great care the foregoing essay on Dostoevsky. When I wrote it I had just published the original French version of a longer book on five European novelists, including Dostoevsky. In that book, *Deceit, Desire, and the Novel*, the chief principle of interpretation is the idea of mimetic desire, which emerged from its creation and which has dominated my work ever since. The present book relies on mimetic desire, therefore, but not in very explicit fashion. In order to fit the original publisher's requirements, I had to keep it short and I did not want to reformulate in such limited space the theoretical apparatus elaborated at length only a short time before. I was afraid it would seem repetitious and cumbersome. As a result, the essay sounds more impressionistic than it really is."]

2. Richard Pevear, introduction to Fyodor Dostoevsky, *Demons* (New York: Knopf, 1994), xix.

CHAPTER 19

1. This paper was delivered in December 1998 at the Christianity and Literature session of the Modern Language Association's national convention in San Francisco. [I have omitted approximately a page of introductory remarks that concerned the specific circumstances of this session.]

CHAPTER 20

1. [René Girard, *A Theater of Envy: William Shakespeare* (Oxford University Press, 1991). This title has been re-released by Saint Augustine's Press (2004).]

2. [Olivier Maurel, *Essais sur le mimétisme* (Paris: L'Harmattan, 2002).]

# Index

*Cultural Memory* | *in the Present*

Martin Seel, *Aesthetics of Appearing*

Nanette Salomon, *Shifting Priorities: Gender and Genre in Seventeenth-Century Dutch Painting*

Jacob Taubes, *The Political Theology of Paul*

Jean-Luc Marion, *The Crossing of the Visible*

Eric Michaud, *An Art for Eternity: The Cult of Art in Nazi Germany*

Anne Freadman, *The Machinery of Talk: Charles Peirce and the Sign Hypothesis*

Stanley Cavell, *Emerson's Transcendental Etudes*

Stuart McLean, *The Event and Its Terrors: Ireland, Famine, Modernity*

Beate Rössler, ed., *Privacies: Philosophical Evaluations*

Bernard Faure, *Double Exposure: Cutting Across Buddhist and Western Discourses*

Alessia Ricciardi, *The Ends Of Mourning: Psychoanalysis, Literature, Film*

Alain Badiou, *Saint Paul: The Foundation of Universalism*

Gil Anidjar, *The Jew, The Arab: A History of the Enemy*

Jonathan Culler and Kevin Lamb, eds., *Just Being Difficult? Academic Writing in the Public Arena*

Jean-Luc Nancy, *A Finite Thinking*, edited by Simon Sparks

Theodor W. Adorno, *Can One Live after Auschwitz? A Philosophical Reader*, edited by Rolf Tiedemann

Patricia Pisters, *The Matrix of Visual Culture: Working with Deleuze in Film Theory*

Talal Asad, *Formations of the Secular: Christianity, Islam, Modernity*

Dorothea von Mücke, *The Rise of the Fantastic Tale*

Marc Redfield, *The Politics of Aesthetics: Nationalism, Gender, Romanticism*

Emmanuel Levinas, *On Escape*

Dan Zahavi, *Husserl's Phenomenology*

Rodolphe Gasché, *The Idea of Form: Rethinking Kant's Aesthetics*

Michael Naas, *Taking on the Tradition: Jacques Derrida and the Legacies of Deconstruction*

Herlinde Pauer-Studer, ed., *Constructions of Practical Reason: Interviews on Moral and Political Philosophy*

Jean-Luc Marion, *Being Given: Toward a Phenomenology of Givenness*

Theodor W. Adorno and Max Horkheimer, *Dialectic of Enlightenment*

Ian Balfour, *The Rhetoric of Romantic Prophecy*

Martin Stokhof, *World and Life as One: Ethics and Ontology in Wittgenstein's Early Thought*

Gianni Vattimo, *Nietzsche: An Introduction*

Jacques Derrida, *Negotiations: Interventions and Interviews, 1971–1998*, ed. Elizabeth Rottenberg

Brett Levinson, *The Ends of Literature: Post-transition and Neoliberalism in the Wake of the "Boom"*

Timothy J. Reiss, *Against Autonomy: Global Dialectics of Cultural Exchange*

Hent de Vries and Samuel Weber, eds., *Religion and Media*

Niklas Luhmann, *Theories of Distinction: Redescribing the Descriptions of Modernity*, ed. and introd. William Rasch

Johannes Fabian, *Anthropology with an Attitude: Critical Essays*

Michel Henry, *I Am the Truth: Toward a Philosophy of Christianity*

Gil Anidjar, *"Our Place in Al-Andalus": Kabbalah, Philosophy, Literature in Arab-Jewish Letters*

Hélène Cixous and Jacques Derrida, *Veils*

F. R. Ankersmit, *Historical Representation*

F. R. Ankersmit, *Political Representation*

Elissa Marder, *Dead Time: Temporal Disorders in the Wake of Modernity (Baudelaire and Flaubert)*

Reinhart Koselleck, *The Practice of Conceptual History: Timing History, Spacing Concepts*

Niklas Luhmann, *The Reality of the Mass Media*

Hubert Damisch, *A Childhood Memory by Piero della Francesca*

Hubert Damisch, *A Theory of /Cloud/: Toward a History of Painting*

Jean-Luc Nancy, *The Speculative Remark (One of Hegel's Bons Mots)*

Jean-François Lyotard, *Soundproof Room: Malraux's Anti-Aesthetics*

Jan Patočka, *Plato and Europe*

Hubert Damisch, *Skyline: The Narcissistic City*

Isabel Hoving, *In Praise of New Travelers: Reading Caribbean Migrant Women Writers*

Richard Rand, ed., *Futures: Of Derrida*

William Rasch, *Niklas Luhmann's Modernity: The Paradox of System Differentiation*

Jacques Derrida and Anne Dufourmantelle, *Of Hospitality*

Jean-François Lyotard, *The Confession of Augustine*

Kaja Silverman, *World Spectators*

Samuel Weber, *Institution and Interpretation: Expanded Edition*

Jeffrey S. Librett, *The Rhetoric of Cultural Dialogue: Jews and Germans in the Epoch of Emancipation*

Ulrich Baer, *Remnants of Song: Trauma and the Experience of Modernity in Charles Baudelaire and Paul Celan*

Samuel C. Wheeler III, *Deconstruction as Analytic Philosophy*

David S. Ferris, *Silent Urns: Romanticism, Hellenism, Modernity*

Rodolphe Gasché, *Of Minimal Things: Studies on the Notion of Relation*

Sarah Winter, *Freud and the Institution of Psychoanalytic Knowledge*

Samuel Weber, *The Legend of Freud: Expanded Edition*

Aris Fioretos, ed., *The Solid Letter: Readings of Friedrich Hölderlin*

J. Hillis Miller / Manuel Asensi, *Black Holes / J. Hillis Miller; or, Boustrophedonic Reading*

Miryam Sas, *Fault Lines: Cultural Memory and Japanese Surrealism*

Peter Schwenger, *Fantasm and Fiction: On Textual Envisioning*

Didier Maleuvre, *Museum Memories: History, Technology, Art*

Jacques Derrida, *Monolingualism of the Other; or, The Prosthesis of Origin*

Andrew Baruch Wachtel, *Making a Nation, Breaking a Nation: Literature and Cultural Politics in Yugoslavia*

Niklas Luhmann, *Love as Passion: The Codification of Intimacy*

Mieke Bal, ed., *The Practice of Cultural Analysis: Exposing Interdisciplinary Interpretation*

Jacques Derrida and Gianni Vattimo, eds., *Religion*